High Performance Python

Micha Gorelick and Ian Ozsvald

Beijing · Cambridge · Farnham · Köln · Sebastopol · Tokyo

High Performance Python

by Micha Gorelick and Ian Ozsvald

Printed in the United States of America.

Published by O'Reilly Media, Inc., 1005 Gravenstein Highway North, Sebastopol, CA 95472.

O'Reilly books may be purchased for educational, business, or sales promotional use. Online editions are also available for most titles (*http://safaribooksonline.com/*). For more information, contact our corporate/institutional sales department: 800-998-9938 or *corporate@oreilly.com*.

Editors: Meghan Blanchette and Rachel Roumeliotis
Production Editor: Matthew Hacker
Copyeditor: Rachel Head
Proofreader: Rachel Monaghan

Indexer: Wendy Catalano
Cover Designer: Karen Montgomery
Interior Designer: David Futato
Illustrator: Rebecca Demarest

September 2014:   First Edition

Revision History for the First Edition:

2014-08-21:   First release

See *http://oreilly.com/catalog/errata.csp?isbn=9781449361594* for release details.

ISBN: 978-1-449-36159-4

[LSI]

Table of Contents

Preface

Python is easy to learn. You're probably here because now that your code runs correctly, you need it to run faster. You like the fact that your code is easy to modify and you can iterate with ideas quickly. The trade-off between *easy to develop* and *runs as quickly as I need* is a well-understood and often-bemoaned phenomenon. There are solutions.

Some people have serial processes that have to run faster. Others have problems that could take advantage of multicore architectures, clusters, or graphics processing units. Some need scalable systems that can process more or less as expediency and funds allow, without losing reliability. Others will realize that their coding techniques, often borrowed from other languages, perhaps aren't as natural as examples they see from others.

In this book we will cover all of these topics, giving practical guidance for understanding bottlenecks and producing faster and more scalable solutions. We also include some war stories from those who went ahead of you, who took the knocks so you don't have to.

Python is well suited for rapid development, production deployments, and scalable systems. The ecosystem is full of people who are working to make it scale on your behalf, leaving you more time to focus on the more challenging tasks around you.

Who This Book Is For

You've used Python for long enough to have an idea about why certain things are slow and to have seen technologies like Cython, numpy, and PyPy being discussed as possible solutions. You might also have programmed with other languages and so know that there's more than one way to solve a performance problem.

While this book is primarily aimed at people with CPU-bound problems, we also look at data transfer and memory-bound solutions. Typically these problems are faced by scientists, engineers, quants, and academics.

We also look at problems that a web developer might face, including the movement of data and the use of just-in-time (JIT) compilers like PyPy for easy-win performance gains.

It might help if you have a background in C (or C++, or maybe Java), but it isn't a prerequisite. Python's most common interpreter (CPython—the standard you normally get if you type python at the command line) is written in C, and so the hooks and libraries all expose the gory inner C machinery. There are lots of other techniques that we cover that don't assume any knowledge of C.

You might also have a lower-level knowledge of the CPU, memory architecture, and data buses, but again, that's not strictly necessary.

Who This Book Is Not For

This book is meant for intermediate to advanced Python programmers. Motivated novice Python programmers may be able to follow along as well, but we recommend having a solid Python foundation.

We don't cover storage-system optimization. If you have a SQL or NoSQL bottleneck, then this book probably won't help you.

What You'll Learn

Your authors have been working with large volumes of data, a requirement for *I want the answers faster!* and a need for scalable architectures, for many years in both industry and academia. We'll try to impart our hard-won experience to save you from making the mistakes that we've made.

At the start of each chapter, we'll list questions that the following text should answer (if it doesn't, tell us and we'll fix it in the next revision!).

We cover the following topics:

- Background on the machinery of a computer so you know what's happening behind the scenes
- Lists and tuples—the subtle semantic and speed differences in these fundamental data structures
- Dictionaries and sets—memory allocation strategies and access algorithms in these important data structures
- Iterators—how to write in a more Pythonic way and open the door to infinite data streams using iteration
- Pure Python approaches—how to use Python and its modules effectively

- Matrices with numpy—how to use the beloved numpy library like a beast
- Compilation and just-in-time computing—processing faster by compiling down to machine code, making sure you're guided by the results of profiling
- Concurrency—ways to move data efficiently
- multiprocessing—the various ways to use the built-in multiprocessing library for parallel computing, efficiently share numpy matrices, and some costs and benefits of interprocess communication (IPC)
- Cluster computing—convert your multiprocessing code to run on a local or remote cluster for both research and production systems
- Using less RAM—approaches to solving large problems without buying a humungous computer
- Lessons from the field—lessons encoded in war stories from those who took the blows so you don't have to

Python 2.7

Python 2.7 is the dominant version of Python for scientific and engineering computing. 64-bit is dominant in this field, along with *nix environments (often Linux or Mac). 64-bit lets you address larger amounts of RAM. *nix lets you build applications that can be deployed and configured in well-understood ways with well-understood behaviors.

If you're a Windows user, then you'll have to buckle up. Most of what we show will work just fine, but some things are OS-specific, and you'll have to research a Windows solution. The biggest difficulty a Windows user might face is the installation of modules: research in sites like StackOverflow should give you the solutions you need. If you're on Windows, then having a virtual machine (e.g., using VirtualBox) with a running Linux installation might help you to experiment more freely.

Windows users should definitely look at a packaged solution like those available through Anaconda, Canopy, Python(x,y), or Sage. These same distributions will make the lives of Linux and Mac users far simpler too.

Moving to Python 3

Python 3 is the future of Python, and everyone is moving toward it. Python 2.7 will nonetheless be around for many years to come (some installations still use Python 2.4 from 2004); its retirement date has been set at 2020.

The shift to Python 3.3+ has caused enough headaches for library developers that people have been slow to port their code (with good reason), and therefore people have been slow to adopt Python 3. This is mainly due to the complexities of switching from a mix of string and Unicode datatypes in complicated applications to the Unicode and byte implementation in Python 3.

Typically, when you want reproducible results based on a set of trusted libraries, you don't want to be at the bleeding edge. High performance Python developers are likely to be using and trusting Python 2.7 for years to come.

Most of the code in this book will run with little alteration for Python 3.3+ (the most significant change will be with `print` turning from a statement into a function). In a few places we specifically look at improvements that Python 3.3+ provides. One item that might catch you out is the fact that / means *integer* division in Python 2.7, but it becomes *float* division in Python 3. Of course—being a good developer, your well-constructed unit test suite will already be testing your important code paths, so you'll be alerted by your unit tests if this needs to be addressed in your code.

`scipy` and `numpy` have been Python 3–compatible since late 2010. `matplotlib` was compatible from 2012, `scikit-learn` was compatible in 2013, and `NLTK` is expected to be compatible in 2014. Django has been compatible since 2013. The transition notes for each are available in their repositories and newsgroups; it is worth reviewing the processes they used if you're going to migrate older code to Python 3.

We encourage you to experiment with Python 3.3+ for new projects, but to be cautious with libraries that have only recently been ported and have few users—you'll have a harder time tracking down bugs. It would be wise to make your code Python 3.3+-compatible (learn about the __future__ imports), so a future upgrade will be easier.

Two good guides are "Porting Python 2 Code to Python 3" (*http://bit.ly/pyporting*) and "Porting to Python 3: An in-depth guide." (*http://python3porting.com/*) With a distribution like Anaconda or Canopy, you can run both Python 2 and Python 3 simultaneously—this will simplify your porting.

License

This book is licensed under Creative Commons Attribution-NonCommercial-NoDerivs 3.0 (*http://bit.ly/CC_A-NC-ND3*).

You're welcome to use this book for noncommercial purposes, including for noncommercial teaching. The license only allows for complete reproductions; for partial reproductions, please contact O'Reilly (see "How to Contact Us" on page xv). Please attribute the book as noted in the following section.

We negotiated that the book should have a Creative Commons license so the contents could spread further around the world. We'd be quite happy to receive a beer if this decision has helped you. We suspect that the O'Reilly staff would feel similarly about the beer.

How to Make an Attribution

The Creative Commons license requires that you attribute your use of a part of this book. Attribution just means that you should write something that someone else can follow to find this book. The following would be sensible: "*High Performance Python* by Micha Gorelick and Ian Ozsvald (O'Reilly). Copyright 2014 Micha Gorelick and Ian Ozsvald, 978-1-449-36159-4."

Errata and Feedback

We encourage you to review this book on public sites like Amazon—please help others understand if they'd benefit from this book! You can also email us at *feedback@highper formancepython.com.*

We're particularly keen to hear about errors in the book, successful use cases where the book has helped you, and high performance techniques that we should cover in the next edition. You can access the page for this book at *http://bit.ly/High_Performance_Python.*

Complaints are welcomed through the instant-complaint-transmission-service `> /dev/null`.

Conventions Used in This Book

The following typographical conventions are used in this book:

Italic
> Indicates new terms, URLs, email addresses, filenames, and file extensions.

`Constant width`
> Used for program listings, as well as within paragraphs to refer to commands, modules, and program elements such as variable or function names, databases, datatypes, environment variables, statements, and keywords.

`Constant width bold`
> Shows commands or other text that should be typed literally by the user.

`Constant width italic`
> Shows text that should be replaced with user-supplied values or by values determined by context.

 This element signifies a question or exercise.

This element signifies a general note.

 This element indicates a warning or caution.

Using Code Examples

Supplemental material (code examples, exercises, etc.) is available for download at *https://github.com/mynameisfiber/high_performance_python*.

This book is here to help you get your job done. In general, if example code is offered with this book, you may use it in your programs and documentation. You do not need to contact us for permission unless you're reproducing a significant portion of the code. For example, writing a program that uses several chunks of code from this book does not require permission. Selling or distributing a CD-ROM of examples from O'Reilly books does require permission. Answering a question by citing this book and quoting example code does not require permission. Incorporating a significant amount of example code from this book into your product's documentation does require permission.

If you feel your use of code examples falls outside fair use or the permission given above, feel free to contact us at *permissions@oreilly.com*.

Safari® Books Online

 *Safari Books Online* is an on-demand digital library that delivers expert content in both book and video form from the world's leading authors in technology and business.

Technology professionals, software developers, web designers, and business and creative professionals use Safari Books Online as their primary resource for research, problem solving, learning, and certification training.

Safari Books Online offers a range of plans and pricing for enterprise, government, education, and individuals.

Members have access to thousands of books, training videos, and prepublication manuscripts in one fully searchable database from publishers like O'Reilly Media, Prentice Hall Professional, Addison-Wesley Professional, Microsoft Press, Sams, Que, Peachpit Press, Focal Press, Cisco Press, John Wiley & Sons, Syngress, Morgan Kaufmann, IBM

Redbooks, Packt, Adobe Press, FT Press, Apress, Manning, New Riders, McGraw-Hill, Jones & Bartlett, Course Technology, and hundreds more. For more information about Safari Books Online, please visit us online.

How to Contact Us

Please address comments and questions concerning this book to the publisher:

O'Reilly Media, Inc.
1005 Gravenstein Highway North
Sebastopol, CA 95472
800-998-9938 (in the United States or Canada)
707-829-0515 (international or local)
707-829-0104 (fax)

To comment or ask technical questions about this book, send email to *bookques tions@oreilly.com*.

For more information about our books, courses, conferences, and news, see our website at *http://www.oreilly.com*.

Find us on Facebook: *http://facebook.com/oreilly*

Follow us on Twitter: *http://twitter.com/oreillymedia*

Watch us on YouTube: *http://www.youtube.com/oreillymedia*

Acknowledgments

Thanks to Jake Vanderplas, Brian Granger, Dan Foreman-Mackey, Kyran Dale, John Montgomery, Jamie Matthews, Calvin Giles, William Winter, Christian Schou Oxvig, Balthazar Rouberol, Matt "snakes" Reiferson, Patrick Cooper, and Michael Skirpan for invaluable feedback and contributions. Ian thanks his wife Emily for letting him disappear for 10 months to write this (thankfully she's terribly understanding). Micha thanks Elaine and the rest of his friends and family for being so patient while he learned to write. O'Reilly are also rather lovely to work with.

Our contributors for the "Lessons from the Field" chapter very kindly shared their time and hard-won lessons. We give thanks to Ben Jackson, Radim Řehůřek, Sebastjan Trebca, Alex Kelly, Marko Tasic, and Andrew Godwin for their time and effort.

## CHAPTER 1

Understanding Performant Python

Questions You'll Be Able to Answer After This Chapter

- What are the elements of a computer's architecture?
- What are some common alternate computer architectures?
- How does Python abstract the underlying computer architecture?
- What are some of the hurdles to making performant Python code?
- What are the different types of performance problems?

Programming computers can be thought of as moving bits of data and transforming them in special ways in order to achieve a particular result. However, these actions have a time cost. Consequently, high performance programming can be thought of as the act of minimizing these operations by either reducing the overhead (i.e., writing more efficient code) or by changing the way that we do these operations in order to make each one more meaningful (i.e., finding a more suitable algorithm).

Let's focus on reducing the overhead in code in order to gain more insight into the actual hardware on which we are moving these bits. This may seem like a futile exercise, since Python works quite hard to abstract away direct interactions with the hardware. However, by understanding both the best way that bits can be moved in the real hardware and the ways that Python's abstractions force your bits to move, you can make progress toward writing high performance programs in Python.

The Fundamental Computer System

The underlying components that make up a computer can be simplified into three basic parts: the computing units, the memory units, and the connections between them. In addition, each of these units has different properties that we can use to understand them. The computational unit has the property of how many computations it can do per second, the memory unit has the properties of how much data it can hold and how fast we can read from and write to it, and finally the connections have the property of how fast they can move data from one place to another.

Using these building blocks, we can talk about a standard workstation at multiple levels of sophistication. For example, the standard workstation can be thought of as having a central processing unit (CPU) as the computational unit, connected to both the random access memory (RAM) and the hard drive as two separate memory units (each having different capacities and read/write speeds), and finally a bus that provides the connections between all of these parts. However, we can also go into more detail and see that the CPU itself has several memory units in it: the L1, L2, and sometimes even the L3 and L4 cache, which have small capacities but very fast speeds (from several kilobytes to a dozen megabytes). These extra memory units are connected to the CPU with a special bus called the *backside bus*. Furthermore, new computer architectures generally come with new configurations (for example, Intel's Nehalem CPUs replaced the frontside bus with the Intel QuickPath Interconnect and restructured many connections). Finally, in both of these approximations of a workstation we have neglected the network connection, which is effectively a very slow connection to potentially many other computing and memory units!

To help untangle these various intricacies, let's go over a brief description of these fundamental blocks.

Computing Units

The computing unit of a computer is the centerpiece of its usefulness—it provides the ability to transform any bits it receives into other bits or to change the state of the current process. CPUs are the most commonly used computing unit; however, graphics processing units (GPUs), which were originally typically used to speed up computer graphics but are becoming more applicable for numerical applications, are gaining popularity due to their intrinsically parallel nature, which allows many calculations to happen simultaneously. Regardless of its type, a computing unit takes in a series of bits (for example, bits representing numbers) and outputs another set of bits (for example, representing the sum of those numbers). In addition to the basic arithmetic operations on integers and real numbers and bitwise operations on binary numbers, some computing units also provide very specialized operations, such as the "fused multiply add" operation, which takes in three numbers, A,B,C, and returns the value A * B + C.

The main properties of interest in a computing unit are the number of operations it can do in one cycle and how many cycles it can do in one second. The first value is measured by its instructions per cycle (IPC),[1] while the latter value is measured by its clock speed. These two measures are always competing with each other when new computing units are being made. For example, the Intel Core series has a very high IPC but a lower clock speed, while the Pentium 4 chip has the reverse. GPUs, on the other hand, have a very high IPC and clock speed, but they suffer from other problems, which we will outline later.

Furthermore, while increasing clock speed almost immediately speeds up all programs running on that computational unit (because they are able to do more calculations per second), having a higher IPC can also drastically affect computing by changing the level of *vectorization* that is possible. Vectorization is when a CPU is provided with multiple pieces of data at a time and is able to operate on all of them at once. This sort of CPU instruction is known as SIMD (Single Instruction, Multiple Data).

In general, computing units have been advancing quite slowly over the past decade (see Figure 1-1). Clock speeds and IPC have both been stagnant because of the physical limitations of making transistors smaller and smaller. As a result, chip manufacturers have been relying on other methods to gain more speed, including hyperthreading, more clever out-of-order execution, and multicore architectures.

Hyperthreading presents a virtual second CPU to the host operating system (OS), and clever hardware logic tries to interleave two threads of instructions into the execution units on a single CPU. When successful, gains of up to 30% over a single thread can be achieved. Typically this works well when the units of work across both threads use different types of execution unit—for example, one performs floating-point operations and the other performs integer operations.

Out-of-order execution enables a compiler to spot that some parts of a linear program sequence do not depend on the results of a previous piece of work, and therefore that both pieces of work could potentially occur in any order or at the same time. As long as sequential results are presented at the right time, the program continues to execute correctly, even though pieces of work are computed out of their programmed order. This enables some instructions to execute when others might be blocked (e.g., waiting for a memory access), allowing greater overall utilization of the available resources.

Finally, and most important for the higher-level programmer, is the prevalence of multi-core architectures. These architectures include multiple CPUs within the same unit, which increases the total capability without running into barriers in making each in-dividual unit faster. This is why it is currently hard to find any machine with less than two cores—in this case, the computer has two physical computing units that are con-nected to each other. While this increases the total number of operations that can be

---

1. Not to be confused with interprocess communication, which shares the same acronym—we'll look at the topic in Chapter 9.

done per second, it introduces intricacies in fully utilizing both computing units at the same time.

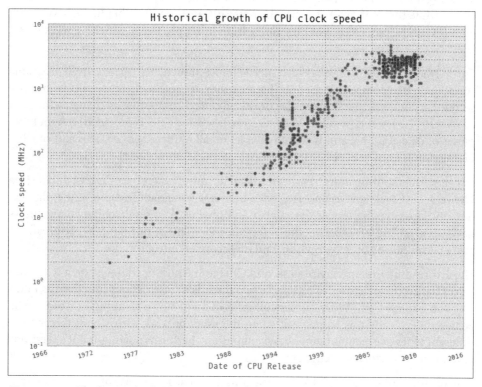

Figure 1-1. Clock speed of CPUs over time (data from CPU DB (http://cpudb.stan ford.edu/))

Simply adding more cores to a CPU does not always speed up a program's execution time. This is because of something known as *Amdahl's law*. Simply stated, Amdahl's law says that if a program designed to run on multiple cores has some routines that must run on one core, this will be the bottleneck for the final speedup that can be achieved by allocating more cores.

For example, if we had a survey we wanted 100 people to fill out, and that survey took 1 minute to complete, we could complete this task in 100 minutes if we had one person asking the questions (i.e., this person goes to participant 1, asks the questions, waits for the responses, then moves to participant 2). This method of having one person asking the questions and waiting for responses is similar to a serial process. In serial processes, we have operations being satisfied one at a time, each one waiting for the previous operation to complete.

However, we could perform the survey in parallel if we had two people asking the questions, which would let us finish the process in only 50 minutes. This can be done because each individual person asking the questions does not need to know anything about the other person asking questions. As a result, the task can be easily split up without having any dependency between the question askers.

Adding more people asking the questions will give us more speedups, until we have 100 people asking questions. At this point, the process would take 1 minute and is simply limited by the time it takes the participant to answer questions. Adding more people asking questions will not result in any further speedups, because these extra people will have no tasks to perform—all the participants are already being asked questions! At this point, the only way to reduce the overall time to run the survey is to reduce the amount of time it takes for an individual survey, the serial portion of the problem, to complete. Similarly, with CPUs, we can add more cores that can perform various chunks of the computation as necessary until we reach a point where the bottleneck is a specific core finishing its task. In other words, the bottleneck in any parallel calculation is always the smaller serial tasks that are being spread out.

Furthermore, a major hurdle with utilizing multiple cores in Python is Python's use of a *global interpreter lock* (GIL). The GIL makes sure that a Python process can only run one instruction at a time, regardless of the number of cores it is currently using. This means that even though some Python code has access to multiple cores at a time, only one core is running a Python instruction at any given time. Using the previous example of a survey, this would mean that even if we had 100 question askers, only one could ask a question and listen to a response at a time. This effectively removes any sort of benefit from having multiple question askers! While this may seem like quite a hurdle, especially if the current trend in computing is to have multiple computing units rather than having faster ones, this problem can be avoided by using other standard library tools, like `multiprocessing`, or technologies such as `numexpr`, Cython, or distributed models of computing.

Memory Units

Memory units in computers are used to store bits. This could be bits representing variables in your program, or bits representing the pixels of an image. Thus, the abstraction of a memory unit applies to the registers in your motherboard as well as your RAM and hard drive. The one major difference between all of these types of memory units is the speed at which they can read/write data. To make things more complicated, the read/write speed is heavily dependent on the way that data is being read.

For example, most memory units perform much better when they read one large chunk of data as opposed to many small chunks (this is referred to as *sequential read* versus *random data*). If the data in these memory units is thought of like pages in a large book, this means that most memory units have better read/write speeds when going through the book page by page rather than constantly flipping from one random page to another. While this fact is generally true across all memory units, the amount that this affects each type is drastically different.

In addition to the read/write speeds, memory units also have *latency*, which can be characterized as the time it takes the device to find the data that is being used. For a spinning hard drive, this latency can be high because the disk needs to physically spin up to speed and the read head must move to the right position. On the other hand, for RAM this can be quite small because everything is solid state. Here is a short description of the various memory units that are commonly found inside a standard workstation, in order of read/write speeds:

Spinning hard drive
> Long-term storage that persists even when the computer is shut down. Generally has slow read/write speeds because the disk must be physically spun and moved. Degraded performance with random access patterns but very large capacity (terabyte range).

Solid state hard drive
> Similar to a spinning hard drive, with faster read/write speeds but smaller capacity (gigabyte range).

RAM
> Used to store application code and data (such as any variables being used). Has fast read/write characteristics and performs well with random access patterns, but is generally limited in capacity (gigabyte range).

L1/L2 cache
> Extremely fast read/write write speeds. Data going to the CPU *must* go through here. Very small capacity (kilobyte range).

Figure 1-2 gives a graphic representation of the differences between these types of memory units by looking at the characteristics of currently available consumer hardware.

A clearly visible trend is that read/write speeds and capacity are inversely proportional —as we try to increase speed, capacity gets reduced. Because of this, many systems implement a tiered approach to memory: data starts in its full state in the hard drive, part of it moves to RAM, then a much smaller subset moves to the L1/L2 cache. This method of tiering enables programs to keep memory in different places depending on access speed requirements. When trying to optimize the memory patterns of a program, we are simply optimizing which data is placed where, how it is laid out (in order to increase the number of sequential reads), and how many times it is moved between the various locations. In addition, methods such as asynchronous I/O and preemptive caching provide ways to make sure that data is always where it needs to be without having to waste computing time—most of these processes can happen independently, while other calculations are being performed!

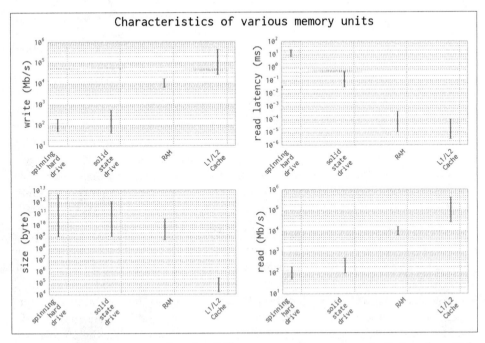

Figure 1-2. Characteristic values for different types of memory units (values from February 2014)

Communications Layers

Finally, let's look at how all of these fundamental blocks communicate with each other. There are many different modes of communication, but they are all variants on a thing called a *bus*.

The *frontside bus*, for example, is the connection between the RAM and the L1/L2 cache. It moves data that is ready to be transformed by the processor into the staging ground to get ready for calculation, and moves finished calculations out. There are other buses, too, such as the external bus that acts as the main route from hardware devices (such as hard drives and networking cards) to the CPU and system memory. This bus is generally slower than the frontside bus.

In fact, many of the benefits of the L1/L2 cache are attributable to the faster bus. Being able to queue up data necessary for computation in large chunks on a slow bus (from RAM to cache) and then having it available at very fast speeds from the backside bus (from cache to CPU) enables the CPU to do more calculations without waiting such a long time.

Similarly, many of the drawbacks of using a GPU come from the bus it is connected on: since the GPU is generally a peripheral device, it communicates through the PCI bus, which is much slower than the frontside bus. As a result, getting data into and out of the GPU can be quite a taxing operation. The advent of heterogeneous computing, or computing blocks that have both a CPU and a GPU on the frontside bus, aims at reducing the data transfer cost and making GPU computing more of an available option, even when a lot of data must be transferred.

In addition to the communication blocks within the computer, the network can be thought of as yet another communication block. This block, however, is much more pliable than the ones discussed previously; a network device can be connected to a memory device, such as a network attached storage (NAS) device or another computing block, as in a computing node in a cluster. However, network communications are generally much slower than the other types of communications mentioned previously. While the frontside bus can transfer dozens of gigabits per second, the network is limited to the order of several dozen megabits.

It is clear, then, that the main property of a bus is its speed: how much data it can move in a given amount of time. This property is given by combining two quantities: how much data can be moved in one transfer (bus width) and how many transfers it can do per second (bus frequency). It is important to note that the data moved in one transfer is always sequential: a chunk of data is read off of the memory and moved to a different place. Thus, the speed of a bus is broken up into these two quantities because individually they can affect different aspects of computation: a large bus width can help vectorized code (or any code that sequentially reads through memory) by making it possible to move all the relevant data in one transfer, while, on the other hand, having a small bus width but a very high frequency of transfers can help code that must do many reads from random parts of memory. Interestingly, one of the ways that these properties are changed by computer designers is by the physical layout of the motherboard: when chips are placed closed to one another, the length of the physical wires joining them is smaller, which can allow for faster transfer speeds. In addition, the number of wires itself dictates the width of the bus (giving real physical meaning to the term!).

Since interfaces can be tuned to give the right performance for a specific application, it is no surprise that there are hundreds of different types. Figure 1-3 (from Wikimedia Commons (*http://commons.wikimedia.org*)) shows the bitrates for a sampling of common interfaces. Note that this doesn't speak at all about the latency of the connections, which dictates how long it takes for a data request to be responded to (while latency is very computer-dependent, there are some basic limitations inherent to the interfaces being used).

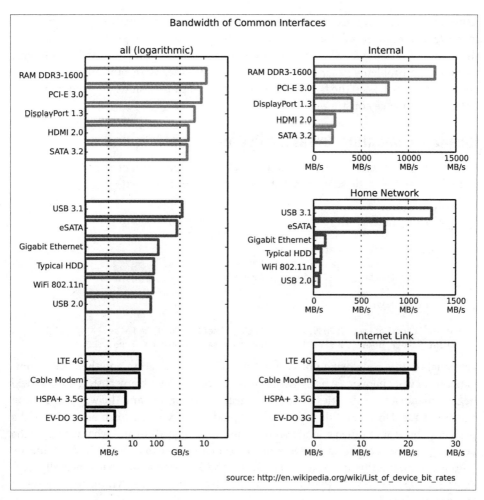

Figure 1-3. Connection speeds of various common interfaces (image by Leadbuffalo (http://bit.ly/interface_speeds) [CC BY-SA 3.0])

Putting the Fundamental Elements Together

Understanding the basic components of a computer is not enough to fully understand the problems of high performance programming. The interplay of all of these components and how they work together to solve a problem introduces extra levels of complexity. In this section we will explore some toy problems, illustrating how the ideal solutions would work and how Python approaches them.

A warning: this section may seem bleak—most of the remarks seem to say that Python is natively incapable of dealing with the problems of performance. This is untrue, for two reasons. Firstly, in all of these "components of performant computing" we have neglected one very important component: the developer. What native Python may lack in performance it gets back right away with speed of development. Furthermore, throughout the book we will introduce modules and philosophies that can help mitigate many of the problems described here with relative ease. With both of these aspects combined, we will keep the fast development mindset of Python while removing many of the performance constraints.

Idealized Computing Versus the Python Virtual Machine

In order to better understand the components of high performance programming, let us look at a simple code sample that checks if a number is prime:

```python
import math
def check_prime(number):
    sqrt_number = math.sqrt(number)
    number_float = float(number)
    for i in xrange(2, int(sqrt_number)+1):
        if (number_float / i).is_integer():
            return False
    return True

print "check_prime(10000000) = ", check_prime(10000000) # False
print "check_prime(10000019) = ", check_prime(10000019) # True
```

Let's analyze this code using our abstract model of computation and then draw comparisons to what happens when Python runs this code. As with any abstraction, we will neglect many of the subtleties in both the idealized computer and the way that Python runs the code. However, this is generally a good exercise to perform before solving a problem: think about the general components of the algorithm and what would be the best way for the computing components to come together in order to find a solution. By understanding this ideal situation and having knowledge of what is actually happening under the hood in Python, we can iteratively bring our Python code closer to the optimal code.

Idealized computing

When the code starts, we have the value of number stored in RAM. In order to calculate sqrt_number and number_float, we need to send that value over to the CPU. Ideally, we could send the value once; it would get stored inside the CPU's L1/L2 cache and the CPU would do the calculations and then send the values back to RAM to get stored. This scenario is ideal because we have minimized the number of reads of the value of number from RAM, instead opting for reads from the L1/L2 cache, which are much faster. Furthermore, we have minimized the number of data transfers through the frontside bus, opting for communications through the faster backside bus instead (which connects the various caches to the CPU). This theme of keeping data where it is needed, and moving it as little as possible, is very important when it comes to optimization. The concept of "heavy data" refers to the fact that it takes time and effort to move data around, which is something we would like to avoid.

For the loop in the code, rather than sending one value of i at a time to the CPU, we would like to send it both number_float and *several* values of i to check at the same time. This is possible because the CPU vectorizes operations with no additional time cost, meaning it can do multiple independent computations at the same time. So, we want to send number_float to the CPU cache, in addition to as many values of i as the cache can hold. For each of the number_float/i pairs, we will divide them and check if the result is a whole number; then we will send a signal back indicating whether any of the values was indeed an integer. If so, the function ends. If not, we repeat. In this way, we only need to communicate back one result for many values of i, rather than depending on the slow bus for every value. This takes advantage of a CPU's ability to *vectorize* a calculation, or run one instruction on multiple data in one clock cycle.

This concept of vectorization is illustrated by the following code:

```
import math
def check_prime(number):
    sqrt_number = math.sqrt(number)
    number_float = float(number)
    numbers = range(2, int(sqrt_number)+1)
    for i in xrange(0, len(numbers), 5):
        # the following line is not valid Python code
        result = (number_float / numbers[i:(i+5)]).is_integer()
        if any(result):
            return False
    return True
```

Here, we set up the processing such that the division and the checking for integers are done on a set of five values of i at a time. If properly vectorized, the CPU can do this line in one step as opposed to doing a separate calculation for every i. Ideally, the any(result) operation would also happen in the CPU without having to transfer the results back to RAM. We will talk more about vectorization, how it works, and when it benefits your code in Chapter 6.

Python's virtual machine

The Python interpreter does a lot of work to try to abstract away the underlying computing elements that are being used. At no point does a programmer need to worry about allocating memory for arrays, how to arrange that memory, or in what sequence it is being sent to the CPU. This is a benefit of Python, since it lets you focus on the algorithms that are being implemented. However, it comes at a huge performance cost.

It is important to realize that at its core, Python is indeed running a set of very optimized instructions. The trick, however, is getting Python to perform them in the correct sequence in order to achieve better performance. For example, it is quite easy to see that, in the following example, `search_fast` will run faster than `search_slow` simply because it skips the unnecessary computations that result from not terminating the loop early, even though both solutions have runtime O(n).

```
def search_fast(haystack, needle):
    for item in haystack:
        if item == needle:
            return True
    return False

def search_slow(haystack, needle):
    return_value = False
    for item in haystack:
        if item == needle:
            return_value = True
    return return_value
```

Identifying slow regions of code through profiling and finding more efficient ways of doing the same calculations is similar to finding these useless operations and removing them; the end result is the same, but the number of computations and data transfers is reduced drastically.

One of the impacts of this abstraction layer is that vectorization is not immediately achievable. Our initial prime number routine will run one iteration of the loop per value of i instead of combining several iterations. However, looking at the abstracted vectorization example, we see that it is not valid Python code, since we cannot divide a float by a list. External libraries such as numpy will help with this situation by adding the ability to do vectorized mathematical operations.

Furthermore, Python's abstraction hurts any optimizations that rely on keeping the L1/L2 cache filled with the relevant data for the next computation. This comes from many factors, the first being that Python objects are not laid out in the most optimal way in memory. This is a consequence of Python being a garbage-collected language—memory is automatically allocated and freed when needed. This creates memory fragmentation that can hurt the transfers to the CPU caches. In addition, at no point is there an opportunity to change the layout of a data structure directly in memory, which means that one transfer on the bus may not contain all the relevant information for a computation, even though it might have all fit within the bus width.

A second, more fundamental problem comes from Python's dynamic types and it not being compiled. As many C programmers have learned throughout the years, the compiler is often smarter than you are. When compiling code that is static, the compiler can do many tricks to change the way things are laid out and how the CPU will run certain instructions in order to optimize them. Python, however, is not compiled: to make matters worse, it has dynamic types, which means that inferring any possible opportunities for optimizations algorithmically is drastically harder since code functionality can be changed during runtime. There are many ways to mitigate this problem, foremost being use of Cython, which allows Python code to be compiled and allows the user to create "hints" to the compiler as to how dynamic the code actually is.

Finally, the previously mentioned GIL can hurt performance if trying to parallelize this code. For example, let's assume we change the code to use multiple CPU cores such that each core gets a chunk of the numbers from 2 to sqrtN. Each core can do its calculation for its chunk of numbers and then, when they are all done, they can compare their calculations. This seems like a good solution since, although we lose the early termination of the loop, we can reduce the number of checks each core has to do by the number of cores we are using (i.e., if we had M cores, each core would have to do sqrtN / M checks). However, because of the GIL, only one core can be used at a time. This means that we would effectively be running the same code as the unparallelled version, but we no longer have early termination. We can avoid this problem by using multiple processes (with the multiprocessing module) instead of multiple threads, or by using Cython or foreign functions.

So Why Use Python?

Python is highly expressive and easy to learn—new programmers quickly discover that they can do quite a lot in a short space of time. Many Python libraries wrap tools written in other languages to make it easy to call other systems; for example, the scikit-learn machine learning system wraps LIBLINEAR and LIBSVM (both of which are written in C), and the numpy library includes BLAS and other C and Fortran libraries. As a result, Python code that properly utilizes these modules can indeed be as fast as comparable C code.

Python is described as "batteries included," as many important and stable libraries are built in. These include:

unicode and bytes
: Baked into the core language

array
: Memory-efficient arrays for primitive types

math
: Basic mathematical operations, including some simple statistics

sqlite3
: A wrapper around the prevalent SQL file-based storage engine SQLite3

collections
: A wide variety of objects, including a deque, counter, and dictionary variants

Outside of the core language there is a huge variety of libraries, including:

numpy
: a numerical Python library (a bedrock library for anything to do with matrices)

scipy
: a very large collection of trusted scientific libraries, often wrapping highly respected C and Fortran libraries

pandas
: a library for data analysis, similar to R's data frames or an Excel spreadsheet, built on scipy and numpy

scikit-learn
: rapidly turning into the default machine learning library, built on scipy

biopython
: a bioinformatics library similar to bioperl

tornado
: a library that provides easy bindings for concurrency

Database bindings
: for communicating with virtually all databases, including Redis, MongoDB, HDF5, and SQL

Web development frameworks
: performant systems for creating websites such as django, pyramid, flask, and tornado

OpenCV
: bindings for computer vision

API bindings
: for easy access to popular web APIs such as Google, Twitter, and LinkedIn

A large selection of managed environments and shells is available to fit various deployment scenarios, including:

- The standard distribution, available at *http://python.org*
- Enthought's EPD and Canopy, a very mature and capable environment
- Continuum's Anaconda, a scientifically focused environment
- Sage, a Matlab-like environment including an integrated development environment (IDE)
- Python(x,y)
- IPython, an interactive Python shell heavily used by scientists and developers

- IPython Notebook, a browser-based frontend to IPython, heavily used for teaching and demonstrations
- BPython, interactive Python shell

One of Python's main strengths is that it enables fast prototyping of an idea. Due to the wide variety of supporting libraries it is easy to test if an idea is feasible, even if the first implementation might be rather flaky.

If you want to make your mathematical routines faster, look to `numpy`. If you want to experiment with machine learning, try `scikit-learn`. If you are cleaning and manipulating data, then `pandas` is a good choice.

In general, it is sensible to raise the question, "If our system runs faster, will we as a team run slower in the long run?" It is always possible to squeeze more performance out of a system if enough man-hours are invested, but this might lead to brittle and poorly understood optimizations that ultimately trip the team up.

One example might be the introduction of Cython ("Cython" on page 140), a compiler-based approach to annotating Python code with C-like types so the transformed code can be compiled using a C compiler. While the speed gains can be impressive (often achieving C-like speeds with relatively little effort), the cost of supporting this code will increase. In particular, it might be harder to support this new module, as team members will need a certain maturity in their programming ability to understand some of the trade-offs that have occurred when leaving the Python virtual machine that introduced the performance increase.

## CHAPTER 2

Profiling to Find Bottlenecks

Questions You'll Be Able to Answer After This Chapter

- How can I identify speed and RAM bottlenecks in my code?
- How do I profile CPU and memory usage?
- What depth of profiling should I use?
- How can I profile a long-running application?
- What's happening under the hood with CPython?
- How do I keep my code correct while tuning performance?

Profiling lets us find bottlenecks so we can do the least amount of work to get the biggest practical performance gain. While we'd like to get huge gains in speed and reductions in resource usage with little work, practically you'll aim for your code to run "fast enough" and "lean enough" to fit your needs. Profiling will let you make the most pragmatic decisions for the least overall effort.

Any measurable resource can be profiled (not just the CPU!). In this chapter we look at both CPU time and memory usage. You could apply similar techniques to measure network bandwidth and disk I/O too.

If a program is running too slowly or using too much RAM, then you'll want to fix whichever parts of your code are responsible. You could, of course, skip profiling and fix what you *believe* might be the problem—but be wary, as you'll often end up "fixing" the wrong thing. Rather than using your intuition, it is far more sensible to first profile, having defined a hypothesis, before making changes to the structure of your code.

Sometimes it's good to be lazy. By profiling first, you can quickly identify the bottlenecks that need to be solved, and then you can solve just enough of these to achieve the performance you need. If you avoid profiling and jump to optimization, then it is quite likely that you'll do more work in the long run. Always be driven by the results of profiling.

Profiling Efficiently

The first aim of profiling is to test a representative system to identify what's slow (or using too much RAM, or causing too much disk I/O or network I/O). Profiling typically adds an overhead (10x to 100x slowdowns can be typical), and you still want your code to be used as similarly to in a real-world situation as possible. Extract a test case and isolate the piece of the system that you need to test. Preferably, it'll have been written to be in its own set of modules already.

The basic techniques that are introduced first in this chapter include the `%timeit` magic in IPython, `time.time()`, and a timing decorator. You can use these techniques to understand the behavior of statements and functions.

Then we will cover `cProfile` ("Using the cProfile Module" on page 31), showing you how to use this built-in tool to understand which functions in your code take the longest to run. This will give you a high-level view of the problem so you can direct your attention to the critical functions.

Next, we'll look at `line_profiler` ("Using line_profiler for Line-by-Line Measurements" on page 37), which will profile your chosen functions on a line-by-line basis. The result will include a count of the number of times each line is called and the percentage of time spent on each line. This is exactly the information you need to understand what's running slowly and why.

Armed with the results of `line_profiler`, you'll have the information you need to move on to using a compiler (Chapter 7).

In Chapter 6 (Example 6-8), you'll learn how to use `perf stat` to understand the number of instructions that are ultimately executed on a CPU and how efficiently the CPU's caches are utilized. This allows for advanced-level tuning of matrix operations. You should take a look at that example when you're done with this chapter.

After `line_profiler` we show you `heapy` ("Inspecting Objects on the Heap with heapy" on page 48), which can track all of the objects inside Python's memory—this is great for hunting down strange memory leaks. If you're working with long-running systems, then `dowser` ("Using dowser for Live Graphing of Instantiated Variables" on page 50) will interest you; it allows you to introspect live objects in a long-running process via a web browser interface.

To help you understand why your RAM usage is high, we'll show you `memory_profil` `er` ("Using memory_profiler to Diagnose Memory Usage" on page 42). It is particularly useful for tracking RAM usage over time on a labeled chart, so you can explain to colleagues why certain functions use more RAM than expected.

 Whatever approach you take to profiling your code, you must remember to have adequate unit test coverage in your code. Unit tests help you to avoid silly mistakes and help to keep your results reproducible. Avoid them at your peril.

Always profile your code before compiling or rewriting your algorithms. You need evidence to determine the most efficient ways to make your code run faster.

Finally, we'll give you an introduction to the Python bytecode inside CPython ("Using the dis Module to Examine CPython Bytecode" on page 52), so you can understand what's happening "under the hood." In particular, having an understanding of how Python's stack-based virtual machine operates will help you to understand why certain coding styles run more slowly than others.

Before the end of the chapter, we'll review how to integrate unit tests while profiling ("Unit Testing During Optimization to Maintain Correctness" on page 56), to preserve the correctness of your code while you make it run more efficiently.

We'll finish with a discussion of profiling strategies ("Strategies to Profile Your Code Successfully" on page 59), so you can reliably profile your code and gather the correct data to test your hypotheses. Here you'll learn about how dynamic CPU frequency scaling and features like TurboBoost can skew your profiling results and how they can be disabled.

To walk through all of these steps, we need an easy-to-analyze function. The next section introduces the Julia set. It is a CPU-bound function that's a little hungry for RAM; it also exhibits nonlinear behavior (so we can't easily predict the outcomes), which means we need to profile it at runtime rather than analyzing it offline.

Introducing the Julia Set

The Julia set (*http://en.wikipedia.org/wiki/Julia_set*) is an interesting CPU-bound problem for us to begin with. It is a fractal sequence that generates a complex output image, named after Gaston Julia.

The code that follows is a little longer than a version you might write yourself. It has a CPU-bound component and a very explicit set of inputs. This configuration allows us to profile both the CPU usage and the RAM usage so we can understand which parts of our code are consuming two of our scarce computing resources. This implementation is *deliberately* suboptimal, so we can identify memory-consuming operations and slow statements. Later in this chapter we'll fix a slow logic statement and a memory-consuming statement, and in Chapter 7 we'll significantly speed up the overall execution time of this function.

We will analyze a block of code that produces both a false grayscale plot (Figure 2-1) and a pure grayscale variant of the Julia set (Figure 2-3), at the complex point c=-0.62772-0.42193j. A Julia set is produced by calculating each pixel in isolation; this is an "embarrassingly parallel problem" as no data is shared between points.

Figure 2-1. Julia set plot with a false grayscale to highlight detail

If we chose a different c, then we'd get a different image. The location we have chosen has regions that are quick to calculate and others that are slow to calculate; this is useful for our analysis.

The problem is interesting because we calculate each pixel by applying a loop that could be applied an indeterminate number of times. On each iteration we test to see if this coordinate's value escapes toward infinity, or if it seems to be held by an attractor. Coordinates that cause few iterations are colored darkly in Figure 2-1, and those that cause a high number of iterations are colored white. White regions are more complex to calculate and so take longer to generate.

We define a set of z-coordinates that we'll test. The function that we calculate squares the complex number z and adds c:

$$f(z) = z^2 + c$$

We iterate on this function while testing to see if the escape condition holds using abs. If the escape function is False, then we break out of the loop and record the number of iterations we performed at this coordinate. If the escape function is never False, then we stop after maxiter iterations. We will later turn this z's result into a colored pixel representing this complex location.

In pseudocode, it might look like:

```
for z in coordinates:
    for iteration in range(maxiter):  # limited iterations per point
        if abs(z) < 2.0:  # has the escape condition been broken?
            z = z*z + c
        else:
            break
    # store the iteration count for each z and draw later
```

To explain this function, let's try two coordinates.

First, we'll use the coordinate that we draw in the top-left corner of the plot at -1.8-1.8j. We must test abs(z) < 2 before we can try the update rule:

```
z = -1.8-1.8j
print abs(z)

2.54558441227
```

We can see that for the top-left coordinate the abs(z) test will be False on the zeroth iteration, so we do not perform the update rule. The output value for this coordinate is 0.

Now let's jump to the center of the plot at z = 0 + 0j and try a few iterations:

```
c = -0.62772-0.42193j
z = 0+0j
for n in range(9):
    z = z*z + c
    print "{}: z={:33}, abs(z)={:0.2f}, c={}".format(n, z, abs(z), c)

0: z=                   (-0.62772-0.42193j), abs(z)=0.76, c=(-0.62772-0.42193j)
1: z=       (-0.4117125265+0.1077777992j), abs(z)=0.43, c=(-0.62772-0.42193j)
2: z=(-0.469828849523-0.510676940018j), abs(z)=0.69, c=(-0.62772-0.42193j)
3: z=(-0.667771789222+0.057931518414j), abs(z)=0.67, c=(-0.62772-0.42193j)
4: z=(-0.185156898345-0.499300067407j), abs(z)=0.53, c=(-0.62772-0.42193j)
5: z=(-0.842737480308-0.237032296351j), abs(z)=0.88, c=(-0.62772-0.42193j)
6: z=(0.026302151203-0.0224179996428j), abs(z)=0.03, c=(-0.62772-0.42193j)
7: z=  (-0.62753076355-0.423109283233j), abs(z)=0.76, c=(-0.62772-0.42193j)
8: z=(-0.412946606356+0.109098183144j), abs(z)=0.43, c=(-0.62772-0.42193j)
```

We can see that each update to z for these first iterations leaves it with a value where
abs(z) < 2 is True. For this coordinate we can iterate 300 times, and still the test will
be True. We cannot tell how many iterations we must perform before the condition
becomes False, and this may be an infinite sequence. The maximum iteration (maxit
er) break clause will stop us iterating potentially forever.

In Figure 2-2 we see the first 50 iterations of the preceding sequence. For 0+0j (the solid
line with circle markers) the sequence appears to repeat every eighth iteration, but each
sequence of seven calculations has a minor deviation from the previous sequence—we
can't tell if this point will iterate forever within the boundary condition, or for a long
time, or maybe for just a few more iterations. The dashed cutoff line shows the boundary at +2.

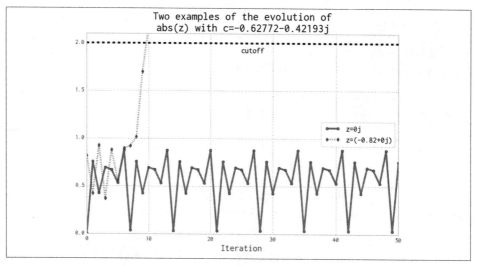

Figure 2-2. Two coordinate examples evolving for the Julia set

For -0.82+0j (the dashed line with diamond markers), we can see that after the ninth update the absolute result has exceeded the +2 cutoff, so we stop updating this value.

Calculating the Full Julia Set

In this section we break down the code that generates the Julia set. We'll analyze it in various ways throughout this chapter. As shown in Example 2-1, at the start of our module we import the time module for our first profiling approach and define some coordinate constants.

Example 2-1. Defining global constants for the coordinate space

```
"""Julia set generator without optional PIL-based image drawing"""
import time

# area of complex space to investigate
x1, x2, y1, y2 = -1.8, 1.8, -1.8, 1.8
c_real, c_imag = -0.62772, -.42193
```

To generate the plot, we create two lists of input data. The first is zs (complex z-coordinates), and the second is cs (a complex initial condition). Neither list varies, and we could optimize cs to a single c value as a constant. The rationale for building two input lists is so that we have some reasonable-looking data to profile when we profile RAM usage later in this chapter.

To build the zs and cs lists, we need to know the coordinates for each z. In Example 2-2 we build up these coordinates using xcoord and ycoord and a specified x_step and y_step. The somewhat verbose nature of this setup is useful when porting the code to other tools (e.g., to numpy) and to other Python environments, as it helps to have everything *very* clearly defined for debugging.

Example 2-2. Establishing the coordinate lists as inputs to our calculation function

```
def calc_pure_python(desired_width, max_iterations):
    """Create a list of complex coordinates (zs) and complex
    parameters (cs), build Julia set, and display"""
    x_step = (float(x2 - x1) / float(desired_width))
    y_step = (float(y1 - y2) / float(desired_width))
    x = []
    y = []
    ycoord = y2
    while ycoord > y1:
        y.append(ycoord)
        ycoord += y_step
    xcoord = x1
    while xcoord < x2:
        x.append(xcoord)
        xcoord += x_step
    # Build a list of coordinates and the initial condition for each cell.
```

```
# Note that our initial condition is a constant and could easily be removed;
# we use it to simulate a real-world scenario with several inputs to
# our function.
zs = []
cs = []
for ycoord in y:
    for xcoord in x:
        zs.append(complex(xcoord, ycoord))
        cs.append(complex(c_real, c_imag))

print "Length of x:", len(x)
print "Total elements:", len(zs)
start_time = time.time()
output = calculate_z_serial_purepython(max_iterations, zs, cs)
end_time = time.time()
secs = end_time - start_time
print calculate_z_serial_purepython.func_name + " took", secs, "seconds"

# This sum is expected for a 1000^2 grid with 300 iterations.
# It catches minor errors we might introduce when we're
# working on a fixed set of inputs.
assert sum(output) == 33219980
```

Having built the zs and cs lists, we output some information about the size of the lists and calculate the output list via calculate_z_serial_purepython. Finally, we sum the contents of output and assert that it matches the expected output value. Ian uses it here to confirm that no errors creep into the book.

As the code is deterministic, we can verify that the function works as we expect by summing all the calculated values. This is useful as a sanity check—when we make changes to numerical code it is *very* sensible to check that we haven't broken the algorithm. Ideally we would use unit tests and we'd test more than one configuration of the problem.

Next, in Example 2-3, we define the calculate_z_serial_purepython function, which expands on the algorithm we discussed earlier. Notably, we also define an output list at the start that has the same length as the input zs and cs lists. You may also wonder why we're using range rather than xrange–this is so, in "Using memory_profiler to Diagnose Memory Usage" on page 42, we can show how wasteful range can be!

Example 2-3. Our CPU-bound calculation function

```python
def calculate_z_serial_purepython(maxiter, zs, cs):
    """Calculate output list using Julia update rule"""
    output = [0] * len(zs)
    for i in range(len(zs)):
        n = 0
        z = zs[i]
        c = cs[i]
        while abs(z) < 2 and n < maxiter:
            z = z * z + c
            n += 1
        output[i] = n
    return output
```

Now we call the calculation routine in Example 2-4. By wrapping it in a __main__ check, we can safely import the module without starting the calculations for some of the profiling methods. Note that here we're not showing the method used to plot the output.

Example 2-4. main for our code

```python
if __name__ == "__main__":
    # Calculate the Julia set using a pure Python solution with
    # reasonable defaults for a laptop
    calc_pure_python(desired_width=1000, max_iterations=300)
```

Once we run the code, we see some output about the complexity of the problem:

```python
# running the above produces:
Length of x: 1000
Total elements: 1000000
calculate_z_serial_purepython took 12.3479790688 seconds
```

In the false-grayscale plot (Figure 2-1), the high-contrast color changes gave us an idea of where the cost of the function was slow-changing or fast-changing. Here, in Figure 2-3, we have a linear color map: black is quick to calculate and white is expensive to calculate.

By showing two representations of the same data, we can see that lots of detail is lost in the linear mapping. Sometimes it can be useful to have various representations in mind when investigating the cost of a function.

Figure 2-3. Julia plot example using a pure grayscale

Simple Approaches to Timing—print and a Decorator

After Example 2-4, we saw the output generated by several print statements in our code. On Ian's laptop this code takes approximately 12 seconds to run using CPython 2.7. It is useful to note that there is always some variation in execution time. You must observe the normal variation when you're timing your code, or you might incorrectly attribute an improvement in your code simply to a random variation in execution time.

Your computer will be performing other tasks while running your code, such as accessing the network, disk, or RAM, and these factors can cause variations in the execution time of your program.

Ian's laptop is a Dell E6420 with an Intel Core I7-2720QM CPU (2.20 GHz, 6 MB cache, Quad Core) and 8 GB of RAM running Ubuntu 13.10.

In calc_pure_python (Example 2-2), we can see several print statements. This is the simplest way to measure the execution time of a piece of code *inside* a function. It is a very basic approach, but despite being quick and dirty it can be very useful when you're first looking at a piece of code.

Using print statements is commonplace when debugging and profiling code. It quickly becomes unmanageable, but is useful for short investigations. Try to tidy them up when you're done with them, or they will clutter your stdout.

A slightly cleaner approach is to use a *decorator*—here, we add one line of code above the function that we care about. Our decorator can be very simple and just replicate the effect of the print statements. Later, we can make it more advanced.

In Example 2-5 we define a new function, timefn, which takes a function as an argument: the inner function, measure_time, takes *args (a variable number of positional arguments) and **kwargs (a variable number of key/value arguments) and passes them through to fn for execution. Around the execution of fn we capture time.time() and then print the result along with fn.func_name. The overhead of using this decorator is small, but if you're calling fn millions of times the overhead might become noticeable. We use @wraps(fn) to expose the function name and docstring to the caller of the decorated function (otherwise, we would see the function name and docstring for the decorator, not the function it decorates).

Example 2-5. Defining a decorator to automate timing measurements

```
from functools import wraps

def timefn(fn):
    @wraps(fn)
    def measure_time(*args, **kwargs):
        t1 = time.time()
        result = fn(*args, **kwargs)
        t2 = time.time()
        print ("@timefn:" + fn.func_name + " took " + str(t2 - t1) + " seconds")
        return result
    return measure_time


@timefn
def calculate_z_serial_purepython(maxiter, zs, cs):
    ...
```

When we run this version (we keep the print statements from before), we can see that the execution time in the decorated version is very slightly quicker than the call from calc_pure_python. This is due to the overhead of calling a function (the difference is very tiny):

```
Length of x: 1000
Total elements: 1000000
@timefn:calculate_z_serial_purepython took 12.2218790054 seconds
calculate_z_serial_purepython took 12.2219250043 seconds
```

 The addition of profiling information will inevitably slow your code down—some profiling options are very informative and induce a heavy speed penalty. The trade-off between profiling detail and speed will be something you have to consider.

We can use the timeit module as another way to get a coarse measurement of the execution speed of our CPU-bound function. More typically, you would use this when timing different types of simple expressions as you experiment with ways to solve a problem.

 Note that the timeit module temporarily disables the garbage collector. This might impact the speed you'll see with real-world operations if the garbage collector would normally be invoked by your operations. See the Python documentation (*http://bit.ly/time it_doc*) for help on this.

From the command line you can run timeit using:

```
$ python -m timeit -n 5 -r 5 -s "import julia1"
   "julia1.calc_pure_python(desired_width=1000,
   max_iterations=300)"
```

Note that you have to import the module as a setup step using -s, as calc_pure_python is inside that module. timeit has some sensible defaults for short sections of code, but for longer-running functions it can be sensible to specify the number of loops, whose results are averaged for each test (-n 5), and the number of repetitions (-r 5). The best result of all the repetitions is given as the answer.

By default, if we run timeit on this function without specifying -n and -r it runs 10 loops with 5 repetitions, and this takes 6 minutes to complete. Overriding the defaults can make sense if you want to get your results a little faster.

We're only interested in the best-case results, as the average and worst case are probably a result of interference by other processes. Choosing the best of five repetitions of five averaged results should give us a fairly stable result:

```
5 loops, best of 5: 13.1 sec per loop
```

Try running the benchmark several times to check if you get varying results—you may need more repetitions to settle on a stable fastest-result time. There is no "correct" configuration, so if you see a wide variation in your timing results, do more repetitions until your final result is stable.

Our results show that the overall cost of calling calc_pure_python is 13.1 seconds (as the best case), while single calls to calculate_z_serial_purepython take 12.2 seconds as measured by the @timefn decorator. The difference is mainly the time taken to create the zs and cs lists.

Inside IPython, we can use the magic %timeit in the same way. If you are developing your code interactively in IPython and the functions are in the local namespace (probably because you're using %run), then you can use:

```
%timeit calc_pure_python(desired_width=1000, max_iterations=300)
```

It is worth considering the variation in load that you get on a normal computer. Many background tasks are running (e.g., Dropbox, backups) that could impact the CPU and disk resources at random. Scripts in web pages can also cause unpredictable resource usage. Figure 2-4 shows the single CPU being used at 100% for some of the timing steps we just performed; the other cores on this machine are each lightly working on other tasks.

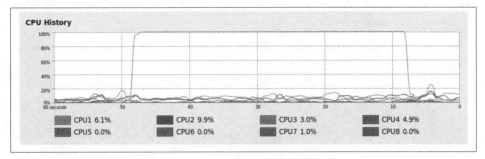

Figure 2-4. System Monitor on Ubuntu showing variation in background CPU usage while we time our function

Occasionally the System Monitor shows spikes of activity on this machine. It is sensible to watch your System Monitor to check that nothing else is interfering with your critical resources (CPU, disk, network).

Simple Timing Using the Unix time Command

We can step outside of Python for a moment to use a standard system utility on Unix-like systems. The following will record various views on the execution time of your program, and it won't care about the internal structure of your code:

```
$ /usr/bin/time -p python julia1_nopil.py
Length of x: 1000
Total elements: 1000000
calculate_z_serial_purepython took 12.7298331261 seconds
real 13.46
user 13.40
sys 0.04
```

Note that we specifically use /usr/bin/time rather than time so we get the system's time and not the simpler (and less useful) version built into our shell. If you try time --verbose and you get an error, you're probably looking at the shell's built-in time command and not the system command.

Using the -p portability flag, we get three results:

- `real` records the wall clock or elapsed time.

- `user` records the amount of time the CPU spent on your task outside of kernel functions.

- `sys` records the time spent in kernel-level functions.

By adding `user` and `sys`, you get a sense of how much time was spent in the CPU. The difference between this and `real` might tell you about the amount of time spent waiting for I/O; it might also suggest that your system is busy running other tasks that are distorting your measurements.

`time` is useful because it isn't specific to Python. It includes the time taken to start the `python` executable, which might be significant if you start lots of fresh processes (rather than having a long-running single process). If you often have short-running scripts where the startup time is a significant part of the overall runtime, then `time` can be a more useful measure.

We can add the `--verbose` flag to get even more output:

```
$ /usr/bin/time --verbose python julia1_nopil.py
Length of x: 1000
Total elements: 1000000
calculate_z_serial_purepython took 12.3145110607 seconds
        Command being timed: "python julia1_nopil.py"
        User time (seconds): 13.46
        System time (seconds): 0.05
        Percent of CPU this job got: 99%
        Elapsed (wall clock) time (h:mm:ss or m:ss): 0:13.53
        Average shared text size (kbytes): 0
        Average unshared data size (kbytes): 0
        Average stack size (kbytes): 0
        Average total size (kbytes): 0
        Maximum resident set size (kbytes): 131952
        Average resident set size (kbytes): 0
        Major (requiring I/O) page faults: 0
        Minor (reclaiming a frame) page faults: 58974
        Voluntary context switches: 3
        Involuntary context switches: 26
        Swaps: 0
        File system inputs: 0
        File system outputs: 1968
        Socket messages sent: 0
        Socket messages received: 0
        Signals delivered: 0
        Page size (bytes): 4096
        Exit status: 0
```

Probably the most useful indicator here is `Major (requiring I/O) page faults`, as this indicates whether the operating system is having to load pages of data from the disk because the data no longer resides in RAM. This will cause a speed penalty.

In our example the code and data requirements are small, so no page faults occur. If you have a memory-bound process, or several programs that use variable and large amounts of RAM, you might find that this gives you a clue as to which program is being slowed down by disk accesses at the operating system level because parts of it have been swapped out of RAM to disk.

Using the cProfile Module

`cProfile` is a built-in profiling tool in the standard library. It hooks into the virtual machine in CPython to measure the time taken to run every function that it sees. This introduces a greater overhead, but you get correspondingly more information. Sometimes the additional information can lead to surprising insights into your code.

`cProfile` is one of three profilers in the standard library; the others are `hotshot` and `profile`. `hotshot` is experimental code, and `profile` is the original pure-Python profiler. `cProfile` has the same interface as `profile`, is supported, and is the default profiling tool. If you're curious about the history of these libraries, see Armin Rigo's 2005 request (*http://bit.ly/cProfile_request*) to include `cProfile` in the standard library.

A good practice when profiling is to generate a *hypothesis* about the speed of parts of your code before you profile it. Ian likes to print out the code snippet in question and annotate it. Forming a hypothesis ahead of time means you can measure how wrong you are (and you will be!) and improve your intuition about certain coding styles.

 You should never avoid profiling in favor of a gut instinct (we warn you—you *will* get it wrong!). It is definitely worth forming a hypothesis ahead of profiling to help you learn to spot possible slow choices in your code, and you should always back up your choices with evidence.

Always be driven by results that you have measured, and always start with some quick-and-dirty profiling to make sure you're addressing the right area. There's nothing more humbling than cleverly optimizing a section of code only to realize (hours or days later) that you missed the slowest part of the process and haven't really addressed the underlying problem at all.

So what's our hypothesis? We know that `calculate_z_serial_purepython` is likely to be the slowest part of the code. In that function, we do a lot of dereferencing and make many calls to basic arithmetic operators and the `abs` function. These will probably show up as consumers of CPU resources.

Here, we'll use the cProfile module to run a variant of the code. The output is spartan but helps us figure out where to analyze further.

The `-s cumulative` flag tells cProfile to sort by cumulative time spent inside each function; this gives us a view into the slowest parts of a section of code. The cProfile output is written to screen directly after our usual print results:

```
$ python -m cProfile -s cumulative julia1_nopil.py
...
        36221992 function calls in 19.664 seconds

   Ordered by: cumulative time

   ncalls  tottime  percall  cumtime  percall filename:lineno(function)
        1    0.034    0.034   19.664   19.664 julia1_nopil.py:1(<module>)
        1    0.843    0.843   19.630   19.630 julia1_nopil.py:23
                                              (calc_pure_python)
        1   14.121   14.121   18.627   18.627 julia1_nopil.py:9
                                              (calculate_z_serial_purepython)
 34219980    4.487    0.000    4.487    0.000 {abs}
  2002000    0.150    0.000    0.150    0.000 {method 'append' of 'list' objects}
        1    0.019    0.019    0.019    0.019 {range}
        1    0.010    0.010    0.010    0.010 {sum}
        2    0.000    0.000    0.000    0.000 {time.time}
        4    0.000    0.000    0.000    0.000 {len}
        1    0.000    0.000    0.000    0.000 {method 'disable' of
                                              '_lsprof.Profiler' objects}
```

Sorting by cumulative time gives us an idea about where the majority of execution time is spent. This result shows us that 36,221,992 function calls occurred in just over 19 seconds (this time includes the overhead of using cProfile). Previously our code took around 13 seconds to execute—we've just added a 5-second penalty by measuring how long each function takes to execute.

We can see that the entry point to the code julia1_cprofile.py on line 1 takes a total of 19 seconds. This is just the __main__ call to calc_pure_python. ncalls is 1, indicating that this line is only executed once.

Inside calc_pure_python, the call to calculate_z_serial_purepython consumes 18.6 seconds. Both functions are only called once. We can derive that approximately 1 second is spent on lines of code inside calc_pure_python, separate to calling the CPU-intensive calculate_z_serial_purepython function. We can't derive *which* lines, however, take the time inside the function using cProfile.

Inside calculate_z_serial_purepython, the time spent on lines of code (without calling other functions) is 14.1 seconds. This function makes 34,219,980 calls to abs, which take a total of 4.4 seconds, along with some other calls that do not cost much time.

What about the {abs} call? This line is measuring the individual calls to the abs function inside calculate_z_serial_purepython. While the per-call cost is negligible (it is recorded as 0.000 seconds), the total time for 34,219,980 calls is 4.4 seconds. We couldn't predict in advance exactly how many calls would be made to abs, as the Julia function has unpredictable dynamics (that's why it is so interesting to look at).

At best we could have said that it will be called a minimum of 1,000,000 times, as we're calculating 1000*1000 pixels. At most it will be called 300,000,000 times, as we calculate 1,000,000 pixels with a maximum of 300 iterations. So, 34 million calls is roughly 10% of the worst case.

If we look at the original grayscale image (Figure 2-3) and, in our mind's eye, squash the white parts together and into a corner, we can estimate that the expensive white region accounts for roughly 10% of the rest of the image.

The next line in the profiled output, {method 'append' of 'list' objects}, details the creation of 2,002,000 list items.

 Why 2,002,000 items? Before you read on, think about how many list items are being constructed.

This creation of the 2,002,000 items is occurring in calc_pure_python during the setup phase.

The zs and cs lists will be 1000*1000 items each, and these are built from a list of 1,000 x- and 1,000 y-coordinates. In total, this is 2,002,000 calls to append.

It is important to note that this cProfile output is not ordered by parent functions; it is summarizing the expense of all functions in the executed block of code. Figuring out what is happening on a line-by-line basis is very hard with cProfile, as we only get profile information for the function calls themselves, not each line within the functions.

Inside calculate_z_serial_purepython we can now account for {abs} and {range}, and in total these two functions cost approximately 4.5 seconds. We know that calculate_z_serial_purepython costs 18.6 seconds in total.

The final line of the profiling output refers to lsprof; this is the original name of the tool that evolved into cProfile and can be ignored.

To get some more control over the results of cProfile, we can write a statistics file and then analyze it in Python:

```
$ python -m cProfile -o profile.stats julia1.py
```

We can load this into Python as follows, and it will give us the same cumulative time report as before:

```
In [1]: import pstats
In [2]: p = pstats.Stats("profile.stats")
In [3]: p.sort_stats("cumulative")
Out[3]: <pstats.Stats instance at 0x177dcf8>
In [4]: p.print_stats()
Tue Jan  7 21:00:56 2014    profile.stats

         36221992 function calls in 19.983 seconds

   Ordered by: cumulative time

   ncalls  tottime  percall  cumtime  percall filename:lineno(function)
        1    0.033    0.033   19.983   19.983 julia1_nopil.py:1(<module>)
        1    0.846    0.846   19.950   19.950 julia1_nopil.py:23
                                              (calc_pure_python)
        1   13.585   13.585   18.944   18.944 julia1_nopil.py:9
                                              (calculate_z_serial_purepython)
 34219980    5.340    0.000    5.340    0.000 {abs}
  2002000    0.150    0.000    0.150    0.000 {method 'append' of 'list' objects}
        1    0.019    0.019    0.019    0.019 {range}
        1    0.010    0.010    0.010    0.010 {sum}
        2    0.000    0.000    0.000    0.000 {time.time}
        4    0.000    0.000    0.000    0.000 {len}
        1    0.000    0.000    0.000    0.000 {method 'disable' of
                                              '_lsprof.Profiler' objects}
```

To trace which functions we're profiling, we can print the caller information. In the following two listings we can see that `calculate_z_serial_purepython` is the most expensive function, and it is called from one place. If it were called from many places, these listings might help us narrow down the locations of the most expensive parents:

```
In [5]: p.print_callers()
   Ordered by: cumulative time

Function                                                 was called by...
                                                             ncalls  tottime  cumtime
julia1_nopil.py:1(<module>)                              <-
julia1_nopil.py:23(calc_pure_python)                     <-          1    0.846   19.950
                                                             julia1_nopil.py:1(<module>)
julia1_nopil.py:9(calculate_z_serial_purepython)         <-          1   13.585   18.944
                                                             julia1_nopil.py:23
                                                             (calc_pure_python)
{abs}                                                    <- 34219980    5.340    5.340
                                                             julia1_nopil.py:9
                                                             (calculate_z_serial_purepython)
{method 'append' of 'list' objects}                      <-  2002000    0.150    0.150
                                                             julia1_nopil.py:23
                                                             (calc_pure_python)
{range}                                                  <-          1    0.019    0.019
```

```
                                                      julia1_nopil.py:9
                                                      (calculate_z_serial_purepython)
{sum}                                            <-    1     0.010     0.010
                                                      julia1_nopil.py:23
                                                      (calc_pure_python)
{time.time}                                      <-    2     0.000     0.000
                                                      julia1_nopil.py:23
                                                      (calc_pure_python)
{len}                                            <-    2     0.000     0.000
                                                      julia1_nopil.py:9
                                                      (calculate_z_serial_purepython)
                                                       2     0.000     0.000
                                                      julia1_nopil.py:23
                                                      (calc_pure_python)
{method 'disable' of '_lsprof.Profiler' objects} <-
```

We can flip this around the other way to show which functions call other functions:

```
In [6]: p.print_callees()
   Ordered by: cumulative time

Function                                              called...
                                                       ncalls  tottime  cumtime
julia1_nopil.py:1(<module>)                      ->     1     0.846    19.950
                                                      julia1_nopil.py:23
                                                      (calc_pure_python)
julia1_nopil.py:23(calc_pure_python)             ->     1    13.585    18.944
                                                      julia1_nopil.py:9
                                                      (calculate_z_serial_purepython)
                                                       2     0.000     0.000
                                                      {len}
                                                 2002000     0.150     0.150
                                                      {method 'append' of 'list'
                                                       objects}
                                                       1     0.010     0.010
                                                      {sum}
                                                       2     0.000     0.000
                                                      {time.time}
julia1_nopil.py:9(calculate_z_serial_purepython) -> 34219980  5.340     5.340
                                                      {abs}
                                                       2     0.000     0.000
                                                      {len}
                                                       1     0.019     0.019
                                                      {range}
{abs}                                            ->
{method 'append' of 'list' objects}              ->
{range}                                          ->
{sum}                                            ->
{time.time}                                      ->
{len}                                            ->
{method 'disable' of '_lsprof.Profiler' objects} ->
```

cProfile is rather verbose, and you need a side screen to see it without lots of word-wrap. Since it is built in, though, it is a convenient tool for quickly identifying bottlenecks. Tools like line_profiler, heapy, and memory_profiler, which we discuss later in this chapter, will then help you to drill down to the specific lines that you should pay attention to.

Using runsnakerun to Visualize cProfile Output

runsnake is a visualization tool for the profile statistics created by cProfile—you can quickly get a sense of which functions are most expensive just by looking at the diagram that's generated.

Use runsnake to get a high-level understanding of a cProfile statistics file, especially when you're investigating a new and large code base. It'll give you a feel for the areas that you should focus on. It might also reveal areas that you hadn't realized would be expensive, potentially highlighting some quick wins for you to focus on.

You can also use it when discussing the slow areas of code in a team, as it is easy to discuss the results.

To install runsnake, issue the command pip install runsnake.

Note that it requires wxPython, and this can be a pain to install into a virtualenv. Ian has resorted to installing this globally on more than one occasion just to analyze a profile file, rather than trying to get it running in a virtualenv.

In Figure 2-5 we have the visual plot of the previous cProfile data. A visual inspection should make it easier to quickly understand that calculate_z_serial_purepython takes the majority of the time and that only a part of the execution time is due to calling other functions (the only one that is significant is abs). You can see that there's little point investing time in the setup routine, as the vast majority of the execution time is in the calculation routine.

With runsnake, you can click on functions and drill into complex nested calls. When you are discussing the reasons for slow execution in a piece of code in a team, this tool is invaluable.

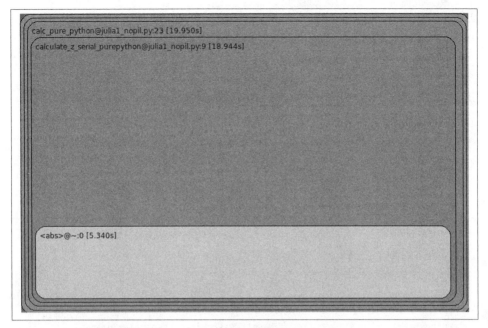

calc_pure_python@julia1_nopil.py:23 [19.950s]

calculate_z_serial_purepython@julia1_nopil.py:9 [18.944s]

<abs>@~:0 [5.340s]

Figure 2-5. RunSnakeRun visualizing a cProfile profile file

Using line_profiler for Line-by-Line Measurements

In Ian's opinion, Robert Kern's `line_profiler` is the strongest tool for identifying the cause of CPU-bound problems in Python code. It works by profiling individual functions on a line-by-line basis, so you should start with `cProfile` and use the high-level view to guide which functions to profile with `line_profiler`.

It is worthwhile printing and annotating versions of the output from this tool as you modify your code, so you have a record of changes (successful or not) that you can quickly refer to. Don't rely on your memory when you're working on line-by-line changes.

To install `line_profiler`, issue the command `pip install line_profiler`.

A decorator (`@profile`) is used to mark the chosen function. The `kernprof.py` script is used to execute your code, and the CPU time and other statistics for each line of the chosen function are recorded.

> The requirement to modify the source code is a minor annoyance, as the addition of a decorator will break your unit tests unless you make a dummy decorator—see "No-op @profile Decorator" on page 57.

The arguments are -l for line-by-line (rather than function-level) profiling and -v for verbose output. Without -v you receive an *.lprof* output that you can later analyze with the line_profiler module. In Example 2-6, we'll do a full run on our CPU-bound function.

Example 2-6. Running kernprof with line-by-line output on a decorated function to record the CPU cost of each line's execution

```
$ kernprof.py -l -v julia1_lineprofiler.py
...
Wrote profile results to julia1_lineprofiler.py.lprof
Timer unit: 1e-06 s

File: julia1_lineprofiler.py
Function: calculate_z_serial_purepython at line 9
Total time: 100.81 s

Line #      Hits    Per Hit   % Time  Line Contents
==============================================================
     9                                 @profile
    10                                 def calculate_z_serial_purepython(maxiter,
                                                                          zs, cs):
    11                                     """Calculate output list using
                                            Julia update rule"""
    12           1     6870.0      0.0     output = [0] * len(zs)
    13     1000001        0.8      0.8     for i in range(len(zs)):
    14     1000000        0.8      0.8         n = 0
    15     1000000        0.8      0.8         z = zs[i]
    16     1000000        0.8      0.8         c = cs[i]
    17    34219980        1.1     36.2         while abs(z) < 2 and n < maxiter:
    18    33219980        1.0     32.6             z = z * z + c
    19    33219980        0.8     27.2             n += 1
    20     1000000        0.9      0.9         output[i] = n
    21           1        4.0      0.0     return output
```

Introducing kernprof.py adds a substantial amount to the runtime. In this example, calculate_z_serial_purepython takes 100 seconds; this is up from 13 seconds using simple print statements and 19 seconds using cProfile. The gain is that we get a line-by-line breakdown of where the time is spent inside the function.

The % Time column is the most helpful—we can see that 36% of the time is spent on the while testing. We don't know whether the first statement (abs(z) < 2) is more expensive than the second (n < maxiter), though. Inside the loop, we see that the update to z is also fairly expensive. Even n += 1 is expensive! Python's dynamic lookup machinery is at work for every loop, even though we're using the same types for each variable in each loop—this is where compiling and type specialization (Chapter 7) give us a massive win. The creation of the output list and the updates on line 20 are relatively cheap compared to the cost of the while loop.

The obvious way to further analyze the `while` statement is to break it up. While there has been some discussion in the Python community around the idea of rewriting the *.pyc* files with more detailed information for multipart, single-line statements, we are unaware of any production tools that offer a more fine-grained analysis than `line_profiler`.

In Example 2-7, we break the `while` logic into several statements. This additional complexity will increase the runtime of the function, as we have more lines of code to execute, but it *might* also help us to understand the costs incurred in this part of the code.

 Before you look at the code, do you think we'll learn about the costs of the fundamental operations this way? Might other factors complicate the analysis?

Example 2-7. Breaking the compound while statement into individual statements to record the cost of each part of the original parts

```
$ kernprof.py -l -v julia1_lineprofiler2.py
...
Wrote profile results to julia1_lineprofiler2.py.lprof
Timer unit: 1e-06 s

File: julia1_lineprofiler2.py
Function: calculate_z_serial_purepython at line 9
Total time: 184.739 s
```

Line #	Hits	Per Hit	% Time	Line Contents
9				@profile
10				def calculate_z_serial_purepython(maxiter, zs, cs):
11				"""Calculate output list using Julia update rule"""
12	1	6831.0	0.0	output = [0] * len(zs)
13	1000001	0.8	0.4	for i in range(len(zs)):
14	1000000	0.8	0.4	n = 0
15	1000000	0.9	0.5	z = zs[i]
16	1000000	0.8	0.4	c = cs[i]
17	34219980	0.8	14.9	while True:
18	34219980	1.0	19.0	not_yet_escaped = abs(z) < 2
19	34219980	0.8	15.5	iterations_left = n < maxiter
20	34219980	0.8	15.1	if not_yet_escaped and iterations_left:
21	33219980	1.0	17.5	z = z * z + c
22	33219980	0.9	15.3	n += 1
23				else:
24	1000000	0.8	0.4	break

```
25    1000000      0.9      0.5        output[i] = n
26          1      5.0      0.0        return output
```

This version takes 184 seconds to execute, while the previous version took 100 seconds. Other factors *did* complicate the analysis. In this case, having extra statements that have to be executed 34,219,980 times each slows down the code. If we hadn't used ker nprof.py to investigate the line-by-line effect of this change, we might have drawn other conclusions about the reason for the slowdown, as we'd have lacked the necessary evidence.

At this point it makes sense to step back to the earlier timeit technique to test the cost of individual expressions:

```
>>> z = 0+0j  # a point in the middle of our image
>>> %timeit abs(z) < 2  # tested inside IPython

10000000 loops, best of 3: 119 ns per loop

>>> n = 1
>>> maxiter = 300
>>> %timeit n < maxiter

10000000 loops, best of 3: 77 ns per loop
```

From this simple analysis it looks as though the logic test on n is almost two times faster than the call to abs. Since the order of evaluation for Python statements is both left to right and opportunistic, it makes sense to put the cheapest test on the left side of the equation. On 1 in every 301 tests for each coordinate the n < maxiter test will be False, so Python wouldn't need to evaluate the other side of the and operator.

We never know whether abs(z) < 2 will be False until we evaluate it, and our earlier observations for this region of the complex plane suggest it is True around 10% of the time for all 300 iterations. If we wanted to have a strong understanding of the time complexity of this part of the code, it would make sense to continue the numerical analysis. In this situation, however, we want an easy check to see if we can get a quick win.

We can form a new hypothesis stating, "By swapping the order of the operators in the while statement we will achieve a reliable speedup." We *can* test this hypothesis using kernprof.py, but the additional overheads of profiling this way might add too much noise. Instead, we can use an earlier version of the code, running a test comparing while abs(z) < 2 and n < maxiter: against while n < maxiter and abs(z) < 2:.

The result was a fairly stable improvement of approximately 0.4 seconds. This result is obviously minor and is very problem-specific, though using a more suitable approach to solve this problem (e.g., swapping to using Cython or PyPy, as described in Chapter 7) would yield greater gains.

We can be confident in our result because:

- We stated a hypothesis that was easy to test.
- We changed our code so that only the hypothesis would be tested (never test two things at once!).
- We gathered enough evidence to support our conclusion.

For completeness, we can run a final kernprof.py on the two main functions including our optimization to confirm that we have a full picture of the overall complexity of our code. Having swapped the two components of the while test on line 17, in Example 2-8 we see a modest improvement from 36.1% of the execution time to 35.9% (this result was stable over repeated runs).

Example 2-8. Swapping the order of the compound while statement to make the test fractionally faster

```
$ kernprof.py -l -v julia1_lineprofiler3.py
...
Wrote profile results to julia1_lineprofiler3.py.lprof
Timer unit: 1e-06 s

File: julia1_lineprofiler3.py
Function: calculate_z_serial_purepython at line 9
Total time: 99.7097 s

Line #      Hits     Per Hit    % Time  Line Contents
==================================================
     9                                  @profile
    10                                  def calculate_z_serial_purepython(maxiter,
                                                                         zs, cs):
    11                                      """Calculate output list using
                                            Julia update rule"""
    12         1      6831.0       0.0      output = [0] * len(zs)
    13   1000001         0.8       0.8      for i in range(len(zs)):
    14   1000000         0.8       0.8          n = 0
    15   1000000         0.9       0.9          z = zs[i]
    16   1000000         0.8       0.8          c = cs[i]
    17  34219980         1.0      35.9          while n < maxiter and abs(z) < 2:
    18  33219980         1.0      32.0              z = z * z + c
    19  33219980         0.8      27.9              n += 1
    20   1000000         0.9       0.9          output[i] = n
    21         1         5.0       0.0      return output
```

As expected, we can see from the output in Example 2-9 that calculate_z_seri al_purepython takes most (97%) of the time of its parent function. The list-creation steps are minor in comparison.

Example 2-9. Testing the line-by-line costs of the setup routine

```
File: julia1_lineprofiler3.py
Function: calc_pure_python at line 24
```

```
Total time: 195.218 s

Line #      Hits      Per Hit    % Time   Line Contents
==================================================
   24                                     @profile
   25                                     def calc_pure_python(draw_output,
                                                               desired_width,
                                                               max_iterations):
...
   44         1        1.0         0.0     zs = []
   45         1        1.0         0.0     cs = []
   46      1001        1.1         0.0     for ycoord in y:
   47   1001000        1.1         0.5         for xcoord in x:
   48   1000000        1.5         0.8             zs.append(
                                                       complex(xcoord, ycoord))
   49   1000000        1.6         0.8             cs.append(
                                                       complex(c_real, c_imag))
   50
   51         1       51.0         0.0     print "Length of x:", len(x)
   52         1       11.0         0.0     print "Total elements:", len(zs)
   53         1        6.0         0.0     start_time = time.time()
   54         1 191031307.0       97.9     output =
                                             calculate_z_serial_purepython
                                             (max_iterations, zs, cs)
   55         1        4.0         0.0     end_time = time.time()
   56         1        2.0         0.0     secs = end_time - start_time
   57         1       58.0         0.0     print calculate_z_serial_purepython
                                             .func_name + " took", secs, "seconds"
   58
                                           # this sum is expected for 1000^2 grid...
   59         1     9799.0         0.0     assert sum(output) == 33219980
```

Using memory_profiler to Diagnose Memory Usage

Just as Robert Kern's line_profiler package measures CPU usage, the memory_pro
filer module by Fabian Pedregosa and Philippe Gervais measures memory usage on
a line-by-line basis. Understanding the memory usage characteristics of your code allows you to ask yourself two questions:

- Could we use *less* RAM by rewriting this function to work more efficiently?
- Could we use *more* RAM and save CPU cycles by caching?

memory_profiler operates in a very similar way to line_profiler, but runs far more
slowly. If you install the psutil package (optional but recommended), memory_profil
er will run faster. Memory profiling may easily make your code run 10 to 100 times
slower. In practice, you will probably use memory_profiler occasionally and line_pro
filer (for CPU profiling) more frequently.

Install `memory_profiler` with the command `pip install memory_profiler` (and optionally `pip install psutil`).

As mentioned, the implementation of `memory_profiler` is not as performant as the implementation of `line_profiler`. It may therefore make sense to run your tests on a smaller problem that completes in a useful amount of time. Overnight runs might be sensible for validation, but you need quick and reasonable iterations to diagnose problems and hypothesize solutions. The code in Example 2-10 uses the full 1,000 × 1,000 grid, and the statistics took about 1.5 hours to collect on Ian's laptop.

 The requirement to modify the source code is a minor annoyance. As with `line_profiler`, a decorator (`@profile`) is used to mark the chosen function. This will break your unit tests unless you make a dummy decorator—see "No-op @profile Decorator" on page 57.

When dealing with memory allocation, you must be aware that the situation is not as clear-cut as it is with CPU usage. Generally, it is more efficient to overallocate memory to a process into a local pool that can be used at leisure, as memory allocation operations are relatively expensive. Furthermore, garbage collection is not instant, so objects may be unavailable but still in the garbage collection pool for some time.

The outcome of this is that it is hard to really understand what is happening with memory usage and release inside a Python program, as a line of code may not allocate a deterministic amount of memory *as observed from outside the process*. Observing the gross trend over a set of lines is likely to lead to better insight than observing the behavior of just one line.

Let's take a look at the output from `memory_profiler` in Example 2-10. Inside `calculate_z_serial_purepython` on line 12, we see that the allocation of 1,000,000 items causes approximately 7 MB of RAM[1] to be added to this process. This does not mean that the `output` list is definitely 7 MB in size, just that the process grew by approximately 7 MB during the internal allocation of the list. On line 13, we see that the process grew by approximately a further 32 MB inside the loop. This can be attributed to the call to `range`. (RAM tracking is further discussed in Example 11-1; the difference between 7 MB and 32 MB is due to the contents of the two lists.) In the parent process on line 46, we see that the allocation of the `zs` and `cs` lists consumes approximately 79 MB. Again,

---

1. `memory_profiler` measures memory usage according to the International Electrotechnical Commission's MiB (mebibyte) of 2^20 bytes. This is slightly different from the more common but also more ambiguous MB (megabyte has two commonly accepted definitions!). 1 MiB is equal to 1.048576 (or approximately 1.05) MB. For the purposes of our discussion, unless dealing with very specific amounts, we'll consider the two equivalent.

it is worth noting that this is not necessarily the true size of the arrays, just the size that the process grew by once these lists had been created.

Example 2-10. memory_profiler's result on both of our main functions, showing an unexpected memory use in calculate_z_serial_purepython

```
$ python -m memory_profiler julia1_memoryprofiler.py
...
Line #    Mem usage    Increment   Line Contents
================================================
     9   89.934 MiB    0.000 MiB   @profile
    10                             def calculate_z_serial_purepython(maxiter,
                                                                     zs, cs):
    11                                 """Calculate output list using...
    12   97.566 MiB    7.633 MiB       output = [0] * len(zs)
    13  130.215 MiB   32.648 MiB       for i in range(len(zs)):
    14  130.215 MiB    0.000 MiB           n = 0
    15  130.215 MiB    0.000 MiB           z = zs[i]
    16  130.215 MiB    0.000 MiB           c = cs[i]
    17  130.215 MiB    0.000 MiB           while n < maxiter and abs(z) < 2:
    18  130.215 MiB    0.000 MiB               z = z * z + c
    19  130.215 MiB    0.000 MiB               n += 1
    20  130.215 MiB    0.000 MiB           output[i] = n
    21  122.582 MiB   -7.633 MiB       return output


Line #    Mem usage      Increment   Line Contents
================================================
    24   10.574 MiB  -112.008 MiB   @profile
    25                              def calc_pure_python(draw_output,
                                                         desired_width,
                                                         max_iterations):
    26                                  """Create a list of complex ...
    27   10.574 MiB    0.000 MiB       x_step = (float(x2 - x1) / ...
    28   10.574 MiB    0.000 MiB       y_step = (float(y1 - y2) / ...
    29   10.574 MiB    0.000 MiB       x = []
    30   10.574 MiB    0.000 MiB       y = []
    31   10.574 MiB    0.000 MiB       ycoord = y2
    32   10.574 MiB    0.000 MiB       while ycoord > y1:
    33   10.574 MiB    0.000 MiB           y.append(ycoord)
    34   10.574 MiB    0.000 MiB           ycoord += y_step
    35   10.574 MiB    0.000 MiB       xcoord = x1
    36   10.582 MiB    0.008 MiB       while xcoord < x2:
    37   10.582 MiB    0.000 MiB           x.append(xcoord)
    38   10.582 MiB    0.000 MiB           xcoord += x_step
    ...
    44   10.582 MiB    0.000 MiB       zs = []
    45   10.582 MiB    0.000 MiB       cs = []
    46   89.926 MiB   79.344 MiB       for ycoord in y:
    47   89.926 MiB    0.000 MiB           for xcoord in x:
    48   89.926 MiB    0.000 MiB               zs.append(complex(xcoord, ycoord))
    49   89.926 MiB    0.000 MiB               cs.append(complex(c_real, c_imag))
    50
```

```
51    89.934 MiB    0.008 MiB    print "Length of x:", len(x)
52    89.934 MiB    0.000 MiB    print "Total elements:", len(zs)
53    89.934 MiB    0.000 MiB    start_time = time.time()
54                               output = calculate_z_serial...
55   122.582 MiB   32.648 MiB    end_time = time.time()
...
```

Another way to visualize the change in memory use is to sample over time and plot the result. memory_profiler has a utility called mprof, used once to sample the memory usage and a second time to visualize the samples. It samples by time and not by line, so it barely impacts the runtime of the code.

Figure 2-6 is created using mprof run julia1_memoryprofiler.py. This writes a statistics file that is then visualized using mprof plot. Our two functions are bracketed: this shows where in time they are entered, and we can see the growth in RAM as they run. Inside calculate_z_serial_purepython, we can see the steady increase in RAM usage throughout the execution of the function; this is caused by all the small objects (int and float types) that are created.

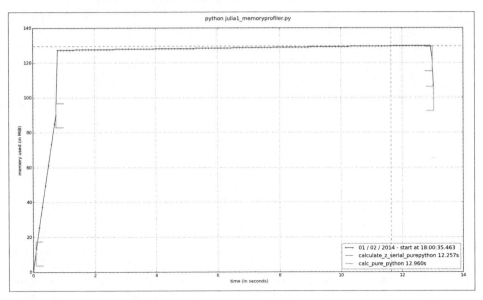

Figure 2-6. memory_profiler report using mprof

In addition to observing the behavior at the function level, we can add labels using a context manager. The snippet in Example 2-11 is used to generate the graph in Figure 2-7. We can see the create_output_list label: it appears momentarily after calculate_z_serial_purepython and results in the process being allocated more

RAM. We then pause for a second; the time.sleep(1) is an artificial addition to make the graph easier to understand.

After the label create_range_of_zs we see a large and quick increase in RAM usage; in the modified code in Example 2-11 you can see this label when we create the itera tions list. Rather than using xrange, we've used range—the diagram should make it clear that a large list of 1,000,000 elements is instantiated just for the purposes of generating an index, and that this is an inefficient approach that will not scale to larger list sizes (we will run out of RAM!). The allocation of the memory used to hold this list will itself take a small amount of time, which contributes nothing useful to this function.

 In Python 3, the behavior of range changes—it works like xrange from Python 2. xrange is deprecated in Python 3, and the 2to3 conversion tool takes care of this change automatically.

Example 2-11. Using a context manager to add labels to the mprof graph

```python
@profile
def calculate_z_serial_purepython(maxiter, zs, cs):
    """Calculate output list using Julia update rule"""
    with profile.timestamp("create_output_list"):
        output = [0] * len(zs)
    time.sleep(1)
    with profile.timestamp("create_range_of_zs"):
        iterations = range(len(zs))
        with profile.timestamp("calculate_output"):
            for i in iterations:
                n = 0
                z = zs[i]
                c = cs[i]
                while n < maxiter and abs(z) < 2:
                    z = z * z + c
                    n += 1
                output[i] = n
    return output
```

In the calculate_output block that runs for most of the graph, we see a very slow, linear increase in RAM usage. This will be from all of the temporary numbers used in the inner loops. Using the labels really helps us to understand at a fine-grained level where memory is being consumed.

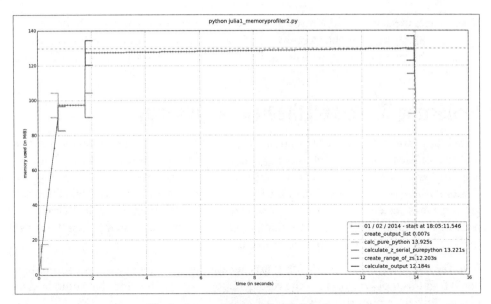

Figure 2-7. memory_profiler report using mprof with labels

Finally, we can change the `range` call into an `xrange`. In Figure 2-8, we see the corresponding decrease in RAM usage in our inner loop.

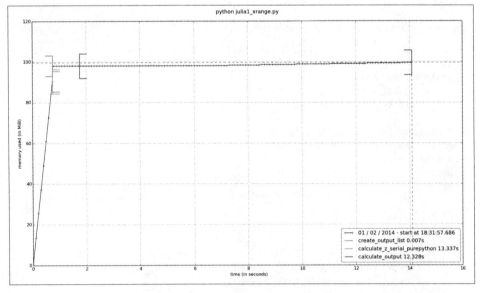

Figure 2-8. memory_profiler report showing the effect of changing range to xrange

If we want to measure the RAM used by several statements we can use the IPython magic %memit, which works just like %timeit. In Chapter 11 we will look at using %memit to measure the memory cost of lists and discuss various ways of using RAM more efficiently.

Inspecting Objects on the Heap with heapy

The Guppy project has a heap inspection tool called heapy that lets us look at the number and size of each object on Python's heap. Looking inside the interpreter and understanding what's held in memory is extremely useful in those rare but difficult debugging sessions where you really need to know how many objects are in use and whether they get garbage collected at appropriate times. If you have a difficult memory leak (probably because references to your objects remain hidden in a complex system), then this is the tool that'll get you to the root of the problem.

If you're reviewing your code to see if it is generating as many objects as you predict, you'll find this tool very useful—the results might surprise you, and that could lead to new optimization opportunities.

To get access to heapy, install the guppy package with the command pip install guppy.

The listing in Example 2-12 is a slightly modified version of the Julia code. The heap object hpy is included in calc_pure_python, and we print out the state of the heap at three places.

Example 2-12. Using heapy to see how object counts evolve during the run of our code

```
def calc_pure_python(draw_output, desired_width, max_iterations):
    ...
    while xcoord < x2:
        x.append(xcoord)
        xcoord += x_step

    from guppy import hpy; hp = hpy()
    print "heapy after creating y and x lists of floats"
    h = hp.heap()
    print h
    print

    zs = []
    cs = []
    for ycoord in y:
        for xcoord in x:
            zs.append(complex(xcoord, ycoord))
            cs.append(complex(c_real, c_imag))

    print "heapy after creating zs and cs using complex numbers"
    h = hp.heap()
    print h
```

```
print

print "Length of x:", len(x)
print "Total elements:", len(zs)
start_time = time.time()
output = calculate_z_serial_purepython(max_iterations, zs, cs)
end_time = time.time()
secs = end_time - start_time
print calculate_z_serial_purepython.func_name + " took", secs, "seconds"

print
print "heapy after calling calculate_z_serial_purepython"
h = hp.heap()
print h
print
```

The output in Example 2-13 shows that the memory use becomes more interesting after creating the zs and cs lists: it has grown by approximately 80 MB due to 2,000,000 complex objects consuming 64,000,000 bytes. These complex numbers represent the majority of the memory usage at this stage. If you wanted to optimize the memory usage in this program, this result would be revealing—we can see both how many objects are being stored and their overall size.

Example 2-13. Looking at the output of heapy to see how our object counts increase at each major stage of our code's execution

```
$ python julia1_guppy.py
heapy after creating y and x lists of floats
Partition of a set of 27293 objects. Total size = 3416032 bytes.
 Index  Count   %    Size   % Cumulative  % Kind (class / dict of class)
     0  10960  40 1050376  31    1050376  31 str
     1   5768  21  465016  14    1515392  44 tuple
     2    199   1  210856   6    1726248  51 dict of type
     3     72   0  206784   6    1933032  57 dict of module
     4   1592   6  203776   6    2136808  63 types.CodeType
     5    313   1  201304   6    2338112  68 dict (no owner)
     6   1557   6  186840   5    2524952  74 function
     7    199   1  177008   5    2701960  79 type
     8    124   0  135328   4    2837288  83 dict of class
     9   1045   4   83600   2    2920888  86 __builtin__.wrapper_descriptor
<91 more rows. Type e.g. '_.more' to view.>

heapy after creating zs and cs using complex numbers
Partition of a set of 2027301 objects. Total size = 83671256 bytes.
 Index     Count   %     Size   % Cumulative  % Kind (class / dict of class)
     0   2000000  99 64000000  76   64000000  76 complex
     1       185   0 16295368  19   80295368  96 list
     2     10962   1  1050504   1   81345872  97 str
     3      5767   0   464952   1   81810824  98 tuple
     4       199   0   210856   0   82021680  98 dict of type
     5        72   0   206784   0   82228464  98 dict of module
```

```
    6    1592   0    203776   0  82432240  99 types.CodeType
    7     319   0    202984   0  82635224  99 dict (no owner)
    8    1556   0    186720   0  82821944  99 function
    9     199   0    177008   0  82998952  99 type
<92 more rows. Type e.g. '_.more' to view.>

Length of x: 1000
Total elements: 1000000
calculate_z_serial_purepython took 13.2436609268 seconds

heapy after calling calculate_z_serial_purepython
Partition of a set of 2127696 objects. Total size = 94207376 bytes.
 Index   Count   %     Size   % Cumulative  % Kind (class / dict of class)
     0 2000000  94 64000000  68   64000000  68 complex
     1     186   0 24421904  26   88421904  94 list
     2  100965   5  2423160   3   90845064  96 int
     3   10962   1  1050504   1   91895568  98 str
     4    5767   0   464952   0   92360520  98 tuple
     5     199   0   210856   0   92571376  98 dict of type
     6      72   0   206784   0   92778160  98 dict of module
     7    1592   0   203776   0   92981936  99 types.CodeType
     8     319   0   202984   0   93184920  99 dict (no owner)
     9    1556   0   186720   0   93371640  99 function
<92 more rows. Type e.g. '_.more' to view.>
```

In the third section, after calculating the Julia result, we have used 94 MB. In addition to the complex numbers we now have a large collection of integers, and more items stored in lists.

hpy.setrelheap() could be used to create a checkpoint of the memory configuration, so subsequent calls to hpy.heap() will generate a delta from this checkpoint. This way you can avoid seeing the internals of Python and prior memory setup before the point of the program that you're analyzing.

Using dowser for Live Graphing of Instantiated Variables

Robert Brewer's dowser hooks into the namespace of the running code and provides a real-time view of instantiated variables via a CherryPy interface in a web browser. Each object that is being tracked has an associated sparkline graphic, so you can watch to see if the quantities of certain objects are growing. This is useful for debugging long-running processes.

If you have a long-running process and you expect different memory behavior to occur depending on the actions you take in the application (e.g., with a web server you might upload data or cause complex queries to run), you can confirm this interactively. There's an example in Figure 2-9.

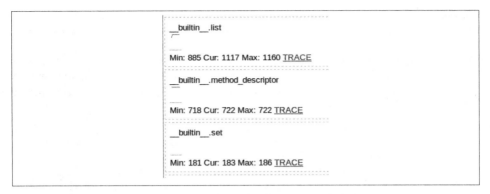

Figure 2-9. Several sparklines shown through CherryPy with dowser

To use it, we add to the Julia code a convenience function (shown in Example 2-14) that can start the CherryPy server.

Example 2-14. Helper function to start dowser in your application

```python
def launch_memory_usage_server(port=8080):
    import cherrypy
    import dowser

    cherrypy.tree.mount(dowser.Root())
    cherrypy.config.update({
        'environment': 'embedded',
        'server.socket_port': port
    })

    cherrypy.engine.start()
```

Before we begin our intensive calculations we launch the CherryPy server, as shown in Example 2-15. Once we have completed our calculations we can keep the console open using the call to time.sleep—this leaves the CherryPy process running so we can continue to introspect the state of the namespace.

Example 2-15. Launching dowser at an appropriate point in our application, which will launch a web server

```python
...
    for xcoord in x:
        zs.append(complex(xcoord, ycoord))
        cs.append(complex(c_real, c_imag))

    launch_memory_usage_server()

...
    output = calculate_z_serial_purepython(max_iterations, zs, cs)
...
    print "now waiting..."
```

```
while True:
    time.sleep(1)
```

By following the TRACE links in Figure 2-9, we can view the contents of each list object (Figure 2-10). We could further drill down into each list, too—this is like using an interactive debugger in an IDE, but you can do this on a deployed server *without* an IDE.

36722880 **list**
list of len 1000: [-1.8, -1.7964, -1.7928, -1.7892, -1.7855999999999999, -1.7819999999999998, -1.778...

36395056 **list**
list of len 1000: [1.8, 1.7964, 1.7928, 1.7892, 1.7855999999999999, 1.7819999999999998, 1.7783999999...

36722016 **list**
list of len 1000000 : [(-1.8+1.8j), (-1.7964+1.8j), (-1.7928+1.8j), (-1.7892+1.8j), (-1.7855999999999...

36722952 **list**
list of len 1000000: [(-0.62772-0.42193j), (-0.62772-0.42193j), (-0.62772-0.42193j), (-0.62772-0.421...

Figure 2-10. 1,000,000 items in a list with dowser

 We prefer to extract blocks of code that can be profiled in controlled conditions. Sometimes this isn't practical, though, and sometimes you just need simpler diagnostics. Watching a live trace of a running process can be a perfect halfway house to gather the necessary evidence without doing lots of engineering.

Using the dis Module to Examine CPython Bytecode

So far we've reviewed various ways to measure the cost of Python code (both for CPU and RAM usage). We haven't yet looked at the underlying bytecode used by the virtual machine, though. Understanding what's going on "under the hood" helps to build a mental model of what's happening in slow functions, and it'll help when you come to compile your code. So, let's introduce some bytecode.

The dis module lets us inspect the underlying bytecode that we run inside the stack-based CPython virtual machine. Having an understanding of what's happening in the virtual machine that runs your higher-level Python code will help you to understand why some styles of coding are faster than others. It will also help when you come to use a tool like Cython, which steps outside of Python and generates C code.

The dis module is built in. You can pass it code or a module, and it will print out a disassembly. In Example 2-16 we disassemble the outer loop of our CPU-bound function.

You should try to disassemble one of your own functions and attempt to *exactly* follow how the disassembled code matches to the disassembled output. Can you match the following dis output to the original function?

Example 2-16. Using the built-in dis to understand the underlying stack-based virtual machine that runs our Python code

```
In [1]: import dis
In [2]: import julia1_nopil

In [3]: dis.dis(julia1_nopil.calculate_z_serial_purepython)
 11           0 LOAD_CONST             1 (0)
              3 BUILD_LIST            1
              6 LOAD_GLOBAL           0 (len)
              9 LOAD_FAST             1 (zs)
             12 CALL_FUNCTION         1
             15 BINARY_MULTIPLY
             16 STORE_FAST            3 (output)

 12          19 SETUP_LOOP          123 (to 145)
             22 LOAD_GLOBAL           1 (range)
             25 LOAD_GLOBAL           0 (len)
             28 LOAD_FAST             1 (zs)
             31 CALL_FUNCTION         1
             34 CALL_FUNCTION         1
             37 GET_ITER
        >>   38 FOR_ITER            103 (to 144)
             41 STORE_FAST            4 (i)

 13          44 LOAD_CONST            1 (0)
             47 STORE_FAST            5 (n)

# ...
# We'll snip the rest of the inner loop for brevity!
# ...

 19     >>  131 LOAD_FAST             5 (n)
            134 LOAD_FAST             3 (output)
            137 LOAD_FAST             4 (i)
            140 STORE_SUBSCR
            141 JUMP_ABSOLUTE        38
        >>  144 POP_BLOCK

 20     >>  145 LOAD_FAST             3 (output)
            148 RETURN_VALUE
```

The output is fairly straightforward, if terse. The first column contains line numbers that relate to our original file. The second column contains several >> symbols; these are the destinations for jump points elsewhere in the code. The third column is the operation address along with the operation name. The fourth column contains the parameters for the operation. The fifth column contains annotations to help line up the bytecode with the original Python parameters.

Refer back to Example 2-3 to match the bytecode to the corresponding Python code. The bytecode starts by putting the constant value 0 onto the stack, and then it builds a single-element list. Next, it searches the namespaces to find the len function, puts it on the stack, searches the namespaces again to find zs, and then puts that onto the stack. On line 12 it calls the len function from the stack, which consumes the zs reference in the stack; then it applies a binary multiply to the last two arguments (the length of zs and the single-element list) and stores the result in output. That's the first line of our Python function now dealt with. Follow the next block of bytecode to understand the behavior of the second line of Python code (the outer for loop).

 The jump points (>>) match to instructions like JUMP_ABSOLUTE and POP_JUMP_IF_FALSE. Go through your own disassembled function and match the jump points to the jump instructions.

Having introduced bytecode, we can now ask: what's the bytecode and time cost of writing a function out explicitly versus using built-ins to perform the same task?

Different Approaches, Different Complexity

There should be one—and preferably only one—obvious way to do it. Although that way may not be obvious at first unless you're Dutch…

— Tim Peters
The Zen of Python

There will be various ways to express your ideas using Python. Generally it should be clear what the most sensible option is, but if your experience is primarily with an older version of Python or another programming language, then you may have other methods in mind. Some of these ways of expressing an idea may be slower than others.

You probably care more about readability than speed for most of your code, so your team can code efficiently, without being puzzled by performant but opaque code. Sometimes you will want performance, though (without sacrificing readability). Some speed testing might be what you need.

Take a look at the two code snippets in Example 2-17. They both do the same job, but the first will generate a lot of additional Python bytecode, which will cause more overhead.

Example 2-17. A naive and a more efficient way to solve the same summation problem

```
def fn_expressive(upper = 1000000):
    total = 0
    for n in xrange(upper):
        total += n
    return total

def fn_terse(upper = 1000000):
    return sum(xrange(upper))

print "Functions return the same result:", fn_expressive() == fn_terse()

Functions return the same result:
True
```

Both functions calculate the sum of a range of integers. A simple rule of thumb (but one you *must* back up using profiling!) is that more lines of bytecode will execute more slowly than fewer equivalent lines of bytecode that use built-in functions. In Example 2-18 we use IPython's %timeit magic function to measure the best execution time from a set of runs.

Example 2-18. Using %timeit to test our hypothesis that using built-in functions should be faster than writing our own functions

```
%timeit fn_expressive()

10 loops, best of 3: 42 ms per loop
100 loops, best of 3: 12.3 ms per loop

%timeit fn_terse()
```

If we use the dis module to investigate the code for each function, as shown in Example 2-19, we can see that the virtual machine has 17 lines to execute with the more expressive function and only 6 to execute with the very readable but more terse second function.

Example 2-19. Using dis to view the number of bytecode instructions involved in our two functions

```
import dis
print fn_expressive.func_name
dis.dis(fn_expressive)

fn_expressive
  2           0 LOAD_CONST               1 (0)
              3 STORE_FAST               1 (total)

  3           6 SETUP_LOOP              30 (to 39)
              9 LOAD_GLOBAL              0 (xrange)
             12 LOAD_FAST                0 (upper)
             15 CALL_FUNCTION            1
```

```
            18 GET_ITER
      >>    19 FOR_ITER              16 (to 38)
            22 STORE_FAST             2 (n)

  4         25 LOAD_FAST              1 (total)
            28 LOAD_FAST              2 (n)
            31 INPLACE_ADD
            32 STORE_FAST             1 (total)
            35 JUMP_ABSOLUTE         19
      >>    38 POP_BLOCK

  5   >>    39 LOAD_FAST              1 (total)
            42 RETURN_VALUE

print fn_terse.func_name
dis.dis(fn_terse)

fn_terse
  8          0 LOAD_GLOBAL            0 (sum)
             3 LOAD_GLOBAL            1 (xrange)
             6 LOAD_FAST              0 (upper)
             9 CALL_FUNCTION          1
            12 CALL_FUNCTION          1
            15 RETURN_VALUE
```

The difference between the two code blocks is striking. Inside fn_expressive(), we maintain two local variables and iterate over a list using a for statement. The for loop will be checking to see if a StopIteration exception has been raised on each loop. Each iteration applies the total.__add__ function, which will check the type of the second variable (n) on each iteration. These checks all add a little expense.

Inside fn_terse(), we call out to an optimized C list comprehension function that knows how to generate the final result without creating intermediate Python objects. This is much faster, although each iteration must still check for the types of the objects that are being added together (in Chapter 4 we look at ways of fixing the type so we don't need to check it on each iteration).

As noted previously, you *must* profile your code—if you just rely on this heuristic, then you will inevitably write slower code at some point. It is definitely worth learning if Python has a shorter and still readable way to solve your problem built in. If so, it is more likely to be easily readable by another programmer, and it will *probably* run faster.

Unit Testing During Optimization to Maintain Correctness

If you aren't already unit testing your code, then you are probably hurting your longer-term productivity. Ian (blushing) is embarrassed to note that once he spent a day optimizing his code, having disabled unit tests because they were inconvenient, only to discover that his significant speedup result was due to breaking a part of the algorithm he was improving. You do not need to make this mistake even once.

In addition to unit testing, you should also strongly consider using `coverage.py`. It checks to see which lines of code are exercised by your tests and identifies the sections that have no coverage. This quickly lets you figure out whether you're testing the code that you're about to optimize, such that any mistakes that might creep in during the optimization process are quickly caught.

No-op @profile Decorator

Your unit tests will fail with a `NameError` exception if your code uses `@profile` from `line_profiler` or `memory_profiler`. The reason is that the unit test framework will not be injecting the `@profile` decorator into the local namespace. The no-op decorator shown here solves this problem. It is easiest to add it to the block of code that you're testing and remove it when you're done.

With the no-op decorator, you can run your tests without modifying the code that you're testing. This means you can run your tests after every profile-led optimization you make so you'll never be caught out by a bad optimization step.

Let's say we have the trivial `ex.py` module shown in Example 2-20. It has a test (for nosetests) and a function that we've been profiling with either `line_profiler` or `memory_profiler`.

Example 2-20. Simple function and test case where we wish to use @profile

```
# ex.py
import unittest

@profile
def some_fn(nbr):
    return nbr * 2


class TestCase(unittest.TestCase):
    def test(self):
        result = some_fn(2)
        self.assertEquals(result, 4)
```

If we run nosetests on our code, we'll get a `NameError`:

```
$ nosetests ex.py
E
======================================================================
ERROR: Failure: NameError (name 'profile' is not defined)
...
NameError: name 'profile' is not defined
```

```
Ran 1 test in 0.001s

FAILED (errors=1)
```

The solution is to add a no-op decorator at the start of ex.py (you can remove it once you're done with profiling). If the @profile decorator is not found in one of the namespaces (because line_profiler or memory_profiler is not being used), then the no-op version we've written is added. If line_profiler or memory_profiler has injected the new function into the namespace, then our no-op version is ignored.

For line_profiler, we can add the code in Example 2-21.

Example 2-21. line_profiler fix to add a no-op @profile decorator to the namespace while unit testing

```
# for line_profiler
if '__builtin__' not in dir() or not hasattr(__builtin__, 'profile'):
    def profile(func):
        def inner(*args, **kwargs):
            return func(*args, **kwargs)
        return inner
```

The __builtin__ test is for nosetests, and the hasattr test is for identifying when the @profile decorator has been injected into the namespace. We can now run noset ests on our code successfully:

```
$ kernprof.py -v -l ex.py
Line #      Hits         Time  Per %%HTMLit   % Time  Line Contents
==============================================================
    11                                              @profile
    12                                              def some_fn(nbr):
    13           1            3 .     3.0    100.0      return nbr * 2


$ nosetests ex.py
.
Ran 1 test in 0.000s
```

For memory_profiler, we use the code in Example 2-22.

Example 2-22. memory_profiler fix to add a no-op @profile decorator to the namespace while unit testing

```
# for memory_profiler
if 'profile' not in dir():
    def profile(func):
        def inner(*args, **kwargs):
            return func(*args, **kwargs)
        return inner
```

We'd expect it to generate output like this:

```
python -m memory_profiler ex.py
...
Line #    Mem usage    Increment   Line Contents
================================================
    11   10.809 MiB    0.000 MiB   @profile
    12                             def some_fn(nbr):
    13   10.809 MiB    0.000 MiB       return nbr * 2


$ nosetests ex.py
.
Ran 1 test in 0.000
```

You can save yourself a few minutes by avoiding the use of these decorators, but once you've lost hours making a false optimization that breaks your code, you'll want to integrate this into your workflow.

Strategies to Profile Your Code Successfully

Profiling requires some time and concentration. You will stand a better chance of understanding your code if you separate the section you want to test from the main body of your code. You can then unit test the code to preserve correctness, and you can pass in realistic fabricated data to exercise the inefficiencies you want to address.

Do remember to disable any BIOS-based accelerators, as they will only confuse your results. On Ian's laptop the Intel TurboBoost feature can temporarily accelerate a CPU above its normal maximum speed if it is cool enough. This means that a cool CPU may run the same block of code faster than a hot CPU. Your operating system may also control the clock speed—a laptop on battery power is likely to more aggressively control CPU speed than a laptop on mains power. To create a more stable benchmarking configuration, we:

- Disable TurboBoost in the BIOS.
- Disable the operating system's ability to override the SpeedStep (you will find this in your BIOS if you're allowed to control it).
- Only use mains power (never battery power).
- Disable background tools like backups and Dropbox while running experiments.
- Run the experiments many times to obtain a stable measurement.
- Possibly drop to run level 1 (Unix) so that no other tasks are running.
- Reboot and rerun the experiments to double-confirm the results.

Try to hypothesize the expected behavior of your code and then validate (or disprove!) the hypothesis with the result of a profiling step. Your choices will not change (you can only use the profiled results to drive your decisions), but your intuitive understanding of the code will improve, and this will pay off in future projects as you will be more likely to make performant decisions. Of course, you will verify these performant decisions by profiling as you go.

Do not skimp on the preparation. If you try to performance test code deep inside a larger project without separating it from the larger project, you are likely to witness side effects that will sidetrack your efforts. It is likely to be harder to unit test a larger project when you're making fine-grained changes, and this may further hamper your efforts. Side effects could include other threads and processes impacting CPU and memory usage and network and disk activity, which will skew your results.

For web servers, investigate `dowser` and `dozer`; you can use these to visualize in real time the behavior of objects in the namespace. Definitely consider separating the code you want to test out of the main web application if possible, as this will make profiling significantly easier.

Make sure your unit tests exercise all the code paths in the code that you're analyzing. Anything you don't test that is used in your benchmarking may cause subtle errors that will slow down your progress. Use `coverage.py` to confirm that your tests are covering all the code paths.

Unit testing a complicated section of code that generates a large numerical output may be difficult. Do not be afraid to output a text file of results to run through `diff` or to use a `pickled` object. For numeric optimization problems, Ian likes to create long text files of floating-point numbers and use `diff`—minor rounding errors show up immediately, even if they're rare in the output.

If your code might be subject to numerical rounding issues due to subtle changes, then you are better off with a large output that can be used for a before-and-after comparison. One cause of rounding errors is the difference in floating-point precision between CPU registers and main memory. Running your code through a different code path can cause subtle rounding errors that might later confound you—it is better to be aware of this as soon as they occur.

Obviously, it makes sense to use a source code control tool while you are profiling and optimizing. Branching is cheap, and it will preserve your sanity.

Wrap-Up

Having looked at profiling techniques, you should have all the tools you need to identify bottlenecks around CPU and RAM usage in your code. Next we'll look at how Python implements the most common containers, so you can make sensible decisions about representing larger collections of data.

## CHAPTER 3

Lists and Tuples

> ## Questions You'll Be Able to Answer After This Chapter
>
> - What are lists and tuples good for?
> - What is the complexity of a lookup in a list/tuple?
> - How is that complexity achieved?
> - What are the differences between lists and tuples?
> - How does appending to a list work?
> - When should I use lists and tuples?

One of the most important things in writing efficient programs is understanding the guarantees of the data structures you use. In fact, a large part of performant programming is understanding what questions you are trying to ask of your data and picking a data structure that can answer these questions quickly. In this chapter, we will talk about the kinds of questions that lists and tuples can answer quickly, and how they do it.

Lists and tuples are a class of data structures called *arrays*. An array is simply a flat list of data with some intrinsic ordering. This *a priori* knowledge of the ordering is important: by knowing that data in our array is at a specific position, we can retrieve it in O(1)! In addition, arrays can be implemented in multiple ways. This demarcates another line between lists and tuples: lists are dynamic arrays while tuples are static arrays.

Let's unpack these previous statements a bit. System memory on a computer can be thought of as a series of numbered buckets, each capable of holding a number. These numbers can be used to represent any variables we care about (integers, floats, strings, or other data structures), since they are simply references to where the data is located in memory.[1]

When we want to create an array (and thus a list or tuple), we first have to allocate a block of system memory (where every section of this block will be used as an integer-sized pointer to actual data). This involves going to kernel, the operating system's subprocess, and requesting the use of N *consecutive* buckets. Figure 3-1 shows an example of the system memory layout for an array (in this case, a list) of size six. Note that in Python lists also store how large they are, so of the six allocated blocks, only five are usable—the first element is the length.

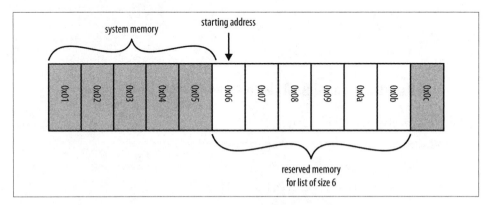

Figure 3-1. Example of system memory layout for an array of size 6

In order to look up any specific element in our list, we simply need to know which element we want and remember which bucket our data started in. Since all of the data will occupy the same amount of space (one "bucket," or, more specifically, one integer-sized pointer to the actual data), we don't need to know anything about the type of data that is being stored to do this calculation.

If you knew where in memory your list of N elements started, how would you find an arbitrary element in the list?

If, for example, we needed to retrieve the first element in our array, we would simply go to the first bucket in our sequence, M, and read out the value inside it. If, on the other hand, we needed the fifth element in our array, we would go to the bucket at position

---

1. In 64-bit computers, having 12 KB of memory gives you 725 buckets and 52 GB of memory gives you 3,250,000,000 buckets!

M+5 and read its content. In general, if we want to retrieve element i from our array, we go to bucket M+i. So, by having our data stored in consecutive buckets, and having knowledge of the ordering of our data, we can locate our data by knowing which bucket to look at in one step (or $O(1)$), regardless of how big our array is (Example 3-1).

Example 3-1. Timings for list lookups for lists of different sizes

```
>>> %%timeit l = range(10)
      ...: l[5]
      ...:
10000000 loops, best of 3: 75.5 ns per loop
>>>
>>> %%timeit l = range(10000000)
      ...: l[100000]
      ...:
10000000 loops, best of 3: 76.3 ns per loop
```

What if we were given an array with an unknown order and wanted to retrieve a particular element? If the ordering were known, we could simply look up that particular value. However, in this case, we must do a search operation. The most basic approach to this problem is called a "linear search," where we iterate over every element in the array and check if it is the value we want, as seen in Example 3-2.

Example 3-2. A linear search through a list

```
def linear_search(needle, array):
    for i, item in enumerate(array):
        if item == needle:
            return i
    return -1
```

This algorithm has a worst-case performance of $O(n)$. This case occurs when we search for something that isn't in the array. In order to know that the element we are searching for isn't in the array, we must first check it against every other element. Eventually, we will reach the final return -1 statement. In fact, this algorithm is exactly the algorithm that list.index() uses.

The only way to increase the speed is by having some other understanding of how the data is placed in memory, or the arrangement of the buckets of data we are holding. For example, hash tables, which are a fundamental data structure powering dictionaries and sets, solve this problem in $O(1)$ by disregarding the original ordering of the data and instead specifying another, more peculiar, organization. Alternatively, if your data is sorted in a way where every item is larger (or smaller) than its neighbor to the left (or right), then specialized search algorithms can be used that can bring your lookup time down to $O(\log n)$. This may seem like an impossible step to take from the constant-time lookups we saw before, but sometimes it is the best option (especially since search algorithms are more flexible and allow you to define searches in creative ways).

Given the following data, write an algorithm to find the index of the value 61:

```
[9, 18, 18, 19, 29, 42, 56, 61, 88, 95]
```

Since you know the data is ordered, how can you do this faster?

Hint: If you split the array in half, you know all the values on the left are smaller than the smallest element in the right set. You can use this!

A More Efficient Search

As alluded to previously, we can achieve better search performance if we first sort our data so that all elements to the left of a particular item are smaller than it (or larger). The comparison is done through the __eq__ and __lt__ magic functions of the object and can be user-defined if using custom objects.

Without the __eq__ and __lt__ methods, a custom object will only compare to objects of the same type and the comparison will be done using the instance's placement in memory.

The two ingredients necessary are the sorting algorithm and the searching algorithm. Python lists have a built-in sorting algorithm that uses Tim sort. Tim sort can sort through a list in O(n) in the best case (and O(n log n) in the worst case). It achieves this performance by utilizing multiple types of sorting algorithms and using heuristics to guess which algorithm will perform the best, given the data (more specifically, it hybridizes insertion and merge sort algorithms).

Once a list has been sorted, we can find our desired element using a binary search (Example 3-3), which has an average case complexity of O(log n). It achieves this by first looking at the middle of the list and comparing this value with the desired value. If this midpoint's value is less than our desired value, then we consider the right half of the list, and we continue halving the list like this until the value is found, or until the value is known not to occur in the sorted list. As a result, we do not need to read all values in the list, as was necessary for the linear search; instead, we only read a small subset of them.

Example 3-3. Efficient searching through a sorted list—binary search

```
def binary_search(needle, haystack):
    imin, imax = 0, len(haystack)
    while True:
        if imin >= imax:
            return -1
        midpoint = (imin + imax) // 2
```

```
    if haystack[midpoint] > needle:
        imax = midpoint
    elif haystack[midpoint] < needle:
        imin = midpoint+1
    else:
        return midpoint
```

This method allows us to find elements in a list without resorting to the potentially heavyweight solution of a dictionary. Especially when the list of data that is being operated on is intrinsically sorted, it is more efficient to simply do a binary search on the list to find an object (and get the O(log n) complexity of the search) rather than converting your data to a dictionary and then doing a lookup on it (although a dictionary lookup takes O(1), converting to a dictionary takes O(n), and a dictionary's restriction of no repeating keys may be undesirable).

In addition, the bisect module simplifies much of this process by giving easy methods to add elements into a list while maintaining its sorting, in addition to finding elements using a heavily optimized binary search. It does this by providing alternative functions that add the element into the correct sorted placement. With the list always being sorted, we can easily find the elements we are looking for (examples of this can be found in the documentation for the bisect module (*http://bit.ly/bisect_doc*)). In addition, we can use bisect to find the closest element to what we are looking for very quickly (Example 3-4). This can be extremely useful for comparing two datasets that are similar but not identical.

Example 3-4. Finding close values in a list with the bisect module

```
import bisect
import random

def find_closest(haystack, needle):
    # bisect.bisect_left will return the first value in the haystack
    # that is greater than the needle
    i = bisect.bisect_left(haystack, needle)
    if i == len(haystack):
        return i - 1
    elif haystack[i] == needle:
        return i
    elif i > 0:
        j = i - 1
        # since we know the value is larger than needle (and vice versa for the
        # value at j), we don't need to use absolute values here
        if haystack[i] - needle > needle - haystack[j]:
            return j
    return i

important_numbers = []
for i in xrange(10):
    new_number = random.randint(0, 1000)
```

```
        bisect.insort(important_numbers, new_number)

# important_numbers will already be in order because we inserted new elements
# with bisect.insort
print important_numbers

closest_index = find_closest(important_numbers, -250)
print "Closest value to -250: ", important_numbers[closest_index]

closest_index = find_closest(important_numbers, 500)
print "Closest value to 500: ", important_numbers[closest_index]

closest_index = find_closest(important_numbers, 1100)
print "Closest value to 1100: ", important_numbers[closest_index]
```

In general, this touches on a fundamental rule of writing efficient code: pick the right data structure and stick with it! Although there may be more efficient data structures for particular operations, the cost of converting to those data structures may negate any efficiency boost.

Lists Versus Tuples

If lists and tuples both use the same underlying data structure, what are the differences between the two? Summarized, the main differences are:

1. Lists are *dynamic* arrays; they are mutable and allow for resizing (changing the number of elements that are held).

2. Tuples are *static* arrays; they are immutable, and the data within them cannot be changed once they have been created.

3. Tuples are cached by the Python runtime, which means that we don't need to talk to the kernel to reserve memory every time we want to use one.

These differences outline the philosophical difference between the two: tuples are for describing multiple properties of one unchanging thing, and lists can be used to store collections of data about completely disparate objects. For example, the parts of a telephone number are perfect for a tuple: they won't change, and if they do they represent a new object or a different phone number. Similarly, the coefficients of a polynomial fit a tuple, since different coefficients represent a different polynomial. On the other hand, the names of the people currently reading this book are better suited for a list: the data is constantly changing both in content and in size but is still always representing the same idea.

It is important to note that both lists and tuples can take mixed types. This can, as we will see, introduce quite some overhead and reduce some potential optimizations. These overheads can be removed if we force all of our data to be of the same type. In Chapter 6 we will talk about reducing both the memory used and the computational overhead by using numpy. In addition, other packages, such as blist and array, can also reduce these overheads for other, nonnumerical situations. This alludes to a major point in performant programming that we will touch on in later chapters: generic code will be much slower than code specifically designed to solve a particular problem.

In addition, the immutability of a tuple as opposed to a list, which can be resized and changed, makes it a very lightweight data structure. This means that there isn't much overhead in memory when storing them, and operations with them are quite straightforward. With lists, as we will learn, their mutability comes at the price of extra memory needed to store them and extra computations needed when using them.

 For the following example datasets, would you use a tuple or a list? Why?

1. First 20 prime numbers
2. Names of programming languages
3. A person's age, weight, and height
4. A person's birthday and birthplace
5. The result of a particular game of pool
6. The results of a continuing series of pool games

Solution:

1. tuple, since the data is static and will not change
2. list, since this dataset is constantly growing
3. list, since the values will need to be updated
4. tuple, since that information is static and will not change
5. tuple, since the data is static
6. list, since more games will be played (in fact, we could use a list of tuples since each individual game's metadata will not change, but we will need to add more of them as more games are played)

Lists as Dynamic Arrays

Once we create a list, we are free to change its contents as needed:

```
>>> numbers = [5, 8, 1, 3, 2, 6]
>>> numbers[2] = 2*numbers[0]  # ❶
>>> numbers
[5, 8, 10, 3, 2, 6]
```

❶ As described previously, this operation is O(1) because we can find the data stored within the zeroth and second elements immediately.

In addition, we can append new data to a list and grow its size:

```
>>> len(numbers)
6
>>> numbers.append(42)
>>> numbers
[5, 8, 10, 3, 2, 6, 42]
>>> len(numbers)
7
```

This is possible because dynamic arrays support a `resize` operation that increases the capacity of the array. When a list of size N is first appended to, Python must create a new list that is big enough to hold the original N items in addition to the extra one that is being appended. However, instead of allocating N+1 items, M items are actually allocated, where M > N, in order to provide extra headroom for future appends. Then, the data from the old list is copied to the new list and the old list is destroyed. The philosophy is that one append is probably the beginning of many appends, and by requesting extra space we can reduce the number of times this allocation must happen and thus the total number of memory copies that are necessary. This is quite important since memory copies can be quite expensive, especially when list sizes start growing. Figure 3-2 shows what this overallocation looks like in Python 2.7. The formula dictating this growth is given in Example 3-5.

Example 3-5. List allocation equation in Python 2.7

```
M = (N >> 3) + (N < 9 ? 3 : 6)
```

N	0	1-4	5-8	9-16	17-25	26-35	36-46	...	991-1120
M	0	4	8	16	25	35	46	...	1120

As we append data, we utilize the extra space and increase the effective size of the list, N. As a result, N grows as we append new data until N == M. At this point, there is no extra space to insert new data into and we must create a *new* list with more extra space. This new list has extra headroom as given by the equation in Example 3-5, and we copy the old data into the new space.

This sequence of events is shown visually in Figure 3-3. The figure follows the various operations being performed on list l in Example 3-6.

Example 3-6. Resizing of a list

```
l = [1, 2]
for i in range(3, 7):
    l.append(i)
```

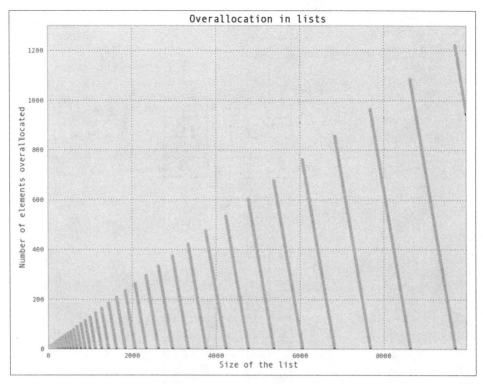

Figure 3-2. Graph showing how many extra elements are being allocated to a list of a particular size

This extra allocation happens on the first append. When a list is directly created, as in the preceding example, only the number of elements needed is allocated.

While the amount of extra headroom allocated is generally quite small, it can add up. This effect becomes especially pronounced when you are maintaining many small lists or when keeping a particularly large list. If we are storing 1,000,000 lists, each containing 10 elements, we would suppose that 10,000,000 elements' worth of memory is being used. In actuality, however, up to 16,000,000 elements could have been allocated if the append operator was used to construct the list. Similarly, for a large list of 100,000,000 elements, we actually have 112,500,007 elements allocated!

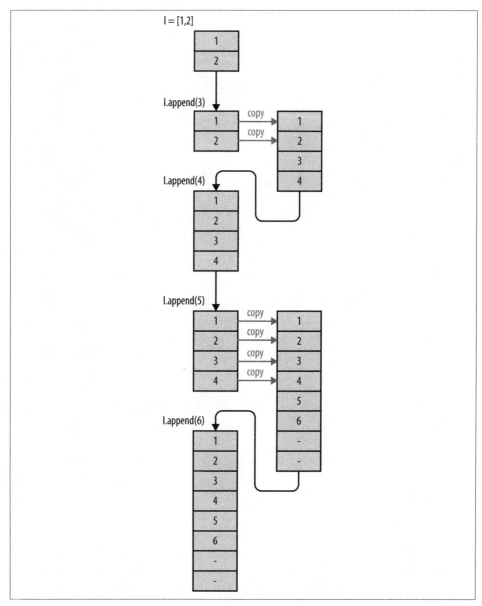

Figure 3-3. Example of how a list is mutated on multiple appends

Tuples As Static Arrays

Tuples are fixed and immutable. This means that once a tuple is created, unlike a list, it cannot be modified or resized:

```
>>> t = (1,2,3,4)
>>> t[0] = 5
Traceback (most recent call last):
  File "<stdin>", line 1, in <module>
TypeError: 'tuple' object does not support item assignment
```

However, although they don't support resizing, we can concatenate two tuples together and form a new tuple. The operation is similar to the `resize` operation on lists, but we do not allocate any extra space for the resulting tuple:

```
>>> t1 = (1,2,3,4)
>>> t2 = (5,6,7,8)
>>> t1 + t2
(1, 2, 3, 4, 5, 6, 7, 8)
```

If we consider this to be comparable to the `append` operation on lists, we see that it performs in $O(n)$ as opposed to the $O(1)$ speed of lists. This is because the allocate/copy operations must happen each time we add something new to the tuple, as opposed to only when our extra headroom ran out for lists. As a result of this, there is no in-place `append`-like operation; addition of two tuples always returns a new tuple that is in a new location in memory.

Not storing the extra headroom for resizing has the advantage of using fewer resources. A list of size 100,000,000 created with any `append` operation actually uses 112,500,007 elements' worth of memory, while a tuple holding the same data will only ever use exactly 100,000,000 elements' worth of memory. This makes tuples lightweight and preferable when data becomes static.

Furthermore, even if we create a list *without* `append` (and thus we don't have the extra headroom introduced by an `append` operation), it will *still* be larger in memory than a tuple with the same data. This is because lists have to keep track of more information about their current state in order to efficiently resize. While this extra information is quite small (the equivalent of one extra element), it can add up if several million lists are in use.

Another benefit of the static nature of tuples is something Python does in the background: resource caching. Python is garbage collected, which means that when a variable isn't used anymore Python frees the memory used by that variable, giving it back to the operating system for use in other applications (or for other variables). For tuples of sizes 1–20, however, when they are no longer in use the space isn't immediately given back to the system, but rather saved for future use. This means that when a new tuple of that size is needed in the future, we don't need to communicate with the operating system to find a region in memory to put the data, since we have a reserve of free memory already.

While this may seem like a small benefit, it is one of the fantastic things about tuples: they can be created easily and quickly since they can avoid communications with the operating system, which can cost your program quite a bit of time. Example 3-7 shows that instantiating a list can be 5.1x slower than instantiating a tuple—which can add up quite quickly if this is done in a fast loop!

Example 3-7. Instantiation timings for lists versus tuples

```
>>> %timeit l = [0,1,2,3,4,5,6,7,8,9]
1000000 loops, best of 3: 285 ns per loop
>>> %timeit t = (0,1,2,3,4,5,6,7,8,9)
10000000 loops, best of 3: 55.7 ns per loop
```

Wrap-Up

Lists and tuples are fast and low-overhead objects to use when your data already has an intrinsic ordering to it. This intrinsic ordering allows you to sidestep the search problem in these structures: if the ordering is known beforehand, then lookups are O(1), avoiding an expensive O(n) linear search. While lists can be resized, you must take care to properly understand how much overallocation is happening to ensure that the dataset can still fit in memory. On the other hand, tuples can be created quickly and without the added overhead of lists, at the cost of not being modifiable. In "Aren't Python Lists Good Enough?" on page 105, we will discuss how to preallocate lists in order to alleviate some of the burden regarding frequent appends to Python lists and look at some other optimizations that can help manage these problems.

In the next chapter, we go over the computational properties of dictionaries, which solve the search/lookup problems with unordered data at the cost of overhead.

Dictionaries and Sets

Questions You'll Be Able to Answer After This Chapter

- What are dictionaries and sets good for?
- How are dictionaries and sets the same?
- What is the overhead when using a dictionary?
- How can I optimize the performance of a dictionary?
- How does Python use dictionaries to keep track of namespaces?

Sets and dictionaries are ideal data structures to be used when your data has no intrinsic order, but does have a unique object that can be used to reference it (the reference object is normally a string, but can be any hashable type). This reference object is called the "key," while the data is the "value." Dictionaries and sets are almost identical, except that sets do not actually contain values: a set is simply a collection of unique keys. As the name implies, sets are very useful for doing set operations.

 A *hashable* type is one that implements both the __hash__ magic function and either __eq__ or __cmp__. All native types in Python already implement these, and any user classes have default values. See "Hash Functions and Entropy" on page 81 for more details.

While we saw in the previous chapter that we are restricted to, at best, $O(\log n)$ lookup time on lists/tuples with no intrinsic order (through a search operation), dictionaries and sets give us $O(n)$ lookups based on the arbitrary index. In addition, like lists/tuples, dictionaries and sets have O(1) insertion time.[1] As we will see in "How Do Dictionaries and Sets Work?" on page 77, this speed is accomplished through the use of an open address hash table as the underlying data structure.

However, there is a cost to using dictionaries and sets. First, they generally take up a larger footprint in memory. Also, although the complexity for insertions/lookups is O(1), the actual speed depends greatly on the hashing function that is in use. If the hash function is slow to evaluate, then any operations on dictionaries or sets will be similarly slow.

Let's look at an example. Say we want to store contact information for everyone in the phone book. We would like to store this in a form that will make it simple to answer the question, "What is John Doe's phone number?" in the future. With lists, we would store the phone numbers and names sequentially and scan through the entire list to find the phone number we required, as shown in Example 4-1.

Example 4-1. Phone book lookup with a list

```
def find_phonenumber(phonebook, name):
    for n, p in phonebook:
        if n == name:
            return p
    return None

phonebook = [
    ("John Doe", "555-555-5555"),
    ("Albert Einstein", "212-555-5555"),
]
print "John Doe's phone number is", find_phonenumber(phonebook, "John Doe")
```

 We could also do this by sorting the list and using the bisect module in order to get O(log n) performance.

With a dictionary, however, we can simply have the "index" be the names and the "values" be the phone numbers, as shown in Example 4-2. This allows us to simply look up the value we need and get a direct reference to it, instead of having to read every value in our dataset.

---

1. As we will discuss in "Hash Functions and Entropy" on page 81, dictionaries and sets are very dependent on their hash functions. If the hash function for a particular datatype is not O(1), any dictionary or set containing that type will no longer have its O(1) guarantee.

Example 4-2. Phone book lookup with a dictionary

```
phonebook = {
    "John Doe": "555-555-5555",
    "Albert Einstein" : "212-555-5555",
}
print "John Doe's phone number is", phonebook["John Doe"]
```

For large phone books, the difference between the O(1) lookup of the dictionary and the O(n) time for linear search over the list (or, at best, the O(log n) with the bisect module) is quite substantial.

 Create a script that times the performance of the list-bisect method versus a dictionary for finding a number in a phone book. How does the timing scale as the size of the phone book grows?

If, on the other hand, we wanted to answer the question, "How many unique first names are there in my phone book?" we could use the power of sets. Recall that a set is simply a collection of *unique* keys—this is the exact property we would like to enforce in our data. This is in stark contrast to a list-based approach, where that property needs to be enforced separately from the data structure by comparing all names with all other names. Example 4-3 illustrates.

Example 4-3. Finding unique names with lists and sets

```
def list_unique_names(phonebook):
    unique_names = []
    for name, phonenumber in phonebook:          # ❶
        first_name, last_name = name.split(" ", 1)
        for unique in unique_names:              # ❷
            if unique == first_name:
                break
        else:
            unique_names.append(first_name)
    return len(unique_names)

def set_unique_names(phonebook):
    unique_names = set()
    for name, phonenumber in phonebook:          # ❸
        first_name, last_name = name.split(" ", 1)
        unique_names.add(first_name)             # ❹
    return len(unique_names)

phonebook = [
    ("John Doe", "555-555-5555"),
    ("Albert Einstein", "212-555-5555"),
    ("John Murphey", "202-555-5555"),
    ("Albert Rutherford", "647-555-5555"),
```

```
        ("Elaine Bodian", "301-555-5555"),
]

print "Number of unique names from set method:", set_unique_names(phonebook)
print "Number of unique names from list method:", list_unique_names(phonebook)
```

❶ ❸ We must go over all the items in our phone book, and thus this loop costs O(n).

❷ Here, we must check the current name against all the unique names we have already seen. If it is a new unique name, we add it to our list of unique names. We then continue through the list, performing this step for every item in the phone book.

❹ For the set method, instead of iterating over all unique names we have already seen, we can simply add the current name to our set of unique names. Because sets guarantee the uniqueness of the keys they contain, if you try to add an item that is already in the set, that item simply won't be added. Furthermore, this operation costs O(1).

The list algorithm's inner loop iterates over unique_names, which starts out as empty and then grows, in the worst case, when all names are unique, to be the size of phone book. This can be seen as performing a linear search for each name in the phone book over a list that is constantly growing. Thus, the complete algorithm performs as O(n log n), since the outer loop contributes the O(n) factor, while the inner loop contributes the O(log n) factor.

On the other hand, the set algorithm has no inner loop; the set.add operation is an O(1) process that completes in a fixed number of operations regardless of how large the phone book is (there are some minor caveats to this, which we will cover while discussing the implementation of dictionaries and sets). Thus, the only nonconstant contribution to the complexity of this algorithm is the loop over the phone book, making this algorithm perform in O(n).

When timing these two algorithms using a phonebook with 10,000 entries and 7,422 unique first names, we see how drastic the difference between O(n) and O(n log n) can be:

```
>>> %timeit list_unique_names(large_phonebook)
1 loops, best of 3: 2.56 s per loop

>>> %timeit set_unique_names(large_phonebook)
100 loops, best of 3: 9.57 ms per loop
```

In other words, the set algorithm gave us a 267x speedup! In addition, as the size of the phonebook grows, the speed gains increase (we get a 557x speedup with a phonebook with 100,000 entries and 15,574 unique first names).

How Do Dictionaries and Sets Work?

Dictionaries and sets use *hash tables* in order to achieve their O(1) lookups and insertions. This efficiency is the result of a very clever usage of a hash function to turn an arbitrary key (i.e., a string or object) into an index for a list. The hash function and list can later be used to determine where any particular piece of data is right away, without a search. By turning the data's key into something that can be used like a list index, we can get the same performance as with a list. In addition, instead of having to refer to data by a numerical index, which itself implies some ordering to the data, we can refer to it by this arbitrary key.

Inserting and Retrieving

In order to create a hash table from scratch, we start with some allocated memory, similar to what we started with for arrays. For an array, if we want to insert data, we simply find the smallest unused bucket and insert our data there (and resize if necessary). For hash tables, we must first figure out the placement of the data in this contiguous chunk of memory.

The placement of the new data is contingent on two properties of the data we are inserting: the hashed value of the key and how the value compares to other objects. This is because when we insert data, the key is first hashed and masked so that it turns into an effective index in an array.[2] The mask makes sure that the hash value, which can take the value of any integer, fits within the allocated number of buckets. So, if we have allocated 8 blocks of memory and our hash value is 28975, we consider the bucket at index 28975 & 0b111 = 7. If, however, our dictionary has grown to require 512 blocks of memory, then the mask becomes 0b111111111 (and in this case, we would consider the bucket at index 28975 & 0b11111111). Now we must check if this bucket is already in use. If it is empty, we can insert the key and the value into this block of memory. We store the key so that we can make sure we are retrieving the correct value on lookups. If it is in use and the value of the bucket is equal to the value we wish to insert (a comparison done with the cmp built-in), then the key/value pair is already in the hash table and we can return. However, if the values don't match, then we must find a new place to put the data.

To find the new index, we compute a new index using a simple linear function, a method called *probing*. Python's probing mechanism adds a contribution from the higher-order bits of the original hash (recall that for a table of length 8 we only considered the last 3 bits of the hash for the initial index, through the use of a mask value of mask = 0b111

---

2. A *mask* is a binary number that truncates the value of a number. So, 0b1111101 & 0b111 = 0b101 = 5 represents the operation of 0b111 masking the number 0b1111101. This operation can also be thought of as taking a certain number of the least-significant digits of a number.

= bin(8 - 1)). Using these higher-order bits gives each hash a different sequence of next possible hashes, which helps to avoid future collisions. There is a lot of freedom when picking the algorithm to generate a new index; however, it is quite important that the scheme visits every possible index in order to evenly distribute the data in the table. How well distributed the data is throughout the hash table is called the "load factor" and is related to the entropy of the hash function. The pseudocode in Example 4-4 illustrates the calculation of hash indices used in CPython 2.7.

Example 4-4. Dictionary lookup sequence

```
def index_sequence(key, mask=0b111, PERTURB_SHIFT=5):
    perturb = hash(key) # ❶
    i = perturb & mask
    yield i
    while True:
        i = ((i << 2) + i + perturb + 1)
        perturb >>= PERTURB_SHIFT
        yield i & mask
```

❶   hash returns an integer, while the actual C code in CPython uses an unsigned integer. Because of this, this pseudocode doesn't 100% replicate the behavior in CPython; however, it is a good approximation.

This probing is a modification of the naive method of "linear probing." In linear probing, we simply yield the values i = (5 * i + 1) & mask, where i is initialized to the hash value of the key and the value '5' is unimportant to the current discussion.[3] An important thing to note is that linear probing only deals with the last several bytes of the hash and disregards the rest (i.e., for a dictionary with eight elements, we only look at the last 3 bits since at that point the mask is 0x111). This means that if hashing two items gives the same last three binary digits, we will not only have a collision, but the sequence of probed indices will be the same. The perturbed scheme that Python uses will start taking into consideration more bits from the items' hashes in order to resolve this problem.

A similar procedure is done when we are performing lookups on a specific key: the given key is transformed into an index and that index is examined. If the key in that index matches (recall that we also store the original key when doing insert operations), then we can return that value. If it doesn't, we keep creating new indices using the same scheme, until we either find the data or hit an empty bucket. If we hit an empty bucket, we can conclude that the data does not exist in the table.

Figure 4-1 illustrates the process of adding some data into a hash table. Here, we chose to create a hash function that simply uses the first letter of the input. We accomplish this by using Python's ord function on the first letter of the input to get the integer

---

3. The value of 5 comes from the properties of a linear congruential generator (LCG), which is used in generating random numbers.

representation of that letter (recall the hash functions must return integers). As we'll see in "Hash Functions and Entropy" on page 81, Python provides hashing functions for most of its types, so typically you won't have to provide one yourself except in extreme situations.

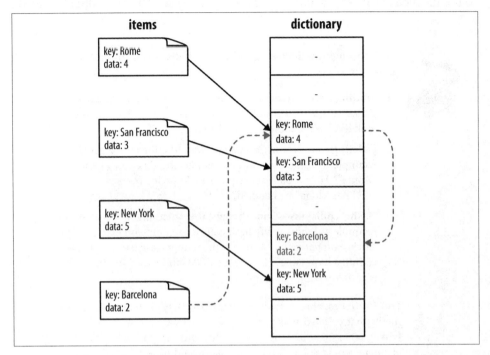

Figure 4-1. The resulting hash table from inserting with collisions

Insertion of the key "Barcelona" causes a collision, and a new index is calculated using the scheme in Example 4-4. This dictionary can also be created in Python using the code in Example 4-5.

Example 4-5. Custom hashing function

```python
class City(str):
    def __hash__(self):
        return ord(self[0])

# We create a dictionary where we assign arbitrary values to cities
data = {
    City("Rome"): 4,
    City("San Francisco"): 3,
    City("New York"): 5,
    City("Barcelona"): 2,
}
```

In this case, "Barcelona" and "Rome" cause the hash collision (Figure 4-1 shows the outcome of this insertion). We see this because for a dictionary with four elements we have a mask value of 0b111. As a result, "Barcelona" will try to use index ord("B") & 0b111 = 66 & 0b111 = 0b1000010 & 0b111 = 0b010 = 2. Similarly, "Rome" will try to use the index ord("R") & 0b111 = 82 & 0b111 = 0b1010010 & 0b111 = 0b010 = 2.

Work through the following problems. A discussion of hash collisions follows:

1. **Finding an element**—Using the dictionary created in Example 4-5, what would a lookup on the key "Johannesburg" look like? What indices would be checked?

2. **Deleting an element**—Using the dictionary created in Example 4-5, how would you handle the deletion of the key "Rome"? How would subsequent lookups for the keys "Rome" and "Barcelona" be handled?

3. **Hash collisions**—Considering the dictionary created in Example 4-5, how many hash collisions could you expect if 500 cities, with names all starting with an uppercase letter, were added into a hash table? How about 1,000 cities? Can you think of a way of lowering this number?

For 500 cities, there would be approximately 474 dictionary elements that collided with a previous value (500–26), with each hash having 500 / 26 = 19.2 cities associated with it. For 1,000 cities, 974 elements would collide and each hash would have 1,000 / 26 = 38.4 cities associated with it. This is because the hash is simply based on the numerical value of the first letter, which can only take a value from A–Z, allowing for only 26 independent hash values. This means that a lookup in this table could require as many as 38 subsequent lookups to find the correct value. In order to fix this, we must increase the number of possible hash values by considering other aspects of the city in the hash. The default hash function on a string considers every character in order to maximize the number of possible values. See "Hash Functions and Entropy" on page 81 for more explanation.

Deletion

When a value is deleted from a hash table, we cannot simply write a NULL to that bucket of memory. This is because we have used NULLs as a sentinel value while probing for hash collisions. As a result, we must write a special value that signifies that the bucket is empty, but there still may be values after it to consider when resolving a hash collision.

These empty slots can be written to in the future and are removed when the hash table is resized.

Resizing

As more items are inserted into the hash table, the table itself must be resized to accommodate it. It can be shown that a table that is no more than two-thirds full will have optimal space savings while still having a good bound on the number of collisions to expect. Thus, when a table reaches this critical point, it is grown. In order to do this, a larger table is allocated (i.e., more buckets in memory are reserved), the mask is adjusted to fit the new table, and all elements of the old table are reinserted into the new one. This requires recomputing indices, since the changed mask will change the resulting index. As a result, resizing large hash tables can be quite expensive! However, since we only do this resizing operation when the table is too small, as opposed to on every insert, the amortized cost of an insert is still $O(1)$.

By default, the smallest size of a dictionary or set is 8 (that is, if you are only storing three values, Python will still allocate eight elements). On resize, the number of buckets increases by 4x until we reach 50,000 elements, after which the size is increased by 2x. This gives the following possible sizes:

```
8, 32, 128, 512, 2048, 8192, 32768, 131072, 262144, ...
```

It is important to note that resizing can happen to make a hash table larger *or* smaller. That is, if sufficiently many elements of a hash table are deleted, the table can be scaled down in size. However, resizing *only happens during an insert.*

Hash Functions and Entropy

Objects in Python are generally hashable, since they already have built-in __hash__ and __cmp__ functions associated with them. For numerical types (int and float), the hash is simply based on the bit value of the number they represent. Tuples and strings have a hash value that is based on their contents. Lists, on the other hand, do not support hashing because their values can change. Since a list's values can change, so could the hash that represents the list, which would change the relative placement of that key in the hash table.[4]

User-defined classes also have default hash and comparison functions. The default __hash__ function simply returns the object's placement in memory as given by the built-in id function. Similarly, the __cmp__ operator compares the numerical value of the object's placement in memory.

---

4. More information about this can be found at *http://wiki.python.org/moin/DictionaryKeys*.

This is generally acceptable, since two instances of a class are generally different and should not collide in a hash table. However, in some cases we would like to use `set` or `dict` objects to disambiguate between items. Take the following class definition:

```
class Point(object):
    def __init__(self, x, y):
        self.x, self.y = x, y
```

If we were to instantiate multiple `Point` objects with the same values for x and y, they would all be independent objects in memory and thus have different placements in memory, which would give them all different hash values. This means that putting them all into a `set` would result in all of them having individual entries:

```
>>> p1 = Point(1,1)
>>> p2 = Point(1,1)
>>> set([p1, p2])
set([<__main__.Point at 0x1099bfc90>, <__main__.Point at 0x1099bfbd0>])
>>> Point(1,1) in set([p1, p2])
False
```

We can remedy this by forming a custom hash function that is based on the actual contents of the object as opposed to the object's placement in memory. The hash function can be arbitrary as long as it consistently gives the same result for the same object. (There are also considerations regarding the entropy of the hashing function, which we will discuss later.) The following redefinition of the `Point` class will yield the results we expect:

```
class Point(object):
    def __init__(self, x, y):
        self.x, self.y = x, y

    def __hash__(self):
        return hash((self.x, self.y))

    def __eq__(self, other):
        return self.x == other.x and self.y == other.y
```

This allows us to create entries in a set or dictionary indexed by the properties of the `Point` object as opposed to the memory address of the instantiated object:

```
>>> p1 = Point(1,1)
>>> p2 = Point(1,1)
>>> set([p1, p2])
set([<__main__.Point at 0x109b95910>])
>>> Point(1,1) in set([p1, p2])
True
```

As alluded to in the earlier note where we discussed hash collisions, a custom-selected hash function should be careful to evenly distribute hash values in order to avoid collisions. Having many collisions will degrade the performance of a hash table: if most keys have collisions, then we need to constantly "probe" the other values, effectively walking a potentially large portion of the dictionary in order to find the key in question. In the worst case, when all keys in a dictionary collide, the performance of lookups in the dictionary is O(n) and thus the same as if we were searching through a list.

If we know that we are storing 5,000 values in a dictionary and we need to create a hashing function for the object we wish to use as a key, we must be aware that the dictionary will be stored in a hash table of size 32,768, and thus only the last 15 bits of our hash are being used to create an index (for a hash table of this size, the mask is bin(32758-1) = 0b111111111111111).

This idea of "how well distributed my hash function is" is called the *entropy* of the hash function. Entropy, defined as:

$$S = -\sum_i p(i) \cdot \log(p(i))$$

where p(i) is the probability that the hash function gives hash i. It is maximized when every hash value has equal probability of being chosen. A hash function that maximizes entropy is called an *ideal* hash function since it guarantees the minimal number of collisions.

For an infinitely large dictionary, the hash function used for integers is ideal. This is because the hash value for an integer is simply the integer itself! For an infinitely large dictionary, the mask value is infinite and thus we consider all bits in the hash value. Thus, given any two numbers, we can guarantee that their hash values will not be the same.

However, if we made this dictionary finite, then we could no longer have this guarantee. For example, for a dictionary with four elements, the mask we use is 0b111. Thus, the hash value for the number 5 is 5 & 0b111 = 5 and the hash value for 501 is 501 & 0b111 = 5, and thus their entries will collide.

 To find the mask for a dictionary with an arbitrary number of elements, N, we first find the minimum number of buckets that dictionary must have to still be two-thirds full (N * 5 / 3). Then, we find the smallest dictionary size that will hold this number of elements (8; 32; 128; 512; 2,048; etc.) and find the number of bits necessary to hold this number. For example, if N=1039, then we must have at least 1,731 buckets, which means we need a dictionary with 2,048 buckets. Thus, the mask is bin(2048 - 1) = 0b11111111111.

There is no single best hash function to use when using a finite dictionary. However, knowing up front what range of values will be used and how large the dictionary will be helps in making a good selection. For example, if we are storing all 676 combinations of two lowercase letters as keys in a dictionary (*aa*, *ab*, *ac*, etc.), then a good hashing function would be the one shown in Example 4-6.

Example 4-6. Optimal two-letter hashing function

```
def twoletter_hash(key):
    offset = ord('a')
    k1, k2 = key
    return (ord(k2) - offset) + 26 * (ord(k1) - offset)
```

This gives no hash collisions for any combination of two lowercase letters, considering a mask of 0b1111111111 (a dictionary of 676 values will be held in a hash table of length 2,048, which has a mask of bin(2048-1) = 0b11111111111).

Example 4-7 very explicitly shows the ramifications of having a bad hashing function for a user-defined class—here, the cost of a bad hash function (in fact, it is the worst possible hash function!) is a 21.8x slowdown of lookups.

Example 4-7. Timing differences between good and bad hashing functions

```
import string
import timeit

class BadHash(str):
    def __hash__(self):
        return 42

class GoodHash(str):
    def __hash__(self):
        """
        This is a slightly optimized version of twoletter_hash
        """
        return ord(self[1]) + 26 * ord(self[0]) - 2619

baddict = set()
gooddict = set()
for i in string.ascii_lowercase:
    for j in string.ascii_lowercase:
        key = i + j
        baddict.add(BadHash(key))
        gooddict.add(GoodHash(key))

badtime = timeit.repeat(
    "key in baddict",
    setup = "from __main__ import baddict, BadHash; key = BadHash('zz')",
    repeat = 3,
    number = 1000000,
)
goodtime = timeit.repeat(
    "key in gooddict",
    setup = "from __main__ import gooddict, GoodHash; key = GoodHash('zz')",
    repeat = 3,
```

```
    number = 1000000,
)

print "Min lookup time for baddict: ", min(badtime)
print "Min lookup time for gooddict: ", min(goodtime)

# Results:
#   Min lookup time for baddict:  16.3375990391
#   Min lookup time for gooddict:  0.748275995255
```

1. Show that for an infinite dictionary (and thus an infinite mask), using an integer's value as its hash gives no collisions.
2. Show that the hashing function given in Example 4-6 is ideal for a hash table of size 1,024. Why is it not ideal for smaller hash tables?

Dictionaries and Namespaces

Doing a lookup on a dictionary is fast; however, doing it unnecessarily will slow down your code, just as any extraneous lines will. One area where this surfaces is in Python's namespace management, which heavily uses dictionaries to do its lookups.

Whenever a variable, function, or module is invoked in Python, there is a hierarchy that determines where it looks for these objects. First, Python looks inside of the locals() array, which has entries for all local variables. Python works hard to make local variable lookups fast, and this is the only part of the chain that doesn't require a dictionary lookup. If it doesn't exist there, then the globals() dictionary is searched. Finally, if the object isn't found there, the __builtin__ object is searched. It is important to note that while locals() and globals() are explicitly dictionaries and __builtin__ is technically a module object, when searching __builtin__ for a given property we are just doing a dictionary lookup inside of *its* locals() map (this is the case for all module objects and class objects!).

To make this clearer, let's look at a simple example of calling functions that are defined in different scopes (Example 4-8). We can disassemble the functions with the dis module (Example 4-9) to get a better understanding of how these namespace lookups are happening.

Example 4-8. Namespace lookups

```
import math
from math import sin

def test1(x):
    """
    >>> %timeit test1(123456)
```

```
      1000000 loops, best of 3: 381 ns per loop
      """
      return math.sin(x)

def test2(x):
      """
      >>> %timeit test2(123456)
      1000000 loops, best of 3: 311 ns per loop
      """
      return sin(x)

def test3(x, sin=math.sin):
      """
      >>> %timeit test3(123456)
      1000000 loops, best of 3: 306 ns per loop
      """
      return sin(x)
```

Example 4-9. Namespace lookups disassembled

```
>>> dis.dis(test1)
  9           0 LOAD_GLOBAL              0 (math)   # Dictionary lookup
              3 LOAD_ATTR                1 (sin)    # Dictionary lookup
              6 LOAD_FAST                0 (x)      # Local lookup
              9 CALL_FUNCTION            1
             12 RETURN_VALUE

>>> dis.dis(test2)
 15           0 LOAD_GLOBAL              0 (sin)    # Dictionary lookup
              3 LOAD_FAST                0 (x)      # Local lookup
              6 CALL_FUNCTION            1
              9 RETURN_VALUE

>>> dis.dis(test3)
 21           0 LOAD_FAST                1 (sin)    # Local lookup
              3 LOAD_FAST                0 (x)      # Local lookup
              6 CALL_FUNCTION            1
              9 RETURN_VALUE
```

The first function, test1, makes the call to sin by explicitly looking at the math library. This is also evident in the bytecode that is produced: first a reference to the math module must be loaded, and then we do an attribute lookup on this module until we finally have a reference to the sin function. This is done through two dictionary lookups, one to find the math module and one to find the sin function within the module.

On the other hand, test2 explicitly imports the sin function from the math module, and the function is then directly accessible within the global namespace. This means we can avoid the lookup of the math module and the subsequent attribute lookup. However, we still must find the sin function within the global namespace. This is yet another reason to be explicit about what functions you are importing from a module.

This practice not only makes code more readable, because the reader knows exactly what functionality is required from external sources, but it also speeds up code!

Finally, `test3` defines the `sin` function as a keyword argument, with its default value being a reference to the `sin` function within the `math` module. While we still do need to find a reference to this function within the module, this is only necessary when the `test3` function is first defined. After this, the reference to the `sin` function is stored within the function definition as a local variable in the form of a default keyword argument. As mentioned previously, local variables do not need a dictionary lookup to be found; they are stored in a very slim array that has very fast lookup times. Because of this, finding the function is quite fast!

While these effects are an interesting result of the way namespaces in Python are managed, `test3` is definitely not "Pythonic." Luckily, these extra dictionary lookups only start to degrade performance when they are called a lot (i.e., in the innermost block of a very fast loop, such as in the Julia set example). With this in mind, a more readable solution would be to set a local variable with the global reference before the loop is started. We'll still have to do the global lookup once whenever the function is called, but all the calls to that function in the loop will be made faster. This speaks to the fact that even minute slowdowns in code can be amplified if that code is being run millions of times. Even though a dictionary lookup may only take several hundred nanoseconds, if we are looping millions of times over this lookup it can quickly add up. In fact, looking at Example 4-10 we see a 9.4% speedup simply by making the `sin` function local to the tight loop that calls it.

Example 4-10. Effects of slow namespace lookups in loops

```
from math import sin

def tight_loop_slow(iterations):
    """
    >>> %timeit tight_loop_slow(10000000)
    1 loops, best of 3: 2.21 s per loop
    """
    result = 0
    for i in xrange(iterations):
        # this call to sin requires a global lookup
        result += sin(i)

def tight_loop_fast(iterations):
    """
    >>> %timeit tight_loop_fast(10000000)
    1 loops, best of 3: 2.02 s per loop
    """
    result = 0
    local_sin = sin
    for i in xrange(iterations):
```

```
# this call to local_sin requires a local lookup
result += local_sin(i)
```

Wrap-Up

Dictionaries and sets provide a fantastic way to store data that can be indexed by a key. The way this key is used, through the hashing function, can greatly affect the resulting performance of the data structure. Furthermore, understanding how dictionaries work gives you a better understanding not only of how to organize your data, but also of how to organize your code, since dictionaries are an intrinsic part of Python's internal functionality.

In the next chapter we will explore generators, which allow us to provide data to code with more control over ordering and without having to store full datasets in memory beforehand. This lets us sidestep many of the possible hurdles that one might encounter when using any of Python's intrinsic data structures.

## CHAPTER 5

Iterators and Generators

Questions You'll Be Able to Answer After This Chapter

- How do generators save memory?
- When is the best time to use a generator?
- How can I use `itertools` to create complex generator workflows?
- When is lazy evaluation beneficial, and when is it not?

When many people with experience in another language start learning Python, they are taken aback by the difference in `for` loop notation. That is to say, instead of writing:

```
# Other languages
for (i=0; i<N; i++) {
    do_work(i);
}
```

they are instead introduced to a new function called `range` or `xrange`:

```
# Python
for i in range(N):
    do_work(i)
```

These two functions provide insight into the paradigm of programming using generators. In order to fully understand generators, let us first make simple implementations of the `range` and `xrange` functions:

```
def range(start, stop, step=1):
    numbers = []
    while start < stop:
        numbers.append(start)
        start += step
```

```
        return numbers

    def xrange(start, stop, step=1):
        while start < stop:
            yield start # ❶
            start += step

    for i in range(1,10000):
        pass

    for i in xrange(1,10000):
        pass
```

❶   This function will yield many values instead of returning one value. This turns
     this regular-looking function into a generator that can be repeatedly polled for
     the next available value.

The first thing to note is that the range implementation must precreate the list of all
numbers within the range. So, if the range is from 1 to 10,000, the function will do 10,000
appends to the numbers list (which, as we discussed in Chapter 3, has overhead associated with it), and then return it. On the other hand, the generator is able to "return"
many values. Every time the code gets to the yield, the function emits its value, and
when another value is requested the function resumes running (maintaining its previous
state) and emits the new value. When the function reaches its end, a StopIteration
exception is thrown indicating that the given generator has no more values. As a result,
even though both functions must, in the end, do the same number of calculations, the
range version of the preceding loop uses 10x more memory (or Nx more memory if we
are ranging from 1 to N).

With this code in mind, we can decompose the for loops that use our implementations
of range and xrange. In Python, for loops require that the object we are looping over
supports iteration. This means that we must be able to create an iterator out of the object
we want to loop over. To create an iterator from almost any object, we can simply use
Python's built-in iter function. This function, for lists, tuples, dictionaries, and sets,
returns an iterator over the items or keys in the object. For more complex objects, iter
returns the result of the __iter__ property of the object. Since xrange already returns
an iterator, calling iter on it is a trivial operation, and it simply returns the original
object (so type(xrange(1,10)) == type(iter(xrange(1,10)))). However, since
range returns a list, we must create a new object, a list iterator, that will iterate over all
values in the list. Once an iterator is created, we simply call the next() function on it,
retrieving new values until a StopIteration exception is thrown. This gives us a good
deconstructed view of for loops, as illustrated in Example 5-1.

Example 5-1. Python for loop deconstructed

```
# The python loop
for i in object:
    do_work(i)

# Is equivalent to
object_iterator = iter(object)
while True:
    try:
        i = object_iterator.next()
        do_work(i)
    except StopIteration:
        break
```

The for loop code shows that we are doing extra work calling iter when using range instead of xrange. When using xrange, we create a generator that is trivially transformed into an iterator (since it is already an iterator!); however, for range we need to allocate a new list and precompute its values, and then we still must create an iterator!

More importantly, precomputing the range list requires allocating enough space for the full dataset and setting each element to the correct value, even though we only ever require one value at a time. This also makes the list allocation useless. In fact, it may even make the loop unrunnable, because range may be trying to allocate more memory than is available (range(100,000,000) would create a list 3.1 GB large!). By timing the results, we can see this very explicitly:

```
def test_range():
    """
    >>> %timeit test_range()
    1 loops, best of 3: 446 ms per loop
    """
    for i in range(1, 10000000):
        pass

def test_xrange():
    """
    >>> %timeit test_xrange()
    1 loops, best of 3: 276 ms per loop
    """
    for i in xrange(1, 10000000):
        pass
```

This may seem like a trivial enough problem to solve—simply replace all range calls with xrange—but the problem is actually a lot deeper. Let's say we had a long list of numbers, and we wanted to know how many of them are divisible by 3. This could look like:

```
divisible_by_three = len([n for n in list_of_numbers if n % 3 == 0])
```

However, this suffers from the same problem as `range` does. Since we are doing list comprehension, we are pregenerating the list of numbers divisible by 3, only to do a calculation on it and forget that list. If this list of numbers was quite large, this could mean allocating a lot of memory—potentially more than is available—for almost no reason.

Recall that we can create a list comprehension using a statement of the form `[<value>` `for <item>` in `<sequence>` if `<condition>]`. This will create a list of all the `<value>` items. Alternatively, we can use similar syntax to create a generator of the `<value>` items instead of a list by doing (`<value>` for `<item>` in `<sequence>` if `<condition>`).

Using this subtle difference between list comprehension and generator comprehension, we can optimize the preceding code for `divisible_by_three`. However, generators do not have a `length` property. As a result, we will have to be a bit clever:

```
divisible_by_three = sum((1 for n in list_of_numbers if n % 3 == 0))
```

Here, we have a generator that emits a value of 1 whenever it encounters a number divisible by 3, and nothing otherwise. By summing all elements in this generator we are essentially doing the same as the list comprehension version. The performance of the two versions of this code is almost equivalent, but the memory impact of the generator version is far less than that of the list comprehension. Furthermore, we are able to simply transform the list version into a generator because all that matters for each element of the list is its current value—either the number is divisible by 3 or it is not; it doesn't matter where its placement is in the list of numbers or what the previous/next values are. More complex functions can also be transformed into generators, but depending on their reliance on state, this can become a difficult thing to do.

Iterators for Infinite Series

Since we only need to store some version of a state and emit only the current value, generators are ideal for infinite series. The Fibonacci series is a great example—it is an infinite series with two state variables (the two last Fibonacci numbers):

```
def fibonacci():
    i, j = 0, 1
    while True:
        yield j
        i, j = j, i + j
```

We see here that although `j` is the value being emitted, we keep track of `i` as well since this holds the state of the Fibonacci series. The amount of state necessary for a calculation is quite important for generators because it translates into the actual memory footprint of the object. This makes it so that if we have a function that uses a lot of state and outputs a very small amount of data, it may be better to have this function precompute the list of data rather than have a generator for it.

One reason why generators aren't used as much as they could be is that a lot of the logic within them can be encapsulated in your logic code. This means that generators are really a way of organizing your code and having smarter loops. For example, we could answer the question, "How many Fibonacci numbers below 5,000 are odd?" in multiple ways:

```
def fibonacci_naive():
    i, j = 0, 1
    count = 0
    while j <= 5000:
        if j % 2:
            count += 1
        i, j = j, i + j
    return count

def fibonacci_transform():
    count = 0
    for f in fibonacci():
        if f > 5000:
            break
        if f % 2:
            count += 1
    return count

from itertools import islice
def fibonacci_succinct():
    is_odd = lambda x : x % 2
    first_5000 = islice(fibonacci(), 0, 5000)
    return sum(1 for x in first_5000 if is_odd(x))
```

All of these methods have similar runtime properties (namely, they all have the same memory footprint and the same performance), but the fibonacci_transform function benefits from several things. Firstly, it is much more verbose than fibonacci_suc cinct, which means it will be easy for another developer to debug and understand. The latter mainly stands as a warning for the next section, where we cover some common workflows using itertools—while the module greatly simplifies many simple actions with iterators, it can also quickly make Python code very un-Pythonic. Conversely, fibonacci_naive is doing multiple things at a time, which hides the actual calculation it is doing! While it is obvious in the generator function that we are iterating over the Fibonacci numbers, we are not overencumbered by the actual calculation. Lastly, fibo nacci_transform is more generalizable. This function could be renamed num_odd_un der_5000 and take in the generator by argument, and thus work over any series.

One last benefit of the fibonacci_transform function is that it supports the notion that in computation there are two phases: generating data and transforming data. This function is very clearly performing a transformation on data, while the fibonacci function generates it. This clear demarcation adds extra clarity and extra functionality: we can move a transformative function to work on a new set of data, or perform multiple transformations on existing data. This paradigm has always been important when creating complex programs; however, generators facilitate this clearly by making generators responsible for creating the data, and normal functions responsible for acting on the generated data.

Lazy Generator Evaluation

As touched on previously, the way we get the memory benefits with a generator is by dealing only with the current values of interest. At any point in our calculation with a generator, we only have the current value and cannot reference any other items in the sequence (algorithms that perform this way are generally called "single pass" or "online"). This can sometimes make generators more difficult to use, but there are many modules and functions that can help.

The main library of interest is `itertools`, in the standard library. It supplies generator versions of Python's built-in functions `map`, `reduce`, `filter`, and `zip` (called `imap`, `ireduce`, `ifilter`, and `izip` in `itertools`), in addition to many other useful functions. Of particular note are:

`islice`
> Allows slicing a potentially infinite generator

`chain`
> Chains together multiple generators

`takewhile`
> Adds a condition that will end a generator

`cycle`
> Makes a finite generator infinite by constantly repeating it

Let's build up an example of using generators to analyze a large dataset. Let's say we've had an analysis routine going over temporal data, one piece of data per second, for the last 20 years—that's 631,152,000 data points! The data is stored in a file, one second per line, and we cannot load the entire dataset into memory. If we wanted to do some simple anomaly detection, we could use generators and never allocate any lists!

The problem will be: given a data file of the form "timestamp, value", find days with a value 3 sigma away from that day's mean. We start by writing the code that will read the file, line by line, and output each line's value as a Python object. We will also create a `read_fake_data` generator to generate fake data we can test our algorithms with. For this function we still take the argument `filename`, so as to have the same function signature as `read_data`; however, we will simply disregard it. These two functions, shown in Example 5-2, are indeed lazily evaluated—we only read the next line in the file, or generate new fake data, when the `next()` property of the generator is called.

Example 5-2. Lazily reading data

```
from random import normalvariate, rand
from itertools import count

def read_data(filename):
    with open(filename) as fd:
        for line in fd:
            data = line.strip().split(',')
            yield map(int, data)

def read_fake_data(filename):
    for i in count():
        sigma = rand() * 10
        yield (i, normalvariate(0, sigma))
```

Now, we can use the `groupby` function in `itertools` to group together timestamps that occur on the same day (Example 5-3). This function works by taking in a sequence of items and a key used to group these items. The output is a generator that produces tuples whose items are the key for the group and a generator for the items in the group. As our key function, we will create a `lambda` function that returns a `date` object. These `date` objects are equal when they occur on the same day, which will group them by day. This "key" function could be anything—we could group our data by hour, by year, or by some property in the actual value. The only limitation is that groups will only be formed for data that is sequential. So, if we had the input A A A A B B A A and had `groupby` group by the letter, we would get three groups, (A, [A, A, A, A]), (B, [B, B]), and (A, [A, A]).

Example 5-3. Grouping our data

```
from datetime import date
from itertools import groupby

def day_grouper(iterable):
    key = lambda (timestamp, value) : date.fromtimestamp(timestamp)
    return groupby(iterable, key)
```

Now to do the actual anomaly detection. We will do this by iterating through a day's values and keeping track of the mean and maximum values. The mean will be calculated using an online mean and standard deviation algorithm.[1] The maximum is kept because it is the best candidate for being anomalous—if the max is more than 3 sigma larger than the mean, then we will return the `date` object representing the day we just analyzed. Otherwise, we will return `False` for posterity; however, we could equally have just ended

---

1. We use Knuth's online mean algorithm. This lets us calculate the mean and the first moment (in this case, the standard deviation) using a single temporary variable. We could also calculate further moments by modifying the equations slightly and adding more state variables (one per moment). More information can be found at *http://www.johndcook.com/standard_deviation.html*.

the function (and implicitly returned None). We output these values because this check_anomaly function is defined as a data filter—a function that returns True for data that should be kept and False for data that should be discarded. This will allow us to filter through the original dataset and only keep days that match our condition. The check_anomaly function is shown in Example 5-4.

Example 5-4. Generator-based anomaly detection

```
import math

def check_anomaly((day, day_data)):
    # We find the mean, standard deviation, and maximum values for the day.
    # Using a single-pass mean/standard deviation algorithm allows us to only
    # read through the day's data once.
    n = 0
    mean = 0
    M2 = 0
    max_value = None
    for timestamp, value in day_data:
        n += 1
        delta = value - mean
        mean = mean + delta/n
        M2 += delta*(value - mean)
        max_value = max(max_value, value)
    variance = M2/(n - 1)
    standard_deviation = math.sqrt(variance)

    # Here is the actual check of whether that day's data is anomalous.  If it
    # is, we return the value of the day; otherwise, we return false.
    if max_value > mean + 3 * standard_deviation:
        return day
    return False
```

One aspect of this function that may seem strange is the extra set of parentheses in the parameter definition. This is not a typo, but a result of this function taking input from the groupby generator. Recall that groupby yields tuples that become the parameters to this check_anomaly function. As a result, we must do tuple expansion in order to properly extract the group key and the group data. Since we are using ifilter, another way of dealing with this instead of having the tuple expansion inside the function definition is to define istarfilter, which is similar to what istarmap does to imap (see the itertools documentation (*http://bit.ly/itertools_doc*) for more information).

Finally, we can put together the chain of generators to get the days that had anomalous data (Example 5-5).

Example 5-5. Chaining together our generators

```
from itertools import ifilter, imap

data = read_data(data_filename)
```

```
data_day = day_grouper(data)
anomalous_dates = ifilter(None, imap(check_anomaly, data_day)) # ❶

first_anomalous_date, first_anomalous_data = anomalous_dates.next()
print "The first anomalous date is: ", first_anomalous_date
```

❶   ifilter will remove any elements that do not satisfy the given filter. By default
     (sending None to the first parameter triggers this), ifilter will filter out any
     elements that evaluate to False. This makes it so we don't include any days that
     check_anomaly didn't think were anomalous.

This method very simply allows us to get the list of days that are anomalous without
having to load the entire dataset. One thing to note is that this code does not actually
do any calculation; it simply sets up the pipeline to do the calculation. The file will never
be read until we do anomalous_dates.next() or somehow iterate on the anoma
lous_dates generator. In fact, we only ever do the analysis when a new value is requested
from anomalous_dates. So, if our full dataset has five anomalous dates, but in our code
we retrieve one and then stop requesting new values, the file will only be read up to the
point where this day's data appears. This is called *lazy evaluation*—only the calculations
that are explicitly requested are performed, which can drastically reduce overall runtime
if there is an early termination condition.

Another nicety about organizing analysis this way is it allows us to do more expansive
calculations easily, without having to rework large parts of the code. For example, if we
want to have a moving window of one day instead of chunking up by days, we can simply
write a new day_grouper that does this and use it instead:

```
from datetime import datetime

def rolling_window_grouper(data, window_size=3600):
    window = tuple(islice(data, 0, window_size))
    while True:
        current_datetime = datetime.fromtimestamp(window[0][0])
        yield (current_datetime, window)
        window = window[1:] + (data.next(),)
```

Now, we simply replace the call to day_grouper in Example 5-5 with a call to roll
ing_window_grouper and we get the desired result. In this version we also see very
explicitly the memory guarantee of this and the previous method—it will store only the
window's worth of data as state (in both cases, one day, or 3,600 data points). We can
change this by opening the file multiple times and using the various life descriptors to
point to the exact data we like (or using the linecache module). However, this is only
necessary if this subsampling of the dataset still doesn't fit in memory.

A final note: in the rolling_window_grouper function, we perform many pop and
append operations on the list window. We can greatly optimize this by using the deque
object in the collections module. This object gives us O(1) appends and removals to

and from the beginning or end of a list (while normal lists are O(1) for appends or removals to/from the end of the list and O(n) for the same operations at the beginning of the list). Using the deque object, we can append the new data to the right (or end) of the list and use deque.popleft() to delete data from the left (or beginning) of the list without having to allocate more space or perform long O(n) operations.

Wrap-Up

By formulating our anomaly-finding algorithm with iterators, we are able to process much more data than could fit into memory. What's more, we are able to do it faster than if we had used lists, since we avoid all the costly append operations.

Since iterators are a primitive type in Python, this should always be a go-to method for trying to reduce the memory footprint of an application. The benefits are that results are lazily evaluated, so you only ever process the data you need, and memory is saved since we don't store previous results unless explicitly required to. In Chapter 11, we will talk about other methods that can be used for more specific problems and introduce some new ways of looking at problems when RAM is an issue.

Another benefit of solving problems using iterators is that it prepares your code to be used on multiple CPUs or multiple computers, as we will see in Chapters 9 and 10. As we discussed in "Iterators for Infinite Series" on page 92, when working with iterators you must always think about the various states that are necessary for your algorithm to work. Once you figure out how to package the state necessary for the algorithm to run, it doesn't matter where it runs. We can see this sort of paradigm, for example, with the multiprocessing and ipython modules, both of which use a map-like function to launch parallel tasks.

## CHAPTER 6

Matrix and Vector Computation

Questions You'll Be Able to Answer After This Chapter

- What are the bottlenecks in vector calculations?
- What tools can I use to see how efficiently the CPU is doing my calculations?
- Why is numpy better at numerical calculations than pure Python?
- What are cache-misses and page-faults?
- How can I track the memory allocations in my code?

Regardless of what problem you are trying to solve on a computer, you will encounter vector computation at some point. Vector calculations are integral to how a computer works and how it tries to speed up runtimes of programs down at the silicon level—the only thing the computer knows how to do is operate on numbers, and knowing how to do several of those calculations at once will speed up your program.

In this chapter, we try to unwrap some of the complexities of this problem by focusing on a relatively simple mathematical problem, solving the diffusion equation, and understanding what is happening at the CPU level. By understanding how different Python code affects the CPU and how to effectively probe these things, we can learn how to understand other problems as well.

We will start by introducing the problem and coming up with a quick solution using pure Python. After identifying some memory issues and trying to fix them using pure Python, we will introduce numpy and identify how and why it speeds up our code. Then we will start doing some algorithmic changes and specialize our code to solve the problem at hand. By removing some of the generality of the libraries we are using, we will yet again be able to gain more speed. Finally, we introduce some extra modules that will help facilitate this sort of process out in the field, and also explore a cautionary tale about optimizing before profiling.

Introduction to the Problem

 This section is meant to give a deeper understanding of the equations we will be solving throughout the chapter. It is not strictly necessary to understand this section in order to approach the rest of the chapter. If you wish to skip this section, make sure to look at the algorithm in Examples 6-1 and 6-2 to understand the code we will be optimizing.

On the other hand, if you read this section and want even more explanation, read Chapter 17 of *Numerical Recipes*, Third Edition, by William Press et al. (Cambridge University Press).

In order to explore matrix and vector computation in this chapter, we will repeatedly use the example of diffusion in fluids. Diffusion is one of the mechanisms that moves fluids and tries to make them uniformly mixed.

In this section we will explore the mathematics behind the diffusion equation. This may seem complicated, but don't worry! We will quickly simplify this to make it more understandable. Also, it is important to note that while having a basic understanding of the final equation we are solving will be useful while reading this chapter, it is not completely necessary; the subsequent chapters will focus mainly on various formulations of the code, not the equation. However, having an understanding of the equations will help you gain intuition about ways of optimizing your code. This is true in general —understanding the motivation behind your code and the intricacies of the algorithm will give you deeper insight about possible methods of optimization.

One simple example of diffusion is dye in water: if you put several drops of dye into water at room temperature it will slowly move out until it fully mixes with the water. Since we are not stirring the water, nor is it warm enough to create convection currents, diffusion will be the main process mixing the two liquids. When solving these equations numerically, we pick what we want the initial condition to look like and are able to evolve the initial condition forward in time to see what it will look like at a later time (see Figure 6-2).

All this being said, the most important thing to know about diffusion for our purposes is its formulation. Stated as a partial differential equation in one dimension (1D), the diffusion equation is written as:

$$\frac{\partial}{\partial t} u(x,\ t) = D \cdot \frac{\partial^2}{\partial x^2} u(x,\ t)$$

In this formulation, u is the vector representing the quantities we are diffusing. For example, we could have a vector with values of 0 where there is only water and 1 where there is only dye (and values in between where there is mixing). In general, this will be a 2D or 3D matrix representing an actual area or volume of fluid. In this way, we could have u be a 3D matrix representing the fluid in a glass, and instead of simply doing the second derivative along the x direction, we'd have to take it over all axes. In addition, D is a physical value that represents properties of the fluid we are simulating. A large value of D represents a fluid that can diffuse very easily. For simplicity, we will set D = 1 for our code, but still include it in the calculations.

The diffusion equation is also called the *heat equation*. In this case, u represents the temperature of a region and D describes how well the material conducts heat. Solving the equation tells us how the heat is being transferred. So, instead of solving for how a couple of drops of dye diffuse through water, we might be solving for how the heat generated by a CPU diffuses into a heat sink.

What we will do is take the diffusion equation, which is continuous in space and time, and approximate it using discrete volumes and discrete times. We will do so using Euler's method. Euler's method simply takes the derivative and writes it as a difference, such that:

$$\frac{\partial}{\partial t} u(x, t) \approx \frac{u(x, t + dt) + u(x, t)}{dt}$$

where dt is now a fixed number. This fixed number represents the time step, or the resolution in time for which we wish to solve this equation. It can be thought of as the frame rate of the movie we are trying to make. As the frame rate goes up (or dt goes down), we get a clearer picture of what happens. In fact, as dt approaches zero, Euler's approximation becomes exact (note, however, that this exactness can only be achieved theoretically, since there is only finite precision on a computer and numerical errors will quickly dominate any results). We can thus rewrite this equation to figure out what u(x, t+dt) is given u(x,t). What this means for us is that we can start with some initial state (u(x,0), representing the glass of water just as we add a drop of dye into it) and churn through the mechanisms we've outlined to "evolve" that initial state and see what it will look like at future times (u(x,dt)). This type of problem is called an "initial value problem" or "Cauchy problem."

Doing a similar trick for the derivative in x using the finite differences approximation, we arrive at the final equation:

$$u(x, t + dt) = u(x, t) + dt * D * \frac{u(x + dx, t) + u(x + dx, t) + 2 \cdot u(x, t)}{dx^2}$$

Here, similar to how dt represents the frame rate, dx represents the resolution of the images—the smaller dx is the smaller a region every cell in our matrix represents. For simplicity, we will simply set D = 1 and dx = 1. These two values become very important when doing proper physical simulations; however, since we are simply solving the diffusion equation for illustrative purposes they are not important to us.

Using this equation, we can solve almost any diffusion problem. However, there are some considerations regarding this equation. Firstly, we said before that the spatial index in u (i.e., the x parameter) will be represented as the indices into a matrix. What happens when we try to find the value at x-dx when x is at the beginning of the matrix? This problem is called the *boundary condition*. You can have fixed boundary conditions that say, "any value out of the bounds of my matrix will be set to 0" (or any other value). Alternatively, you can have periodic boundary conditions that say that the values will wrap around (i.e., if one of the dimensions of your matrix has length N, the value in that dimension at index -1 is the same as at N-1, and the value at N is the same as at index 0. In other words, if you are trying to access the value at index i, you will get the value at index (i%N)).

Another consideration is how we are going to store the multiple time components of u. We could have one matrix for every time value we do our calculation for. At minimum, it seems that we will need two matrices: one for the current state of the fluid and one for the next state of the fluid. As we'll see, there are very drastic performance considerations for this particular question.

So, what does it look like to solve this problem in practice? Example 6-1 contains some pseudocode to illustrate the way we can use our equation to solve the problem.

Example 6-1. Pseudocode for 1D diffusion

```
# Create the initial conditions
u = vector of length N
for i in range(N):
    u = 0 if there is water, 1 if there is dye

# Evolve the initial conditions
D = 1
t = 0
dt = 0.0001
while True:
    print "Current time is: %f" % t
    unew = vector of size N

    # Update step for every cell
    for i in range(N):
```

```
    unew[i] = u[i] + D * dt * (u[(i+1)%N] + u[(i-1)%N] - 2 * u[i])
# Move the updated solution into u
u = unew

visualize(u)
```

This code will take some initial condition of the dye in water and tell us what the system looks like at every 0.0001-second interval in the future. The results of this can be seen in Figure 6-1, where we evolve our very concentrated drop of dye (represented by the top-hat function) into the future. We can see how, far into the future, the dye becomes well mixed, to the point where everywhere has a similar concentration of the dye.

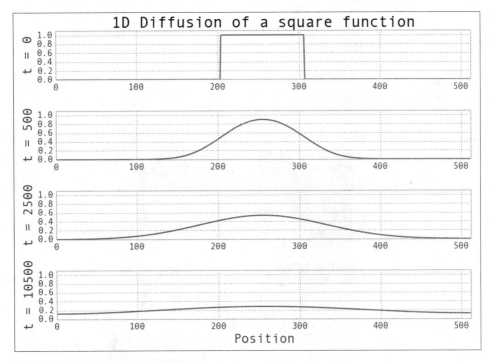

Figure 6-1. Example of 1D diffusion

For the purposes of this chapter, we will be solving the 2D version of the preceding equation. All this means is that instead of operating over a vector (or in other words, a matrix with one index), we will be operating over a 2D matrix. The only change to the equation (and thus the subsequent code) is that we must now also take the second derivative in the y direction. This simply means that the original equation we were working with becomes:

$$\frac{\partial}{\partial t}u(x, y, t) = D \cdot \left(\frac{\partial^2}{\partial x^2}u(x, y, t) + \frac{\partial^2}{\partial y^2}u(x, y, t) \right)$$

This numerical diffusion equation in 2D translates to the pseudocode in Example 6-2, using the same methods we used before.

Example 6-2. Algorithm for calculating 2D diffusion

```
for i in range(N):
    for j in range(M):
        unew[i][j] = u[i][j] + dt * (                               \
            (u[(i+1)%N][j] + u[(i-1)%N][j] - 2 * u[i][j]) + \ # d^2 u / dx^2
            (u[i][(j+1)%M] + u[j][(j-1)%M] - 2 * u[i][j])   \ # d^2 u / dy^2
        )
```

We can now put all of this together and write the full Python 2D diffusion code that we will use as the basis for our benchmarks for the rest of this chapter. While the code looks more complicated, the results are similar to that of the 1D diffusion (as can be seen in Figure 6-2).

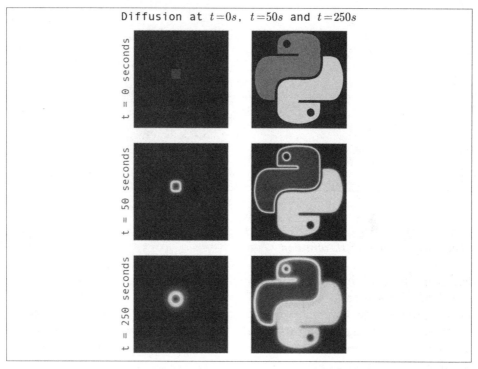

Figure 6-2. Example of diffusion for two sets of initial conditions

If you'd like to do some additional reading on the topics in this section, check out the Wikipedia page on the diffusion equation (*http://bit.ly/diffusion_eq*) and Chapter 7 (*http://bit.ly/Gurevich*) of "Numerical methods for complex systems," by S. V. Gurevich.

Aren't Python Lists Good Enough?

Let's take our pseudocode from Example 6-1 and formalize it so we can better analyze its runtime performance. The first step is to write out the evolution function that takes in the matrix and returns its evolved state. This is shown in Example 6-3.

Example 6-3. Pure Python 2D diffusion

```
grid_shape = (1024, 1024)

def evolve(grid, dt, D=1.0):
    xmax, ymax = grid_shape
    new_grid = [[0.0,] * ymax for x in xrange(xmax)]
    for i in xrange(xmax):
        for j in xrange(ymax):
            grid_xx = grid[(i+1)%xmax][j] + grid[(i-1)%xmax][j] - 2.0 * grid[i][j]
            grid_yy = grid[i][(j+1)%ymax] + grid[i][(j-1)%ymax] - 2.0 * grid[i][j]
            new_grid[i][j] = grid[i][j] + D * (grid_xx + grid_yy) * dt
    return new_grid
```

 Instead of preallocating the new_grid list, we could have built it up in the for loop by using appends. While this would have been noticeably faster than what we have written, the conclusions we draw are still applicable. We chose this method because it is more illustrative.

The global variable grid_shape designates how big a region we will simulate; and, as explained in "Introduction to the Problem" on page 100, we are using periodic boundary conditions (which is why we use modulo for the indices). In order to actually use this code, we must initialize a grid and call evolve on it. The code in Example 6-4 is a very generic initialization procedure that will be reused throughout the chapter (its performance characteristics will not be analyzed since it must only run once, as opposed to the evolve function, which is called repeatedly).

Example 6-4. Pure Python 2D diffusion initialization

```
def run_experiment(num_iterations):
    # Setting up initial conditions ❶
    xmax, ymax = grid_shape
    grid = [[0.0,] * ymax for x in xrange(xmax)]

    block_low = int(grid_shape[0] * .4)
    block_high = int(grid_shape[0] * .5)
    for i in xrange(block_low, block_high):
```

```
        for j in xrange(block_low, block_high):
            grid[i][j] = 0.005

    # Evolve the initial conditions
    start = time.time()
    for i in range(num_iterations):
        grid = evolve(grid, 0.1)
    return time.time() - start
```

❶ The initial conditions used here are the same as in the square example in
    Figure 6-2.

The values for dt and grid elements have been chosen to be sufficiently small that the
algorithm is stable. See William Press et al.'s *Numerical Recipes* (*http://www.nr.com/*),
Third Edition, for a more in-depth treatment of this algorithm's convergence characteristics.

Problems with Allocating Too Much

By using line_profiler on the pure Python evolution function, we can start to unravel
what is contributing to a possibly slow runtime. Looking at the profiler output in
Example 6-5, we see that most of the time spent in the function is spent doing the
derivative calculation and updating the grid.[1] This is what we want, since this is a purely
CPU-bound problem—any time spent not solving the CPU-bound problem is an obvious place for optimization.

Example 6-5. Pure Python 2D diffusion profiling

```
$ kernprof.py -lv diffusion_python.py
Wrote profile results to diffusion_python.py.lprof
Timer unit: 1e-06 s

File: diffusion_python.py
Function: evolve at line 8
Total time: 16.1398 s

Line #      Hits         Time  Per Hit   % Time  Line Contents
==============================================================
     8                                           @profile
     9                                           def evolve(grid, dt, D=1.0):
    10          10           39      3.9      0.0      xmax, ymax = grid_shape # ❶
    11     2626570      2159628      0.8     13.4      new_grid = ...
    12        5130         4167      0.8      0.0      for i in xrange(xmax): # ❷
    13     2626560      2126592      0.8     13.2          for j in xrange(ymax):
```

---

1. This is the code from Example 6-3, truncated to fit within the page margins. Recall that kernprof.py requires
   functions to be decorated with @profile in order to be profiled (see "Using line_profiler for Line-by-Line
   Measurements" on page 37).

14	2621440	4259164	1.6	26.4	`grid_xx = ...`
15	2621440	4196964	1.6	26.0	`grid_yy = ...`
16	2621440	3393273	1.3	21.0	`new_grid[i][j] = ...`
17	10	10	1.0	0.0	`return grid #` ❸

❶   This statement takes such a long time per hit because `grid_shape` must be retrieved from the local namespace (see "Dictionaries and Namespaces" on page 85 for more information).

❷   This line has 5,130 hits associated with it, which means the grid we operated over had xmax = 512. This comes from 512 evaluations for each value in xrange plus one evaluation of the termination condition of the loop, and all this happened 10 times.

❸   This line has 10 hits associated with it, which informs us that the function was profiled over 10 runs.

However, the output also shows that we are spending 20% of our time allocating the new_grid list. This is a waste, because the properties of new_grid do not change—no matter what values we send to evolve, the new_grid list will always be the same shape and size and contain the same values. A simple optimization would be to allocate this list once and simply reuse it. This sort of optimization is similar to moving repetitive code outside of a fast loop:

```
from math import sin

def loop_slow(num_iterations):
    """
    >>> %timeit loop_slow(int(1e4))
    100 loops, best of 3: 2.67 ms per loop
    """
    result = 0
    for i in xrange(num_iterations):
        result += i * sin(num_iterations) # ❶
    return result

def loop_fast(num_iterations):
    """
    >>> %timeit loop_fast(int(1e4))
    1000 loops, best of 3: 1.38 ms per loop
    """
    result = 0
    factor = sin(num_iterations)
    for i in xrange(num_iterations):
        result += i
    return result * factor
```

❶   The value of sin(num_iterations) doesn't change throughout the loop, so there is no use recalculating it every time.

We can do a similar transformation to our diffusion code, as illustrated in Example 6-6. In this case, we would want to instantiate `new_grid` in Example 6-4 and send it in to our `evolve` function. That function will do the same as it did before: read the `grid` list and write to the `new_grid` list. Then, we can simply swap `new_grid` with `grid` and continue again.

Example 6-6. Pure Python 2D diffusion after reducing memory allocations

```python
def evolve(grid, dt, out, D=1.0):
    xmax, ymax = grid_shape
    for i in xrange(xmax):
        for j in xrange(ymax):
            grid_xx = grid[(i+1)%xmax][j] + grid[(i-1)%xmax][j] - 2.0 * grid[i][j]
            grid_yy = grid[i][(j+1)%ymax] + grid[i][(j-1)%ymax] - 2.0 * grid[i][j]
            out[i][j] = grid[i][j] + D * (grid_xx + grid_yy) * dt

def run_experiment(num_iterations):
    # Setting up initial conditions
    xmax,ymax = grid_shape
    next_grid = [[0.0,] * ymax for x in xrange(xmax)]
    grid = [[0.0,] * ymax for x in xrange(xmax)]

    block_low = int(grid_shape[0] * .4)
    block_high = int(grid_shape[0] * .5)
    for i in xrange(block_low, block_high):
        for j in xrange(block_low, block_high):
            grid[i][j] = 0.005

    start = time.time()
    for i in range(num_iterations):
        evolve(grid, 0.1, next_grid)
        grid, next_grid = next_grid, grid
    return time.time() - start
```

We can see from the line profile of the modified version of the code in Example 6-7[2] that this small change has given us a 21% speedup. This leads us to a conclusion similar to the conclusion made during our discussion of `append` operations on lists (see "Lists as Dynamic Arrays" on page 67): memory allocations are not cheap. Every time we request memory in order to store a variable or a list, Python must take its time to talk to the operating system in order to allocate the new space, and then we must iterate over the newly allocated space to initialize it to some value. Whenever possible, reusing space that has already been allocated will give performance speedups. However, be careful when implementing these changes. While the speedups can be substantial, as always, you should profile to make sure you are achieving the results you want and are not simply polluting your code base.

---

2. The code profiled here is the code from Example 6-6; it has been truncated to fit within the page margins.

Example 6-7. Line profiling Python diffusion after reducing allocations

```
$ kernprof.py -lv diffusion_python_memory.py
Wrote profile results to diffusion_python_memory.py.lprof
Timer unit: 1e-06 s

File: diffusion_python_memory.py
Function: evolve at line 8
Total time: 13.3209 s
```

Line #	Hits	Time	Per Hit	% Time	Line Contents
8					@profile
9					def evolve(grid, dt, out, D=1.0):
10	10	15	1.5	0.0	xmax, ymax = grid_shape
11	5130	3853	0.8	0.0	for i in xrange(xmax):
12	2626560	1942976	0.7	14.6	for j in xrange(ymax):
13	2621440	4059998	1.5	30.5	grid_xx = ...
14	2621440	4038560	1.5	30.3	grid_yy = ...
15	2621440	3275454	1.2	24.6	out[i][j] = ...

Memory Fragmentation

The Python code we wrote in Example 6-6 still has a problem that is at the heart of using Python for these sorts of vectorized operations: Python doesn't natively support vectorization. There are two reasons for this: Python lists store pointers to the actual data, and Python bytecode is not optimized for vectorization, so for loops cannot predict when using vectorization would be beneficial.

The fact that Python lists store *pointers* means that instead of actually holding the data we care about, lists store locations where that data can be found. For most uses, this is good because it allows us to store whatever type of data we like inside of a list. However, when it comes to vector and matrix operations, this is a source of a lot of performance degradation.

The degradation occurs because every time we want to fetch an element from the grid matrix, we must do multiple lookups. For example, doing grid[5][2] requires us to first do a list lookup for index 5 on the list grid. This will return a pointer to where the data at that location is stored. Then we need to do another list lookup on this returned object, for the element at index 2. Once we have this reference, we have the location where the actual data is stored.

The overhead for one such lookup is not big and can be, in most cases, disregarded. However, if the data we wanted was located in one contiguous block in memory, we could move *all* of the data in one operation instead of needing two operations for each element. This is one of the major points with data fragmentation: when your data is fragmented, you must move each piece over individually instead of moving the entire block over. This means you are invoking more memory transfer overhead, and you are forcing the CPU to wait while data is being transferred. We will see with perf just how important this is when looking at the cache-misses.

This problem of getting the right data to the CPU when it is needed is related to the so-called "Von Neumann bottleneck." This refers to the fact that there is limited bandwidth between the memory and the CPU as a result of the tiered memory architecture that modern computers use. If we could move data infinitely fast, we would not need any cache, since the CPU could retrieve any data it needed instantly. This would be a state where the bottleneck is nonexistent.

Since we can't move data infinitely fast, we must prefetch data from RAM and store it in smaller but faster CPU caches so that hopefully, when the CPU needs a piece of data, it will be located in a location that can be read from quickly. While this is a severely idealized way of looking at the architecture, we can still see some of the problems with it—how do we know what data will be needed in the future? The CPU does a good job with mechanisms called *branch prediction* and *pipelining*, which try to predict the next instruction and load the relevant portions of memory into the cache while still working on the current instruction. However, the best way to minimize the effects of the bottleneck is to be smart about how we allocate our memory and how we do our calculations over our data.

Probing how well memory is being moved to the CPU can be quite hard; however, in Linux the perf tool can be used to get amazing amounts of insight into how the CPU is dealing with the program being run. For example, we can run perf on the pure Python code from Example 6-6 and see just how efficiently the CPU is running our code. The results are shown in Example 6-8. Note that the output in this and the following perf examples has been truncated to fit within the margins of the page. The removed data included variances for each measurement, indicating how much the values changed throughout multiple benchmarks. This is useful for seeing how much a measured value is dependent on the actual performance characteristics of the program versus other system properties, such as other running programs using system resources.

Example 6-8. Performance counters for pure Python 2D diffusion with reduced memory allocations

```
$ perf stat -e cycles,stalled-cycles-frontend,stalled-cycles-backend,instructions,\
    cache-references,cache-misses,branches,branch-misses,task-clock,faults,\
    minor-faults,cs,migrations -r 3 python diffusion_python_memory.py

 Performance counter stats for 'python diffusion_python_memory.py' (3 runs):

    329,155,359,015 cycles                    #    3.477 GHz
     76,800,457,550 stalled-cycles-frontend   #   23.33% frontend cycles idle
     46,556,100,820 stalled-cycles-backend    #   14.14% backend  cycles idle
    598,135,111,009 instructions              #    1.82  insns per cycle
                                              #    0.13  stalled cycles per insn
         35,497,196 cache-references          #    0.375 M/sec
```

```
     10,716,972 cache-misses          #    30.191 % of all cache refs
133,881,241,254 branches              # 1414.067 M/sec
  2,891,093,384 branch-misses         #     2.16% of all branches
  94678.127621 task-clock             #     0.999 CPUs utilized
          5,439 page-faults           #     0.057 K/sec
          5,439 minor-faults          #     0.057 K/sec
            125 context-switches      #     0.001 K/sec
              6 CPU-migrations        #     0.000 K/sec

    94.749389121 seconds time elapsed
```

Understanding perf

Let's take a second to understand the various performance metrics that perf is giving us and their connection to our code. The task-clock metric tells us how many clock cycles our task took. This is different from the total runtime, because if our program took 1 second to run but used two CPUs, then the task-clock would be 1000 (task-clock is generally in milliseconds). Conveniently, perf does the calculation for us and tells us, next to this metric, how many CPUs were utilized. This number isn't exactly 1 because there were periods where the process relied on other subsystems to do instructions for it (for example, when memory was allocated).

context-switches and CPU-migrations tell us about how the program is halted in order to wait for a kernel operation to finish (such as I/O), let other applications run, or to move execution to another CPU core. When a context-switch happens, the program's execution is halted and another program is allowed to run instead. This is a *very* time-intensive task and is something we would like to minimize as much as possible, but we don't have too much control over when this happens. The kernel delegates when programs are allowed to be switched out; however, we can do things to disincentivize the kernel from moving *our* program. In general, the kernel suspends a program when it is doing I/O (such as reading from memory, disk, or the network). As we'll see in later chapters, we can use asynchronous routines to make sure that our program still uses the CPU even when waiting for I/O, which will let us keep running without being context-switched. In addition, we could set the nice value of our program in order to give our program priority and stop the kernel from context switching it. Similarly, CPU-migrations happen when the program is halted and resumed on a different CPU than the one it was on before, in order to have all CPUs have the same level of utilization. This can be seen as an especially bad context switch, since not only is our program being temporarily halted, but we lose whatever data we had in the L1 cache (recall that each CPU has its own L1 cache).

A page-fault is part of the modern Unix memory allocation scheme. When memory is allocated, the kernel doesn't do much except give the program a reference to memory. However, later, when the memory is first used, the operating system throws a minor page fault interrupt, which pauses the program that is being run and properly allocates the memory. This is called a *lazy allocation system*. While this method is quite an op-timization over previous memory allocation systems, minor page faults are quite an expensive operation since most of the operations are done outside the scope of the program you are running. There is also a major page fault, which happens when the program requests data from a device (disk, network, etc.) that hasn't been read yet. These are even more expensive operations, since not only do they interrupt your program, but they also involve reading from whichever device the data lives on. This sort of page fault does not generally affect CPU-bound work; however, it will be a source of pain for any program that does disk or network reads/writes.

Once we have data in memory and we reference it, the data makes its way through the various tiers of memory (see "Communications Layers" on page 7 for a discussion of this). Whenever we reference data that is in our cache, the cache-references metric increases. If we did not already have this data in the cache and need to fetch it from RAM, this counts as a cache-miss. We won't get a cache miss if we are reading data we have read recently (that data will still be in the cache), or data that is located *near* data we have recently (data is sent from RAM into the cache in chunks). Cache misses can be a source of slowdowns when it comes to CPU-bound work, since not only do we need to wait to fetch the data from RAM, but we also interrupt the flow of our execution pipeline (more on this in a second). We will be discussing how to reduce this effect by optimizing the layout of data in memory later in this chapter.

instructions tells us how many instructions our code is issuing to the CPU. Because of pipelining, these instructions can be run several at a time, which is what the insns per cycle annotation tells us. To get a better handle on this pipelining, stalled-cycles-frontend and stalled-cycles-backend tell us how many cycles our program was waiting for the frontend or backend of the pipeline to be filled. This can happen because of a cache miss, a mispredicted branch, or a resource conflict. The frontend of the pipeline is responsible for fetching the next instruction from memory and decoding it into a valid operation, while the backend is responsible for actually running the operation. With pipelining, the CPU is able to run the current operation while fetching and preparing the next one.

A branch is a time in the code where the execution flow changes. Think of an if..then statement—depending on the result of the conditional, we will either be executing one section of code or another. This is essentially a branch in the execution of the code—the next instruction in the program could be one of two things. In order to optimize this, especially with regard to the pipeline, the CPU tries to guess which direction the branch will take and preload the relevant instructions. When this prediction is incorrect, we will get some stalled-cycles and a branch-miss. Branch misses can be quite con-fusing and result in many strange effects (for example, some loops will run substantially faster on sorted lists than unsorted lists simply because there will be fewer branch misses).

If you would like a more thorough explanation of what is going on at the CPU level with the various performance metrics, check out Gurpur M. Prabhu's fantastic "Computer Architecture Tutorial." (*http://bit.ly/ca_tutorial*) It deals with the problems at a very low level, which gives you a good understanding of what is going on under the hood when you run your code.

Making Decisions with perf's Output

With all this in mind, the performance metrics in Example 6-8 are telling us that while running our code, the CPU had to reference the L1/L2 cache 35,497,196 times. Of those references, 10,716,972 (or 30.191%) were requests for data that wasn't in memory at the time and had to be retrieved. In addition, we can see that in each CPU cycle we are able to perform an average of 1.82 instructions, which tells us the total speed boost from pipelining, out-of-order execution, and hyperthreading (or any other CPU feature that lets you run more than one instruction per clock cycle).

Fragmentation increases the number of memory transfers to the CPU. Additionally, since you don't have multiple pieces of data ready in the CPU cache when a calculation is requested, it means you cannot vectorize the calculations. As explained in "Communications Layers" on page 7, vectorization of computations (or having the CPU do multiple computations at a time) can only occur if we can fill the CPU cache with all the relevant data. Since the bus can only move contiguous chunks of memory, this is only possible if the grid data is stored sequentially in RAM. Since a list stores pointers to data instead of the actual data, the actual values in the grid are scattered throughout memory and cannot be copied all at once.

We can alleviate this problem by using the array module instead of lists. These objects store data sequentially in memory, so that a slice of the array actually represents a continuous range in memory. However, this doesn't completely fix the problem—now we have data that is stored sequentially in memory, but Python still does not know how to vectorize our loops. What we would like is for any loop that does arithmetic on our array one element at a time to work on chunks of data, but as mentioned previously, there is no such bytecode optimization in Python (partly due to the extremely dynamic nature of the language).

Why doesn't having the data we want stored sequentially in memory automatically give us vectorization? If we looked at the raw machine code that the CPU is running, vectorized operations (such as multiplying two arrays) use a different part of the CPU, and different instructions, than non-vectorized operations. In order for Python to use these special instructions, we must have a module that was created to use them. We will soon see how numpy gives us access to these specialized instructions.

Furthermore, because of implementation details, using the array type when creating lists of data that must be iterated on is actually *slower* than simply creating a list. This is because the array object stores a very low-level representation of the numbers it stores, and this must be converted into a Python-compatible version before being returned to the user. This extra overhead happens every time you index an array type. That implementation decision has made the array object less suitable for math and more suitable for storing fixed-type data more efficiently in memory.

Enter numpy

In order to deal with the fragmentation we found using perf, we must find a package that can efficiently vectorize operations. Luckily, numpy has all of the features we need —it stores data in contiguous chunks of memory and supports vectorized operations on its data. As a result, any arithmetic we do on numpy arrays happens in chunks without us having to explicitly loop over each element. Not only does this make it much easier to do matrix arithmetic this way, but it is also faster. Let's look at an example:

```
from array import array
import numpy

def norm_square_list(vector):
    """
    >>> vector = range(1000000)
    >>> %timeit norm_square_list(vector_list)
    1000 loops, best of 3: 1.16 ms per loop
    """
    norm = 0
    for v in vector:
        norm += v*v
    return norm

def norm_square_list_comprehension(vector):
    """
    >>> vector = range(1000000)
    >>> %timeit norm_square_list_comprehension(vector_list)
    1000 loops, best of 3: 913 μs per loop
    """
```

```
    return sum([v*v for v in vector])

def norm_squared_generator_comprehension(vector):
    """
    >>> vector = range(1000000)
    >>> %timeit norm_square_generator_comprehension(vector_list)
    1000 loops, best of 3: 747 µs per loop
    """
    return sum(v*v for v in vector)

def norm_square_array(vector):
    """
    >>> vector = array('l', range(1000000))
    >>> %timeit norm_square_array(vector_array)
    1000 loops, best of 3: 1.44 ms per loop
    """
    norm = 0
    for v in vector:
        norm += v*v
    return norm

def norm_square_numpy(vector):
    """
    >>> vector = numpy.arange(1000000)
    >>> %timeit norm_square_numpy(vector_numpy)
    10000 loops, best of 3: 30.9 µs per loop
    """
    return numpy.sum(vector * vector) # ❶

def norm_square_numpy_dot(vector):
    """
    >>> vector = numpy.arange(1000000)
    >>> %timeit norm_square_numpy_dot(vector_numpy)
    10000 loops, best of 3: 21.8 µs per loop
    """
    return numpy.dot(vector, vector) # ❷
```

❶ This creates two implied loops over vector, one to do the multiplication and one to do the sum. These loops are similar to the loops from norm_square_list_comprehension, but they are executed using numpy's optimized numerical code.

❷ This is the preferred way of doing vector norms in numpy by using the vectorized numpy.dot operation. The less efficient norm_square_numpy code is provided for illustration.

The simpler `numpy` code runs 37.54x faster than `norm_square_list` and 29.5x faster than the "optimized" Python list comprehension. The difference in speed between the pure Python looping method and the list comprehension method shows the benefit of doing more calculation behind the scenes rather than explicitly doing it in your Python code. By performing calculations using Python's already-built machinery, we get the speed of the native C code that Python is built on. This is also partly the same reasoning behind why we have such a drastic speedup in the `numpy` code: instead of using the very generalized list structure, we have a very finely tuned and specially built object for dealing with arrays of numbers.

In addition to more lightweight and specialized machinery, the `numpy` object also gives us memory locality and vectorized operations, which are incredibly important when dealing with numerical computations. The CPU is exceedingly fast, and most of the time simply getting it the data it needs faster is the best way to optimize code quickly. Running each function using the `perf` tool we looked at earlier shows that the `array` and pure Python functions takes $\sim 1 \times 10^{11}$ instructions, while the `numpy` version takes $\sim 3 \times 10^9$ instructions. In addition, the `array` and pure Python versions have $\sim 80\%$ cache misses, while `numpy` has $\sim 55\%$.

In our `norm_square_numpy` code, when doing `vector * vector`, there is an *implied* loop that numpy will take care of. The implied loop is the same loop we have explicitly written out in the other examples: loop over all items in `vector`, multiplying each item by itself. However, since we tell `numpy` to do this instead of explicitly writing it out in Python code, it can take advantage of all the optimizations it wants. In the background, `numpy` has very optimized C code that has been specifically made to take advantage of any vectorization the CPU has enabled. In addition, `numpy` arrays are represented sequentially in memory as low-level numerical types, which gives them the same space requirements as `array` objects (from the `array` module).

As an extra bonus, we can reformulate the problem as a dot product, which `numpy` supports. This gives us a single operation to calculate the value we want, as opposed to first taking the product of the two vectors and then summing them. As you can see in Figure 6-3, this operation, `norm_numpy_dot`, outperforms all the others by quite a substantial margin—this is thanks to the specialization of the function, and because we don't need to store the intermediate value of `vector * vector` as we did in `norm_numpy`.

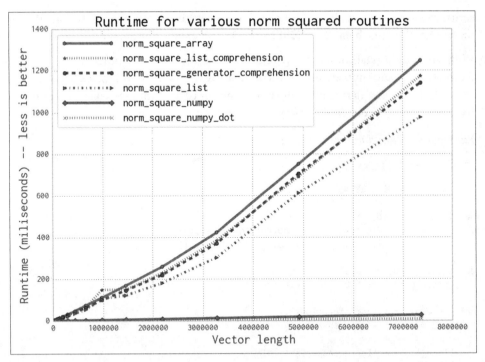

Figure 6-3. Runtimes for the various norm squared routines with vectors of different length

Applying numpy to the Diffusion Problem

Using what we've learned about numpy, we can easily adapt our pure Python code to be vectorized. The only new functionality we must introduce is numpy's roll function. This function does the same thing as our modulo-index trick, but it does so for an entire numpy array. In essence, it vectorizes this reindexing:

```
>>> import numpy as np
>>> np.roll([1,2,3,4], 1)
array([4, 1, 2, 3])

>>> np.roll([[1,2,3],[4,5,6]], 1, axis=1)
array([[3, 1, 2],
       [6, 4, 5]])
```

The roll function creates a new numpy array, which can be thought of as both good and bad. The downside is that we are taking time to allocate new space, which then needs to be filled with the appropriate data. On the other hand, once we have created this new rolled array we will be able to vectorize operations on it quite quickly and not suffer from cache misses from the CPU cache. This can substantially affect the speed of the actual calculation we must do on the grid. Later in this chapter, we will rewrite this so that we get the same benefit without having to constantly allocate more memory.

With this additional function we can rewrite the Python diffusion code from Example 6-6 using simpler, and vectorized, numpy arrays. In addition, we break up the calculation of the derivatives, grid_xx and grid_yy, into a separate function. Example 6-9 shows our initial numpy diffusion code.

Example 6-9. Initial numpy diffusion

```python
import numpy as np

grid_shape = (1024, 1024)

def laplacian(grid):
    return np.roll(grid, +1, 0) + np.roll(grid, -1, 0) + \
           np.roll(grid, +1, 1) + np.roll(grid, -1, 1) - 4 * grid

def evolve(grid, dt, D=1):
    return grid + dt * D * laplacian(grid)

def run_experiment(num_iterations):
    grid = np.zeros(grid_shape)

    block_low = int(grid_shape[0] * .4)
    block_high = int(grid_shape[0] * .5)
    grid[block_low:block_high, block_low:block_high] = 0.005

    start = time.time()
    for i in range(num_iterations):
        grid = evolve(grid, 0.1)
    return time.time() - start
```

Immediately we see that this code is much shorter. This is generally a good indication of performance: we are doing a lot of the heavy lifting outside of the Python interpreter, and hopefully inside a module specially built for performance and for solving a particular problem (however, this should always be tested!). One of the assumptions here is that numpy is using better memory management in order to give the CPU the data it needs faster. However, since whether or not this happens relies on the actual implementation of numpy, let's profile our code to see whether our hypothesis is correct. Example 6-10 shows the results.

Example 6-10. Performance counters for numpy 2D diffusion

```
$ perf stat -e cycles,stalled-cycles-frontend,stalled-cycles-backend,instructions,\
    cache-references,cache-misses,branches,branch-misses,task-clock,faults,\
    minor-faults,cs,migrations -r 3 python diffusion_numpy.py

 Performance counter stats for 'python diffusion_numpy.py' (3 runs):
```

```
   10,194,811,718 cycles                     #      3.332 GHz
    4,435,850,419 stalled-cycles-frontend    #     43.51% frontend cycles idle
    2,055,861,567 stalled-cycles-backend     #     20.17% backend  cycles idle
   15,165,151,844 instructions               #      1.49  insns per cycle
                                             #      0.29  stalled cycles per insn
      346,798,311 cache-references           #    113.362 M/sec
          519,793 cache-misses               #      0.150 % of all cache refs
    3,506,887,927 branches                   #   1146.334 M/sec
        3,681,441 branch-misses              #      0.10% of all branches
    3059.219862 task-clock                   #      0.999 CPUs utilized
          751,707 page-faults                #      0.246 M/sec
          751,707 minor-faults               #      0.246 M/sec
                8 context-switches           #      0.003 K/sec
                1 CPU-migrations             #      0.000 K/sec

    3.061883218 seconds time elapsed
```

This shows that the simple change to numpy has given us a 40x speedup over the pure Python implementation with reduced memory allocations (Example 6-8). How was this achieved?

First of all, we can thank the vectorization that numpy gives. Although the numpy version seems to be running fewer instructions per cycle, each of the instructions does much more work. That is to say, one vectorized instruction can multiply four (or more) numbers in an array together instead of requiring four independent multiplication instructions. Overall this results in fewer total instructions necessary to solve the same problem.

There are also several other factors that contribute to the numpy version requiring a lower absolute number of instructions to solve the diffusion problem. One of them has to do with the full Python API being available when running the pure Python version, but not necessarily for the numpy version—for example, the pure Python grids can be appended to in pure Python, but not in numpy. Even though we aren't explicitly using this (or other) functionality, there is overhead in providing a system where it *could* be available. Since numpy can make the assumption that the data being stored is always going to be numbers, everything regarding the arrays can be optimized for operations over numbers. We will continue on the track of removing necessary functionality in favor of performance when we talk about Cython (see "Cython" on page 140), where it is even possible to remove list bounds checking to speed up list lookups.

Normally, the number of instructions doesn't necessarily correlate to performance—the program with fewer instructions may not issue them efficiently, or they may be slow instructions. However, we see that in addition to reducing the number of instructions, the numpy version has also reduced a large inefficiency: cache misses (0.15% cache misses instead of 30.2%). As explained in "Memory Fragmentation" on page 109, cache misses slow down computations because the CPU must wait for data to be retrieved from slower memory instead of having it immediately available in its cache. In fact, memory fragmentation is such a dominant factor in performance that if we disable vectorization[3] in numpy but keep everything else the same, we still see a sizable speed increase compared to the pure Python version (Example 6-11).

Example 6-11. Performance counters for numpy 2D diffusion without vectorization

```
$ perf stat -e cycles,stalled-cycles-frontend,stalled-cycles-backend,instructions,\
    cache-references,cache-misses,branches,branch-misses,task-clock,faults,\
    minor-faults,cs,migrations -r 3 python diffusion_numpy.py

Performance counter stats for 'python diffusion_numpy.py' (3 runs):

    48,923,515,604 cycles                     #    3.413 GHz
    24,901,979,501 stalled-cycles-frontend    #   50.90% frontend cycles idle
     6,585,982,510 stalled-cycles-backend     #   13.46% backend  cycles idle
    53,208,756,117 instructions               #    1.09  insns per cycle
                                              #    0.47  stalled cycles per insn
        83,436,665 cache-references           #    5.821 M/sec
         1,211,229 cache-misses               #    1.452 % of all cache refs
     4,428,225,111 branches                   #  308.926 M/sec
         3,716,789 branch-misses              #    0.08% of all branches
    14334.244888 task-clock                   #    0.999 CPUs utilized
           751,185 page-faults                #    0.052 M/sec
           751,185 minor-faults               #    0.052 M/sec
                24 context-switches           #    0.002 K/sec
                 5 CPU-migrations             #    0.000 K/sec

      14.345794896 seconds time elapsed
```

This shows us that the dominant factor in our 40x speedup when introducing numpy is not the vectorized instruction set, but rather the memory locality and reduced memory fragmentation. In fact, we can see from the preceding experiment that vectorization accounts for only about 15% of that 40x speedup.[4]

This realization that memory issues are the dominant factor in slowing down our code doesn't come as too much of a shock. Computers are very well designed to do exactly the calculations we are requesting them to do with this problem—multiplying and adding numbers together. The bottleneck is in getting those numbers to the CPU fast enough to see it do the calculations as fast as it can.

Memory Allocations and In-Place Operations

In order to optimize the memory-dominated effects, let us try using the same method we used in Example 6-6 in order to reduce the number of allocations we make in our

---

3. We do this by compiling numpy with the -O0 flag. For this experiment we built numpy 1.8.0 with the command:
   `$ OPT='-O0' FOPT='-O0' BLAS=None LAPACK=None ATLAS=None python setup.py build`.

4. This is very contingent on what CPU is being used.

numpy code. Allocations are quite a bit worse than the cache misses we discussed previously. Instead of simply having to find the right data in RAM when it is not found in the cache, an allocation also must make a request to the operating system for an available chunk of data and then reserve it. The request to the operating system generates quite a lot more overhead than simply filling a cache—while filling a cache miss is a hardware routine that is optimized on the motherboard, allocating memory requires talking to another process, the kernel, in order to complete.

In order to remove the allocations in Example 6-9, we will preallocate some scratch space at the beginning of the code and then only use in-place operations. In-place operations, such as +=, *=, etc., reuse one of the inputs as their output. This means that we don't need to allocate space to store the result of the calculation.

To show this explicitly, we will look at how the id of a numpy array changes as we perform operations on it (Example 6-12). The id is a good way of tracking this for numpy arrays, since the id has to do with what section of memory is being referenced. If two numpy arrays have the same id, then they are referencing the same section of memory.[5]

Example 6-12. In-place operations reducing memory allocations

```
>>> import numpy as np
>>> array1 = np.random.random((10,10))
>>> array2 = np.random.random((10,10))
>>> id(array1)
140199765947424  # ❶
>>> array1 += array2
>>> id(array1)
140199765947424  # ❷
>>> array1 = array1 + array2
>>> id(array1)
140199765969792  # ❸
```

❶ ❷ These two ids are the same, since we are doing an in-place operation. This means that the memory address of array1 does not change; we are simply changing the data contained within it.

❸ Here, the memory address has changed. When doing array1 + array2, a new memory address is allocated and filled with the result of the computation. This does have benefits, however, for when the original data needs to be preserved (i.e., array3 = array1 + array2 allows you to keep using array1 and array2, while in-place operations destroy some of the original data).

---

5. This is not strictly true, since two numpy arrays can reference the same section of memory but use different striding information in order to represent the same data in different ways. These two numpy arrays will have different ids. There are many subtleties to the id structure of numpy arrays that are outside the scope of this discussion.

Furthermore, we see an expected slowdown from the non-in-place operation. For small numpy arrays, this overhead can be as much as 50% of the total computation time. For larger computations, the speedup is more in the single-percent region, but this still represents a lot of time if this is happening millions of times. In Example 6-13, we see that using in-place operations gives us a 20% speedup for small arrays. This margin will become larger as the arrays grow, since the memory allocations become more strenuous.

Example 6-13. In-place operations reducing memory allocations

```
>>> %%timeit array1, array2 = np.random.random((10,10)), np.random.random((10,10))
# ❶
... array1 = array1 + array2
...
100000 loops, best of 3: 3.03 us per loop

>>> %%timeit array1, array2 = np.random.random((10,10)), np.random.random((10,10))
... array1 += array2
...
100000 loops, best of 3: 2.42 us per loop
```

❶   Note that we use `%%timeit` instead of `%timeit`, which allows us to specify code to set up the experiment that doesn't get timed.

The downside is that while rewriting our code from Example 6-9 to use in-place operations is not very complicated, it does make the resulting code a bit harder to read. In Example 6-14 we can see the results of this refactoring. We instantiate `grid` and `next_grid` vectors, and we constantly swap them with each other. `grid` is the current information we know about the system and, after running `evolve`, `next_grid` contains the updated information.

Example 6-14. Making most numpy operations in-place

```
def laplacian(grid, out):
    np.copyto(out, grid)
    out *= -4
    out += np.roll(grid, +1, 0)
    out += np.roll(grid, -1, 0)
    out += np.roll(grid, +1, 1)
    out += np.roll(grid, -1, 1)

def evolve(grid, dt, out, D=1):
    laplacian(grid, out)
    out *= D * dt
    out += grid

def run_experiment(num_iterations):
    next_grid = np.zeros(grid_shape)
    grid = np.zeros(grid_shape)

    block_low = int(grid_shape[0] * .4)
```

```
block_high = int(grid_shape[0] * .5)
grid[block_low:block_high, block_low:block_high] = 0.005

start = time.time()
for i in range(num_iterations):
    evolve(grid, 0.1, next_grid)
    grid, next_grid = next_grid, grid          # ❶
return time.time() - start
```

❶ Since the output of evolve gets stored in the output vector next_grid, we must
   swap these two variables so that, for the next iteration of the loop, grid has the
   most up-to-date information. This swap operation is quite cheap because only
   the references to the data are changed, not the data itself.

It is important to remember that since we want each operation to be in-place, whenever
we do a vector operation we must have it be on its own line. This can make something
as simple as A = A * B + C become quite convoluted. Since Python has a heavy emphasis
on readability, we should make sure that the changes we have made give us sufficient
speedups to be justified.

Comparing the performance metrics from Examples 6-15 and 6-10, we see that
removing the spurious allocations sped up our code by 29%. This comes partly from a
reduction in the number of cache misses, but mostly from a reduction in page faults.

Example 6-15. Performance metrics for numpy with in-place memory operations

```
$ perf stat -e cycles,stalled-cycles-frontend,stalled-cycles-backend,instructions,\
  cache-references,cache-misses,branches,branch-misses,task-clock,faults,\
  minor-faults,cs,migrations -r 3 python diffusion_numpy_memory.py

Performance counter stats for 'python diffusion_numpy_memory.py' (3 runs):

    7,864,072,570 cycles                     #    3.330 GHz
    3,055,151,931 stalled-cycles-frontend    #   38.85% frontend cycles idle
    1,368,235,506 stalled-cycles-backend     #   17.40% backend  cycles idle
   13,257,488,848 instructions               #    1.69  insns per cycle
                                             #    0.23  stalled cycles per insn
      239,195,407 cache-references           #  101.291 M/sec
        2,886,525 cache-misses               #    1.207 % of all cache refs
    3,166,506,861 branches                   # 1340.903 M/sec
        3,204,960 branch-misses              #    0.10% of all branches
    2361.473922 task-clock                   #    0.999 CPUs utilized
            6,527 page-faults                #    0.003 M/sec
            6,527 minor-faults               #    0.003 M/sec
                6 context-switches           #    0.003 K/sec
                2 CPU-migrations             #    0.001 K/sec

    2.363727876 seconds time elapsed
```

Selective Optimizations: Finding What Needs to Be Fixed

Looking at the code from Example 6-14, it seems like we have addressed most of the issues at hand: we have reduced the CPU burden by using numpy, and we have reduced the number of allocations necessary to solve the problem. However, there is always more investigation to be done. If we do a line profile on that code (Example 6-16), we see that the majority of our work is done within the laplacian function. In fact, 93% of the time evolve takes to run is spent in laplacian.

Example 6-16. Line profiling shows that laplacian is taking too much time

```
Wrote profile results to diffusion_numpy_memory.py.lprof
Timer unit: 1e-06 s

File: diffusion_numpy_memory.py
Function: laplacian at line 8
Total time: 3.67347 s

Line #      Hits         Time  Per Hit   % Time  Line Contents
==============================================================
     8                                           @profile
     9                                           def laplacian(grid, out):
    10         500       162009    324.0      4.4      np.copyto(out, grid)
    11         500       111044    222.1      3.0      out *= -4
    12         500       464810    929.6     12.7      out += np.roll(grid, +1, 0)
    13         500       432518    865.0     11.8      out += np.roll(grid, -1, 0)
    14         500      1261692   2523.4     34.3      out += np.roll(grid, +1, 1)
    15         500      1241398   2482.8     33.8      out += np.roll(grid, -1, 1)

File: diffusion_numpy_memory.py
Function: evolve at line 17
Total time: 3.97768 s

Line #      Hits         Time  Per Hit   % Time  Line Contents
==============================================================
    17                                           @profile
    18                                           def evolve(grid, dt, out, D=1):
    19         500      3691674   7383.3     92.8      laplacian(grid, out)
    20         500       111687    223.4      2.8      out *= D * dt
    21         500       174320    348.6      4.4      out += grid
```

There could be many reasons why laplacian is so slow. However, there are two main high-level issues to consider. First, it looks like the calls to np.roll are allocating new vectors (we can verify this by looking at the documentation for the function). This means that even though we removed seven memory allocations in our previous refactoring, there are still four outstanding allocations. Furthermore, np.roll is a very generalized function that has a lot of code to deal with special cases. Since we know exactly what we want to do (move just the first column of data to be the last in every dimension), we can rewrite this function to eliminate most of the spurious code. We could even merge the `np.roll` logic with the add operation that happens with the rolled data to make a very specialized `roll_add` function that does exactly what we want with the fewest number of allocations and the least extra logic.

Example 6-17 shows what this refactoring would look like. All we need to do is create our new `roll_add` function and have `laplacian` use it. Since `numpy` supports fancy indexing, implementing such a function is just a matter of not jumbling up the indices. However, as stated earlier, while this code may be more performant, it is much less readable.

 Notice the extra work that has gone into having an informative docstring for the function, in addition to full tests. When you are taking a route similar to this one it is important to maintain the readability of the code, and these steps go a long way to making sure that your code is always doing what it was intended to do and that future programmers can modify your code and know what things do and when things are not working.

Example 6-17. Creating our own roll function

```
import numpy as np

def roll_add(rollee, shift, axis, out):
    """
    Given a matrix, rollee, and an output matrix, out, this function will
    perform the calculation:

        >>> out += np.roll(rollee, shift, axis=axis)

    This is done with the following assumptions:
        * rollee is 2D
        * shift will only ever be +1 or -1
        * axis will only ever be 0 or 1 (also implied by the first assumption)

    Using these assumptions, we are able to speed up this function by avoiding
    extra machinery that numpy uses to generalize the `roll` function and also
    by making this operation intrinsically in-place.
    """
    if shift == 1 and axis == 0:
        out[1:, :] += rollee[:-1, :]
        out[0 , :] += rollee[-1, :]
    elif shift == -1 and axis == 0:
        out[:-1, :] += rollee[1:, :]
        out[-1 , :] += rollee[0, :]
    elif shift == 1 and axis == 1:
        out[:, 1:] += rollee[:, :-1]
        out[:, 0 ] += rollee[:, -1]
    elif shift == -1 and axis == 1:
        out[:, :-1] += rollee[:, 1:]
```

```
            out[:,  -1] += rollee[:,  0]

def test_roll_add():
    rollee = np.asarray([[1,2],[3,4]])
    for shift in (-1, +1):
        for axis in (0, 1):
            out = np.asarray([[6,3],[9,2]])
            expected_result = np.roll(rollee, shift, axis=axis) + out
            roll_add(rollee, shift, axis, out)
            assert np.all(expected_result == out)

def laplacian(grid, out):
    np.copyto(out, grid)
    out *= -4
    roll_add(grid, +1, 0, out)
    roll_add(grid, -1, 0, out)
    roll_add(grid, +1, 1, out)
    roll_add(grid, -1, 1, out)
```

If we look at the performance counters in Example 6-18 for this rewrite, we see that while it is considerably faster than Example 6-14 (70% faster, in fact), most of the counters are about the same. The number of page-faults went down, but not by 70%. Similarly, cache-misses and cache-references went down, but not enough to account for the entire speedup. One of the most important metrics here is the instructions metric. The instructions metric counts how many CPU instructions had to be issued to run the program—in other words, how many things the CPU had to do. Somehow, the change to the customized roll_add function reduced the total number of instructions necessary by about 2.86x. This is because instead of having to rely on the entire machinery of numpy to roll our matrix, we are able to create shorter and simpler machinery that can take advantage of assumptions about our data (namely, that our data is two-dimensional and that we will only ever be rolling by 1). This theme of trimming out unnecessary machinery in both numpy and Python in general will continue in "Cython" on page 140.

Example 6-18. Performance metrics for numpy with in-place memory operations and custom laplacian function

```
$ perf stat -e cycles,stalled-cycles-frontend,stalled-cycles-backend,instructions,\
    cache-references,cache-misses,branches,branch-misses,task-clock,faults,\
    minor-faults,cs,migrations -r 3 python diffusion_numpy_memory2.py

 Performance counter stats for 'python diffusion_numpy_memory2.py' (3 runs):

      4,303,799,244 cycles                    #    3.108 GHz
      2,814,678,053 stalled-cycles-frontend   #   65.40% frontend cycles idle
      1,635,172,736 stalled-cycles-backend    #   37.99% backend  cycles idle
      4,631,882,411 instructions              #    1.08  insns per cycle
                                              #    0.61  stalled cycles per insn
        272,151,957 cache-references          #  196.563 M/sec
```

```
    2,835,948 cache-misses            #     1.042 % of all cache refs
  621,565,054 branches                #   448.928 M/sec
    2,905,879 branch-misses           #     0.47% of all branches
 1384.555494 task-clock               #     0.999 CPUs utilized
        5,559 page-faults             #     0.004 M/sec
        5,559 minor-faults            #     0.004 M/sec
            6 context-switches        #     0.004 K/sec
            3 CPU-migrations          #     0.002 K/sec
  1.386148918 seconds time elapsed
```

numexpr: Making In-Place Operations Faster and Easier

One downfall of numpy's optimization of vector operations is that it only occurs on one operation at a time. That is to say, when we are doing the operation A * B + C with numpy vectors, first the entire A * B operation completes, and the data is stored in a temporary vector; then this new vector is added with C. The in-place version of the diffusion code in Example 6-14 shows this quite explicitly.

However, there are many modules that can help with this. numexpr is a module that can take an entire vector expression and compile it into very efficient code that is optimized to minimize cache misses and temporary space used. In addition, the expressions can utilize multiple CPU cores (see Chapter 9 for more information) and specialized instructions for Intel chips to maximize the speedup.

It is very easy to change code to use numexpr: all that's required is to rewrite the expressions as strings with references to local variables. The expressions are compiled behind the scenes (and cached so that calls to the same expression don't incur the same cost of compilation) and run using optimized code. Example 6-19 shows the simplicity of changing the evolve function to use numexpr. In this case, we chose to use the out parameter of the evaluate function so that numexpr doesn't allocate a new vector to which to return the result of the calculation.

Example 6-19. Using numexpr to further optimize large matrix operations

```
from numexpr import evaluate

def evolve(grid, dt, next_grid, D=1):
    laplacian(grid, next_grid)
    evaluate("next_grid*D*dt+grid", out=next_grid)
```

An important feature of numexpr is its consideration of CPU caches. It specifically moves data around so that the various CPU caches have the correct data in order to minimize cache misses. When we run perf on the updated code (Example 6-20), we see a speedup. However, if we look at the performance on a smaller, 512×512 grid (see Figure 6-4, at the end of the chapter) we see a ~15% decrease in speed. Why is this?

Example 6-20. Performance metrics for numpy with in-place memory operations, custom laplacian function, and numexpr

```
$ perf stat -e cycles,stalled-cycles-frontend,stalled-cycles-backend,instructions,\
    cache-references,cache-misses,branches,branch-misses,task-clock,faults,\
    minor-faults,cs,migrations -r 3 python diffusion_numpy_memory2_numexpr.py

Performance counter stats for 'python diffusion_numpy_memory2_numexpr.py' (3 runs):

    5,940,414,581 cycles                    #    1.447 GHz
    3,706,635,857 stalled-cycles-frontend   #   62.40% frontend cycles idle
    2,321,606,960 stalled-cycles-backend    #   39.08% backend  cycles idle
    6,909,546,082 instructions              #    1.16  insns per cycle
                                            #    0.54  stalled cycles per insn
      261,136,786 cache-references          #   63.628 M/sec
       11,623,783 cache-misses              #    4.451 % of all cache refs
      627,319,686 branches                  #  152.851 M/sec
        8,443,876 branch-misses             #    1.35% of all branches
     4104.127507 task-clock                 #    1.364 CPUs utilized
            9,786 page-faults               #    0.002 M/sec
            9,786 minor-faults              #    0.002 M/sec
            8,701 context-switches          #    0.002 M/sec
               60 CPU-migrations            #    0.015 K/sec

      3.009811418 seconds time elapsed
```

Much of the extra machinery we are bringing into our program with numexpr deals with cache considerations. When our grid size is small and all the data we need for our calculations fits in the cache, this extra machinery simply adds more instructions that don't help performance. In addition, compiling the vector operation that we encoded as a string adds a large overhead. When the total runtime of the program is small, this overhead can be quite noticeable. However, as we increase the grid size, we should expect to see numexpr utilize our cache better than native numpy does. In addition, numexpr utilizes multiple cores to do its calculation and tries to saturate each of the cores' caches. When the size of the grid is small, the extra overhead of managing the multiple cores overwhelms any possible increase in speed.

The particular computer we are running the code on has a 20,480 KB cache (Intel® Xeon® E5-2680). Since we are operating on two arrays, one for input and one for output, we can easily do the calculation for the size of the grid that will fill up our cache. The number of grid elements we can store in total is 20,480 KB / 64 bit = 2,560,000. Since we have two grids, this number is split between two objects (so each one can be at most 2,560,000 / 2 = 1,280,000 elements). Finally, taking the square root of this number gives us the size of the grid that uses that many grid elements. All in all, this means that approximately two 2D arrays of size 1,131 × 1,131 would fill up the cache ($\sqrt{20480KB / 64bit / 2} = 1131$). In practice, however, we do not get to fill up the cache ourselves (other programs will fill up parts of the cache), so realistically we can probably fit two 800 × 800 arrays. Looking at Tables 6-1 and 6-2, we see that when the grid size jumps from 512 × 512 to 1,024 × 1,024, the `numexpr` code starts to outperform pure `numpy`.

A Cautionary Tale: Verify "Optimizations" (scipy)

An important thing to take away from this chapter is the approach we took to every optimization: profile the code to get a sense of what is going on, come up with a possible solution to fix slow parts, then profile to make sure the fix actually worked. Although this sounds straightforward, things can get complicated quickly, as we saw with how the performance of `numexpr` depended greatly on the size of the grid we were considering.

Of course, our proposed solutions don't always work as expected. While writing the code for this chapter, this author saw that the `laplacian` function was the slowest routine and hypothesized that the `scipy` routine would be considerably faster. This thinking came from the fact that Laplacians are a common operation in image analysis and probably have a very optimized library to speed up the calls. `scipy` has an image submodule, so we must be in luck!

The implementation was quite simple (Example 6-21) and required little thought about the intricacies of implementing the periodic boundary conditions (or "wrap" condition, as `scipy` calls it).

Example 6-21. Using scipy's laplace filter

```
from scipy.ndimage.filters import laplace

def laplacian(grid, out):
    laplace(grid, out, mode='wrap')
```

Ease of implementation is quite important, and definitely won this method some points before we considered performance. However, once we benchmarked the `scipy` code (Example 6-22), we got the revelation: this method offers no substantial speedup compared to the code it was based on (Example 6-14). In fact, as we increase the grid size, this method starts performing worse (see Figure 6-4 at the end of the chapter).

Example 6-22. Performance metrics for diffusion with scipy's laplace function

```
$ perf stat -e cycles,stalled-cycles-frontend,stalled-cycles-backend,instructions,\
    cache-references,cache-misses,branches,branch-misses,task-clock,faults,\
    minor-faults,cs,migrations -r 3 python diffusion_scipy.py

 Performance counter stats for 'python diffusion_scipy.py' (3 runs):

     6,573,168,470 cycles                    #    2.929 GHz
     3,574,258,872 stalled-cycles-frontend   #   54.38% frontend cycles idle
     2,357,614,687 stalled-cycles-backend    #   35.87% backend  cycles idle
     9,850,025,585 instructions              #    1.50  insns per cycle
                                             #    0.36  stalled cycles per insn
```

```
    415,930,123 cache-references        #   185.361 M/sec
      3,188,390 cache-misses            #     0.767 % of all cache refs
  1,608,887,891 branches                #   717.006 M/sec
      4,017,205 branch-misses           #     0.25% of all branches
    2243.897843 task-clock              #     0.994 CPUs utilized
          7,319 page-faults             #     0.003 M/sec
          7,319 minor-faults            #     0.003 M/sec
             12 context-switches        #     0.005 K/sec
              1 CPU-migrations          #     0.000 K/sec

    2.258396667 seconds time elapsed
```

Comparing the performance metrics of the `scipy` version of the code with those of our custom `laplacian` function (Example 6-18), we can start to get some indication as to why we aren't getting the speedup we were expecting from this rewrite.

The metrics that stand out the most are `page-faults` and `instructions`. Both of these values are substantially larger for the `scipy` version. The increase in `page-faults` shows us that while the `scipy` `laplacian` function has support for in-place operations, it is still allocating a lot of memory. In fact, the number of `page-faults` in the `scipy` version is larger than in our first rewrite of the `numpy` code (Example 6-15).

Most importantly, however, is the `instructions` metric. This shows us that the `scipy` code is requesting that the CPU do over double the amount of work as our custom `laplacian` code. Even though these instructions are more optimized (as we can see with the higher `insns per cycle` count, which says how many instructions the CPU can do in one clock cycle), the extra optimization doesn't win out over the sheer number of added instructions. This could be in part due to the fact that the `scipy` code is written very generally, so that it can process all sorts of inputs with different boundary conditions (which requires extra code and thus more instructions). We can see this, in fact, by the high number of `branches` that the `scipy` code requires.

Wrap-Up

Looking back on our optimizations, we seem to have taken two main routes: reducing the time taken to get data to the CPU and reducing the amount of work that the CPU had to do. Tables 6-1 and 6-2 show a comparison of the results achieved by our various optimization efforts, for various dataset sizes, in relation to the original pure Python implementation.

Figure 6-4 shows graphically how all these methods compared to each other. We can see three bands of performance that correspond to these two methods: the band along the bottom shows the small improvement made in relation to our pure Python implementation by our first effort at reducing memory allocations, the middle band shows what happened when we used `numpy` and further reduced allocations, and the upper band illustrates the results achieved by reducing the work done by our process.

Table 6-1. Total runtime of all schemes for various grid sizes and 500 iterations of the evolve function

Method	256 × 256	512 × 512	1,024 × 1,024	2,048 × 2,048	4,096 × 4,096
Python	2.32s	9.49s	39.00s	155.02s	617.35s
Python + memory	2.56s	10.26s	40.87s	162.88s	650.26s
numpy	0.07s	0.28s	1.61s	11.28s	45.47s
numpy + memory	0.05s	0.22s	1.05s	6.95s	28.14s
numpy + memory + laplacian	0.03s	0.12s	0.53s	2.68s	10.57s
numpy + memory + laplacian + numexpr	0.04s	0.13s	0.50s	2.42s	9.54s
numpy + memory + scipy	0.05s	0.19s	1.22s	6.06s	30.31s

Table 6-2. Speedup compared to naive Python (Example 6-3) for all schemes and various grid sizes over 500 iterations of the evolve function

Method	256 × 256	512 × 512	1,024 × 1,024	2,048 × 2,048	4,096 × 4,096
Python	0.00x	0.00x	0.00x	0.00x	0.00x
Python + memory	0.90x	0.93x	0.95x	0.95x	0.95x
numpy	32.33x	33.56x	24.25x	13.74x	13.58x
numpy + memory	42.63x	42.75x	37.13x	22.30x	21.94x
numpy + memory + laplacian	77.98x	78.91x	73.90x	57.90x	58.43x
numpy + memory + laplacian + numexpr	65.01x	74.27x	78.27x	64.18x	64.75x
numpy + memory + scipy	42.43x	51.28x	32.09x	25.58x	20.37x

One important lesson to take away from this is that you should always take care of any administrative things the code must do during initialization. This may include allocating memory, or reading configuration from a file, or even precomputing some values that will be needed throughout the lifetime of the program. This is important for two reasons. First, you are reducing the total number of times these tasks must be done by doing them once up front, and you know that you will be able to use those resources without too much penalty in the future. Secondly, you are not disrupting the flow of the program; this allows it to pipeline more efficiently and keep the caches filled with more pertinent data.

We also learned more about the importance of data locality and how important simply getting data to the CPU is. CPU caches can be quite complicated, and often it is best to allow the various mechanisms designed to optimize them take care of the issue. However, understanding what is happening and doing all that is possible to optimize how memory is handled can make all the difference. For example, by understanding how caches work we are able to understand that the decrease in performance that leads to a saturated speedup no matter the grid size in Figure 6-4 can probably be attributed to the L3 cache being filled up by our grid. When this happens, we stop benefiting from the tiered memory approach to solving the Von Neumann bottleneck.

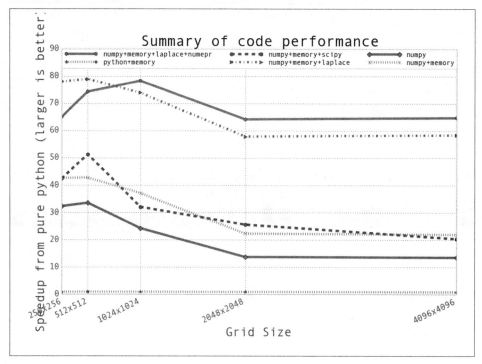

Figure 6-4. Summary of speedups from the methods attempted in this chapter

Another important lesson concerns the use of external libraries. Python is fantastic for its ease of use and readability, which allow you to write and debug code fast. However, tuning performance down to the external libraries is essential. These external libraries can be extremely fast, because they can be written in lower-level languages—but since they interface with Python, you can also still write code that used them quickly.

Finally, we learned the importance of benchmarking everything and forming hypotheses about performance before running the experiment. By forming a hypothesis before running the benchmark, we are able to form conditions to tell us whether our optimization actually worked. Was this change able to speed up runtime? Did it reduce the number of allocations? Is the number of cache misses lower? Optimization can be an art at times because of the vast complexity of computer systems, and having a quantitative probe into what is actually happening can help enormously.

One last point about optimization is that a lot of care must be taken to make sure that the optimizations you make generalize to different computers (the assumptions you make and the results of benchmarks you do may be dependent on the architecture of the computer you are running on, how the modules you are using were compiled, etc.). In addition, when making these optimizations it is incredibly important to consider other developers and how the changes will affect the readability of your code. For example, we realized that the solution we implemented in Example 6-17 was potentially vague, so care was taken to make sure that the code was fully documented and tested to help not only us, but also help other people in the team.

In the next chapter we will talk about how to create your own external modules that can be finely tuned to solve specific problems with much greater efficiencies. This allows us to follow the rapid prototyping method of making our programs—first solve the problem with slow code, then identify the elements that are slow, and finally find ways to make those elements faster. By profiling often and only trying to optimize sections of code we *know* are slow, we can save ourselves time while still making our programs run as fast as possible.

## CHAPTER 7

Compiling to C

Questions You'll Be Able to Answer After This Chapter

- How can I have my Python code run as lower-level code?
- What is the difference between a JIT compiler and an AOT compiler?
- What tasks can compiled Python code perform faster than native Python?
- Why do type annotations speed up compiled Python code?
- How can I write modules for Python using C or Fortran?
- How can I use libraries from C or Fortran in Python?

The easiest way to get your code to run faster is to make it do less work. Assuming you've already chosen good algorithms and you've reduced the amount of data you're processing, the easiest way to execute fewer instructions is to compile your code down to machine code.

Python offers a number of options for this, including pure C-based compiling approaches like Cython, Shed Skin, and Pythran; LLVM-based compiling via Numba; and the replacement virtual machine PyPy, which includes a built-in just-in-time (JIT) compiler. You need to balance the requirements of code adaptability and team velocity when deciding which route to take.

Each of these tools adds a new dependency to your toolchain, and additionally Cython requires you to write in a new language type (a hybrid of Python and C), which means you need a new skill. Cython's new language may hurt your team's velocity, as team members without knowledge of C may have trouble supporting this code; in practice, though, this is probably a small concern as you'll only use Cython in well-chosen, small regions of your code.

It is worth noting that performing CPU and memory profiling on your code will probably start you thinking about higher-level algorithmic optimizations that you might apply. These algorithmic changes (e.g., additional logic to avoid computations or caching to avoid recalculation) could help you avoid doing unnecessary work in your code, and Python's expressivity helps you to spot these algorithmic opportunities. Radim Řehůřek discusses how a Python implementation can beat a pure C implementation in "Making Deep Learning Fly with RadimRehurek.com" on page 328.

In this chapter, we'll review:

- Cython—This is the most commonly used tool for compiling to C, covering both numpy and normal Python code (requires some knowledge of C)
- Shed Skin—An automatic Python-to-C converter for non-numpy code
- Numba—A new compiler specialized for numpy code
- Pythran—A new compiler for both numpy and non-numpy code
- PyPy—A stable just-in-time compiler for non-numpy code that is a replacement for the normal Python executable

Later in the chapter we'll look at foreign function interfaces, which allow C code to be compiled into extension modules for Python. Python's native API is used along with ctypes and cffi (from the authors of PyPy), along with the f2py Fortran-to-Python converter.

What Sort of Speed Gains Are Possible?

Gains of an order or magnitude or more are quite possible if your problem yields to a compiled approach. Here, we'll look at various ways to achieve speedups of one to two orders of magnitude on a single core, along with using multiple cores through OpenMP.

Python code that tends to run faster after compiling is probably mathematical, and it probably has lots of loops that repeat the same operations many times. Inside these loops, you're probably making lots of temporary objects.

Code that calls out to external libraries (e.g., regular expressions, string operations, calls to database libraries) is unlikely to show any speedup after compiling. Programs that are I/O-bound are also unlikely to show significant speedups.

Similarly, if your Python code focuses on calling vectorized numpy routines it may not run any faster after compilation—it'll only run faster if the code being compiled is mainly Python (and probably if it is mainly looping). We looked at numpy operations in Chapter 6; compiling doesn't really help because there aren't many intermediate objects.

Overall, it is very unlikely that your compiled code will run any faster than a handcrafted C routine, but it is also unlikely to run much slower. It is quite possible that the generated

C code from your Python will run as fast as a handwritten C routine, unless the C coder has particularly good knowledge of ways to tune the C code to the target machine's architecture.

For math-focused code it is possible that a handcoded Fortran routine will beat an equivalent C routine, but again, this probably requires expert-level knowledge. Overall, a compiled result (probably using Cython, Pythran, or Shed Skin) will be as close to a handcoded-in-C result as most programmers will need.

Keep the diagram in Figure 7-1 in mind when you profile and work on your algorithm. A small amount of work understanding your code through profiling should enable you to make smarter choices at an algorithmic level. After this some focused work with a compiler should buy you an additional speedup. It will probably be possible to keep tweaking your algorithm, but don't be surprised to see increasingly small improvements coming from increasingly large amounts of work on your part. Know when additional effort probably isn't useful.

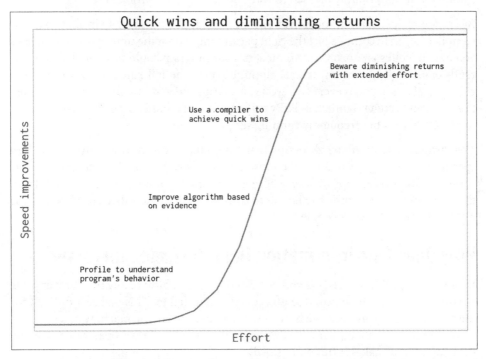

Figure 7-1. *Some effort profiling and compiling brings a lot of reward, but continued effort tends to pay increasingly less*

If you're dealing with Python code and batteries-included libraries, without numpy, then Cython, Shed Skin, and PyPy are your main choices. If you're working with numpy, then

Cython, Numba, and Pythran are the right choices. These tools all support Python 2.7, and some support Python 3.2+.

Some of the following examples require a little understanding of C compilers and C code. If you lack this knowledge, then you should learn a little C and compile a working C program before diving in too deeply.

JIT Versus AOT Compilers

The tools we'll look at roughly split into two sets: tools for compiling ahead of time (Cython, Shed Skin, Pythran) and compiling "just in time" (Numba, PyPy).

By compiling ahead of time (AOT), you create a static library that's specialized to your machine. If you download numpy, scipy, or scikit-learn, it will compile parts of the library using Cython on your machine (or you'll use a prebuilt compiled library if you're using a distribution like Continuum's Anaconda). By compiling ahead of use, you'll have a library that can instantly be used to work on solving your problem.

By compiling just in time, you don't have to do much (if any) work up front; you let the compiler step in to compile just the right parts of the code at the time of use. This means you have a "cold start" problem—if most of your program could be compiled and currently none of it is, when you start running your code it'll run very slowly while it compiles. If this happens every time you run a script and you run the script many times, this cost can become significant. PyPy suffers from this problem, so you may not want to use it for short but frequently running scripts.

The current state of affairs shows us that compiling ahead of time buys us the best speedups, but often this requires the most manual effort. Just-in-time compiling offers some impressive speedups with very little manual intervention, but it can also run into the problem just described. You'll have to consider these trade-offs when choosing the right technology for your problem.

Why Does Type Information Help the Code Run Faster?

Python is dynamically typed—a variable can refer to an object of any type, and any line of code can change the type of the object that is referred to. This makes it difficult for the virtual machine to optimize how the code is executed at the machine code level, as it doesn't know which fundamental datatype will be used for future operations. Keeping the code generic makes it run more slowly.

In the following example, v is either a floating-point number or a pair of floating-point numbers that represent a complex number. Both conditions could occur in the same loop at different points in time, or in related serial sections of code:

```
v = -1.0
print type(v), abs(v)
```

```
<type 'float'> 1.0
v = 1-1j
print type(v), abs(v)
<type 'complex'> 1.41421356237
```

The abs function works differently depending on the underlying datatype. abs for an integer or a floating-point number simply results in turning a negative value into a positive value. abs for a complex number involves taking the square root of the sum of the squared components:

$$abs(c) = \sqrt{c.real^2 + c.imag^2}$$

The machine code for the complex example involves more instructions and will take longer to run. Before calling abs on a variable, Python first has to look up the type of the variable and then decide which version of a function to call—this overhead adds up when you make a lot of repeated calls.

Inside Python every fundamental object, like an integer, will be wrapped up in a higher-level Python object (e.g., an int for an integer). The higher-level object has extra functions like __hash__ to assist with storage and __str__ for printing.

Inside a section of code that is CPU-bound, it is often the case that the types of variables do not change. This gives us an opportunity for static compilation and faster code execution.

If all we want are a lot of intermediate mathematical operations, then we don't need the higher-level functions, and we may not need the machinery for reference counting either. We can drop down to the machine code level and do our calculations quickly using machine code and bytes, rather than manipulating the higher-level Python objects, which involves greater overhead. To do this we determine the types of our objects ahead of time, so we can generate the correct C code.

Using a C Compiler

In the following examples we'll use gcc and g++ from the GNU C Compiler toolset. You could use an alternative compiler (e.g., Intel's icc or Microsoft's cl) if you configure your environment correctly. Cython uses gcc; Shed Skin uses g++.

gcc is a very good choice for most platforms; it is well supported and quite advanced. It is often possible to squeeze out more performance using a tuned compiler (e.g., Intel's icc may produce faster code than gcc on Intel devices), but the cost is that you have to gain some more domain knowledge and learn how to tune the flags on the alternative compiler.

C and C++ are often used for static compilation rather than other languages like Fortran due to their ubiquity and the wide range of supporting libraries. The compiler and the converter (Cython, etc., are the converters in this case) have an opportunity to study the annotated code to determine whether static optimization steps (like inlining functions and unrolling loops) can be applied. Aggressive analysis of the intermediate abstract syntax tree (performed by Pythran, Numba, and PyPy) provides opportunities for combining knowledge of Python's way of expressing things to inform the underlying compiler how best to take advantage of the patterns that have been seen.

Reviewing the Julia Set Example

Back in Chapter 2 we profiled the Julia set generator. This code uses integers and complex numbers to produce an output image. The calculation of the image is CPU-bound.

The main cost in the code was the CPU-bound nature of the inner loop that calculates the output list. This list can be drawn as a square pixel array, where each value represents the cost to generate that pixel.

The code for the inner function is shown in Example 7-1.

Example 7-1. Reviewing the Julia function's CPU-bound code

```
def calculate_z_serial_purepython(maxiter, zs, cs):
    """Calculate output list using Julia update rule"""
    output = [0] * len(zs)
    for i in range(len(zs)):
        n = 0
        z = zs[i]
        c = cs[i]
        while n < maxiter and abs(z) < 2:
            z = z * z + c
            n += 1
        output[i] = n
    return output
```

On Ian's laptop the original Julia set calculation on a 1,000 × 1,000 grid with maxit er=300 takes approximately 11 seconds using a pure Python implementation running on CPython 2.7.

Cython

Cython (*http://cython.org/*) is a compiler that converts type-annotated Python into a compiled extension module. The type annotations are C-like. This extension can be imported as a regular Python module using import. Getting started is simple, but it does have a learning curve that must be climbed with each additional level of complexity and optimization. For Ian, this is the tool of choice for turning calculation-bound functions into faster code, due to its wide usage, its maturity, and its OpenMP support.

With the OpenMP standard it is possible to convert parallel problems into multiprocessing-aware modules that run on multiple CPUs on one machine. The threads are hidden from your Python code; they operate via the generated C code.

Cython (announced in 2007) is a fork of Pyrex (announced in 2002) that expands the capabilities beyond the original aims of Pyrex. Libraries that use Cython include `scipy`, `scikit-learn`, `lxml`, and `zmq`.

Cython can be used via a `setup.py` script to compile a module. It can also be used interactively in IPython via a "magic" command. Typically the types are annotated by the developer, although some automated annotation is possible.

Compiling a Pure-Python Version Using Cython

The easy way to begin writing a compiled extension module involves three files. Using our Julia set as an example, they are:

- The calling Python code (the bulk of our Julia code from earlier)
- The function to be compiled in a new *.pyx* file
- A *setup.py* that contains the instructions for calling Cython to make the extension module

Using this approach, the *setup.py* script is called to use Cython to compile the *.pyx* file into a compiled module. On Unix-like systems, the compiled module will probably be a *.so* file; on Windows it should be a *.pyd* (DLL-like Python library).

For the Julia example, we'll use:

- *julia1.py* to build the input lists and call the calculation function
- *cythonfn.pyx*, which contains the CPU-bound function that we can annotate
- *setup.py*, which contains the build instructions

The result of running *setup.py* is a module that can be imported. In our *julia1.py* script in Example 7-2 we only need to make some tiny changes to `import` the new module and call our function.

Example 7-2. Importing the newly compiled module into our main code

```
...
import calculate  # as defined in setup.py
...
def calc_pure_python(desired_width, max_iterations):
    # ...
    start_time = time.time()
    output = calculate.calculate_z(max_iterations, zs, cs)
    end_time = time.time()
```

```
    secs = end_time - start_time
    print "Took", secs, "seconds"
...
```

In Example 7-3, we will start with a pure Python version without type annotations.

Example 7-3. Unmodified pure-Python code in cythonfn.pyx (renamed from .py) for Cython's setup.py

```
# cythonfn.pyx
def calculate_z(maxiter, zs, cs):
    """Calculate output list using Julia update rule"""
    output = [0] * len(zs)
    for i in range(len(zs)):
        n = 0
        z = zs[i]
        c = cs[i]
        while n < maxiter and abs(z) < 2:
            z = z * z + c
            n += 1
        output[i] = n
    return output
```

The *setup.py* script shown in Example 7-4 is short; it defines how to convert *cythonfn.pyx* into *calculate.so*.

Example 7-4. setup.py, which converts cythonfn.pyx into C code for compilation by Cython

```
from distutils.core import setup
from distutils.extension import Extension
from Cython.Distutils import build_ext

setup(
        cmdclass = {'build_ext': build_ext},
        ext_modules = [Extension("calculate", ["cythonfn.pyx"])]
        )
```

When we run the *setup.py* script in Example 7-5 with the argument `build_ext`, Cython will look for *cythonfn.pyx* and build *calculate.so*.

> Remember that this is a manual step—if you update your *.pyx* or *setup.py* and forget to rerun the build command, you won't have an updated *.so* module to import. If you're unsure whether you compiled the code, check the timestamp for the *.so* file. If in doubt, delete the generated C files and the *.so* file and build them again.

Example 7-5. Running setup.py to build a new compiled module

```
$ python setup.py build_ext --inplace
running build_ext
cythoning cythonfn.pyx to cythonfn.c
building 'calculate' extension
gcc -pthread -fno-strict-aliasing -DNDEBUG -g -fwrapv -O2 -Wall
    -Wstrict-prototypes -fPIC -I/usr/include/python2.7 -c cythonfn.c
    -o build/temp.linux-x86_64-2.7/cythonfn.o
gcc -pthread -shared -Wl,-O1 -Wl,-Bsymbolic-functions -Wl,
    -Bsymbolic-functions -Wl,-z,
    reliu build/temp.linux-x86_64-2.7/cythonfn.o -o calculate.so
```

The `--inplace` argument tells Cython to build the compiled module into the current directory rather than into a separate *build* directory. After the build has completed we'll have the intermediate *cythonfn.c*, which is rather hard to read, along with *calculate.so*.

Now when the *julia1.py* code is run the compiled module is imported, and the Julia set is calculated on Ian's laptop in 8.9 seconds, rather than the more usual 11 seconds. This is a small improvement for very little effort.

Cython Annotations to Analyze a Block of Code

The preceding example shows that we can quickly build a compiled module. For tight loops and mathematical operations, this alone often leads to a speedup. Obviously, we should not opimize blindly, though—we need to know what is slow so we can decide where to focus our efforts.

Cython has an annotation option that will output an HTML file that we can view in a browser. To generate the annotation we use the command `cython -a cythonfn.pyx`, and the output file *cythonfn.html* is generated. Viewed in a browser, it looks something like Figure 7-2. A similar image is available in the Cython documentation (*http://bit.ly/cythonize*).

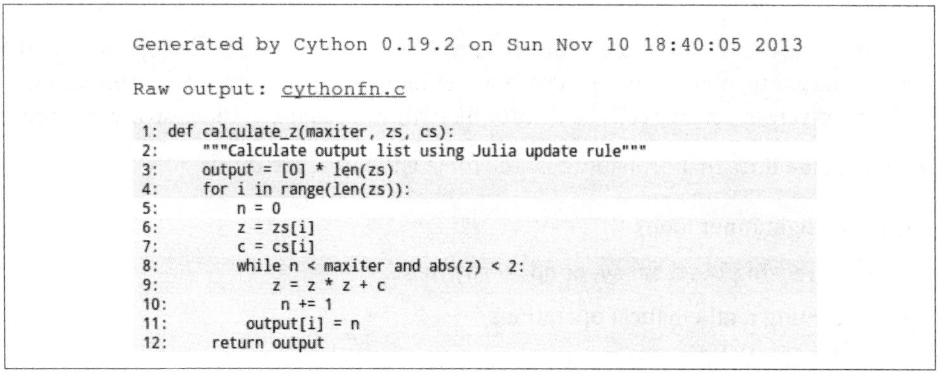

```
Generated by Cython 0.19.2 on Sun Nov 10 18:40:05 2013

Raw output: cythonfn.c

 1: def calculate_z(maxiter, zs, cs):
 2:     """Calculate output list using Julia update rule"""
 3:     output = [0] * len(zs)
 4:     for i in range(len(zs)):
 5:         n = 0
 6:         z = zs[i]
 7:         c = cs[i]
 8:         while n < maxiter and abs(z) < 2:
 9:             z = z * z + c
10:             n += 1
11:         output[i] = n
12:     return output
```

Figure 7-2. Colored Cython output of unannotated function

Each line can be expanded with a double-click to show the generated C code. More yellow means "more calls into the Python virtual machine," while more white means "more non-Python C code." The goal is to remove as many of the yellow lines as possible and to end up with as much white as possible.

Although "more yellow lines" means more calls into the virtual machine, this won't necessarily cause your code to run slower. Each call into the virtual machine has a cost, but the cost of those calls will only be significant if the calls occur inside large loops. Calls outside of large loops (e.g., the line used to create output at the start of the function) are not expensive relative to the cost of the inner calculation loop. Don't waste your time on the lines that don't cause a slowdown.

In our example, the lines with the most calls back into the Python virtual machine (the "most yellow") are lines 4 and 8. From our previous profiling work we know that line 8 is likely to be called over 30 million times, so that's a great candidate to focus on.

Lines 9, 10, and 11 are almost as yellow, and we also know they're inside the tight inner loop. In total they'll be responsible for the bulk of the execution time of this function, so we need to focus on these first. Refer back to "Using line_profiler for Line-by-Line Measurements" on page 37 if you need to remind yourself of how much time is spent in this section.

Lines 6 and 7 are less yellow, and since they're only called 1 million times they'll have a much smaller effect on the final speed, so we can focus on them later. In fact, since they are list objects there's actually nothing we can do to speed up their access except, as you'll see in "Cython and numpy" on page 154, replace the list objects with numpy arrays, which will buy a small speed advantage.

To better understand the yellow regions, you can expand each line with a double-click. In Figure 7-3 we can see that to create the output list we iterate over the length of zs, building new Python objects that are reference-counted by the Python virtual machine. Even though these calls are expensive, they won't really affect the execution time of this function.

To improve the execution time of our function, we need to start declaring the types of objects that are involved in the expensive inner loops. These loops can then make fewer of the relatively expensive calls back into the Python virtual machine, saving us time.

In general the lines that probably cost the most CPU time are those:

- Inside tight inner loops
- Dereferencing list, array, or np.array items
- Performing mathematical operations

```
Generated by Cython 0.19.2 on Sun Nov 10 18:40:05 2013

Raw output: cythonfn.c

 1: def calculate_z(maxiter, zs, cs):
 2:     """Calculate output list using Julia update rule"""
 3:     output = [0] * len(zs)

    /* "cythonfn.pyx":3
     * def calculate_z(maxiter, zs, cs):
     *     """Calculate output list using Julia update rule"""
     *     output = [0] * len(zs)            # <<<<<<<<<<<<<<
     *     for i in range(len(zs)):
     *         n = 0
     */
    __pyx_t_1 = PyObject_Length(__pyx_v_zs); if (unlikely(__pyx_t_1 == -1)) {__pyx_filename = __pyx_f[0];
    __pyx_t_2 = PyList_New(1 * ((__pyx_t_1<0) ? 0:__pyx_t_1)); if (unlikely(!__pyx_t_2)) {__pyx_filename =
    __Pyx_GOTREF(__pyx_t_2);
    { Py_ssize_t __pyx_temp;
      for (__pyx_temp=0; __pyx_temp < __pyx_t_1; __pyx_temp++) {
        __Pyx_INCREF(__pyx_int_0);
        PyList_SET_ITEM(__pyx_t_2, __pyx_temp, __pyx_int_0);
        __Pyx_GIVEREF(__pyx_int_0);
      }
    }
    __pyx_v_output = ((PyObject*)__pyx_t_2);
    __pyx_t_2 = 0;

 4:     for i in range(len(zs)):
 5:         n = 0
 6:         z = zs[i]
 7:         c = cs[i]
 8:         while n < maxiter and abs(z) < 2:
 9:             z = z * z + c
10:             n += 1
11:         output[i] = n
12:     return output
```

Figure 7-3. C code behind a line of Python code

 If you don't know which lines are most frequently executed, then use a profiling tool—line_profiler, discussed in "Using line_profiler for Line-by-Line Measurements" on page 37, would be the most appropriate. You'll learn which lines are executed most frequently and which lines cost the most inside the Python virtual machine, so you'll have clear evidence of which lines you need to focus on to get the best speed gain.

Adding Some Type Annotations

Figure 7-2 showed that almost every line of our function is calling back into the Python virtual machine. All of our numeric work is also calling back into Python as we are using the higher-level Python objects. We need to convert these into local C objects, and then, after doing our numerical coding, we need to convert the result back to a Python object.

In Example 7-6 we see how to add some primitive types using the cdef syntax.

It is important to note that these types will only be understood by Cython, and *not* by Python. Cython uses these types to convert the Python code to C objects, which do not have to call back into the Python stack; this means the operations run at a faster speed, but with a loss of flexibility and a loss of development speed.

The types we add are:

- `int` for a signed integer
- `unsigned int` for an integer that can only be positive
- `double complex` for double-precision complex numbers

The `cdef` keyword lets us declare variables inside the function body. These must be declared at the top of the function, as that's a requirement from the C language specification.

Example 7-6. Adding primitive C types to start making our compiled function run faster by doing more work in C and less via the Python virtual machine

```
def calculate_z(int maxiter, zs, cs):
    """Calculate output list using Julia update rule"""
    cdef unsigned int i, n
    cdef double complex z, c
    output = [0] * len(zs)
    for i in range(len(zs)):
        n = 0
        z = zs[i]
        c = cs[i]
        while n < maxiter and abs(z) < 2:
            z = z * z + c
            n += 1
        output[i] = n
    return output
```

When adding Cython annotations, you're adding non-Python code to the *.pyx* file. This means you lose the interactive nature of developing Python in the interpreter. For those of you familiar with coding in C, we go back to the code-compile-run-debug cycle.

You might wonder if we could add a type annotation to the lists that we pass in. We can use the `list` keyword, but practically this has no effect for this example. The `list` objects still have to be interrogated at the Python level to pull out their contents, and this is very slow.

The act of giving types to some of the primitive objects is reflected in the annotated output in Figure 7-4. Critically, lines 11 and 12—two of our most frequently called lines—have now turned from yellow to white, indicating that they no longer call back to the Python virtual machine. We can anticipate a great speedup compared to the previous version. Line 10 is called over 30 million times, so we'll still want to focus on it.

```
Generated by Cython 0.19.2 on Sun Nov 10 19:05:41 2013

Raw output: cythonfn.c

 1: def calculate_z(int maxiter, zs, cs):
 2:     """Calculate output list using Julia update rule"""
 3:     cdef unsigned int i, n
 4:     cdef double complex z, c
 5:     output = [0] * len(zs)
 6:     for i in range(len(zs)):
 7:         n = 0
 8:         z = zs[i]
 9:         c = cs[i]
10:         while n < maxiter and abs(z) < 2:
11:             z = z * z + c
12:             n += 1
13:         output[i] = n
14:     return output
```

Figure 7-4. Our first type annotations

After compiling, this version takes 4.3 seconds to complete. With only a few changes to the function we are running at twice the speed of the original Python version.

It is important to note that the reason we are gaining speed is because more of the frequently performed operations are being pushed down to the C level—in this case, the updates to z and n. This means that the C compiler can optimize how the lower-level functions are operating on the bytes that represent these variables, without calling into the relatively slow Python virtual machine.

We can see in Figure 7-4 that the while loop is still somewhat expensive (it is yellow). The expensive call is in to Python for the abs function for the complex z. Cython does not provide a native abs for complex numbers; instead, we can provide our own local expansion.

As noted earlier in this chapter, abs for a complex number involves taking the square root of the sum of the squares of the real and imaginary components. In our test, we want to see if the square root of the result is less than 2. Rather than taking the square root we can instead square the other side of the comparison, so we turn < 2 into < 4. This avoids us having to calculate the square root as the final part of the abs function.

In essence, we started with:

$$\sqrt{c.real^2 + c.imag^2} < \sqrt{4}$$

and we have simplified the operation to:

$$c.real^2 + c.imag^2 < 4$$

If we retained the `sqrt` operation in the following code, we would still see an improvement in execution speed. One of the secrets to optimizing code is to make it do as little work as possible. Removing a relatively expensive operation by considering the ultimate aim of a function means that the C compiler can focus on what it is good at, rather than trying to intuit the programmer's ultimate needs.

Writing equivalent but more specialized code to solve the same problem is known as *strength reduction*. You trade worse flexibility (and possibly worse readability) for faster execution.

This mathematical unwinding leads to the next example, Example 7-7, where we have replaced the relatively expensive `abs` function with a simplified line of expanded mathematics.

Example 7-7. Expanding the abs function using Cython

```
def calculate_z(int maxiter, zs, cs):
    """Calculate output list using Julia update rule"""
    cdef unsigned int i, n
    cdef double complex z, c
    output = [0] * len(zs)
    for i in range(len(zs)):
        n = 0
        z = zs[i]
        c = cs[i]
        while n < maxiter and (z.real * z.real + z.imag * z.imag) < 4:
            z = z * z + c
            n += 1
        output[i] = n
    return output
```

By annotating the code, we see a small improvement in the cost of the `while` statement on line 10 (Figure 7-5). Now it involves fewer calls into the Python virtual machine. It isn't immediately obvious how much of a speed gain we'll get, but we know that this line is called over 30 million times so we anticipate a good improvement.

This change has a dramatic effect—by reducing the number of Python calls in the innermost loop, we greatly reduce the calculation time of the function. This new version completes in just 0.25 seconds, an amazing 40x speedup over the original version.

```
Generated by Cython 0.19.2 on Sun Nov 10 19:21:24 2013

Raw output: cythonfn.c

 1: def calculate_z(int maxiter, zs, cs):
 2:     """Calculate output list using Julia update rule"""
 3:     cdef unsigned int i, n
 4:     cdef double complex z, c
 5:     output = [0] * len(zs)
 6:     for i in range(len(zs)):
 7:         n = 0
 8:         z = zs[i]
 9:         c = cs[i]
10:         while n < maxiter and (z.real * z.real + z.imag * z.imag) < 4:
11:             z = z * z + c
12:             n += 1
13:         output[i] = n
14:     return output
```

Figure 7-5. Expanded math to get a final win

Cython supports several methods of compiling to C, some easier than the full-type-annotation method described here. You should familiarize yourself with the Pure Python Mode if you'd like an easier start to using Cython and look at `pyximport` to ease the introduction of Cython to colleagues.

For a final possible improvement on this piece of code, we can disable bounds checking for each dereference in the list. The goal of the bounds checking is to ensure that the program does not access data outside of the allocated array—in C it is easy to accidentally access memory outside the bounds of an array, and this will give unexpected results (and probably a segmentation fault!).

By default, Cython protects the developer from accidentally addressing outside of the list's limits. This protection costs a little bit of CPU time, but it occurs in the outer loop of our function so in total it won't account for much time. It is normally safe to disable bounds checking unless you are performing your own calculations for array addressing, in which case you will have to be careful to stay within the bounds of the list.

Cython has a set of flags that can be expressed in various ways. The easiest is to add them as single-line comments at the start of the *.pyx* file. It is also possible to use a decorator or compile-time flag to change these settings. To disable bounds checking, we add a directive for Cython inside a comment at the start of the *.pyx* file:

```
#cython: boundscheck=False
def calculate_z(int maxiter, zs, cs):
```

As noted, disabling the bounds checking will only save a little bit of time as it occurs in the outer loop, not in the inner loop, which is more expensive. For this example, it doesn't save us any more time.

Try disabling bounds checking and wraparound checking if your CPU-bound code is in a loop that is dereferencing items frequently.

Shed Skin

Shed Skin (*http://code.google.com/p/shedskin/*) is an experimental Python-to-C++ compiler that works with Python 2.4–2.7. It uses type inference to *automatically* inspect a Python program to annotate the types used for each variable. This annotated code is then translated into C code for compilation with a standard compiler like g++. The automatic introspection is a very interesting feature of Shed Skin; the user only has to provide an example of how to call the function with the right kind of data, and Shed Skin will figure the rest out.

The benefit of type inference is that the programmer does not need to explicitly specify types by hand. The cost is that the analyzer has to be able to infer types for every variable in the program. In the current version, up to thousands of lines of Python can be automatically converted into C. It uses the Boehm mark-sweep garbage collector to dynamically manage memory. The Boehm garbage collector is also used in Mono and the GNU Compiler for Java. One negative for Shed Skin is that it uses external implementations for the standard libraries. Anything that has not been implemented (which includes numpy) will not be supported.

The project has over 75 examples, including many math-focused pure Python modules and even a fully working Commodore 64 emulator. Each runs significantly faster after being compiled with Shed Skin compared to running natively in CPython.

Shed Skin can build standalone executables that don't depend on an installed Python installation or extension modules for use with import in regular Python code.

Compiled modules manage their own memory. This means that memory from a Python process is copied in and results are copied back—there is no explicit sharing of memory. For large blocks of memory (e.g., a large matrix) the cost of performing the copy may be significant; we look at this briefly toward the end of this section.

Shed Skin provides a similar set of benefits to PyPy (see "PyPy" on page 160). Therefore, PyPy might be easier to use, as it doesn't require any compilation steps. The way that Shed Skin automatically adds type annotations might be interesting to some users, and the generated C may be easier to read than Cython's generated C if you intend to modify the resulting C code. We strongly suspect that the automatic type introspection code will be of interest to other compiler writers in the community.

Building an Extension Module

For this example, we will build an extension module. We can import the generated module just as we did with the Cython examples. We could also compile this module into a standalone executable.

In Example 7-8 we have a code example in a separate module; it contains normal Python code that is not annotated in any way. Also note that we have added a __main__ test— this makes this module self-contained for type analysis. Shed Skin can use this __main__ block, which provides example arguments, to infer the types that are passed into cal culate_z and from there infer the types used inside the CPU-bound function.

Example 7-8. Moving our CPU-bound function to a separate module (as we did with Cython) to allow Shed Skin's automatic type inference system to run

```python
# shedskinfn.py
def calculate_z(maxiter, zs, cs):
    """Calculate output list using Julia update rule"""
    output = [0] * len(zs)
    for i in range(len(zs)):
        n = 0
        z = zs[i]
        c = cs[i]
        while n < maxiter and abs(z) < 2:
            z = z * z + c
            n += 1
        output[i] = n
    return output


if __name__ == "__main__":
    # make a trivial example using the correct types to enable type inference
    # call the function so Shed Skin can analyze the types
    output = calculate_z(1, [0j], [0j])
```

We can import this module, as in Example 7-9, both before it has been compiled and after, in the usual way. Since the code isn't modified (unlike with Cython), we can call the original Python module before compilation. You won't get a speed improvement if you haven't compiled your code, but you can debug in a lightweight way using the normal Python tools.

Example 7-9. Importing the external module to allow Shed Skin to compile just that module

```python
...
import shedskinfn
...
def calc_pure_python(desired_width, max_iterations):
    #...
    start_time = time.time()
```

```
    output = shedskinfn.calculate_z(max_iterations, zs, cs)
    end_time = time.time()
    secs = end_time - start_time
    print "Took", secs, "seconds"
...
```

As seen in Example 7-10, we can ask Shed Skin to provide an annotated output of its analysis using shedskin -ann shedskinfn.py, and it generates *shedskinfn.ss.py*. We only need to "seed" the analysis with the dummy __main__ function if we're compiling an extension module.

Example 7-10. Examining the annotated output from Shed Skin to see which types it has inferred

```
# shedskinfn.ss.py
def calculate_z(maxiter, zs, cs):        # maxiter: [int],
                                         # zs: [list(complex)],
                                         # cs: [list(complex)]
    """Calculate output list using Julia update rule"""
    output = [0] * len(zs)               # [list(int)]
    for i in range(len(zs)):             # [__iter(int)]
        n = 0                            # [int]
        z = zs[i]                        # [complex]
        c = cs[i]                        # [complex]
        while n < maxiter and abs(z) < 2: # [complex]
            z = z * z + c                # [complex]
            n += 1                       # [int]
        output[i] = n                    # [int]
    return output                        # [list(int)]


if __name__ == "__main__":               # []
    # make a trivial example using the correct types to enable type inference
    # call the function so Shed Skin can analyze the types
    output = calculate_z(1, [0j], [0j])  # [list(int)]
```

The __main__ types are analyzed, and then, inside calculate_z, variables like z and c can be inferred from the objects they interact with.

We compile this module using shedskin --extmod shedskinfn.py. The following are generated:

- *shedskinfn.hpp* (the C++ header file)
- *shedskinfn.cpp* (the C++ source file)
- *Makefile*

By running make, we generate *shedskinfn.so*. We can use this in Python with import shedskinfn. The execution time for julia1.py using *shedskinfn.so* is 0.4s—this is a huge win compared to the uncompiled version for doing very little work.

We can also expand the `abs` function, as we did with Cython in Example 7-7. After running this version (with just the one `abs` line being modified) and using some additional flags, `--nobounds --nowrap`, we get a final execution time of 0.3 seconds. This is slightly slower (by 0.05 seconds) than the Cython version, but *we didn't have to specify all that type information*. This makes experimenting with Shed Skin very easy. PyPy runs the same version of the code at a similar speed.

 Just because Cython, PyPy, and Shed Skin share similar runtimes on this example does not mean that this is a general result. To get the best speedups for your project, you must investigate these different tools and run your own experiments.

Shed Skin allows you to specify extra compile-time flags, like `-ffast-math` or `-O3`, and you can add profile-guided optimization (PGO) in two passes (one to gather execution statistics, and a second to optimize the generated code in light of those statistics) to try to make additional speed improvements. Profile-guided optimization didn't make the Julia example run any faster, though; in practice, it often provides little or no real gain.

You should note that by default integers are 32 bits; if you want larger ranges with a 64-bit integer, then specify the `--long` flag. You should also avoid allocating small objects (e.g., new tuples) inside tight inner loops, as the garbage collector doesn't handle these as efficiently as it could.

The Cost of the Memory Copies

In our example, Shed Skin copies Python `list` objects into the Shed Skin environment by flattening the data into basic C types; it then converts the result from the C function back into a Python `list` at the end of executing the function. These conversions and copies take time. Might this account for the missing 0.05 seconds that we noted in the previous result?

We can modify our *shedskinfn.py* file to remove the actual work, just so we can calculate the cost of copying data into and out of the function via Shed Skin. The following variant of `calculate_z` is all we need:

```
def calculate_z(maxiter, zs, cs):
    """Calculate output list using Julia update rule"""
    output = [0] * len(zs)
    return output
```

When we execute `julia1.py` using this skeleton function, the execution time is approximately 0.05s (and obviously, it does not calculate the correct result!). This time is the cost of copying 2,000,000 complex numbers into `calculate_z` and copying 1,000,000 integers out again. In essence, Shed Skin and Cython are generating the same machine code; the execution speed difference comes down to Shed Skin running in a separate memory space, and the overhead required for copying data across. On the flip side, with Shed Skin you don't have to do the up-front annotation work, which offers quite a time savings.

Cython and numpy

List objects (for background, see Chapter 3) have an overhead for each dereference, as the objects they reference can occur anywhere in memory. In contrast, array objects store primitive types in contiguous blocks of RAM, which enables faster addressing.

Python has the `array` module, which offers 1D storage for basic primitives (including integers, floating-point numbers, characters, and Unicode strings). Numpy's `numpy.array` module allows multidimensional storage and a wider range of primitive types, including complex numbers.

When iterating over an `array` object in a predictable fashion, the compiler can be instructed to avoid asking Python to calculate the appropriate address and instead to move to the next primitive item in the sequence by going directly to its memory address. Since the data is laid out in a contiguous block it is trivial to calculate the address of the next item in C using an offset, rather than asking CPython to calculate the same result, which would involve a slow call back into the virtual machine.

You should note that if you run the following `numpy` version *without* any Cython annotations (i.e., just run it as a plain Python script), it'll take about 71 seconds to run— far in excess of the plain Python `list` version, which takes around 11 seconds. The slowdown is because of the overhead of dereferencing individual elements in the `numpy` lists—it was never designed to be used this way, even though to a beginner this might feel like the intuitive way of handling operations. By compiling the code, we remove this overhead.

Cython has two special syntax forms for this. Older versions of Cython had a special access type for `numpy` arrays, but more recently the generalized buffer interface protocol has been introduced through the `memoryview`—this allows the same low-level access to any object that implements the buffer interface, including `numpy` arrays and Python arrays.

An added bonus of the buffer interface is that blocks of memory can easily be shared with other C libraries, without any need to convert them from Python objects into another form.

The code block in Example 7-11 looks a little like the original implementation, except that we have added `memoryview` annotations. The function's second argument is `double complex[:] zs`, which means we have a double-precision complex object using the buffer protocol (specified using []), which contains a one-dimensional data block (specified by the single colon :).

Example 7-11. Annotated numpy version of the Julia calculation function

```
# cython_np.pyx
import numpy as np
cimport numpy as np

def calculate_z(int maxiter, double complex[:] zs, double complex[:] cs):
    """Calculate output list using Julia update rule"""
    cdef unsigned int i, n
    cdef double complex z, c
    cdef int[:] output = np.empty(len(zs), dtype=np.int32)
    for i in range(len(zs)):
        n = 0
        z = zs[i]
        c = cs[i]
        while n < maxiter and (z.real * z.real + z.imag * z.imag) < 4:
            z = z * z + c
            n += 1
        output[i] = n
    return output
```

In addition to specifying the input arguments using the buffer annotation syntax we also annotate the output variable, assigning a 1D numpy array to it via empty. The call to empty will allocate a block of memory but will not initialize the memory with sane values, so it could contain anything. We will overwrite the contents of this array in the inner loop so we don't need to reassign it with a default value. This is slightly faster than allocating and setting the contents of the array with a default value.

We also expanded the call to abs using the faster, more explicit math version. This version runs in 0.23 seconds—a slightly faster result than the original Cythonized version of the pure Python Julia example in Example 7-7. The pure Python version has an overhead every time it dereferences a Python complex object, but these dereferences occur in the outer loop and so don't account for much of the execution time. After the outer loop we make native versions of these variables, and they operate at "C speed." The inner loop for both this numpy example and the former pure Python example are doing the same work on the same data, so the time difference is accounted for by the outer loop dereferences and the creation of the output arrays.

Parallelizing the Solution with OpenMP on One Machine

As a final step in the evolution of this version of the code, let us look at the use of the OpenMP C++ extensions to parallelize our embarrassingly parallel problem. If your problem fits this pattern, then you can quickly take advantage of multiple cores in your computer.

OpenMP (Open Multi-Processing) is a well-defined cross-platform API that supports parallel execution and memory sharing for C, C++, and Fortran. It is built into most modern C compilers, and if the C code is written appropriately the parallelization occurs at the compiler level, so it comes with relatively little effort to the developer through Cython.

With Cython, OpenMP can be added by using the prange (parallel range) operator and adding the -fopenmp compiler directive to setup.py. Work in a prange loop can be performed in parallel because we disable the global interpreter lock (GIL).

A modified version of the code with prange support is shown in Example 7-12. with nogil: specifies the block where the GIL is disabled; inside this block we use prange to enable an OpenMP parallel for loop to independently calculate each i.

 When disabling the GIL we must *not* operate on regular Python objects (e.g., lists); we must only operate on primitive objects and objects that support the memoryview interface. If we operated on normal Python objects in parallel, we would have to solve the associated memory management problems that the GIL deliberately avoids. Cython does not prevent us from manipulating Python objects, and only pain and confusion can result if you do this!

Example 7-12. Adding prange to enable parallelization using OpenMP

```
# cython_np.pyx
from cython.parallel import prange
import numpy as np
cimport numpy as np

def calculate_z(int maxiter, double complex[:] zs, double complex[:] cs):
    """Calculate output list using Julia update rule"""
    cdef unsigned int i, length
    cdef double complex z, c
    cdef int[:] output = np.empty(len(zs), dtype=np.int32)
    length = len(zs)
    with nogil:
        for i in prange(length, schedule="guided"):
            z = zs[i]
            c = cs[i]
            output[i] = 0
            while output[i] < maxiter and (z.real * z.real + z.imag * z.imag) < 4:
                z = z * z + c
                output[i] += 1
    return output
```

To compile *cython_np.pyx* we have to modify the *setup.py* script as shown in Example 7-13. We tell it to inform the C compiler to use -fopenmp as an argument during compilation to enable OpenMP and to link with the OpenMP libraries.

Example 7-13. Adding the OpenMP compiler and linker flags to setup.py for Cython

```
#setup.py
from distutils.core import setup
from distutils.extension import Extension
from Cython.Distutils import build_ext

setup(
        cmdclass = {'build_ext': build_ext},
        ext_modules = [Extension("calculate",
                                ["cython_np.pyx"],
                                extra_compile_args=['-fopenmp'],
                                extra_link_args=['-fopenmp'])]
        )
```

With Cython's `prange`, we can choose different scheduling approaches. With `static`, the workload is distributed evenly across the available CPUs. Some of our calculation regions are expensive in time, and some are cheap. If we ask Cython to schedule the work chunks equally using `static` across the CPUs, then the results for some regions will complete faster than others and those threads will then sit idle.

Both the `dynamic` and `guided` schedule options attempt to mitigate this problem by allocating work in smaller chunks dynamically at runtime so that the CPUs are more evenly distributed when the workload's calculation time is variable. For your code, the correct choice will vary depending on the nature of your workload.

By introducing OpenMP and using `schedule="guided"`, we drop our execution time to approximately 0.07s—the `guided` schedule will dynamically assign work, so fewer threads will wait for new work.

We could also have disabled the bounds checking for this example using `#cython:` `boundscheck=False`, but it wouldn't improve our runtime.

Numba

Numba (*http://numba.pydata.org/*) from Continuum Analytics is a just-in-time compiler that specializes in `numpy` code, which it compiles via the LLVM compiler (*not* via `g++` or `gcc`,as used by our earlier examples) at runtime. It doesn't require a precompilation pass, so when you run it against new code it compiles each annotated function for your hardware. The beauty is that you provide a decorator telling it which functions to focus on and then you let Numba take over. It aims to run on all standard `numpy` code.

It is a younger project (we're using v0.13) and the API can change a little with each release, so consider it to be more useful in a research environment at present. If you use `numpy` arrays and have nonvectorized code that iterates over many items, then Numba should give you a quick and very painless win.

One drawback when using Numba is the toolchain—it uses LLVM, and this has many dependencies. We recommend that you use Continuum's Anaconda distribution, as everything is provided; otherwise, getting Numba installed in a fresh environment can be a very time-consuming task.

Example 7-14 shows the addition of the @jit decorator to our core Julia function. This is all that's required; the fact that numba has been imported means that the LLVM machinery kicks in at execution time to compile this function behind the scenes.

Example 7-14. Applying the @jit decorator to a function

```
from numba import jit
...
@jit()
def calculate_z_serial_purepython(maxiter, zs, cs, output):
```

If the @jit decorator is removed, then this is just the numpy version of the Julia demo running with Python 2.7, and it takes 71 seconds. Adding the @jit decorator drops the execution time to 0.3 seconds. This is very close to the result we achieved with Cython, but without all of the annotation effort.

If we run the same function a second time in the same Python session, then it runs even faster—there's no need to compile the target function on the second pass if the argument types are the same, so the overall execution speed is faster. On the second run the Numba result is equivalent to the Cython with numpy result we obtained before (so it came out as fast as Cython for very little work!). PyPy has the same warmup requirement.

When debugging with Numba it is useful to note that you can ask Numba to show the type of the variable that it is dealing with inside a compiled function. In Example 7-15 we can see that zs is recognized by the JIT compiler as a complex array.

Example 7-15. Debugging inferred types

```
print("zs has type:", numba.typeof(zs))
    array(complex128, 1d, C))
```

Numba supports other forms of introspection too, such as inspect_types, which lets you review the compiled code to see where type information has been inferred. If types have been missed, then you can refine how the function is expressed to help Numba spot more type inference opportunities.

Numba's premium version, NumbaPro (*http://docs.continuum.io/numbapro/*), has experimental support of a prange parallelization operator using OpenMP. Experimental GPU support is also available. This project aims to make it trivial to convert slower looping Python code using numpy into very fast code that could run on a CPU or a GPU; it is one to watch.

Pythran

Pythran (*http://pythonhosted.org/pythran/*) is a Python-to-C++ compiler for a subset of Python that includes partial numpy support. It acts a little like Numba and Cython—you annotate a function's arguments, and then it takes over with further type annotation and code specialization. It takes advantage of vectorization possibilities and of OpenMP-based parallelization possibilities. It runs using Python 2.7 only.

One very interesting feature of Pythran is that it will attempt to automatically spot parallelization opportunities (e.g., if you're using a map), and turn this into parallel code without requiring extra effort from you. You can also specify parallel sections using pragma omp directives; in this respect, it feels very similar to Cython's OpenMP support.

Behind the scenes, Pythran will take both normal Python and numpy code and attempt to aggressively compile them into very fast C++—even faster than the results of Cython. You should note that this project is young, and you may encounter bugs; you should also note that the development team are very friendly and tend to fix bugs in a matter of hours.

Take another look at the diffusion equation in Example 6-9. We've extracted the calculation part of the routine to a separate module so it can be compiled into a binary library. A nice feature of Pythran is that we *do not make Python-incompatible code*. Think back to Cython and how we had to create *.pyx* files with annotated Python that couldn't be run by Python directly. With Pythran, we add one-line comments that the Pythran compiler can spot. This means that if we delete the generated *.so* compiled module we can just run our code using Python alone—this is great for debugging.

In Example 7-16 you can see our earlier heat equation example. The evolve function has a one-line comment that annotates the type information for the function (since it is a comment, if you run this without Pythran, Python will just ignore the comment). When Pythran runs, it sees that comment and propagates the type information (much as we saw with Shed Skin) through each related function.

Example 7-16. Adding a one-line comment to annotate the entry point to evolve()

```
import numpy as np
def laplacian(grid):
    return np.roll(grid, +1, 0) +
                np.roll(grid, -1, 0) +
                np.roll(grid, +1, 1) +
                np.roll(grid, -1, 1) - 4 * grid

#pythran export evolve(float64[][], float)
def evolve(grid, dt, D=1):
    return grid + dt * D * laplacian(grid)
```

We can compile this module using `pythran diffusion_numpy.py` and it will output *diffusion_numpy.so*. From a test function, we can import this new module and call `evolve`. On Ian's laptop *without* Pythran this function executes on a 8,192 × 8,192 grid in 3.8 seconds. With Pythran this drops to 1.5 seconds. Clearly, if Pythran supports the functions that you need, it can offer some very impressive performance gains for very little work.

The reason for the speedup is that Pythran has its own version of the `roll` function, which has less functionality—it therefore compiles to less-complex code that might run faster. This also means it is less flexible than the `numpy` version (Pythran's authors note that it only implements parts of `numpy`), but when it works it can outperform the results of the other tools we've seen.

Now let's apply the same technique to the Julia expanded-math example. Just by adding the one-line annotation to `calculate_z`, we drop the execution time to 0.29 seconds—little slower than the Cython output. Adding a one-line OpenMP declaration in front of the outer loop drops the execution time to 0.1 seconds, which is not far off of Cython's best OpenMP output. The annotated code can be seen in Example 7-17.

Example 7-17. Annotating calculate_z for Pythran with OpenMP support

```
#pythran export calculate_z(int, complex[], complex[], int[])
def calculate_z(maxiter, zs, cs, output):
    #omp parallel for schedule(guided)
    for i in range(len(zs)):
```

The technologies we've seen so far all involve using a compiler in addition to the normal CPython interpreter. Let's now look at PyPy, which provides an entirely new interpreter.

PyPy

PyPy (*http://pypy.org/*) is an alternative implementation of the Python language that includes a tracing just-in-time compiler; it is compatible with Python 2.7 and an experimental Python 3.2 version is available.

PyPy is a drop-in replacement for CPython and offers all the built-in modules. The project comprises the RPython Translation Toolchain, which is used to build PyPy (and could be used to build other interpreters). The JIT compiler in PyPy is very effective, and good speedups can be seen with little or no work on your part. See "PyPy for Successful Web and Data Processing Systems" on page 339 for a large PyPy deployment success story.

PyPy runs our pure-Python Julia demo without any modifications. With CPython it takes 11 seconds, and with PyPy it takes 0.3 seconds. This means that PyPy achieves a result that's very close to the Cython example in Example 7-7, without *any effort at all* —that's pretty impressive! As we observed in our discussion of Numba, if the calculations are run again *in the same session*, then the second (and subsequent) runs are faster than the first as they are already compiled.

The fact that PyPy supports all the built-in modules is interesting—this means that multiprocessing works as it does in CPython. If you have a problem that runs with the batteries-included modules and can run in parallel with multiprocessing, expect that all the speed gains you might hope to get will be available.

PyPy's speed has evolved over time. The chart in Figure 7-6 from *speed.pypy.org* will give you an idea about its maturity. These speed tests reflect a wide range of use cases, not just mathematical operations. It is clear that PyPy offers a faster experience than CPython.

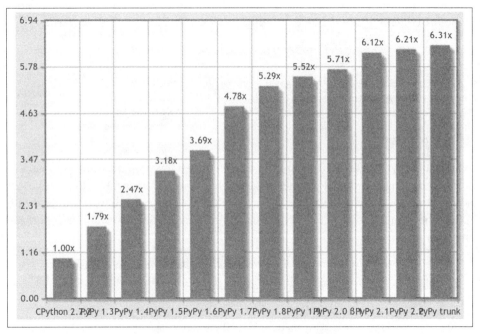

Figure 7-6. Each new version of PyPy offers speed improvements

Garbage Collection Differences

PyPy uses a different type of garbage collector to CPython, and this can cause some nonobvious behavior changes to your code. Whereas CPython uses reference counting, PyPy uses a modified mark and sweep approach that may clean up an unused object much later. Both are correct implementations of the Python specification; you just have to be aware that some code modifications might be required when swapping.

Some coding approaches seen in CPython depend on the behavior of the reference counter—particularly the flushing of files if they're opened and written to without an explicit file close. With PyPy the same code will run, but the updates to the file might get flushed to disk later, when the garbage collector next runs. An alternative form that works in both PyPy and Python is to use a context manager using with to open and automatically close files. The "Differences Between PyPy and CPython" page (*http://bit.ly/PyPy_CPy_diff*) on the PyPy website lists the details; implementation details for the garbage collector (*http://bit.ly/PyPy_garbage*) are also available on the website.

Running PyPy and Installing Modules

If you've never run an alternative Python interpreter, you might benefit from a short example. Assuming you've downloaded and extracted PyPy, you'll now have a folder structure containing a *bin* directory. Run it as shown in Example 7-18 to start PyPy.

Example 7-18. Running PyPy to see that it implements Python 2.7.3

```
$ ./bin/pypy
Python 2.7.3 (84efb3ba05f1, Feb 18 2014, 23:00:21)
[PyPy 2.3.0-alpha0 with GCC 4.6.3] on linux2
Type "help", "copyright", "credits" or "license" for more information.
And now for something completely different: ``<arigato> (not thread-safe, but
well, nothing is)''
```

Note that PyPy 2.3 runs as Python 2.7.3. Now we need to set up pip, and we'll want to install ipython (note that IPython starts with the same Python 2.7.3 build as we've just seen). The steps shown in Example 7-19 are the same as you might have performed with CPython if you've installed pip without the help of an existing distribution or package manager.

Example 7-19. Installing pip for PyPy to install third-party modules like IPython

```
$ mkdir sources  # make a local download directory
$ cd sources
# fetch distribute and pip
$ curl -O http://python-distribute.org/distribute_setup.py
$ curl -O https://raw.github.com/pypa/pip/master/contrib/get-pip.py
# now run the setup files for these using pypy
$ ../bin/pypy ./distribute_setup.py
...
$ ../bin/pypy get-pip.py
...
$ ../bin/pip install ipython
...
$ ../bin/ipython
Python 2.7.3 (84efb3ba05f1, Feb 18 2014, 23:00:21)
Type "copyright", "credits" or "license" for more information.

IPython 2.0.0—An enhanced Interactive Python.
```

```
?           -> Introduction and overview of IPython's features.
%quickref -> Quick reference.
help        -> Python's own help system.
object?   -> Details about 'object', use 'object??' for extra details.
```

Note that PyPy does *not* support projects like numpy in a usable way (there is a bridge layer via cpyext (*http://bit.ly/PyPy_compatibility*), but it is too slow to be useful with numpy), so don't go looking for strong numpy support with PyPy. PyPy does have an experimental port of numpy known as "numpypy" (installation instructions are available on Ian's blog (*http://bit.ly/install_numpy*)), but it doesn't offer any useful speed advantages at present.[1]

If you need other packages, anything that is pure Python will *probably* install, while anything that relies on C extension libraries *probably* won't work in a useful way. PyPy doesn't have a reference-counting garbage collector, and anything that is compiled for CPython will use library calls that support CPython's garbage collector. PyPy has a workaround, but it adds a lot of overhead; in practice, it isn't useful to try to force older extension libraries to work with PyPy directly. The PyPy advice is to try to remove any C extension code if possible (it might just be there to make the Python code go fast, and that's now PyPy's job). The PyPy wiki maintains a list of compatible modules (*http://bit.ly/compatible_mods*).

Another downside of PyPy is that it can use a lot of RAM. Each release is better in this respect, but in practice it may use more RAM than CPython. RAM is fairly cheap, though, so it makes sense to try to trade it for enhanced performance. Some users have also reported *lower* RAM usage when using PyPy. As ever, perform an experiment using representative data if this is important to you.

PyPy is bound by the global interpreter lock, but the development team are working on a project called software transactional memory (STM) (*http://bit.ly/PyPy_STM*) to attempt to remove the need for the GIL. STM is a little like database transactions. It is a concurrency control mechanism that applies to memory access; it can roll back changes if conflicting operations occur to the same memory space. The goal of STM integration is to enable highly concurrent systems to have a form of concurrency control, losing some efficiency on operations but gaining programmer productivity by not forcing the user to handle all aspects of concurrent access control.

For profiling, the recommended tools are jitviewer (*https://bitbucket.org/pypy/jitviewer*) and logparser (*http://bit.ly/PyPy_logparser*).

---

1. This may change during 2014; see *http://bit.ly/numpypy*.

When to Use Each Technology

If you're working on a numeric project, then each of these technologies could be useful to you. Table 7-1 summarizes the main options.

Pythran probably offers the best gains on numpy problems for the least effort, if your problem fits into the restricted scope of the supported functions. It also offers some easy OpenMP parallelization options. It is also a relatively young project.

Table 7-1. Summary of compiler options

	Cython	Shed Skin	Numba	Pythran	PyPy
Mature	Y	Y	–	–	Y
Widespread	Y	–	–	–	–
numpy support	Y	–	Y	Y	–
Nonbreaking code changes	–	Y	Y	Y	Y
Needs C knowledge	Y	–	–	–	–
Supports OpenMP	Y	–	Y	Y	Y

Numba may offer quick wins for little effort, but it too has limitations that might stop it working well on your code. It is also a relatively young project.

Cython probably offers the best results for the widest set of problems, but it does require more effort and has an additional "support tax" due to its use of the mix of Python with C annotations.

PyPy is a strong option if you're not using numpy or other hard-to-port C extensions.

Shed Skin may be useful if you want to compile to C and you're not using numpy or other external libraries.

If you're deploying a production tool, then you probably want to stick with well-understood tools—Cython should be your main choice, and you may want to check out "Making Deep Learning Fly with RadimRehurek.com" on page 328. PyPy is also being used in production settings (see "PyPy for Successful Web and Data Processing Systems" on page 339).

If you're working with light numeric requirements, note that Cython's buffer interface accepts array.array matrices—this is an easy way to pass a block of data to Cython for fast numeric processing without having to add numpy as a project dependency.

Overall, Pythran and Numba are young but very promising projects, whereas Cython is very mature. PyPy is regarded as being fairly mature now and should definitely be evaluated for long-running processes.

In a class run by Ian in 2014, a capable student implemented a C version of the Julia algorithm and was disappointed to see it execute more slowly than his Cython version.

It transpired that he was using 32-bit floats on a 64-bit machine—these run more slowly than 64-bit doubles on a 64-bit machine. The student, despite being a good C programmer, didn't know that this could involve a speed cost. He changed his code and the C version, despite being significantly shorter than the autogenerated Cython version, ran at roughly the same speed. The act of writing the raw C version, comparing its speed, and figuring out how to fix it took longer than using Cython in the first place.

This is just an anecdote; we're not suggesting that Cython will generate the best code, and competent C programmers can probably figure out how to make *their* code run faster than the version generated by Cython. It is worth noting, though, that the assumption that hand-written C will be faster than converted Python is not a safe assumption. You must always benchmark and make decisions using evidence. C compilers are pretty good at converting code into fairly efficient machine code, and Python is pretty good at letting you express your problem in an easy-to-understand language—combine these two powers sensibly.

Other Upcoming Projects

The PyData compilers page (*http://compilers.pydata.org/*) lists a set of high performance and compiler tools. Theano (*http://deeplearning.net/software/theano/*) is a higher-level language allowing the expression of mathematical operators on multidimensional arrays; it has tight integration with numpy and can export compiled code for CPUs and GPUs. Interestingly, it has found favor with the deep-learning AI community. Parakeet (*http://www.parakeetpython.com/*) focuses on compiling operations involving dense numpy arrays using a subset of Python; it too supports GPUs.

PyViennaCL (*http://bit.ly/PyViennaCL*) is a Python binding to the ViennaCL numerical computation and linear algebra library. It supports GPUs and CPUs using numpy. ViennaCL is written in C++ and generates code for CUDA, OpenCL, and OpenMP. It supports dense and sparse linear algebra operations, BLAS, and solvers.

Nuitka (*http://nuitka.net/pages/overview.html*) is a Python compiler that aims to be an alternative to the usual CPython interpreter, with the option of creating compiled executables. It supports all of Python 2.7, though in our testing it didn't produce any noticeable speed gains for our plain Python numerical tests.

Pyston (*https://github.com/dropbox/pyston*) is the latest entrant to the field. It uses the LLVM compiler and is being supported by Dropbox. It may suffer from the same issue that PyPy faces, with a lack of support for extension modules, but there are project plans to try to address this. Without addressing this issue it is unlikely that numpy support would be practical.

In our community we're rather blessed with a wide array of compilation options. Whilst they all have trade-offs, they also offer a lot of power so that complex projects can take advantage of the full power of CPUs and multicore architectures.

A Note on Graphics Processing Units (GPUs)

GPUs are a sexy technology at the moment, and we're choosing to delay covering them until at least the next edition. This is because the field is rapidly changing, and it is quite likely that anything we say now will have changed by the time you read it. Critically, it isn't just that the lines of code you write might have to change, but that you might have to substantially change how you go about solving your problems as architectures evolve.

Ian worked on a physics problem using the NVIDIA GTX 480 GPU for a year using Python and PyCUDA. By the year's end, the full power of the GPU was harnessed and the system ran fully 25x faster than the same function on a quad-core machine. The quad-core variant was written in C with a parallel library, while the GPU variant was mostly expressed in CUDA's C wrapped in PyCUDA for data handling. Shortly after this, the GTX 5xx series of GPUs were launched, and many of the optimizations that applied to the 4xx series changed. Roughly a year's worth of work ultimately was abandoned in favor of an easier-to-maintain C solution running on CPUs.

This is an isolated example, but it highlights the danger of writing low-level CUDA (or OpenCL) code. Libraries that sit on top of GPUs and offer a higher-level functionality are far more likely to be generally usable (e.g., libraries that offer image analysis or video transcoding interfaces), and we'd urge you to consider these rather than looking at coding for GPUs directly.

Projects that aim to manage GPUs for you include Numba, Parakeet, and Theano.

A Wish for a Future Compiler Project

Among the current compiler options, we have some strong technology components. Personally, we'd like to see Shed Skin's annotation engine become generalized so that it could work with other tools—for example, making an output that's Cython-compatible to smooth the learning curve when starting with Cython (particularly when using numpy). Cython is mature and integrates tightly into Python and numpy, and more people would use it if the learning curve and support requirement weren't quite so daunting.

A longer-term wish would be to see some sort of Numba- and PyPy-like solution that offers JIT behavior on both regular Python code and numpy code. No one solution offers this at present; a tool that solves this problem would be a strong contender to replace the regular CPython interpreter that we all currently use, without requiring the developers to modify their code.

Friendly competition and a large marketplace for new ideas make our ecosystem a rich place indeed.

Foreign Function Interfaces

Sometimes the automatic solutions just don't cut it and you need to write some custom C or FORTRAN code yourself. This could be because the compilation methods don't find some potential optimizations, or because you want to take advantage of libraries or language features that aren't available in Python. In all of these cases you'll need to use foreign function interfaces, which give you access to code written and compiled in another language.

For the rest of this chapter, we will attempt to use an external library to solve the 2D diffusion equation in the same way we did in Chapter 6.[2] The code for this library, shown in Example 7-20, could be representative of a library you've installed, or some code that you have written. The methods we'll look at serve as great ways to take small parts of your code and move them to another language in order to do very targeted language-based optimizations.

Example 7-20. Sample C code for solving the 2D diffusion problem

```
void evolve(double in[][512], double out[][512], double D, double dt) {
    int i, j;
    double laplacian;
    for (i=1; i<511; i++) {
        for (j=1; j<511; j++) {
            laplacian = in[i+1][j] + in[i-1][j] + in[i][j+1] + in[i][j-1]\
                - 4 * in[i][j];
            out[i][j] = in[i][j] + D * dt * laplacian;
        }
    }
}
```

In order to use this code, we must compile it into a shared module that creates a *.so* file. We can do this using gcc (or any other C compiler) by following these steps:

```
$ gcc -O3 -std=gnu99 -c diffusion.c
$ gcc -shared -o diffusion.so diffusion.o
```

We can place this final shared library file anywhere that is accessible to our Python code, but standard *nix organization stores shared libraries in */usr/lib* and */usr/local/lib*.

ctypes

The most basic foreign function interface in CPython[3] is through the ctypes module. The bare-bones nature of this module can be quite inhibitive at times—you are in charge

---

2. For simplicity, we will not implement the boundary conditions.

3. This is very CPython-dependent. Other version of Python may have their own versions of ctypes, which may work very differently.

of doing everything, and it can take quite a while to make sure that you have everything in order. This extra level of complexity is evident in our `ctypes` diffusion code, shown in Example 7-21.

Example 7-21. ctypes 2D diffusion code

```python
import ctypes

grid_shape = (512, 512)
_diffusion = ctypes.CDLL("../diffusion.so") # ❶

# Create references to the C types that we will need to simplify future code
TYPE_INT = ctypes.c_int
TYPE_DOUBLE = ctypes.c_double
TYPE_DOUBLE_SS = ctypes.POINTER(ctypes.POINTER(ctypes.c_double))

# Initialize the signature of the evolve function to:
# void evolve(int, int, double**, double**, double, double)
_diffusion.evolve.argtypes = [
    TYPE_INT,
    TYPE_INT,
    TYPE_DOUBLE_SS,
    TYPE_DOUBLE_SS,
    TYPE_DOUBLE,
    TYPE_DOUBLE,
]
_diffusion.evolve.restype = None

def evolve(grid, out, dt, D=1.0):
    # First we convert the Python types into the relevant C types
    cX = TYPE_INT(grid_shape[0])
    cY = TYPE_INT(grid_shape[1])
    cdt = TYPE_DOUBLE(dt)
    cD = TYPE_DOUBLE(D)
    pointer_grid = grid.ctypes.data_as(TYPE_DOUBLE_SS) # ❷
    pointer_out = out.ctypes.data_as(TYPE_DOUBLE_SS)

    # Now we can call the function
    _diffusion.evolve(cX, cY, pointer_grid, pointer_out, cD, cdt) # ❸
```

❶   This is similar to importing the `diffusion.so` library.

❷   grid and out are both numpy arrays.

❸   We finally have all the setup necessary and can call the C function directly.

This first thing that we do is "import" our shared library. This is done with the `ctypes.CDLL` call. In this line we can specify any shared library that Python can access (for example, the `ctypes-opencv` module loads the `libcv.so` library). From this, we get a `_diffusion` object that contains all the members that the shared library contains. In this example, `diffusion.so` only contains one function, `evolve`, which is not a property of the object. If `diffusion.so` had many functions and properties, we could access them all through the `_diffusion` object.

However, even though the `_diffusion` object has the `evolve` function available within it, it doesn't know how to use it. C is statically typed, and the function has a very specific signature. In order to properly work with the `evolve` function, we must explicitly set the input argument types and the return type. This can become quite tedious when developing libraries in tandem with the Python interface, or when dealing with a quickly changing library. Furthermore, since ctypes can't check if you have given it the correct types, if you make a mistake your code may silently fail or segfault!

Furthermore, in addition to setting the arguments and return type of the function object, we also need to convert any data we care to use with it (this is called "casting"). Every argument we send to the function must be carefully casted into a native C type. Sometimes this can get quite tricky, since Python is very relaxed about its variable types. For example, if we had `num1 = 1e5` we would have to know that this is a Python `float`, and thus we should use a `ctype.c_float`. On the other hand, for `num2 = 1e300` we would have to use `ctype.c_double`, because it would overflow a standard C `float`.

That being said, `numpy` provides a `.ctypes` property to its arrays that makes it easily compatible with `ctypes`. If `numpy` didn't provide this functionality, we would have had to initialize a `ctypes` array of the correct type, and then find the location of our original data and have our new `ctypes` object point there.

 Unless the object you are turning into a `ctype` object implements a buffer (as do the `array` module, `numpy` arrays, `cStringIO`, etc.), your data will be copied into the new object. In the case of casting an `int` to a `float`, this doesn't mean much for the performance of your code. However, if you are casting a very long Python list, this can incur quite a penalty! In these cases, using the `array` module or a `numpy` array, or even building up your own buffered object using the `struct` module, would help. This does, however, hurt the readability of your code, since these objects are generally less flexible than their native Python counterparts.

This can get even more complicated if you have to send the library a complicated data structure. For example, if your library expects a C `struct` representing a point in space with the properties x and y, you would have to define:

```
from ctypes import Structure
class cPoint(Structure):
    _fields_ = ("x", c_int), ("y", c_int)
```

At this point you could start creating C-compatible objects by initializing a `cPoint` object (i.e., `point = cPoint(10, 5)`). This isn't a terrible amount of work, but it can become tedious and results in some fragile code. What happens if a new version of the library is released that slightly changes the structure? This will make your code very hard to maintain and generally results in stagnant code, where the developers simply decide never to upgrade the underlying libraries that are being used.

For these reasons, using the `ctypes` module is great if you already have a good understanding of C and want to be able to tune every aspect of the interface. It has great portability since it is part of the standard library, and if your task is simple, it provides simple solutions. Just be careful, because the complexity of `ctypes` solutions (and similar low-level solutions) quickly becomes unmanageable.

cffi

Realizing that `ctypes` can be quite cumbersome to use at times, `cffi` attempts to simplify many of the standard operations that programmers use. It does this by having an internal C parser that can understand function and structure definitions.

As a result, we can simply write the C code that defines the structure of the library we wish to use, and then `cffi` will do all the heavy work for us: it imports the module and makes sure we specify the correct types to the resulting functions. In fact, this work can be almost trivial if the source for the library is available, since the header files (the files ending in *.h*) will include all the relevant definitions we need. Example 7-22 shows the `cffi` version of the 2D diffusion code.

Example 7-22. cffi 2D diffusion code

```
from cffi import FFI

ffi = FFI()
ffi.cdef(r'''
    void evolve(
        int Nx, int Ny,
        double **in, double **out,
        double D, double dt
    ); # ❶
''')
lib = ffi.dlopen("../diffusion.so")

def evolve(grid, dt, out, D=1.0):
    X, Y = grid_shape
    pointer_grid = ffi.cast('double**', grid.ctypes.data) # ❷
    pointer_out = ffi.cast('double**', out.ctypes.data)
    lib.evolve(X, Y, pointer_grid, pointer_out, D, dt)
```

❶   The contents of this definition can normally be acquired from the manual of the library that you are using or by looking at the library's header files.

❷   While we still need to cast nonnative Python objects for use with our C module, the syntax is very familiar to those with experience in C.

In the preceding code, we can think of the cffi initialization as being two-stepped. First, we create an FFI object and give it all the global C declarations we need. This can include datatypes in addition to function signatures. Then, we can import a shared library using dlopen into its own namespace that is a child namespace of FFI. This means we could have loaded up two libraries with the same evolve function into variables lib1 and lib2 and uses them independently (which is fantastic for debugging and profiling!).

In addition to simply importing a shared C library, cffi allows you to simply write C code and have it be just-in-time compiled using the verify function. This has many immediate benefits—you can easily rewrite small portions of your code to be in C without invoking the large machinery of a separate C library. Alternatively, if there is a library you wish to use, but some glue code in C is required to have the interface work perfectly, you can simply inline it into your cffi code as shown in Example 7-23 to have everything be in a centralized location. In addition, since the code is being just-in-time compiled, you can specify compile instructions to every chunk of code you need to compile. Note, however, that this compilation has a one-time penalty every time the verify function is run to actually perform the compilation.

Example 7-23. cffi with inline 2D diffusion code

```
ffi = FFI()
ffi.cdef(r'''
    void evolve(
        int Nx, int Ny,
        double **in, double **out,
        double D, double dt
    );
''')
lib = ffi.verify(r'''
void evolve(int Nx, int Ny,
        double in[][Ny], double out[][Ny],
        double D, double dt) {
    int i, j;
    double laplacian;
    for (i=1; i<Nx-1; i++) {
        for (j=1; j<Ny-1; j++) {
            laplacian = in[i+1][j] + in[i-1][j] + in[i][j+1] + in[i][j-1]\
                - 4 * in[i][j];
            out[i][j] = in[i][j] + D * dt * laplacian;
        }
    }
}
''', extra_compile_args=["-O3",]) # ❶
```

❶   Since we are just-in-time compiling this code, we can also provide relevant compilation flags.

Another benefit of the `verify` functionality is how it plays very nicely with complicated `cdef` statements. For example, if we were using a library with a very complicated structure, but only wanted to use a part of it, we could use the partial struct definition. To do this, we add a . . . in the struct definition in `ffi.cdef` and `#include` the relevant header file in a later `verify`.

For example, suppose we were working with a library with header `complicated.h` that included a structure that looked like this:

```
struct Point {
    double x;
    double y;
    bool isActive;
    char *id;
    int num_times_visited;
}
```

If we only cared about the x and y properties, we could write some simple `cffi` code that only cares about those values:

```
from cffi import FFI

ffi = FFI()
ffi.cdef(r"""
    struct Point {
        double x;
        double y;
        ...;
    };
    struct Point do_calculation();
""")
lib = ffi.verify(r"""
    #include <complicated.h>
""")
```

We could then run the `do_calculation` function from the `complicated.h` library and get returned to us a `Point` object with its x and y properties accessible. This is amazing for portability, since this code will run just fine on systems with a different implementation of `Point` or when new versions of `complicated.h` come out, as long as they all have the x and y properties.

All of these niceties really make `cffi` an amazing tool to have when you're working with C code in Python. It is much simpler than `ctypes`, while still giving you the same amount of fine-grained control you may want when working directly with a foreign function interface.

f2py

For many scientific applications, Fortran is still the gold standard. While its days of being a general-purpose language are over, it still has many niceties that make vector operations easy to write, and quite quick. In addition, there are many performance math libraries written in Fortran (LAPACK (*http://www.netlib.org/lapack/*), BLAS (*http://www.netlib.org/blas/*), etc.), and being able to use them in your performance Python code may be critical.

For such situations, f2py (*http://bit.ly/f2py_mod*) provides a dead-simple way of importing Fortran code into Python. This module is able to be so simple because of the explicitness of types in Fortran. Since the types can be easily parsed and understood, f2py can easily make a CPython module that uses the native foreign function support within C to use the Fortran code. This means that when you are using f2py, you are actually autogenerating a C module that knows how to use Fortran code! As a result, a lot of the confusion inherent in the ctypes and cffi solutions simply doesn't exist.

In Example 7-24 we can see some simple f2py-compatible code for solving the diffusion equation. In fact, all native Fortran code is f2py-compatible; however, the annotations to the function arguments (the statements prefaced by !f2py) simplify the resulting Python module and make for an easier-to-use interface. The annotations implicitly tell f2py whether we intend for an argument to be only an output or only an input; to be something we want to modify in place or hidden completely. The hidden type is particularly useful for the sizes of vectors: while Fortran may need those numbers explicitly, our Python code already has this information on hand. When we set the type as "hidden," f2py can automatically fill those values for us, essentially keeping them hidden from us in the final Python interface.

Example 7-24. Fortran 2D diffusion code with f2py annotations

```
SUBROUTINE evolve(grid, next_grid, D, dt, N, M)
    !f2py threadsafe
    !f2py intent(in) grid
    !f2py intent(inplace) next_grid
    !f2py intent(in) D
    !f2py intent(in) dt
    !f2py intent(hide) N
    !f2py intent(hide) M
    INTEGER :: N, M
    DOUBLE PRECISION, DIMENSION(N,M) :: grid, next_grid
    DOUBLE PRECISION, DIMENSION(N-2, M-2) :: laplacian
    DOUBLE PRECISION :: D, dt

    laplacian = grid(3:N, 2:M-1) + grid(1:N-2, 2:M-1) + &
                grid(2:N-1, 3:M) + grid(2:N-1, 1:M-2) - 4 * grid(2:N-1, 2:M-1)
    next_grid(2:N-1, 2:M-1) = grid(2:N-1, 2:M-1) + D * dt * laplacian
END SUBROUTINE evolve
```

To build the code into a Python module, we run the following command:

```
$ f2py -c -m diffusion --fcompiler=gfortran --opt='-O3' diffusion.f90
```

This will create a *diffusion.so* file that can be imported directly into Python.

If we play around with the resulting module interactively, we can see the niceties that f2py has given us thanks to our annotations and its ability to parse the Fortran code:

```
In [1]: import diffusion

In [2]: diffusion?
Type:        module
String form: <module 'diffusion' from 'diffusion.so'>
File:        .../examples/compilation/f2py/diffusion.so
Docstring:
This module 'diffusion' is auto-generated with f2py (version:2).
Functions:
  evolve(grid,next_grid,d,dt)
.

In [3]: diffusion.evolve?
Type:        fortran
String form: <fortran object>
Docstring:
evolve(grid,next_grid,d,dt)

Wrapper for ``evolve``.

Parameters
grid : input rank-2 array('d') with bounds (n,m)
next_grid :  rank-2 array('d') with bounds (n,m)
d : input float
dt : input float
```

This code shows that the result from the f2py generation is automatically documented, and the interface is quite simplified. For example, instead of us having to extract the sizes of the vectors, f2py has figured out how to automatically find this information and simply hides it in the resulting interface. In fact, the resulting evolve function looks exactly the same in its signature as the pure Python version we wrote in Example 6-14.

The only thing we must be careful of is the ordering of the numpy arrays in memory. Since most of what we do with numpy and Python focuses on code derived from C, we always use the C convention for ordering data in memory (called *row-major ordering*). Fortran uses a different convention (*column-major ordering*) that we must make sure our vectors abide by. These orderings simply state whether, for a 2D array, columns or

rows are contiguous in memory.[4] Luckily, this simply means we specify the or
der='F' parameter to numpy when declaring our vectors.

 The difference between row-major ordering and column-major
ordering means that the matrix [[1, 2], [3, 4]] gets stored in
memory as [1, 2, 3, 4] for row-major ordering and [1, 3, 2,
4] for column-major ordering. The difference is simply convention and doesn't have any real implications for performance when
used properly.

This results in the following code to use our Fortran subroutine. This code looks exactly
the same as what we used in Example 6-14, except for the import from the f2py-derived
library and the explicit Fortran ordering of our data:

```
from diffusion import evolve

def run_experiment(num_iterations):
    next_grid = np.zeros(grid_shape, dtype=np.double, order='F') # ➊
    grid = np.zeros(grid_shape, dtype=np.double, order='F')

    # ... standard initialization ...

    for i in range(num_iterations):
        evolve(grid, next_grid, 1.0, 0.1)
        grid, next_grid = next_grid, grid
```

➊ FORTRAN orders numbers differently in memory, so we must remember to set
our numpy arrays to use that standard.

CPython Module

Finally, we can always go right down to the CPython API level and write a CPython
module. This requires us to write code in the same way that CPython is developed and
take care of all of the interactions between our code and the implementation of CPython.

This has the advantage that it is incredibly portable, depending on the Python version.
We don't require any external modules or libraries, just a C compiler and Python! However, this doesn't necessarily scale well to new versions of Python. For example, CPython
modules written for Python 2.7 work with Python 3.

That portability comes at a big cost, though—you are responsible for every aspect of
the interface between your Python code and the module. This can make even the simplest tasks take dozens of lines of code. For example, to interface with the diffusion

---

4. For more information, see the Wikipedia page (*http://bit.ly/row-major_order*).

library from Example 7-20, we must write 28 lines of code simply to read the arguments to a function and parse them (Example 7-25). Of course, this does mean that you have incredibly fine-grained control over what is happening. This goes all the way down to being able to manually change the reference counts for Python's garbage collection (which can be the cause of a lot of pain when creating CPython modules that deal with native Python types). Because of this, the resulting code tends to be minutely faster than other interface methods.

 All in all, this method should be left as a last resort. While it is quite informative to write a CPython module, the resulting code is not as reusable or maintainable as other potential methods. Making subtle changes in the module can often require completely reworking it. In fact, we include the module code and the required *setup.py* to compile it (Example 7-26) as a cautionary tale.

Example 7-25. CPython module to interface to the 2D diffusion library

```
// python_interface.c
// - cpython module interface for diffusion.c
#define NPY_NO_DEPRECATED_API NPY_1_7_API_VERSION

#include <Python.h>
#include <numpy/arrayobject.h>
#include "diffusion.h"

/* Docstrings */
static char module_docstring[] =
    "Provides optimized method to solve the diffusion equation";
static char cdiffusion_evolve_docstring[] =
    "Evolve a 2D grid using the diffusion equation";

PyArrayObject* py_evolve(PyObject* self, PyObject* args) {
    PyArrayObject* data;
    PyArrayObject* next_grid;
    double dt, D=1.0;

    /* The "evolve" function will have the signature:
     *      evolve(data, next_grid, dt, D=1)
     */
    if (!PyArg_ParseTuple(args, "OOd|d", &data, &next_grid, &dt, &D)) {
        PyErr_SetString(PyExc_RuntimeError, "Invalid arguments");
        return NULL;
    }

    /* Make sure that the numpy arrays are contiguous in memory */
    if (!PyArray_Check(data) || !PyArray_ISCONTIGUOUS(data)) {
        PyErr_SetString(PyExc_RuntimeError,"data is not a contiguous array.");
        return NULL;
    }
```

```c
    if (!PyArray_Check(next_grid) || !PyArray_ISCONTIGUOUS(next_grid)) {
        PyErr_SetString(PyExc_RuntimeError,"next_grid is not a contiguous array.");
        return NULL;
    }

    /* Make sure that grid and next_grid are of the same type and have the same
     * dimensions
     */
    if (PyArray_TYPE(data) != PyArray_TYPE(next_grid)) {
        PyErr_SetString(PyExc_RuntimeError,
                        "next_grid and data should have same type.");
        return NULL;
    }
    if (PyArray_NDIM(data) != 2) {
        PyErr_SetString(PyExc_RuntimeError,"data should be two dimensional");
        return NULL;
    }
    if (PyArray_NDIM(next_grid) != 2) {
        PyErr_SetString(PyExc_RuntimeError,"next_grid should be two dimensional");
        return NULL;
    }
    if ((PyArray_DIM(data,0) != PyArrayDim(next_grid,0)) ||
        (PyArray_DIM(data,1) != PyArrayDim(next_grid,1))) {
        PyErr_SetString(PyExc_RuntimeError,
                        "data and next_grid must have the same dimensions");
        return NULL;
    }

    /* Fetch the size of the grid we are working with */
    const int N = (int) PyArray_DIM(data, 0);
    const int M = (int) PyArray_DIM(data, 1);

    evolve(
        N,
        M,
        PyArray_DATA(data),
        PyArray_DATA(next_grid),
        D,
        dt
    );

    Py_XINCREF(next_grid);
    return next_grid;
}

/* Module specification */
static PyMethodDef module_methods[] = {
/* { method name , C function  , argument types , docstring                  } */
   { "evolve"    , py_evolve   , METH_VARARGS   , cdiffusion_evolve_docstring }   ,
   { NULL        , NULL        , 0              , NULL                        }
};
```

```
/* Initialize the module */
PyMODINIT_FUNC initcdiffusion(void)
{
    PyObject *m = Py_InitModule3("cdiffusion", module_methods, module_docstring);
    if (m == NULL)
        return;

    /* Load `numpy` functionality. */
    import_array();
}
```

In order to build this code, we need to create a *setup.py* script that uses the distutils module to figure out how to build the code such that it is Python-compatible (Example 7-26). In addition to the standard distutils module, numpy provides its own module to help with adding numpy integration in your CPython modules.

Example 7-26. Setup file for the CPython module diffusion interface

```
"""
setup.py for cpython diffusion module.  The extension can be built by running

    $ python setup.py build_ext --inplace

which will create the __cdiffusion.so__ file, which can be directly imported into
Python.
"""

from distutils.core import setup, Extension
import numpy.distutils.misc_util

__version__ = "0.1"

cdiffusion = Extension(
    'cdiffusion',
    sources = ['cdiffusion/cdiffusion.c', 'cdiffusion/python_interface.c'],
    extra_compile_args = ["-O3", "-std=c99", "-Wall", "-p", "-pg", ],
    extra_link_args = ["-lc"],
)

setup (
    name = 'diffusion',
    version = __version__,
    ext_modules = [cdiffusion,],
    packages = ["diffusion", ],
    include_dirs = numpy.distutils.misc_util.get_numpy_include_dirs(),
)
```

The result from this is a cdiffusion.so file that can be imported directly from Python and used quite easily. Since we had complete control over the signature of the resulting function and exactly how our C code interacted with the library, we were able to (with some hard work) create a module that is easy to use:

```
from cdiffusion import evolve

def run_experiment(num_iterations):
    next_grid = np.zeros(grid_shape, dtype=np.double)
    grid = np.zeros(grid_shape, dtype=np.double)

    # ... standard initialization ...

    for i in range(num_iterations):
        evolve(grid, next_grid, 1.0, 0.1)
        grid, next_grid = next_grid, grid
```

Wrap-Up

The various strategies introduced in this chapter allow you to specialize your code to different degrees in order to reduce the number of instructions the CPU must execute and increase the efficiency of your programs. Sometimes this can be done algorithmically, although often it must be done manually (see "JIT Versus AOT Compilers" on page 138). Furthermore, sometimes these methods must be employed simply to use libraries that have already been written in other languages. Regardless of the motivation, Python allows us to benefit from the speedups that other languages can offer on some problems, while still maintaining verbosity and flexibility when it is needed.

It is important to note, though, that these optimizations are done in order to optimize the efficiency of CPU instructions only. If you have I/O-bound processes coupled to a CPU-bound problem, simply compiling your code may not provide any reasonable speedups. For these problems, we must rethink our solutions and potentially use parallelism to run different tasks at the same time.

## CHAPTER 8

Concurrency

Questions You'll Be Able to Answer After This Chapter

- What is concurrency and how is it helpful?
- What is the difference between concurrency and parallelism?
- Which tasks can be done concurrently and which can't?
- What are the various paradigms for concurrency?
- When is the right time to take advantage of concurrency?
- How can concurrency speed up my programs?

I/O can be quite burdensome to the flow of a program. Every time your code reads from a file or writes to a network socket, it must pause to contact the kernel, request that the operation happen, and then wait for it to complete. This may not seem like the end of the world, especially after you realize that a similar operation happens every time memory is allocated; however, if we look back to Figure 1-3 we see that most of the I/O operations we perform are on devices that are orders of magnitude slower than the CPU.

For example, in the time it takes to write to a network socket, an operation that typically takes about 1 ms, we could have completed 2,400,000 instructions on a 2.4 GHz computer. Worst of all, our program is halted for much of this 1 ms time—our execution is paused and we are waiting for a signal that the write operation has completed. This time spent in a paused state is called "I/O wait."

Concurrency helps us utilize this wasted time by allowing us to perform other operations while waiting for an I/O operation to complete. For example, in Figure 8-1 we see a depiction of a program that must run three tasks, all of which have periods of I/O wait within them. If we run them serially, then we suffer the I/O wait penalty three times.

However, if we run these tasks concurrently we can essentially hide the wait time by running another task in the meantime. It is important to note that this is all still happening on a single thread and still only uses one CPU at a time!

While concurrency isn't limited to I/O, this is where we see the greatest benefits. In a concurrent program, instead of having your code run serially—that is, from one line to the next—your code is written to handle *events*, and different parts of your code run when different events happen.

By modeling a program in this way, we are able to deal with the particular event that we are concerned with: I/O wait.

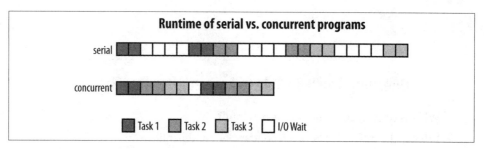

Figure 8-1. Comparison between serial and concurrent programs

Introduction to Asynchronous Programming

When a program enters I/O wait, the execution is paused so that the kernel can perform the low-level operations associated with the I/O request (this is called a *context switch*) and is not resumed until the I/O operation is completed. Context switching is quite a heavy operation. It requires us to save the state of our program (losing any sort of caching we had at the CPU level) and give up the use of the CPU. Later, when we are allowed to run again, we must spend time reinitializing our program on the motherboard and getting ready to resume (of course, all this happens behind the scenes).

With concurrency, on the other hand, we typically have a thing called an "event loop" running that manages what gets to run in our program, and when. In essence, an event loop is simply a list of functions that need to be run. The function at the top of the list gets run, then the next, etc. Example 8-1 shows a simple example of an event loop.

Example 8-1. Toy event loop

```
from Queue import Queue
from functools import partial

eventloop = None

class EventLoop(Queue):
    def start(self):
```

```
        while True:
            function = self.get()
            function()

def do_hello():
    global eventloop
    print "Hello"
    eventloop.put(do_world)

def do_world():
    global eventloop
    print "world"
    eventloop.put(do_hello)

if __name__ == "__main__":
    eventloop = EventLoop()
    eventloop.put(do_hello)
    eventloop.start()
```

This may not seem like a big change; however, we can couple event loops with asynchronous (async) I/O operations for massive gains when performing I/O tasks. These operations are nonblocking, meaning if we do a network write with an async function, it will return right away even though the write has not happened yet. When the write has completed, an event fires so our program knows about it.

Putting these two concepts together, we can have a program that, when an I/O operation is requested, runs other functions while waiting for the original I/O operation to complete. This essentially allows us to still do meaningful calculations while we would otherwise have been in I/O wait.

 Switching from function to function does have a cost. The kernel must take the time to set up the function to be called in memory, and the state of our caches won't be as predictable. It is because of this that concurrency gives the best results when your program has a lot of I/O wait—while this switching does have a cost to it, it can be much less than what is gained by making use of I/O wait time.

Programming using event loops can take two forms: callbacks or futures. In the callback paradigm, functions are called with an argument that is generally called the *callback*. Instead of the function returning its value, it calls the callback function with the value instead. This sets up long chains of functions that are called, with each getting the result of the previous function in the chain. Example 8-2 is a simple example of the callback paradigm.

Example 8-2. Example with callbacks

```
from functools import partial
def save_value(value, callback):
```

```
    print "Saving {} to database".format(value)
    save_result_to_db(result, callback) # ❶

def print_response(db_response):
    print "Response from database: {}".format(db_response)

if __name__ == "__main__":
    eventloop.put(
        partial(save_value, "Hello World", print_response)
    )
```

❶   save_result_to_db is an asynchronous function; it will return immediately and the function will end and allow other code to run. However, once the data is ready, print_response will be called.

With futures, on the other hand, an asynchronous function returns a *promise* of a future result instead of the actual result. Because of this, we must wait for the future that is returned by this sort of asynchronous function to complete and be filled with the value we desire (either by doing a yield on it or by running a function that explicitly waits for a value to be ready). While waiting for the future object to be filled with the data we requested, we can do other calculations. If we couple this with the concept of generators —functions that can be paused and whose execution can later be resumed—we can write asynchronous code that looks very close to serial code in form:

```
@coroutine
def save_value(value, callback):
    print "Saving {} to database".format(value)
    db_response = yield save_result_to_db(result, callback) # ❶
    print "Response from database: {}".format(db_response)

if __name__ == "__main__":
    eventloop.put(
        partial(save_value, "Hello World")
    )
```

❶   In this case, save_result_to_db returns a Future type. By yielding from it, we ensure that save_value gets paused until the value is ready, then resumes and completes its operations.

In Python, coroutines are implemented as generators. This is convenient because generators already have the machinery to pause their execution and resume later. So, what happens is our coroutine will yield a future and the event loop will wait until that future has its value ready. Once this happens, the event loop will resume execution of that function, sending back to it the value of the future.

For Python 2.7 implementations of future-based concurrency, things can get a bit strange when we're trying to use coroutines as actual functions. Remember that generators cannot return values, so there are various ways libraries deal with this issue.

In Python 3.4, however, new machinery has been introduced in order to easily create coroutines and have them still return values.

In this chapter we will analyze a web crawler that fetches data from an HTTP server that has latency built into it. This represents the general response time latency that will occur whenever we're dealing with I/O. We will first create a serial crawler that looks like the naive Python solution to this problem. Then we will go through two solutions in Python 2.7: gevent and tornado. Finally, we will look at the asyncio library in Python 3.4 and see what the future of asynchronous programming in Python looks like.

 The web server we implemented can support multiple connections at a time. This will be true for most services that you will be performing I/O with—most databases can support multiple requests at a time, and most web servers support 10K+ simultaneous connections. However, when interacting with a service that cannot handle multiple connections at a time,[1] we will always have the same performance as the serial case.

Serial Crawler

For the control in our experiment with concurrency we will write a serial web scraper that takes a list of URLs, fetches them, and sums the total length of the content from the pages. We will use a custom HTTP server that takes two parameters, name and delay. The delay field will tell the server how long, in milliseconds, to pause before responding. The name field is simply for logging purposes.

By controlling the delay parameter, we can simulate the time it takes a server to respond to our query. In the real world, this could correspond to a slow web server, a strenuous database call, or any I/O call that takes a long time to perform. For the serial case, this simply represents more time that our program will be stuck in I/O wait, but in the concurrent examples later it will represent more time the program can spend doing other things.

In addition, we chose to use the requests module to perform the HTTP call. This choice is because of the simplicity of the module. We use HTTP in general for this section because it is a simple example of I/O and HTTP requests can be performed quite easily. In general, any call to an HTTP library can be replaced with any I/O. The serial version of our HTTP crawler is shown in Example 8-3.

---

1. With some databases, such as Redis, this is a design choice made specifically to maintain data consistency.

Example 8-3. Serial HTTP scraper

```
import requests
import string
import random

def generate_urls(base_url, num_urls):
    """
    We add random characters to the end of the URL to break any caching
    mechanisms in the requests library or the server
    """
    for i in xrange(num_urls):
        yield base_url + "".join(random.sample(string.ascii_lowercase, 10))

def run_experiment(base_url, num_iter=500):
    response_size = 0
    for url in generate_urls(base_url, num_iter):
        response = requests.get(url)
        response_size += len(response.text)
    return response_size

if __name__ == "__main__":
    import time
    delay = 100
    num_iter = 500
    base_url = "http://127.0.0.1:8080/add?name=serial&delay={}&".format(delay)

    start = time.time()
    result = run_experiment(base_url, num_iter)
    end = time.time()
    print("Result: {}, Time: {}".format(result, end - start))
```

When running this code, an interesting metric to look at is the start and stop time of each request as seen by the HTTP server. This tells us how efficient our code was during I/O wait—since our task is simply to launch HTTP requests and then sum the number of characters that were returned, we should be able to launch more HTTP requests, and process any responses, while waiting for other requests to complete.

We can see from Figure 8-2 that, as expected, there is no interleaving of our requests. We do one request at a time and wait for the previous request to complete before we move to the next request. In fact, the total runtime of the serial process makes perfect sense, knowing this: since each request takes 0.1s (because of our delay parameter) and we are doing 500 requests, we expect the total runtime to be about 50 seconds.

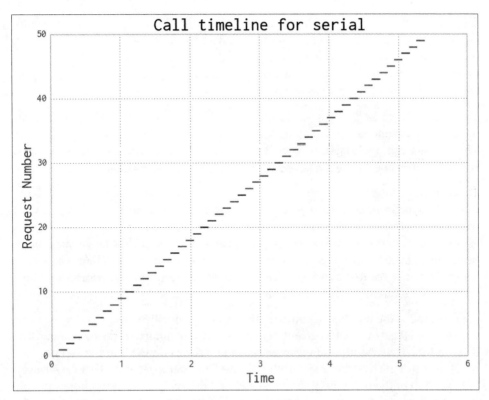

Figure 8-2. Chronology of HTTP requests for Example 8-3

gevent

One of the simplest asynchronous libraries is gevent. It follows the paradigm of having asynchronous functions return futures, which means most of the logic in your code can stay the same. In addition, gevent monkey-patches the standard I/O functions to be asynchronous, so most of the time you can simply use the standard I/O packages and benefit from asynchronous behavior.

gevent provides two mechanisms to enable asynchronous programming—as we've just mentioned, it patches the standard library with asynchronous I/O functions, and it also has a Greenlet object that can be used for concurrent execution. A *greenlet* is a type of coroutine and can be thought of as a thread (see Chapter 9 for a discussion of threads); however, all greenlets run on the same physical thread. That is, instead of using multiple CPUs to run all the greenlets, gevent's scheduler switches between them during I/O wait by use of an event loop. For the most part, gevent tries to make the handling of the event loop as transparent as possible through the use of wait functions. The wait function will start an event loop and run it as long as needed, until all the greenlets have finished. Because of this, most of your gevent code will run serially; then, at some point you will set up many greenlets to do some concurrent task, and start the event loop with the wait function. While the wait function is executing, all of the concurrent tasks you have queued up will run until completion (or some stopping condition), and then your code will go back to being serial again.

The futures are created with gevent.spawn, which takes a function and the arguments to that function and launches a greenlet that is responsible for running that function. The greenlet can be thought of as a future, since once the function you've specified completes, its value will be contained within the greenlet's value field.

This patching of Python standard modules can make it harder to control the subtleties of which asynchronous functions get run, and when. For example, one thing we want to make sure of when doing async I/O is that we don't open too many files or connections at one time. If we do this, we can overload the remote server or slow down our process by having to context-switch between too many operations. It wouldn't be as efficient to launch as many greenlets as we have URLs to fetch; we need a mechanism to limit how many HTTP requests we make at a time.

We can control the number of concurrent requests manually by using a *semaphore* to only do HTTP gets from 100 greenlets at a time. A semaphore works by making sure that only a certain number of coroutines can enter the context block at a time. As a result, we can launch all the greenlets that we need in order to fetch the URLs right away, but only 100 of them will be able to make HTTP calls at a time. Semaphores are one type of locking mechanism used a lot in various parallel code flows. By restricting the progression of your code based on various rules, locks can help you make sure that the various components of your program don't interfere with each other.

Now that we have all the futures set up and have put in a locking mechanism to control the flow of the greenlets, we can wait until we start having results by using the ge vent.iwait function, which will take a sequence of futures and iterate over the ready items. Conversely, we could have used gevent.wait, which would block execution of our program until all requests are done.

We go through the trouble of chunking our requests instead of sending them all at once because overloading the event loop can cause performance decreases (and this is true for all asynchronous programming). From experimentation, we generally see that 100 or so open connections at a time is optimal (see Figure 8-3). If we were to use less, we would still have wasted time during I/O wait. With more, we are switching contexts too often in the event loop and adding unnecessary overhead to our program. That being said, this value of 100 depends on many things—the computer the code is being run on, the implementation of the event loop, the properties of the remote host, the expected response time of the remote server, etc. We recommend doing some experimentation before settling on a choice. Example 8-4 shows the code for the gevent version of our HTTP crawler.

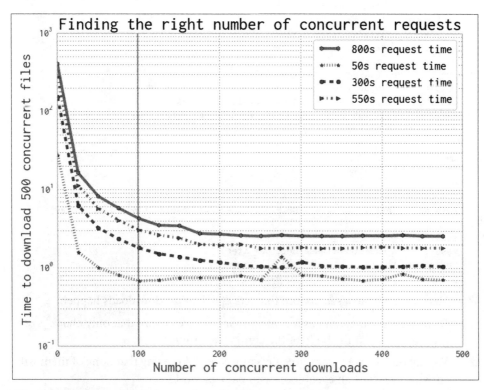

Figure 8-3. Finding the right number of concurrent requests

Example 8-4. gevent HTTP scraper

```
from gevent import monkey
monkey.patch_socket()

import gevent
from gevent.coros import Semaphore
import urllib2
import string
import random

def generate_urls(base_url, num_urls):
    for i in xrange(num_urls):
        yield base_url + "".join(random.sample(string.ascii_lowercase, 10))

def chunked_requests(urls, chunk_size=100):
    semaphore = Semaphore(chunk_size) # ❶
    requests = [gevent.spawn(download, u, semaphore) for u in urls] # ❷
```

```
        for response in gevent.iwait(requests):
            yield response

def download(url, semaphore):
    with semaphore: # ❸
        data = urllib2.urlopen(url)
        return data.read()

def run_experiment(base_url, num_iter=500):
    urls = generate_urls(base_url, num_iter)
    response_futures = chunked_requests(urls, 100) # ❹
    response_size = sum(len(r.value) for r in response_futures)
    return response_size

if __name__ == "__main__":
    import time
    delay = 100
    num_iter = 500
    base_url = "http://127.0.0.1:8080/add?name=gevent&delay={}&".format(delay)

    start = time.time()
    result = run_experiment(base_url, num_iter)
    end = time.time()
    print("Result: {}, Time: {}".format(result, end - start))
```

❶   Here we generate a semaphore that lets chunk_size downloads happen.

❸   By using the semaphore as a context manager, we ensure that only chunk_size greenlets can run the body of the context at a time.

❷   We can queue up as many greenlets as we need, knowing that none of them will run until we start an event loop with wait or iwait.

❹   response_futures now holds an iterator of completed futures, all of which have our desired data in the .value property.

Alternatively, we can use grequests to greatly simplify our gevent code. While gevent provides all sorts of lower-level concurrent socket operations, grequests is a combination of the requests HTTP library and gevent; the result is a very simple API for making concurrent HTTP requests (it even handles the semaphore logic for us). With grequests, our code becomes a lot simpler, more understandable, and more maintainable, while still resulting in comparable speedups to the lower-level gevent code (see Example 8-5).

Example 8-5. grequests HTTP scraper

```
import grequests

def run_experiment(base_url, num_iter=500):
    urls = generate_urls(base_url, num_iter)
    response_futures = (grequests.get(u) for u in urls) # ❶
```

```
responses = grequests.imap(response_futures, size = 100) # ❷
response_size = sum(len(r.text) for r in responses)
return response_size
```

❶ First we create the requests and get futures back. We chose to do this as a generator so that later we only need to evaluate as many requests as we are ready to issue.

❷ Now we can take the future objects and map them into real response objects. The `.imap` function gives us a generator that yields response objects for which we have retrieved data.

An important thing to note is that we have used `gevent` and `grequests` to make our I/O requests asynchronous, but we are not doing any non-I/O computations while in I/O wait. Figure 8-4 shows the massive speedup we get. By launching more requests while waiting for previous requests to finish, we are able to achieve a 69x speed increase! We can explicitly see how new requests are being sent out before previous requests finish by how the horizontal lines representing the requests stack on each other. This is in sharp contrast to the case of the serial crawler (Figure 8-2), where a line only starts when the previous line finishes. Furthermore, we can see more interesting effects going on with the shape of the `gevent` request timeline. For example, at around the first 100th request, we see a pause where new requests are not launched. This is because it is the first time that our semaphore is hit, and we are able to lock the semaphore before any previous requests finish. After this, the semaphore goes into an equilibrium where it locks just as another request finishes and unlocks it.

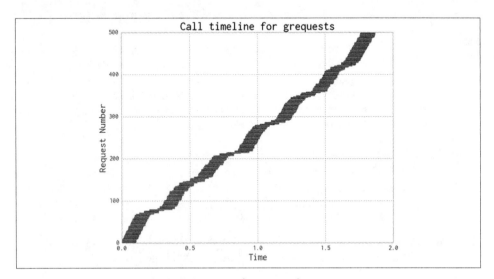

Figure 8-4. Chronology of HTTP requests for Example 8-5

tornado

Another very frequently used package for asynchronous I/O in Python is tornado, a package developed by Facebook primarily for HTTP clients and servers. In contrast to gevent, tornado chooses to use the callback method for async behavior. However, in the 3.x release coroutine-like behavior was added in a way that is compatible with old code.

In Example 8-6, we implement the same web crawler as we did for gevent, but using the tornado I/O loop (its version of an event loop) and HTTP client. This saves us the trouble of having to batch our requests and deal with other, more low-level aspects of our code.

Example 8-6. tornado HTTP scraper

```python
from tornado import ioloop
from tornado.httpclient import AsyncHTTPClient
from tornado import gen

from functools import partial
import string
import random

AsyncHTTPClient.configure("tornado.curl_httpclient.CurlAsyncHTTPClient",
max_clients=100) # ❶

def generate_urls(base_url, num_urls):
    for i in xrange(num_urls):
        yield base_url + "".join(random.sample(string.ascii_lowercase, 10))

@gen.coroutine
def run_experiment(base_url, num_iter=500):
    http_client = AsyncHTTPClient()
    urls = generate_urls(base_url, num_iter)
    responses = yield [http_client.fetch(url) for url in urls] # ❷
    response_sum = sum(len(r.body) for r in responses)
    raise gen.Return(value=response_sum) # ❸

if __name__ == "__main__":
    #... initialization ...

    _ioloop = ioloop.IOLoop.instance()
    run_func = partial(run_experiment, base_url, num_iter)
    result = _ioloop.run_sync(run_func) # ❹
```

❶   We can configure our HTTP client and pick what backend library we wish to use and how many requests we would like to batch together.

❷ We generate many futures and then `yield` back to the I/O loop. This function will resume, and the `responses` variable will be filled with all of the futures, results when they are ready.

❸ Coroutines in `tornado` are backed by Python generators. In order to return a value from them, we must raise a special exception that `gen.coroutine` turns into a return value.

❹ `ioloop.run_sync` will start the `IOLoop` just for the duration of the runtime of the specified function. `ioloop.start()`, on the other hand, starts an `IOLoop` that must be terminated manually.

An important difference between the `tornado` code from Example 8-6 and the `gevent` code from Example 8-4 is when the event loop runs. For `gevent`, the event loop is only running while the `iwait` function is running. On the other hand, in `tornado` the event loop is running the entire time and controls the complete execution flow of the program, not just the asynchronous I/O parts.

This makes `tornado` ideal for applications that are mostly I/O-bound and where most, if not all, of the application should be asynchronous. This is where `tornado` makes its biggest claim to fame, as a performant web server. In fact, Micha has on many occasions written `tornado`-backed databases and data structures that require a lot of I/O.[2] On the other hand, since `gevent` makes no requirements of your program as a whole, it is an ideal solution for a mainly CPU-based problems that sometimes involve heavy I/O— for example, a program that does a lot of computations over a dataset and then must send the results back to the database for storage. This becomes even simpler with the fact that most databases have simple HTTP APIs, which means you can even use `grequests`.

We can see just how much control the `tornado` event loop has if we look at the older-style `tornado` code that utilizes callbacks in Example 8-7. We can see that in order to start the code we must add the entry point for our program into the I/O loop, and then start it. Then, in order for the program to terminate, we must carefully carry around the `stop` function for our I/O loop and call it when appropriate. As a result, programs that must explicitly carry callbacks become incredibly burdensome and quickly unmaintainable. One reason this happens is that tracebacks can no longer hold valuable information about what function called what and how we got into an exception to begin with. Even simply knowing which functions are called at all can become hard, since we are constantly making partial functions to fill in parameters. It is no surprise that this is often called "callback hell."

---

2. For example, `fuggetaboutit` (*http://bit.ly/fuggetaboutit*) is a special type of probabilistic data structure (see "Probabilistic Data Structures" on page 305) that uses the `tornado` `IOLoop` to schedule time-based tasks.

Example 8-7. tornado crawler with callbacks

```python
from tornado import ioloop
from tornado.httpclient import AsyncHTTPClient

from functools import partial

AsyncHTTPClient.configure("tornado.curl_httpclient.CurlAsyncHTTPClient",
                          max_clients=100)

def fetch_urls(urls, callback):
    http_client = AsyncHTTPClient()
    urls = list(urls)
    responses = []
    def _finish_fetch_urls(result): # ❶
        responses.append(result)
        if len(responses) == len(urls):
            callback(responses)
    for url in urls:
        http_client.fetch(url, callback=_finish_fetch_urls)

def run_experiment(base_url, num_iter=500, callback=None):
    urls = generate_urls(base_url, num_iter)
    callback_passthrou = partial(_finish_run_experiment,
            callback=callback) # ❷
    fetch_urls(urls, callback_passthrou)

def _finish_run_experiment(responses, callback):
    response_sum = sum(len(r.body) for r in responses)
    print response_sum
    callback()

if __name__ == "__main__":
    # ... initialization ...

    _ioloop = ioloop.IOLoop.instance()
    _ioloop.add_callback(run_experiment, base_url, num_iter, _ioloop.stop) # ❸

    _ioloop.start()
```

❸   We send `_ioloop.stop` as the callback to `run_experiment` so that once the experiment is done, it shuts off the I/O loop for us.

❷   Callback-type async code involves a lot of partial function creation. This is because we often need to preserve the original callback we were sent, even though we currently need to transfer the runtime to another function.

❶   Sometimes games with scope are a necessary evil, in order to preserve state while not cluttering the global namespace.

Another interesting difference between gevent and tornado is the way the internals change the request call graphs. Compare Figure 8-5 with Figure 8-4. For the gevent call graph, we see some areas where the diagonal line seems to get thinner, and others where it seems to get much thicker. The thinner regions show times when we are waiting for old requests to finish before launching new ones. The thicker regions represent areas where we are too busy to read the responses from requests that should have already finished. Both these types of regions represent times when the event loop isn't doing its job optimally: times when we are either underutilizing or overutilizing our resources.

On the other hand, the call graph for `tornado` is much more uniform. This shows that 'tornado` is better able to optimize our resource use. This can be attributed to many things. A contributing factor here is that because the semaphore logic limiting the number of concurrent requests to 100 is internal to `tornado`, it can better allocate resources. This includes preallocating and reusing connections in a smarter way. In addition, there are many smaller effects resulting from the modules' choices with regard to their communications with the kernel in order to coordinate receiving results from asynchronous operations.

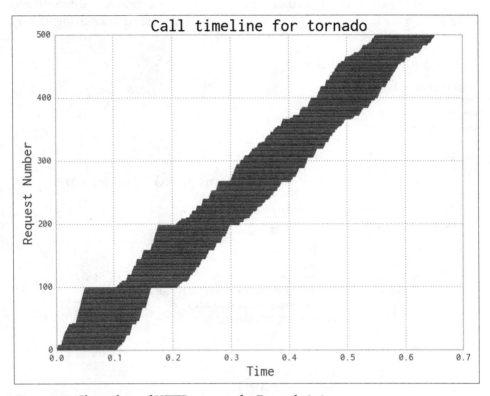

Figure 8-5. Chronology of HTTP requests for Example 8-6

AsyncIO

In response to the popularity of using async functionality to deal with heavy-I/O systems, Python 3.4+ introduced a revamping of the old `asyncio` standard library module. This module draws much of its influence from the `gevent` and `tornado` method of concurrency, where coroutines are defined and yielded from in order to halt the execution of the current function and allow other coroutines to run. As in `tornado`, the event loop is explicitly started in order to start the execution of the coroutines. In addition, Python 3 introduced a new keyword, `yield from`, that greatly simplifies dealing with these coroutines (we no longer have to raise an exception to return a value from a coroutine, as we did in Example 8-6).

It is important to note that the `asyncio` library is very low-level and does not provide much higher-level functionality to the user. For example, while there is a very full socket API, there is no easy way to do HTTP requests. As a result, we chose to use the `aiohttp` library in Example 8-8. However, the adoption of the `asyncio` library is just starting to ramp up, and the landscape of helper modules is probably going to be changing very quickly.

Example 8-8. asyncio HTTP scraper

```python
import asyncio
import aiohttp
import random
import string

def generate_urls(base_url, num_urls):
    for i in range(num_urls):
        yield base_url + "".join(random.sample(string.ascii_lowercase, 10))

def chunked_http_client(num_chunks):
    semaphore = asyncio.Semaphore(num_chunks) # ❶
    @asyncio.coroutine
    def http_get(url): # ❷
        nonlocal semaphore
        with (yield from semaphore):
            response = yield from aiohttp.request('GET', url)
            body = yield from response.content.read()
            yield from response.wait_for_close()
        return body
    return http_get

def run_experiment(base_url, num_iter=500):
    urls = generate_urls(base_url, num_iter)
    http_client = chunked_http_client(100)
    tasks = [http_client(url) for url in urls] # ❸
    responses_sum = 0
    for future in asyncio.as_completed(tasks): # ❹
        data = yield from future
```

```
        responses_sum += len(data)
    return responses_sum

if __name__ == "__main__":
    import time
    delay = 100
    num_iter = 500
    base_url = "http://127.0.0.1:8080/add?name=asyncio&delay={}&".format(delay)
    loop = asyncio.get_event_loop()

    start = time.time()
    result = loop.run_until_complete(run_experiment(base_url, num_iter))
    end = time.time()
    print("{} {}".format(result, end-start))
```

❶   As in the gevent example, we must use a semaphore to limit the number of requests.

❷   We return a new coroutine that will asynchronously download files and respect the locking of the semaphore.

❸   The http_client function returns futures. To keep track of progress, we save the futures into a list.

❹   As with gevent, we can wait for futures to become ready and iterate over them.

One of the fantastic benefits of the asyncio module is its familiar API compared to the standard library, which simplifies making helper modules. We are able to get the same sort of results as we would with tornado or gevent, but if we wanted to, we could dive deeper into the stack and make our own async protocols using a wide array of supported structures. In addition, because it is a standard library module, we are assured that this module will always be PEP-compliant and reasonably maintained.[3]

Furthermore, the asyncio library allows us to unify modules like tornado and ge vent by having them run in the same event loop. In fact, the Python 3.4 version of tornado is backed by the asyncio library. As a result, even though tornado and ge vent have different use cases, the underlying event loop will be unified, which will make changing from one paradigm to the other mid-code trivial. You can even make your own wrappers on top of the asyncio module quite easily, in order to interact with asynchronous operations in the most efficient way possible for the problem you are solving.

---

3. Python Enhancement Proposals (PEPs) are how the Python community decides on changes and advances the language. Because it's part of the standard library, asyncio will always comply with the newest PEP standards for the language and take advantage of any new features.

Although it's only supported in Python 3.4 and higher,[4] this module at the very least is a great sign of more work being put into asynchronous I/O in the future. As Python starts dominating more and more processing pipelines (from data processing to web request processing), this shift makes perfect sense.

Figure 8-6 shows the request timeline for the `asyncio` version of our HTTP scraper.

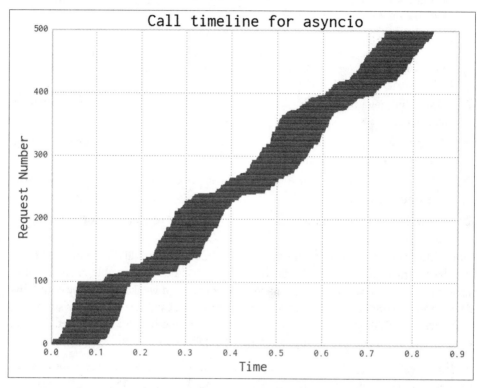

Figure 8-6. Chronology of HTTP requests for Example 8-8

Database Example

To make the preceding examples more concrete, we will create another toy problem that is mostly CPU-bound but contains a potentially limiting I/O component. We will be calculating primes and saving the found primes into a database. The database could be anything, and the problem is representative of any sort of problem where your program has heavy calculations to do, and the results of those calculations must be stored

---

4. Most performance applications and modules are still in the Python 2.7 ecosystem.

into a database, potentially incurring a heavy I/O penalty. The only restrictions we are putting on our database are:

- It has an HTTP API so that we can use code like that in the earlier examples.[5]
- Response times are on the order of 50 ms.
- The database can satisfy many requests at a time.[6]

We start with some simple code that calculates primes and makes a request to the database's HTTP API every time a prime is found·

```python
from tornado.httpclient import HTTPClient
import math

httpclient = HTTPClient()
def save_prime_serial(prime):
    url = "http://127.0.0.1:8080/add?prime={}".format(prime)
    response = httpclient.fetch(url)
    finish_save_prime(response, prime)

def finish_save_prime(response, prime):
    if response.code != 200:
        print "Error saving prime: {}".format(prime)

def check_prime(number):
    if number % 2 == 0:
        return False
    for i in xrange(3, int(math.sqrt(number)) + 1, 2):
        if number % i == 0:
            return False
    return True

def calculate_primes_serial(max_number):
    for number in xrange(max_number):
        if check_prime(number):
            save_prime_serial(number)
    return
```

Just as in our serial example (Example 8-3), the request times for each database save (50 ms) do not stack, and we must pay this penalty for each prime we find. As a result, searching up to max_number = 8,192 (which results in 1,028 primes) takes 55.2s. We know, however, that because of the way our serial requests work, we are spending 51.4s at minimum doing I/O! So, simply because we are pausing our program while doing I/O, we are wasting 93% of our time.

---

5. This is not necessary; it just serves to simplify our code.
6. This is true for all distributed databases and other popular databases, such as Postgres, MongoDB, Riak, etc.

What we want to do instead is to find a way to change our request scheme so that we can issue many requests asynchronously at a time, so that we don't have such a burdensome I/O wait. In order to do this, we create an `AsyncBatcher` class that takes care of batching requests for us and making the requests when necessary:

```python
import grequests
from itertools import izip

class AsyncBatcher(object):
    __slots__ = ["batch", "batch_size", "save", "flush"]
    def __init__(self, batch_size):
        self.batch_size = batch_size
        self.batch = []

    def save(self, prime):
        url = "http://127.0.0.1:8080/add?prime={}".format(prime)
        self.batch.append((url,prime))
        if len(self.batch) == self.batch_size:
            self.flush()

    def flush(self):
        responses_futures = (grequests.get(url) for url, _ in self.batch)
        responses = grequests.map(responses_futures)
        for response, (url, prime) in izip(responses, self.batch):
            finish_save_prime(response, prime)
        self.batch = []
```

Now, we can proceed almost in the same way as we did before. The only main difference is that we add our new primes to our `AsyncBatcher` and let it take care of when to send the requests. In addition, since we are batching we must make sure to send the last batch even if it is not full (which means making a call to `AsyncBatcher.flush()`):

```python
def calculate_primes_async(max_number):
    batcher = AsyncBatcher(100) # ❶
    for number in xrange(max_number):
        if check_prime(number):
            batcher.save(number)
    batcher.flush()
    return
```

❶ We choose to batch at 100 requests, for similar reasons to those illustrated in Figure 8-3.

With this change, we are able to bring our runtime for `max_number = 8,192` down to 4.09s. This represents a 13.5x speedup without our having to do much work. In a constrained environment such as a real-time data pipeline, this extra speed could mean the difference between a system being able to keep up with demand and falling behind (in which case a queue will be required; you'll learn about these in Chapter 10).

In Figure 8-7 we can see a summary of how these changes affect the runtime of our code for different workloads. The speedup in the async code over the serial code is significant, although we are still a ways away from the speeds achieved in the raw CPU problem. For this to be completely remedied, we would need to use modules like `multiprocess ing` to have a completely separate process that can deal with the I/O burden of our program without slowing down the CPU portion of the problem.

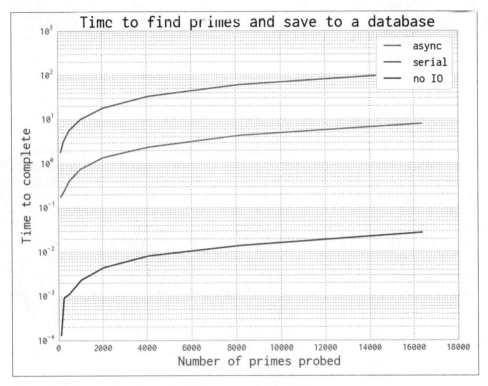

Figure 8-7. Processing times for different numbers of primes

Wrap-Up

When solving problems in real-world and production systems, it is often necessary to communicate with some outside source. This outside source could be a database running on another server, another worker computer, or a data service that is providing the raw data that must be processed. Whenever this is the case, your problem can quickly become I/O-bound, meaning that most of the runtime is dominated by dealing with input/output.

Concurrency helps with I/O-bound problems by allowing you to interleave computation with potentially multiple I/O operations. This allows you to exploit the fundamental difference between I/O and CPU operations in order to speed up overall runtime.

As we saw, gevent provides the highest-level interface for asynchronous I/O. On the other hand, tornado lets you manually control how the event loop is running, allowing you to use the event loop to schedule any sort of task you want. Finally, asyncio in Python 3.4+ allows full control of an asynchronous I/O stack. In addition to the various levels of abstraction, every library uses a different paradigm for its syntax (the differences stem mainly from the lack of native support for concurrency before Python 3 and the introduction of the yield from statement). We recommend gaining some experience in a range of methods and picking one based on how much low-level control is necessary.

Finally, there are small speed differences between the three libraries we approached. Many of these speed differences are based on how coroutines are scheduled. For example, tornado does an incredible job of launching asynchronous operations and resuming the coroutine quickly. On the other hand, even though asyncio seems to perform slightly worse, it allows much lower-level access into the API and can be tuned dramatically.

In the next chapter, we will take this concept of interleaving computation from I/O-bound problems and apply it to CPU-bound problems. With this new ability, we will be able to perform not only multiple I/O operations at once, but also many computational operations. This capability will allow us to start to make fully scalable programs where we can achieve more speed by simply adding more computer resources that can each handle a chunk of the problem.

## CHAPTER 9

The multiprocessing Module

Questions You'll Be Able to Answer After This Chapter

- What does the multiprocessing module offer?
- What's the difference between processes and threads?
- How do I choose the right size for a process pool?
- How do I use nonpersistent queues for work processing?
- What are the costs and benefits of interprocess communication?
- How can I process numpy data with many CPUs?
- Why do I need locking to avoid data loss?

CPython doesn't use multiple CPUs by default. This is partly due to Python's being designed back in a single-core era, and partly because parallelizing can actually be quite difficult to do efficiently. Python gives us the tools to do it but leaves us to make our own choices. It is painful to see your multicore machine using just one CPU on a long-running process, though, so in this chapter we'll review ways of using all the machine's cores at once.

It is important to note that we mentioned *CPython* above (the common implementation that we all use). There's nothing in the Python language that stops it from using multicore systems. CPython's implementation cannot efficiently use multiple cores, but other implementations (e.g., PyPy with the forthcoming software transactional memory) may not be bound by this restriction.

We live in a multicore world—4 cores are common in laptops, 8-core desktop configurations will be popular soon, and 10-, 12-, and 15-core server CPUs are available. If your job can be split to run on multiple CPUs *without* too much engineering effort, then this is a wise direction to consider.

When used to parallelize a problem over a set of CPUs you can expect *up to* an n-times (nx) speedup with n cores. If you have a quad-core machine and you can use all four cores for your task, it might run in a quarter of the original runtime. You are unlikely to see a greater than 4x speedup; in practice, you'll probably see gains of 3–4x.

Each additional process will increase the communication overhead and decrease the available RAM, so you rarely get a full nx speedup. Depending on which problem you are solving, the communication overhead can even get so large that you can see very significant slowdowns. These sorts of problems are often where the complexity lies for any sort of parallel programming and normally require a change in algorithm. This is why parallel programming is often considered an art.

If you're not familiar with Amdahl's law (*http://bit.ly/law_Amdahl*), then it is worth doing some background reading. The law shows that if only a small part of your code can be parallelized, it doesn't matter how many CPUs you throw at it; overall, it still won't run much faster. Even if a large fraction of your runtime could be parallelized, there's a finite number of CPUs that can be used efficiently to make the overall process run faster, before you get to a point of diminishing returns.

The multiprocessing module lets you use process- and thread-based parallel processing, share work over queues, and share data among processes. It is mostly focused on single-machine multicore parallelism (there are better options for multimachine parallelism). A very common use is to parallelize a task over a set of processes for a CPU-bound problem. You might also use it to parallelize an I/O-bound problem, but as we saw in Chapter 8, there are better tools for this (e.g., the new asyncio module in Python 3.4+ and gevent or tornado in Python 2+).

 OpenMP is a low-level interface to multiple cores—you might wonder whether to focus on it rather than multiprocessing. We introduced it with Cython and Pythran back in Chapter 7, but we don't cover it in this chapter. multiprocessing works at a higher level, sharing Python data structures, while OpenMP works with C primitive objects (e.g., integers and floats) once you've compiled to C. It only makes sense to use it if you're compiling your code; if you're not compiling (e.g., if you're using efficient numpy code and you want to run on many cores), then sticking with multiprocessing is probably the right approach.

To parallelize your task, you have to think a little differently to the normal way of writing a serial process. You must also accept that debugging a parallelized task is *harder*—often, it can be very frustrating. We'd recommend keeping the parallelism as simple as possible (even if you're not squeezing every last drop of power from your machine) so that your development velocity is kept high.

One particularly difficult topic is the sharing of state in a parallel system—it feels like it should be easy, but incurs lots of overheads and can be hard to get right. There are many use cases, each with different trade-offs, so there's definitely no one solution for everyone. In "Verifying Primes Using Interprocess Communication" on page 232 we'll go through state sharing with an eye on the synchronization costs. Avoiding shared state will make your life far easier.

In fact, an algorithm can be analyzed to see how well it'll perform in a parallel environment almost entirely by how much state must be shared. For example, if we can have multiple Python processes all solving the same problem without communicating with one another (a situation known as *embarrassingly parallel*), not much of a penalty will be incurred as we add more and more Python processes.

On the other hand, if each process needs to communicate with every other Python process, the communication overhead will slowly overwhelm the processing and slow things down. This means that as we add more and more Python processes, we can actually slow down our overall performance.

As a result, sometimes some counterintuitive algorithmic changes must be made in order to efficiently solve a problem in parallel. For example, when solving the diffusion equation (Chapter 6) in parallel, each process actually does some redundant work that another process also does. This redundancy reduces the amount of communication required and speeds up the overall calculation!

Here are some typical jobs for the multiprocessing module:

- Parallelize a CPU-bound task with Process or Pool objects.
- Parallelize an I/O-bound task in a Pool with threads using the (oddly named) dummy module.
- Share pickled work via a Queue.
- Share state between parallelized workers, including bytes, primitive datatypes, dictionaries, and lists.

If you come from a language where threads are used for CPU-bound tasks (e.g., C++ or Java), then you should know that while threads in Python are OS-native (they're not simulated, they are actual operating system threads), they are bound by the global interpreter lock (GIL), so only one thread may interact with Python objects at a time.

By using processes we run a number of Python interpreters in parallel, each with a private memory space with its own GIL, and each runs in series (so there's no competition for each GIL). This is the easiest way to speed up a CPU-bound task in Python. If we need to share state, then we need to add some communication overhead; we'll explore that in "Verifying Primes Using Interprocess Communication" on page 232.

If you work with numpy arrays, you might wonder if you can create a larger array (e.g., a large 2D matrix) and ask processes to work on segments of the array in parallel. You can, but it is hard to discover how by trial and error, so in "Sharing numpy Data with multiprocessing" on page 248 we'll work through sharing a 6.4 GB numpy array across four CPUs. Rather than sending partial copies of the data (which would at least double the working size required in RAM and create a massive communication overhead), we share the underlying bytes of the array among the processes. This is an ideal approach to sharing a large array among local workers on one machine.

 Here, we discuss multiprocessing on *nix-based machines (this chapter is written using Ubuntu; the code should run unchanged on a Mac). For Windows machines, you should check the official documentation (*http://bit.ly/multi_Windows*).

In this following chapter we'll hardcode the number of processes (NUM_PROCESSES=4) to match the four physical cores on Ian's laptop. By default, multiprocessing will use as many cores as it can see (the machine presents eight—four CPUs and four hyper-threads). Normally you'd avoid hardcoding the number of processes to create unless you were specifically managing your resources.

An Overview of the Multiprocessing Module

The multiprocessing module was introduced in Python 2.6 (*http://bit.ly/stan dard_addition*) by taking the existing pyProcessing module and folding it into Python's built-in library set. Its main components are:

Process

> A forked copy of the current process; this creates a new process identifier and the task runs as an independent child process in the operating system. You can start and query the state of the Process and provide it with a target method to run.

Pool

> Wraps the Process or threading.Thread API into a convenient pool of workers that share a chunk of work and return an aggregated result.

Queue

> A FIFO queue allowing multiple producers and consumers.

Pipe

A uni- or bidirectional communication channel between two processes.

Manager

A high-level managed interface to share Python objects between processes.

ctypes

Allows sharing of primitive datatypes (e.g., integers, floats, and bytes) between processes after they have forked.

Synchronization primitives

Locks and semaphores to synchronize control flow between processes.

 In Python 3.2, the concurrent.futures module was introduced (via PEP 3148 (*http://bit.ly/concurrent_add*)); this provides the core behavior of multiprocessing, with a simpler interface based on Java's java.util.concurrent. It is available as a backport to earlier versions of Python (*https://pypi.python.org/pypi/futures*). We don't cover it here as it isn't as flexible as multiprocessing, but we suspect that with the growing adoption of Python 3+ we'll see it replace multiprocessing over time.

In the rest of the chapter we'll introduce a set of examples to demonstrate common ways of using this module.

We'll estimate pi using a Monte Carlo approach with a Pool of processes or threads, using normal Python and numpy. This is a simple problem with well-understood complexity, so it parallelizes easily; we can also see an unexpected result from using threads with numpy. Next, we'll search for primes using the same Pool approach; we'll investigate the nonpredictable complexity of searching for primes and look at how we can efficiently (and inefficiently!) split the workload to best use our computing resources. We'll finish the primes search by switching to queues, where we introduce Process objects in place of a Pool and use a list of work and poison pills to control the lifetime of workers.

Next, we'll tackle interprocess communication (IPC) to validate a small set of possible-primes. By splitting each number's workload across multiple CPUs, we use IPC to end the search early if a factor is found so that we can significantly beat the speed of a single-CPU search process. We'll cover shared Python objects, OS primitives, and a Redis server to investigate the complexity and capability trade-offs of each approach.

We can share a 6.4 GB numpy array across four CPUs to split a large workload *without* copying data. If you have large arrays with parallelizable operations, then this technique should buy you a great speedup since you have to allocate less space in RAM and copy less data. Finally, we'll look at synchronizing access to a file and a variable (as a Value) between processes without corrupting data to illustrate how to correctly lock shared state.

 PyPy (discussed in Chapter 7) has full support for the `multiprocess` `ing` library, and the following CPython examples (though not the `numpy` examples, at the time of writing) all run far quicker using Py-Py. If you're only using CPython code (no C extensions or more complex libraries) for parallel processing, then PyPy might be a quick win for you.

This chapter (and the entire book) focuses on Linux. Linux has a forking process to create new processes by cloning the parent process. Windows lacks `fork`, so the `multi` `processing` module imposes some Windows-specific restrictions (*http://bit.ly/ multi_Windows*) that we urge you to review if you're using that platform.

Estimating Pi Using the Monte Carlo Method

We can estimate pi by throwing thousands of imaginary darts into a "dartboard" represented by a unit circle. The relationship between the number of darts falling inside the circle's edge and outside it will allow us to approximate pi.

This is an ideal first problem as we can split the total workload evenly across a number of processes, each one running on a separate CPU. Each process will end at the same time as the workload for each is equal, so we can investigate the speedups available as we add new CPUs and hyperthreads to the problem.

In Figure 9-1 we throw 10,000 darts into the unit square, and a percentage of them fall into the quarter of the unit circle that's drawn. This estimate is rather bad—10,000 dart throws does not reliably give us a three-decimal-place result. If you ran your own code you'd see this estimate vary between 3.0 and 3.2 on each run.

To be confident of the first three decimal places, we need to generate 10,000,000 random dart throws.[1] This is inefficient (and better methods for pi's estimation exist), but it is rather convenient to demonstrate the benefits of parallelization using `multiprocessing`.

With the Monte Carlo method, we use the Pythagorean theorem (*http://en.wikipe dia.org/wiki/Pythagorean_theorem*) to test if a dart has landed inside our circle:

$$\sqrt{(x^2 + y^2)} \le 1^2$$

---

1. See *http://math.missouristate.edu/assets/Math/brett.pptx*.

As we're using a unit circle, we can optimize this by removing the square root operation ($1^2 = 1$), leaving us a simplified expression to implement:

$$x^2 + y^2 \leq 1$$

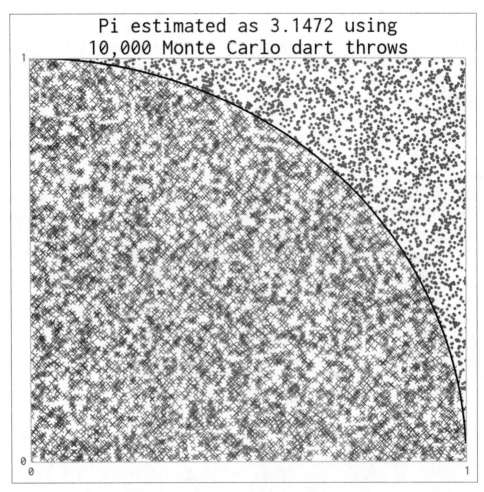

Figure 9-1. Estimating pi using the Monte Carlo method

We'll look at a loop version of this in Example 9-1. We'll implement both a normal Python version and, later, a numpy version, and we'll use both threads and processes to parallelize the problem.

Estimating Pi Using Processes and Threads

It is easier to understand a normal Python implementation, so we'll start with that in this section, using float objects in a loop. We'll parallelize this using processes to use all of our available CPUs, and we'll visualize the state of the machine as we use more CPUs.

Using Python Objects

The Python implementation is easy to follow, but it carries an overhead as each Python float object has to be managed, referenced, and synchronized in turn. This overhead slows down our runtime, but it has bought us thinking time, as the implementation was quick to put together. By parallelizing this version, we get additional speedups for very little extra work.

Figure 9-2 shows three implementations of the Python example:

- No use of multiprocessing (named "Series")
- Using threads
- Using processes

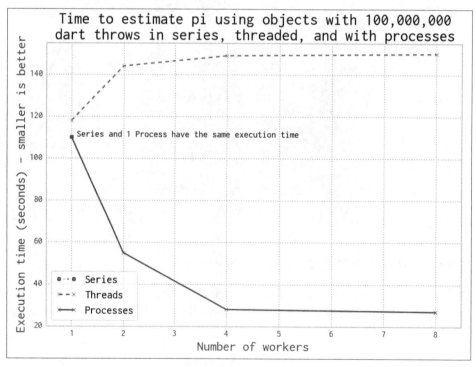

Figure 9-2. Working in series, with threads and with processes

When we use more than one thread or process, we're asking Python to calculate the same total number of dart throws and to divide the work evenly between workers. If we want 100,000,000 dart throws in total using our Python implementation and we use two workers, then we'll be asking both threads or both processes to generate 50,000,000 dart throws per worker.

Using one thread takes approximately 120 seconds. Using two or more threads takes *longer*. By using two or more processes, we make the runtime *shorter*. The cost of using no processes or threads (the series implementation) is the same as running with one process.

By using processes, we get a linear speedup when using two or four cores on Ian's laptop. For the eight-worker case we're using Intel's Hyper-Threading Technology—the laptop only has four physical cores, so we get barely any additional speedup by running eight processes.

Example 9-1 shows the Python version of our pi estimator. If we're using threads each instruction is bound by the GIL, so although each thread could run on a separate CPU, it will only execute when no other threads are running. The process version is not bound by this restriction, as each forked process has a private Python interpreter running as a single thread—there's no GIL contention as no objects are shared. We use Python's built-in random number generator, but see "Random Numbers in Parallel Systems" on page 217 for some notes about the dangers of parallelized random number sequences.

Example 9-1. Estimating pi using a loop in Python

```
def estimate_nbr_points_in_quarter_circle(nbr_estimates):
    nbr_trials_in_quarter_unit_circle = 0
    for step in xrange(int(nbr_estimates)):
        x = random.uniform(0, 1)
        y = random.uniform(0, 1)
        is_in_unit_circle = x * x + y * y <= 1.0
        nbr_trials_in_quarter_unit_circle += is_in_unit_circle

    return nbr_trials_in_quarter_unit_circle
```

Example 9-2 shows the __main__ block. Note that we build the Pool before we start the timer. Spawning threads is relatively instant; spawning processes involves a fork, and this takes a measurable fraction of a second. We ignore this overhead in Figure 9-2, as this cost will be a tiny fraction of the overall execution time.

Example 9-2. main for estimating pi using a loop

```
from multiprocessing import Pool
...

if __name__ == "__main__":
    nbr_samples_in_total = 1e8
    nbr_parallel_blocks = 4
```

```
pool = Pool(processes=nbr_parallel_blocks)
nbr_samples_per_worker = nbr_samples_in_total / nbr_parallel_blocks
print "Making {} samples per worker".format(nbr_samples_per_worker)
nbr_trials_per_process = [nbr_samples_per_worker] * nbr_parallel_blocks
t1 = time.time()
nbr_in_unit_circles = pool.map(calculate_pi, nbr_trials_per_process)
pi_estimate = sum(nbr_in_unit_circles) * 4 / nbr_samples_in_total
print "Estimated pi", pi_estimate
print "Delta:", time.time() - t1
```

We create a list containing nbr_estimates divided by the number of workers. This new argument will be sent to each worker. After execution, we'll receive the same number of results back; we'll sum these to estimate the number of darts in the unit circle.

We import the process-based Pool from multiprocessing. We could also have used from multiprocessing.dummy import Pool to get a threaded version—the "dummy" name is rather misleading (we confess to not understanding why it is named this way); it is simply a light wrapper around the threading module to present the same interface as the process-based Pool.

 It is worth noting that each process we create consumes some RAM from the system. You can expect a forked process using the standard libraries to take on the order of 10–20MB of RAM; if you're using many libraries and lots of data, then you might expect each forked copy to take hundreds of megabytes. On a system with a RAM constraint, this might be a significant issue—if you run out of RAM and the system reverts to using the disk's swap space, then any parallelization advantage will be massively lost to the slow paging of RAM back and forth to disk!

The following figures plot the average CPU utilization of Ian's laptop's four physical cores and their four associated hyperthreads (each hyperthread runs on unutilized silicon in a physical core). The data gathered for these figures *includes* the startup time of the first Python process and the cost of starting subprocesses. The CPU sampler records the entire state of the laptop, not just the CPU time used by this task.

Note that the following diagrams are created using a different timing method with a slower sampling rate than Figure 9-2, so the overall runtime is a little longer.

The execution behavior in Figure 9-3 with one process in the pool (along with the parent process) shows some overhead in the first seconds as the pool is created, and then a consistent close-to-100% CPU utilization throughout the run. With one process, we're efficiently using one core.

Next we'll add a second process, effectively saying Pool(processes=2). As you can see in Figure 9-4, adding a second process roughly halves the execution time to 56 seconds, and two CPUs are fully occupied. This is the best result we can expect—we've efficiently used all the new computing resources and we're not losing any speed to other overheads like communication, paging to disk, or contention with competing processes that want to use the same CPUs.

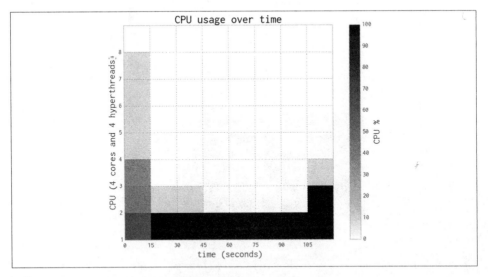

Figure 9-3. Estimating pi using Python objects and one process

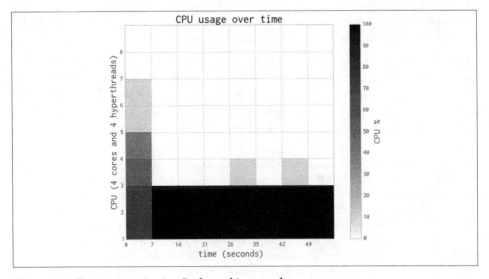

Figure 9-4. Estimating pi using Python objects and two processes

Figure 9-5 shows the results when using all four physical CPUs—now we are using all of the raw power of this laptop. Execution time is roughly a quarter that of the single-process version, at 27 seconds.

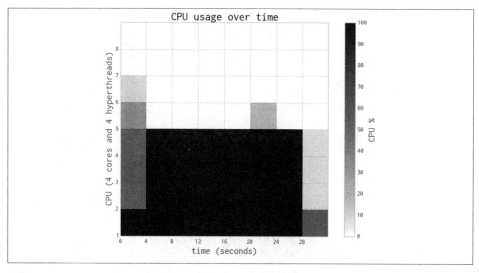

Figure 9-5. Estimating pi using Python objects and four processes

By switching to eight processes, as seen in Figure 9-6, we cannot achieve more than a tiny speedup compared to the four-process version. That is because the four hyper-threads are only able to squeeze a little extra processing power out of the spare silicon on the CPUs, and the four CPUs are already maximally utilized.

These diagrams show that we're efficiently using more of the available CPU resources at each step, and that the HyperThread resources are a poor addition. The biggest problem when using hyperthreads is that CPython is using a lot of RAM—hyperthreading is not cache-friendly, so the spare resources on each chip are very poorly utilized. As we'll see in the next section, numpy makes better use of these resources.

In our experience, hyperthreading can give up to a 30% performance gain *if* there are enough spare computing resources. This works if, for example, you have a mix of floating-point and integer arithmetic rather than just the floating-point operations we have here. By mixing the resource requirements, the hyperthreads can schedule more of the CPU's silicon to be working concurrently. Generally, we see hyperthreads as an added bonus and not a resource to be optimized against, as adding more CPUs is probably more economical than tuning your code (which adds a support overhead).

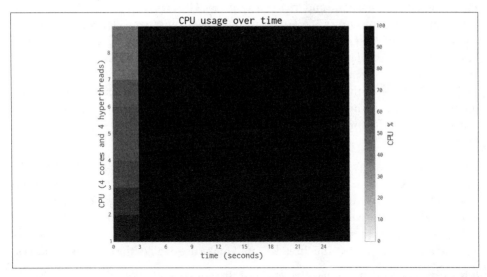

Figure 9-6. Estimating pi using Python objects and eight processes with little additional gain

Now we'll switch to using threads in one process, rather than multiple processes. As you'll see, the overhead caused by the "GIL battle" actually makes our code run *slower*.

Figure 9-7 shows two threads fighting on a dual-core system with Python 2.6 (the same effect occurs with Python 2.7)—this is the GIL battle image taken with permission from David Beazley's blog post, "The Python GIL Visualized." (*http://bit.ly/GIL_visualized*) The darker red tone shows Python threads repeatedly trying to get the GIL but failing. The lighter green tone represents a running thread. White shows the brief periods when a thread is idle. We can see that there's an overhead when adding threads to a CPU-bound task in CPython. The context-switching overhead actually adds to the overall runtime. David Beazley explains this in "Understanding the Python GIL." (*http://www.dabeaz.com/GIL/*) Threads in Python are great for I/O-bound tasks, but they're a poor choice for CPU-bound problems.

Figure 9-7. Python threads fighting on a dual-core machine

Each time a thread wakes up and tries to acquire the GIL (whether it is available or not), it uses some system resources. If one thread is busy, then the other will repeatedly awaken and try to acquire the GIL. These repeated attempts become expensive. David Beazley has an interactive set of plots (*http://bit.ly/Beazley_plots*) that demonstrate the problem; you can zoom in to see every failed attempt at GIL acquisition for multiple threads on multiple CPUs. Note that this is only a problem with multiple threads running on a multicore system—a single-core system with multiple threads has no "GIL battle." This is easily seen in the four-thread zoomable visualization (*http://bit.ly/fourthread*) on David's site.

If the threads weren't fighting for the GIL but were passing it back and forth efficiently, we wouldn't expect to see any of the dark red tone; instead, we might expect the waiting thread to carry on waiting without consuming resources. Avoiding the battle for the GIL would make the overall runtime shorter, but it would still be no faster than using a single thread, due to the GIL. If there were no GIL, each thread could run in parallel without any waiting and so the threads would make use of all of the system's resources.

It is worth noting that the negative effect of threads on CPU-bound problems is reasonably solved in Python 3.2+ (*http://docs.python.org/dev/whatsnew/3.2.html*):

> The mechanism for serializing execution of concurrently running Python threads (generally known as the GIL or Global Interpreter Lock) has been rewritten. Among the objectives were more predictable switching intervals and reduced overhead due to lock contention and the number of ensuing system calls. The notion of a "check interval" to allow thread switches has been abandoned and replaced by an absolute duration expressed in seconds.
>
> — Raymond Hettinger

Figure 9-8 shows the results of running the same code that we used in Figure 9-5, but with threads in place of processes. Although a number of CPUs are being used, they each share the workload lightly. If each thread was running without the GIL, then we'd see 100% CPU utilization on the four CPUs. Instead, each CPU is partially utilized (due to the GIL), and in addition they are running slower than we'd like due to the GIL battle.

Compare this to Figure 9-3, where one process executes the same job in approximately 120 seconds rather than 160 seconds.

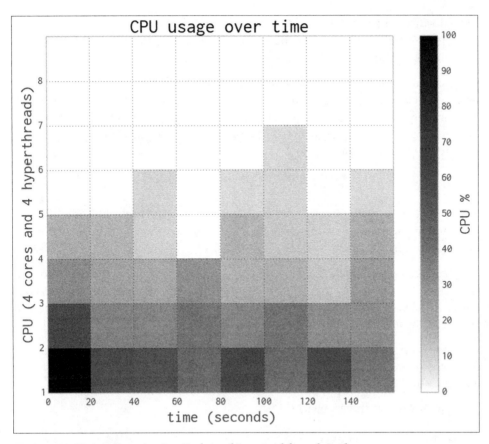

Figure 9-8. Estimating pi using Python objects and four threads

Random Numbers in Parallel Systems

Generating good random number sequences is a hard problem, and it is easy to get it wrong if you try to do it yourself. Getting a good sequence quickly in parallel is even harder—suddenly you have to worry about whether you'll get repeating or correlated sequences in the parallel processes.

We've used Python's built-in random number generator in Example 9-1, and we'll use the numpy random number generator in the next section, in Example 9-3. In both cases the random number generators are seeded in their forked process. For the Python random example the seeding is handled internally by multiprocessing—if during a fork it sees that random is in the namespace, then it'll force a call to seed the generators in each of the new processes.

In the forthcoming numpy example, we have to do this explicitly. If you forget to seed the random number sequence with numpy, then each of your forked processes will generate an identical sequence of random numbers.

If you care about the quality of the random numbers used in the parallel processes, we urge you to research this topic, as we don't discuss it here. *Probably* the numpy and Python random number generators are good enough, but if significant outcomes depend on the quality of the random sequences (e.g., for medical or financial systems), then you must read up on this area.

Using numpy

In this section we switch to using numpy. Our dart-throwing problem is ideal for numpy vectorized operations—we generate the same estimate over 50 times faster than the previous Python examples.

The main reason that numpy is faster than pure Python when solving the same problem is that it is creating and manipulating the same object types at a very low level in contiguous blocks of RAM, rather than creating many higher-level Python objects that each require individual management and addressing.

As numpy is far more cache-friendly, we'll also get a small speed boost when using the four hyperthreads. We didn't get this in the pure Python version, as caches aren't used efficiently by larger Python objects.

In Figure 9-9 we see three scenarios:

- No use of multiprocessing (named "Series")
- Using threads
- Using processes

The serial and single-worker versions execute at the same speed—there's no overhead to using threads with numpy (and with only one worker, there's also no gain).

When using multiple processes, we see a classic 100% utilization of each additional CPU. The result mirrors the plots shown in Figures 9-3, 9-4, 9-5, and 9-6, but the code obviously runs much faster using numpy.

Interestingly, the threaded version runs *faster* with more threads—this is the opposite behavior to the pure Python case, where threads made the example run slower. As discussed on the SciPy wiki (*http://wiki.scipy.org/ParallelProgramming*), by working outside of the GIL numpy can achieve some level of additional speedup around threads.

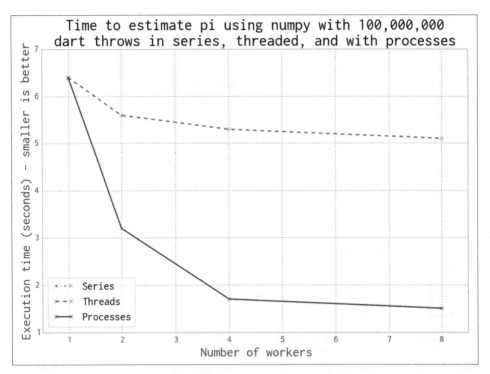

Figure 9-9. Working in series, threaded, and with processes using numpy

Using processes gives us a predictable speedup, just as it did in the pure Python example. A second CPU doubles the speed, and using four CPUs quadruples the speed.

Example 9-3 shows the vectorized form of our code. Note that the random number generator is seeded when this function is called. For the threaded version this isn't necessary, as each thread shares the same random number generator and they access it in series. For the process version, as each new process is a fork, all the forked versions will share the *same state*. This means the random number calls in each will return the same sequence! Calling seed() should ensure that each of the forked processes generates a unique sequence of random numbers. Look back at "Random Numbers in Parallel Systems" on page 217 for some notes about the dangers of parallelized random number sequences.

Example 9-3. Estimating pi using numpy

```
def estimate_nbr_points_in_quarter_circle(nbr_samples):
    # set random seed for numpy in each new process
    # else the fork will mean they all share the same state
    np.random.seed()
    xs = np.random.uniform(0, 1, nbr_samples)
    ys = np.random.uniform(0, 1, nbr_samples)
    estimate_inside_quarter_unit_circle = (xs * xs + ys * ys) <= 1
```

```
nbr_trials_in_quarter_unit_circle = np.sum(estimate_inside_quarter_unit_circle)
return nbr_trials_in_quarter_unit_circle
```

A short code analysis shows that the calls to random run a little slower on this machine when executed with multiple threads and the call to (xs * xs + ys * ys) <= 1 parallelizes well. Calls to the random number generator are GIL-bound as the internal state variable is a Python object.

The process to understand this was basic but reliable:

1. Comment out all of the numpy lines, and run with *no* threads using the serial version. Run several times and record the execution times using time.time() in __main__.

2. Add a line back (first, we added xs = np.random.uniform(...), and run several times, again recording completion times.

3. Add the next line back (now adding ys = ...), run again, and record completion time.

4. Repeat, including the nbr_trials_in_quarter_unit_circle = np.sum(...) line.

5. Repeat this process again, but this time with four threads. Repeat line by line.

6. Compare the difference in runtime at each step for no threads and four threads.

Because we're running code in parallel, it becomes harder to use tools like line_pro filer or cProfile. Recording the raw runtimes and observing the differences in behavior with different configurations takes some patience but gives solid evidence from which to draw conclusions.

 If you want to understand the serial behavior of the uniform call, take a look at the mtrand code in the numpy source (*http://bit.ly/ mtrand_code*) and follow the call to uniform in *mtrand.pyx*. This is a useful exercise if you haven't looked at the numpy source code before.

The libraries used when building numpy are important for some of the parallelization opportunities. Depending on the underlying libraries used when building numpy (e.g., whether Intel's Math Kernel Library or OpenBLAS were included or not), you'll see different speedup behavior.

You can check your numpy configuration using numpy.show_config(). There are some example timings (*http://bit.ly/BLAS_benchmarking*) on StackOverflow if you're curious about the possibilities. Only some numpy calls will benefit from parallelization by external libraries.

Finding Prime Numbers

Next, we'll look at testing for prime numbers over a large number range. This is a different problem to estimating pi, as the workload varies depending on your location in the number range and each individual number's check has an unpredictable complexity. We can create a serial routine that checks for primality and then pass sets of possible factors to each process for checking. This problem is embarrassingly parallel, which means there is no state that needs to be shared.

The multiprocessing module makes it easy to control the workload, so we shall investigate how we can tune the work queue to use (and misuse!) our computing resources and explore an easy way to use our resources slightly more efficiently. This means we'll be looking at *load balancing* to try to efficiently distribute our varying-complexity tasks to our fixed set of resources.

We'll use a slightly improved algorithm from the one earlier in the book (see "Idealized Computing Versus the Python Virtual Machine" on page 10) that exits early if we have an even number; see Example 9-4.

Example 9-4. Finding prime numbers using Python

```
def check_prime(n):
    if n % 2 == 0:
        return False
    from_i = 3
    to_i = math.sqrt(n) + 1
    for i in xrange(from_i, int(to_i), 2):
        if n % i == 0:
            return False
    return True
```

How much variety in the workload do we see when testing for a prime with this approach? Figure 9-10 shows the increasing time cost to check for primality as the possibly-prime n increases from 10,000 to 1,000,000.

Most numbers are non-prime; they're drawn with a dot. Some can be cheap to check for, while others require the checking of many factors. Primes are drawn with an x and form the thick darker band; they're the most expensive to check for. The time cost of checking a number increases as n increases, as the range of possible factors to check increases with the square root of n. The sequence of primes is not predictable, so we can't determine the expected cost of a range of numbers (we could estimate it, but we can't be sure of its complexity).

For the figure, we test each n 20 times and take the fastest result to remove jitter from the results.

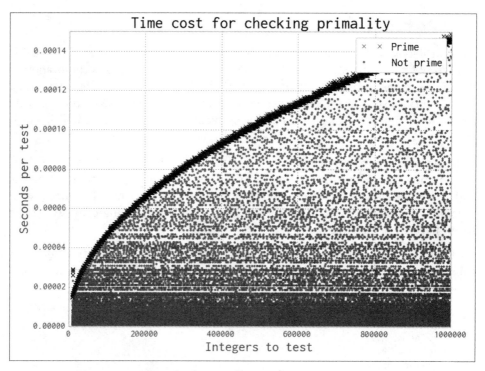

Figure 9-10. Time required to check primality as n increases

When we distribute work to a `Pool` of processes, we can specify how much work is passed to each worker. We could divide all of the work evenly and aim for one pass, or we could make many chunks of work and pass them out whenever a CPU is free. This is controlled using the `chunksize` parameter. Larger chunks of work mean less communication overhead, while smaller chunks of work mean more control over how resources are allocated.

For our prime finder, a single piece of work is a number n that is checked by `check_prime`. A `chunksize` of 10 would mean that each process handles a list of 10 integers, one list at a time.

In Figure 9-11 we can see the effect of varying the `chunksize` from 1 (every job is a single piece of work) to 64 (every job is a list of 64 numbers). Although having many tiny jobs gives us the greatest flexibility, it also imposes the greatest communication overhead. All four CPUs will be utilized efficiently, but the communication pipe will become a bottleneck as each job and result is passed through this single channel. If we double the `chunksize` to 2 our task gets solved twice as quickly, as we have less contention on the communication pipe. We might naively assume that by increasing the `chunk size` we will continue to improve the execution time. However, as you can see in the figure, we will again come to a point of diminishing returns.

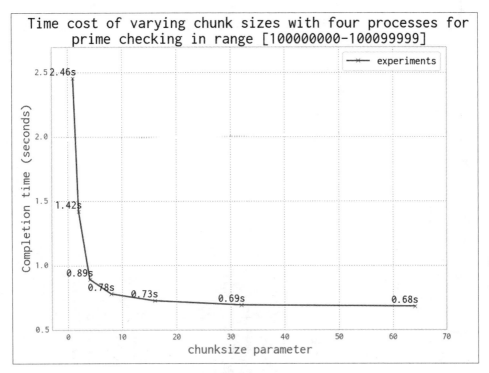

Figure 9-11. Choosing a sensible chunksize value

We can continue to increase the chunksize until we start to see a worsening of behavior. In Figure 9-12 we expand the range of chunk sizes, making them not just tiny but also huge. At the larger end of the scale the worst result shown is 1.32 seconds, where we've asked for chunksize to be 50000—this means our 100,000 items are divided into two work chunks, leaving two CPUs idle for that entire pass. With a chunksize of 10000 items, we are creating 10 chunks of work; this means that 4 chunks of work will run twice in parallel, followed by the 2 remaining chunks. This leaves two CPUs idle in the third round of work, which is an inefficient usage of resources.

An optimal solution in this case is to divide the total number of jobs by the number of CPUs. This is the default behavior in multiprocessing, shown as the "default" black dot in the figure.

As a general rule, the default behavior is sensible; only tune it if you expect to see a real gain, and definitely confirm your hypothesis against the default behavior.

Unlike the Monte Carlo pi problem, our prime testing calculation has varying complexity—sometimes a job exits quickly (an even number is detected the fastest), and sometimes the number is large and a prime (this takes a much longer time to check).

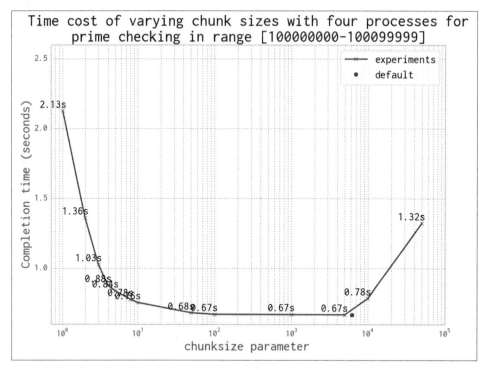

Figure 9-12. Choosing a sensible chunksize value (continued)

What happens if we randomize our job sequence? For this problem we squeeze out a 2% performance gain, as you can see in Figure 9-13. By randomizing we reduce the likelihood of the final job in the sequence taking longer than the others, leaving all but one CPU active.

As our earlier example using a `chunksize` of `10000` demonstrated, misaligning the workload with the number of available resources leads to inefficiency. In that case, we created three rounds of work: the first two rounds used 100% of the resources and the last round only 50%.

Figure 9-14 shows the odd effect that occurs when we misalign the number of chunks of work against the number of processors. Mismatches will underutilize the available resources. The slowest overall runtime occurs when only one chunk of work is created: this leaves three unutilized. Two work chunks leave two CPUs unutilized, and so on; only once we have four work chunks are we using all of our resources. But if we add a fifth work chunk, then again we're underutilizing our resources—four CPUs will work on their chunks, and then one CPU will run to calculate the fifth chunk.

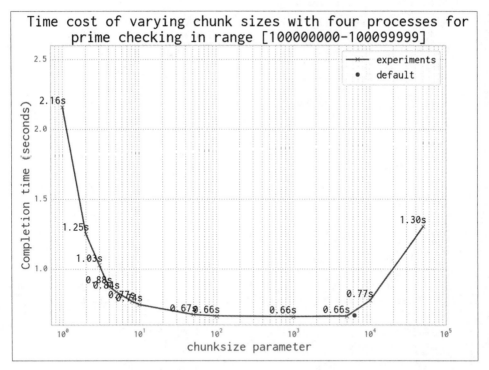

Figure 9-13. Randomizing the job sequence

As we increase the number of chunks of work, we see that the inefficiencies decrease—the difference in runtime between 29 and 32 work chunks is approximately 0.01 seconds. The general rule is to make lots of small jobs for efficient resource utilization if your jobs have varying runtimes.

Here are some strategies for efficiently using multiprocessing for embarrassingly parallel problems:

- Split your jobs into independent units of work.
- If your workers take varying amounts of time, then consider randomizing the sequence of work (another example would be for processing variable-sized files).
- Sorting your work queue so slowest jobs go first may be an equally useful strategy.
- Use the default chunksize unless you have verified reasons for adjusting it.
- Align the number of jobs with the number of physical CPUs (again, the default chunksize takes care of this for you, although it will use any hyperthreads by default, which may not offer any additional gain).

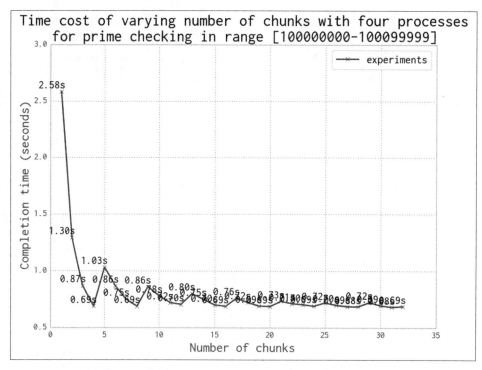

Figure 9-14. The danger of choosing an inappropriate number of chunks

Note that by default `multiprocessing` will see hyperthreads as additional CPUs. This means that on Ian's laptop it will allocate eight processes when only four will really be running at 100% speed. The additional four processes could be taking up valuable RAM while barely offering any additional speed gain.

With a `Pool`, we can split up a chunk of predefined work up front among the available CPUs. This is less helpful if we have dynamic workloads, though, and particularly if we have workloads that arrive over time. For this sort of workload we might want to use a `Queue`, introduced in the next section.

If you're working on long-running scientific problems where each job takes many seconds (or longer) to run, then you might want to review Gael Varoquaux's `joblib` (*https://pythonhosted.org/joblib/*). This tool supports lightweight pipelining; it sits on top of `multiprocessing` and offers an easier parallel interface, result caching, and debugging features.

Queues of Work

`multiprocessing.Queue` objects give us nonpersistent queues that can send any pickle-able Python objects between processes. They carry an overhead, as each object must be pickled to be sent and then unpickled in the consumer (along with some locking operations). In the following example, we'll see that this cost is not negligible. However, if your workers are processing larger jobs, then the communication overhead is probably acceptable.

Working with the queues is fairly easy. In this example, we'll check for primes by consuming a list of candidate numbers and posting confirmed primes back to a `defi nite_primes_queue`. We'll run this with one, two, four, and eight processes and confirm that all of the latter take longer than just running a single process that checks the same range.

A `Queue` gives us the ability to perform lots of interprocess communication using native Python objects. This can be useful if you're passing around objects with lots of state. Since the `Queue` lacks persistence, though, you probably don't want to use them for jobs that might require robustness in the face of failure (e.g., if you lose power or a hard drive gets corrupted).

Example 9-5 shows the `check_prime` function. We're already familiar with the basic primality test. We run in an infinite loop, blocking (waiting until work is available) on `possible_primes_queue.get()` to consume an item from the queue. Only one process can get an item at a time, as the `Queue` object takes care of synchronizing the accesses. If there's no work in the queue, then the `.get()` blocks until a task is available. When primes are found they are put back on the `definite_primes_queue` for consumption by the parent process.

Example 9-5. Using two Queues for IPC

```
FLAG_ALL_DONE = b"WORK_FINISHED"
FLAG_WORKER_FINISHED_PROCESSING = b"WORKER_FINISHED_PROCESSING"

def check_prime(possible_primes_queue, definite_primes_queue):
    while True:
        n = possible_primes_queue.get()
        if n == FLAG_ALL_DONE:
            # flag that our results have all been pushed to the results queue
            definite_primes_queue.put(FLAG_WORKER_FINISHED_PROCESSING)
            break
        else:
            if n % 2 == 0:
                continue
            for i in xrange(3, int(math.sqrt(n)) + 1, 2):
                if n % i == 0:
                    break
```

```
        else:
            definite_primes_queue.put(n)
```

We define two flags: one is fed by the parent process as a poison pill to indicate that there is no more work available, while the second is fed by the worker to confirm that it has seen the poison pill and has closed itself down. The first poison pill is also known as a *sentinel* (*http://en.wikipedia.org/wiki/Sentinel_value*), as it guarantees the termination of the processing loop.

When dealing with queues of work and remote workers it can be helpful to use flags like these to record that the poison pills were sent and to check that responses were sent from the children in a sensible time window, indicating that they are shutting down. We don't handle that process here, but adding some timekeeping is a fairly simple addition to the code. The receipt of these flags can be logged or printed during debugging.

The Queue objects are created out of a Manager in Example 9-6. We'll use the familiar process of building a list of Process objects that each contain a forked process. The two queues are sent as arguments, and multiprocessing handles their synchronization. Having started the new processes, we hand a list of jobs to the possible_primes_queue and end with one poison pill per process. The jobs will be consumed in FIFO order, leaving the poison pills for last. In check_prime we use a blocking .get(), as the new processes will have to wait for work to appear in the queue. Since we use flags, we could add some work, deal with the results, and then iterate by adding more work, and signal the end of life of the workers by adding the poison pills later.

Example 9-6. Building two Queues for IPC

```
if __name__ == "__main__":
    primes = []

    manager = multiprocessing.Manager()
    possible_primes_queue = manager.Queue()
    definite_primes_queue = manager.Queue()

    NBR_PROCESSES = 2
    pool = Pool(processes=NBR_PROCESSES)
    processes = []
    for _ in range(NBR_PROCESSES):
        p = multiprocessing.Process(target=check_prime,
                                    args=(possible_primes_queue,
                                          definite_primes_queue))
        processes.append(p)
        p.start()

    t1 = time.time()
    number_range = xrange(100000000, 101000000)

    # add jobs to the inbound work queue
    for possible_prime in number_range:
```

```
        possible_primes_queue.put(possible_prime)

    # add poison pills to stop the remote workers
    for n in xrange(NBR_PROCESSES):
        possible_primes_queue.put(FLAG_ALL_DONE)
```

To consume the results we start another infinite loop in Example 9-7, using a block-ing .get() on the definite_primes_queue. If the finished-processing flag is found, then we take a count of the number of processes that have signaled their exit. If not, then we have a new prime and we add this to the primes list. We exit the infinite loop when all of our processes have signaled their exit.

Example 9-7. Using two Queues for IPC

```
    processors_indicating_they_have_finished = 0
    while True:
        new_result = definite_primes_queue.get()  # block while waiting for results
        if new_result == FLAG_WORKER_FINISHED_PROCESSING:
            processors_indicating_they_have_finished += 1
            if processors_indicating_they_have_finished == NBR_PROCESSES:
                break
        else:
            primes.append(new_result)
    assert processors_indicating_they_have_finished == NBR_PROCESSES

    print "Took:", time.time() - t1
    print len(primes), primes[:10], primes[-10:]
```

There is quite an overhead to using a Queue, due to the pickling and synchronization. As you can see in Figure 9-15, using a Queue-less single-process solution is significantly faster than using two or more processes. The reason in this case is because our workload is very light—the communication cost dominates the overall time for this task. With Queues, two processes complete this example a little faster than one process, while four and eight processes are each slower.

If your task has a long completion time (at least a sizable fraction of a second) with a small amount of communication, then a Queue approach might be the right answer. You will have to verify whether the communication cost makes this approach useful enough.

You might wonder what happens if we remove the redundant half of the job queue (all the even numbers—these are rejected very quickly in check_prime). Halving the size of the input queue halves our execution time in each case, but it still doesn't beat the single-process non-Queue example! This helps to illustrate that the communication cost is the dominating factor in this problem.

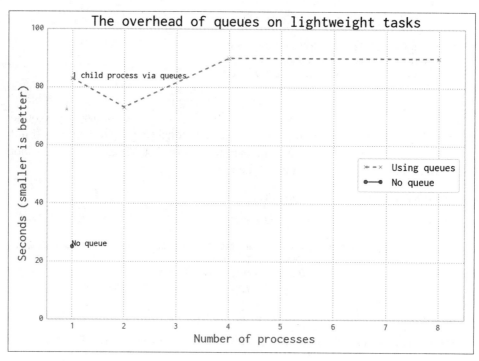

Figure 9-15. Cost of using Queue objects

Asynchronously adding jobs to the Queue

By adding a Thread into the main process, we can feed jobs asynchronously into the possible_primes_queue. In Example 9-8 we define a feed_new_jobs function: it performs the same job as the job setup routine that we had in __main__ before, but it does it in a separate thread.

Example 9-8. Asynchronous job feeding function

```
def feed_new_jobs(number_range, possible_primes_queue, nbr_poison_pills):
    for possible_prime in number_range:
        possible_primes_queue.put(possible_prime)
    # add poison pills to stop the remote workers
    for n in xrange(nbr_poison_pills):
        possible_primes_queue.put(FLAG_ALL_DONE)
```

Now, in Example 9-9, our __main__ will set up the Thread using the possi ble_primes_queue and then move on to the result-collection phase *before* any work has been issued. The asynchronous job feeder could consume work from external sources (e.g., from a database or I/O-bound communication) while the __main__ thread handles each processed result. This means that the input sequence and output sequence do not need to be created in advance; they can both be handled on the fly.

Example 9-9. Using a thread to set up an asynchronous job feeder

```
if __name__ == "__main__":
    primes = []
    manager = multiprocessing.Manager()
    possible_primes_queue = manager.Queue()

    ...

    import threading
    thrd = threading.Thread(target=feed_new_jobs,
                            args=(number_range,
                                  possible_primes_queue,
                                  NBR_PROCESSES))
    thrd.start()

    # deal with the results
```

If you want robust asynchronous systems, you should almost certainly look to an external library that is mature. `gevent`, `tornado`, and `Twisted` are strong candidates, and Python 3.4's `tulip` is a new contender. The examples we've looked at here will get you started, but pragmatically they are more useful for very simple systems and education than for production systems.

 Another single-machine queue you might want to investigate is PyRes (*https://github.com/binarydud/pyres*). This module uses Redis (introduced in "Using Redis as a Flag" on page 241) to store the queue's state. Redis is a non-Python data storage system, which means a queue of data held in Redis is readable outside of Python (so you can inspect the queue's state) and can be shared with non-Python systems.

Be *very aware* that asynchronous systems require a special level of patience—you will end up tearing out your hair while you are debugging. We'd suggest:

- Applying the "Keep It Simple, Stupid" principle
- Avoiding asynchronous self-contained systems (like our example) if possible, as they will grow in complexity and quickly become hard to maintain
- Using mature libraries like `gevent` (described in the previous chapter) that give you tried-and-tested approaches to dealing with certain problem sets

Furthermore, we strongly suggest using an external queue system (e.g., Gearman, 0MQ, Celery, PyRes, or HotQueue) that gives you external visibility on the state of the queues. This requires more thought, but is likely to save you time due to increased debug efficiency and better system visibility for production systems.

Verifying Primes Using Interprocess Communication

Prime numbers are numbers that have no factor other than themselves and 1. It stands to reason that the most common factor is 2 (every even number cannot be a prime). After that, the low prime numbers (e.g., 3, 5, 7) become common factors of larger non-primes (e.g., 9, 15, 21, respectively).

Let's say that we're given a large number and we're asked to verify if it is prime. We will probably have a large space of factors to search. Figure 9-16 shows the frequency of each factor for non-primes up to 10,000,000. Low factors are far more likely to occur than high factors, but there's no predictable pattern.

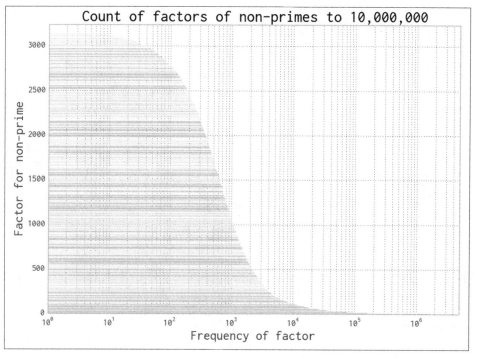

Figure 9-16. The frequency of factors of non-primes

Let's define a new problem—suppose we have a *small* set of numbers and our task is to efficiently use our CPU resources to figure out if each number is a prime, one number at a time. Possibly we'll have just one large number to test. It no longer makes sense to use one CPU to do the check; we want to coordinate the work across many CPUs.

For this section we'll look at some larger numbers, one with 15 digits and four with 18 digits:

- Small non-prime: 112272535095295
- Large non-prime 1: 00109100129100369
- Large non-prime 2: 100109100129101027
- Prime 1: 100109100129100151
- Prime 2: 100109100129162907

By using a smaller non-prime and some larger non-primes, we get to verify that our chosen process is not just faster at checking for primes but also is not getting slower at checking non-primes. We'll assume that we don't know the size or type of numbers that we're being given, so we want the fastest possible result for all our use cases.

Cooperation comes at a cost—the cost of synchronizing data and checking the shared data can be quite high. We'll work through several approaches here that can be used in different ways for task coordination. Note that we're *not* covering the somewhat specialized message passing interface (MPI) here; we're looking at batteries-included modules and Redis (which is very common).

If you want to use MPI, we assume you already know what you're doing. The MPI4PY (*http://bit.ly/MPI4PY_proj*) project would be a good place to start. It is an ideal technology if you want to control latency when lots of processes are collaborating, whether you have one or many machines.

For the following runs, each test is performed 20 times and the minimum time is taken to show the fastest speed that is possible for that method. In these examples we're using various techniques to share a flag (often as 1 byte). We could use a basic object like a Lock, but then we'd only be able to share 1 bit of state. We're choosing to show you how to share a primitive type so that more expressive state sharing is possible (even though we don't need a more expressive state for this example).

We must emphasize that sharing state tends to make things *complicated*—you can easily end up in another hair-pulling state. Be careful and try to keep things as simple as they can be. It might be the case that less efficient resource usage is trumped by developer time spent on other challenges.

First we'll discuss the results and then we'll work through the code.

Figure 9-17 shows the first approaches to trying to use interprocess communication to test for primality faster. The benchmark is the Serial version, which does not use any interprocess communication; each attempt to speed up our code must at least be faster than this.

The Less Naive Pool version has a predictable (and good) speed. It is good enough to be rather hard to beat. Don't overlook the obvious in your search for high-speed solutions—sometimes a dumb and good-enough solution is all you need.

The approach for the Less Naive Pool solution is to take our number under test, divide its possible-factor range evenly among the available CPUs, and then push the work out to each CPU. If any CPU finds a factor, it will exit early, but it won't communicate this fact; the other CPUs will continue to work through their part of the range. This means for an 18-digit number (our four larger examples), the search time is the same whether it is prime or non-prime.

The Redis and Manager solutions are slower when it comes to testing a larger number of factors for primality due to the communication overhead. They use a shared flag to indicate that a factor has been found and the search should be called off.

Redis lets you share state not just with other Python processes, but also with other tools and other machines, and even to expose that state over a web-browser interface (which might be useful for remote monitoring). The Manager is a part of `multiprocessing`; it provides a high-level synchronized set of Python objects (including primitives, the `list`, and the `dict`).

For the larger non-prime cases, although there is a cost to checking the shared flag, this is dwarfed by the saving in search time made by signaling early that a factor has been found.

For the prime cases, though, there is no way to exit early as no factor will be found, so the cost of checking the shared flag will become the dominating cost.

Figure 9-18 shows that we can get a considerably faster result with a bit of effort. The Less Naive Pool result is still our benchmark, but the RawValue and MMap (memory-map) results are much faster than the previous Redis and Manager results. The real magic comes by taking the fastest solution and performing some less-obvious code manipulations to make a near-optimal MMap solution—this final version is faster than the Less Naive Pool solution for non-primes and almost as fast as it for primes.

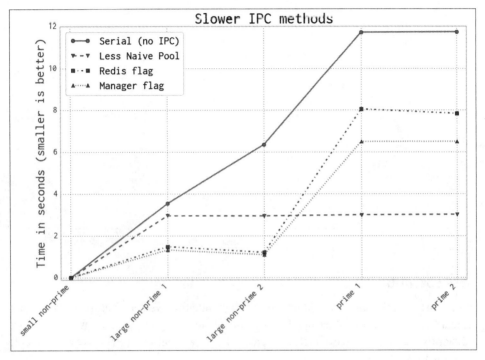

Figure 9-17. The slower ways to use IPC to validate primality

In the following sections, we'll work through various ways of using IPC in Python to solve our cooperative search problem. We hope you'll see that IPC is fairly easy, but generally comes with a cost.

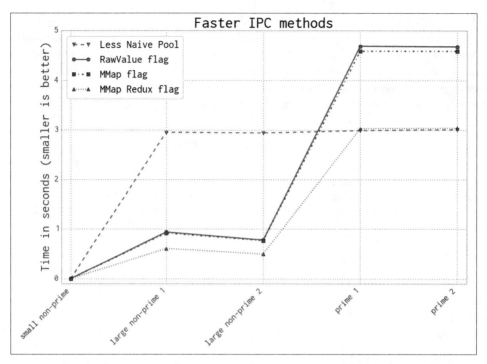

Figure 9-18. The faster ways to use IPC to validate primality

Serial Solution

We'll start with the same serial factor-checking code that we used before, shown again in Example 9-10. As noted earlier, for any non-prime with a large factor, we could more efficiently search the space of factors in parallel. Still, a serial sweep will give us a sensible baseline to work from.

Example 9-10. Serial verification

```
def check_prime(n):
    if n % 2 == 0:
        return False
    from_i = 3
    to_i = math.sqrt(n) + 1
    for i in xrange(from_i, int(to_i), 2):
        if n % i == 0:
            return False
    return True
```

Naive Pool Solution

The Naive Pool solution works with a `multiprocessing.Pool`, similar to what we saw in "Finding Prime Numbers" on page 221 and "Estimating Pi Using Processes and

Threads" on page 210 with four forked processes. We have a number to test for primality, and we divide the range of possible factors into four tuples of subranges and send these into the Pool.

In Example 9-11 we use a new method, create_range.create (which we won't show —it's quite boring), that splits the work space into equal-sized regions, where each item in ranges_to_check is a pair of lower and upper bounds to search between. For the first 18-digit non-prime (100109100129100369), with four processes we'll have the factor ranges ranges_to_check == [(3, 79100057), (79100057, 158200111), (158200111, 237300165), (237300165, 316400222)] (where 316400222 is the square root of 100109100129100369 plus one). In __main__ we first establish a Pool; check_prime then splits the ranges_to_check for each possibly-prime number n via a map. If the result is False, then we have found a factor and we do not have a prime.

Example 9-11. Naive Pool solution

```
def check_prime(n, pool, nbr_processes):
    from_i = 3
    to_i = int(math.sqrt(n)) + 1
    ranges_to_check = create_range.create(from_i, to_i, nbr_processes)
    ranges_to_check = zip(len(ranges_to_check) * [n], ranges_to_check)
    assert len(ranges_to_check) == nbr_processes
    results = pool.map(check_prime_in_range, ranges_to_check)
    if False in results:
        return False
    return True

if __name__ == "__main__":
    NBR_PROCESSES = 4
    pool = Pool(processes=NBR_PROCESSES)
    ...
```

We modify the previous check_prime in Example 9-12 to take a lower and upper bound for the range to check. There's no value in passing a complete list of possible factors to check, so we save time and memory by passing just two numbers that define our range.

Example 9-12. check_prime_in_range

```
def check_prime_in_range((n, (from_i, to_i))):
    if n % 2 == 0:
        return False
    assert from_i % 2 != 0
    for i in xrange(from_i, int(to_i), 2):
        if n % i == 0:
            return False
    return True
```

For the "small non-prime" case the verification time via the Pool is 0.1 seconds, a significantly longer time than the original 0.000002 seconds in the Serial solution. Despite this one worse result, the overall result is a speedup across the board. We might accept that one slower result isn't a problem—but what if we might get lots of smaller non-primes to check? It turns out we can avoid this slowdown; we'll see that next with the Less Naive Pool solution.

A Less Naive Pool Solution

The previous solution was inefficient at validating the smaller non-prime. For any smaller (less than 18 digits) non-prime it is likely to be slower than the serial method, due to the overhead of sending out partitioned work and not knowing if a very small factor (which are the more likely factors) will be found. If a small factor is found, then the process will still have to wait for the other larger factor searches to complete.

We could start to signal between the processes that a small factor has been found, but since this happens so frequently, it will add a lot of communication overhead. The solution presented in Example 9-13 is a more pragmatic approach—a serial check is performed quickly for likely small factors, and if none are found, then a parallel search is started. Combining a serial precheck before launching a relatively more expensive parallel operation is a common approach to avoiding some of the costs of parallel computing.

Example 9-13. Improving the Naive Pool solution for the small-non-prime case

```
def check_prime(n, pool, nbr_processes):
    # cheaply check high-probability set of possible factors
    from_i = 3
    to_i = 21
    if not check_prime_in_range((n, (from_i, to_i))):
        return False

    # continue to check for larger factors in parallel
    from_i = to_i
    to_i = int(math.sqrt(n)) + 1
    ranges_to_check = create_range.create(from_i, to_i, nbr_processes)
    ranges_to_check = zip(len(ranges_to_check) * [n], ranges_to_check)
    assert len(ranges_to_check) == nbr_processes
    results = pool.map(check_prime_in_range, ranges_to_check)
    if False in results:
        return False
    return True
```

The speed of this solution is equal to or better than that of the original serial search for each of our test numbers. This is our new benchmark.

Importantly, this Pool approach gives us an optimal case for the prime-checking situation. If we have a prime, then there's no way to exit early; we have to manually check all possible factors before we can exit.

There's no faster way to check though these factors: any approach that adds complexity will have more instructions, so the check-all-factors case will cause the most instructions to be executed. See the various mmap solutions covered later for a discussion on how to get as close to this current result for primes as possible.

Using Manager.Value as a Flag

The multiprocessing.Manager() lets us share higher-level Python objects between processes as managed shared objects; the lower-level objects are wrapped in proxy objects. The wrapping and safety has a speed cost but also offers great flexibility. You can share both lower-level objects (e.g., integers and floats) and lists and dictionaries.

In Example 9-14 we create a Manager and then create a 1-byte (character) manager.Value(b"c", FLAG_CLEAR) flag. You could create any of the ctypes primitives (which are the same as the array.array primitives) if you wanted to share strings or numbers.

Note that FLAG_CLEAR and FLAG_SET are assigned a byte (b'0' and b'1', respectively). We chose to use the leading b to be very explicit (it might default to a Unicode or string object if left as an implicit string, depending on your environment and Python version).

Now we can flag across all of our processes that a factor has been found, so the search can be called off early. The difficulty is balancing the cost of reading the flag against the speed saving that is possible. Because the flag is synchronized, we don't want to check it too frequently—this adds more overhead.

Example 9-14. Passing a Manager.Value object as a flag

```
SERIAL_CHECK_CUTOFF = 21
CHECK_EVERY = 1000
FLAG_CLEAR = b'0'
FLAG_SET = b'1'
print "CHECK_EVERY", CHECK_EVERY

if __name__ == "__main__":
    NBR_PROCESSES = 4
    manager = multiprocessing.Manager()
    value = manager.Value(b'c', FLAG_CLEAR)  # 1-byte character
    ...
```

check_prime_in_range will now be aware of the shared flag, and the routine will be checking to see if a prime has been spotted by another process. Even though we've yet to begin the parallel search, we must clear the flag as shown in Example 9-15 before we start the serial check. Having completed the serial check, if we haven't found a factor, then we know that the flag must still be false.

Example 9-15. Clearing the flag with a Manager.Value

```
def check_prime(n, pool, nbr_processes, value):
    # cheaply check high-probability set of possible factors
    from_i = 3
    to_i = SERIAL_CHECK_CUTOFF
    value.value = FLAG_CLEAR
    if not check_prime_in_range((n, (from_i, to_i), value)):
        return False

    from_i = to_i
    ...
```

How frequently should we check the shared flag? Each check has a cost, both because we're adding more instructions to our tight inner loop and because checking requires a lock to be made on the shared variable, which adds more cost. The solution we've chosen is to check the flag every 1,000 iterations. Every time we check we look to see if value.value has been set to FLAG_SET, and if so, we exit the search. If in the search the process finds a factor, then it sets value.value = FLAG_SET and exits (see Example 9-16).

Example 9-16. Passing a Manager.Value object as a flag

```
def check_prime_in_range((n, (from_i, to_i), value)):
    if n % 2 == 0:
        return False
    assert from_i % 2 != 0
    check_every = CHECK_EVERY
    for i in xrange(from_i, int(to_i), 2):
        check_every -= 1
        if not check_every:
            if value.value == FLAG_SET:
                return False
            check_every = CHECK_EVERY

        if n % i == 0:
            value.value = FLAG_SET
            return False
    return True
```

The 1,000-iteration check in this code is performed using a check_every local counter. It turns out that this approach, although readable, is suboptimal for speed. By the end of this section we'll replace it with a less readable but significantly faster approach.

You might be curious about the total number of times we check for the shared flag. In the case of the two large primes, with four processes we check for the flag 316,405 times (we check it this many times in all of the following examples). Since each check has an overhead due to locking, this cost really adds up.

Using Redis as a Flag

Redis is a key/value in-memory storage engine. It provides its own locking and each operation is atomic, so we don't have to worry about using locks from inside Python (or from any other interfacing language).

By using Redis we make the data storage language-agnostic—any language or tool with an interface to Redis can share data in a compatible way. You could share data between Python, Ruby, C++, and PHP equally easily. You can share data on the local machine or over a network; to share to other machines all you need to do is change the Redis default of sharing only on localhost.

Redis lets you store:

- Lists of strings
- Sets of strings
- Sorted sets of strings
- Hashes of strings

Redis stores everything in RAM and snapshots to disk (optionally using journaling) and supports master/slave replication to a cluster of instances. One possibility with Redis is to use it to share a workload across a cluster, where other machines read and write state and Redis acts as a fast centralized data repository.

We can read and write a flag as a text string (all values in Redis are strings) in just the same way as we have been using Python flags previously. We create a StrictRedis interface as a global object, which talks to the external Redis server. We could create a new connection inside check_prime_in_range, but this is slower and can exhaust the limited number of Redis handles that are available.

We talk to the Redis server using a dictionary-like access. We can set a value using rds[SOME_KEY] = SOME_VALUE and read the string back using rds[SOME_KEY].

Example 9-17 is very similar to the previous Manager example—we're using Redis as a substitute for the local Manager. It comes with a similar access cost. You should note that Redis supports other (more complex) data structures; it is a powerful storage engine that we're using just to share a flag for this example. We encourage you to familiarize yourself with its features.

Example 9-17. Using an external Redis server for our flag

```
FLAG_NAME = b'redis_primes_flag'
FLAG_CLEAR = b'0'
FLAG_SET = b'1'

rds = redis.StrictRedis()
```

```
def check_prime_in_range((n, (from_i, to_i))):
    if n % 2 == 0:
        return False
    assert from_i % 2 != 0
    check_every = CHECK_EVERY
    for i in xrange(from_i, int(to_i), 2):
        check_every -= 1
        if not check_every:
            flag = rds[FLAG_NAME]
            if flag == FLAG_SET:
                return False
            check_every = CHECK_EVERY

        if n % i == 0:
            rds[FLAG_NAME] = FLAG_SET
            return False
    return True


def check_prime(n, pool, nbr_processes):
    # cheaply check high-probability set of possible factors
    from_i = 3
    to_i = SERIAL_CHECK_CUTOFF
    rds[FLAG_NAME] = FLAG_CLEAR
    if not check_prime_in_range((n, (from_i, to_i))):
        return False


    ...
    if False in results:
        return False
    return True
```

To confirm that the data is stored outside of these Python instances, we can invoke `redis-cli` at the command line, as in Example 9-18, and get the value stored in the key `redis_primes_flag`. You'll note that the returned item is a string (not an integer). All values returned from Redis are strings, so if you want to manipulate them in Python, you'll have to convert them to an appropriate datatype first.

Example 9-18. redis-cli example

```
$ redis-cli
redis 127.0.0.1:6379> GET "redis_primes_flag"
"0"
```

One powerful argument in favor of the use of Redis for data sharing is that it lives outside of the Python world—non-Python developers on your team will understand it, and many tools exist for it. They'll be able to look at its state while reading (but not necessarily running and debugging) your code and follow what's happening. From a team-velocity perspective this might be a big win for you, despite the communication overhead of using Redis. Whilst Redis is an additional dependency on your project, you should note that it is a very commonly deployed tool, and is well debugged and well understood. Consider it a powerful tool to add to your armory.

Redis has many configuration options. By default it uses a TCP interface (that's what we're using), although the benchmark documentation notes that sockets might be much faster. It also states that while TCP/IP lets you share data over a network between different types of OS, other configuration options are likely to be faster (but also to limit your communication options):

> When the server and client benchmark programs run on the same box, both the TCP/IP loopback and unix domain sockets can be used. It depends on the platform, but unix domain sockets can achieve around 50% more throughput than the TCP/IP loopback (on Linux for instance). The default behavior of redis-benchmark is to use the TCP/IP loopback. The performance benefit of unix domain sockets compared to TCP/IP loopback tends to decrease when pipelining is heavily used (i.e. long pipelines).
>
> — Redis documentation (*http://redis.io/topics/benchmarks*)

Using RawValue as a Flag

`multiprocessing.RawValue` is a thin wrapper around a `ctypes` block of bytes. It lacks synchronization primitives, so there's little to get in our way in our search for the fastest way to set a flag between processes. It will be almost as fast as the following `mmap` example (it is only slower because a few more instructions get in the way).

Again, we could use any `ctypes` primitive; there's also a `RawArray` option for sharing an array of primitive objects (which will behave similarly to `array.array`). `RawValue` avoids any locking—it is faster to use, but you don't get atomic operations.

Generally, if you avoid the synchronization that Python provides during IPC, you'll come unstuck (once again, back to that pulling-your-hair-out situation). *However*, in this problem it doesn't matter if one or more processes set the flag at the same time— the flag only gets switched in one direction, and every other time it is read it is just to learn if the search can be called off.

Because we never reset the state of the flag during the parallel search, we don't need synchronization. Be aware that this may not apply to your problem. If you avoid synchronization, please make sure you are doing it for the right reasons.

If you want to do things like update a shared counter, look at the documentation for the `Value` and use a context manager with `value.get_lock()` (*http://bit.ly/value_doc*), as the implicit locking on a `Value` doesn't allow for atomic operations.

This example looks very similar to the previous `Manager` example. The only difference is that in Example 9-19 we create the `RawValue` as a 1-character (byte) flag.

Example 9-19. Creating and passing a RawValue

```
if __name__ == "__main__":
    NBR_PROCESSES = 4
    value = multiprocessing.RawValue(b'c', FLAG_CLEAR)  # 1-byte character
    pool = Pool(processes=NBR_PROCESSES)
    ...
```

The flexibility to use managed and raw values is a benefit of the clean design for data sharing in multiprocessing.

Using mmap as a Flag

Finally, we get to the fastest way of sharing bytes. Example 9-20 shows a memory-mapped (shared memory) solution using the mmap module. The bytes in a shared memory block are not synchronized, and they come with very little overhead. They act like a file—in this case, they are a block of memory with a file-like interface. We have to seek to a location and read or write sequentially. Typically mmap is used to give a short (memory-mapped) view into a larger file, but in our case, rather than specifying a file number as the first argument, we instead pass -1 to indicate that we want an anonymous block of memory. We could also specify whether we want read-only or write-only access (we want both, which is the default).

Example 9-20. Using a shared memory flag via mmap

```
sh_mem = mmap.mmap(-1, 1)  # memory map 1 byte as a flag


def check_prime_in_range((n, (from_i, to_i))):
    if n % 2 == 0:
        return False
    assert from_i % 2 != 0
    check_every = CHECK_EVERY
    for i in xrange(from_i, int(to_i), 2):
        check_every -= 1
        if not check_every:
            sh_mem.seek(0)
            flag = sh_mem.read_byte()
            if flag == FLAG_SET:
                return False
            check_every = CHECK_EVERY

        if n % i == 0:
            sh_mem.seek(0)
            sh_mem.write_byte(FLAG_SET)
            return False
    return True


def check_prime(n, pool, nbr_processes):
```

```
# cheaply check high-probability set of possible factors
from_i = 3
to_i = SERIAL_CHECK_CUTOFF
sh_mem.seek(0)
sh_mem.write_byte(FLAG_CLEAR)
if not check_prime_in_range((n, (from_i, to_i))):
    return False


...

if False in results:
    return False
return True
```

mmap supports a number of methods that can be used to move around in the file that it represents (including find, readline, and write). We are using it in the most basic way —we seek to the start of the memory block before each read or write and, since we're sharing just 1 byte, we use read_byte and write_byte to be explict.

There is no Python overhead for locking and no interpretation of the data; we're dealing with bytes directly with the operating system, so this is our fastest communication method.

Using mmap as a Flag Redux

While the previous mmap result was the best overall, we couldn't help but think that we should be able to get back to the Naive Pool result for the most expensive case of having primes. The goal is to accept that there is no early exit from the inner loop and to minimize the cost of anything extraneous.

This section presents a slightly more complex solution. The same changes can be made to the other flag-based approaches we've seen, although this mmap result will still be fastest.

In our previous examples, we've used CHECK_EVERY. This means we have the check_next local variable to track, decrement, and use in Boolean tests—and each operation adds a bit of extra time to every iteration. In the case of validating a large prime, this extra management overhead occurs over 300,000 times.

The first optimization, shown in Example 9-21, is to realize that we can replace the decremented counter with a look-ahead value, and then we only have to do a Boolean comparison on the inner loop. This removes a decrement, which, due to Python's interpreted style, is quite slow. This optimization works in this test in CPython 2.7, but it is unlikely to offer any benefit in a smarter compiler (e.g., PyPy or Cython). This step saved 0.7 seconds when checking one of our large primes.

Example 9-21. Starting to optimize away our expensive logic

```
def check_prime_in_range((n, (from_i, to_i))):
    if n % 2 == 0:
        return False
    assert from_i % 2 != 0
    check_next = from_i + CHECK_EVERY
    for i in xrange(from_i, int(to_i), 2):
        if check_next == i:
            sh_mem.seek(0)
            flag = sh_mem.read_byte()
            if flag == FLAG_SET:
                return False
            check_next += CHECK_EVERY

        if n % i == 0:
            sh_mem.seek(0)
            sh_mem.write_byte(FLAG_SET)
            return False
    return True
```

We can also entirely replace the logic that the counter represents, as shown in Example 9-22, by unrolling our loop into a two-stage process. First, the outer loop covers the expected range, but in steps, on CHECK_EVERY. Second, a new inner loop replaces the check_every logic—it checks the local range of factors and then finishes. This is equivalent to the if not check_every: test. We follow this with the previous sh_mem logic to check the early-exit flag.

Example 9-22. Optimizing away our expensive logic

```
def check_prime_in_range((n, (from_i, to_i))):
    if n % 2 == 0:
        return False
    assert from_i % 2 != 0
    for outer_counter in xrange(from_i, int(to_i), CHECK_EVERY):
        upper_bound = min(int(to_i), outer_counter + CHECK_EVERY)
        for i in xrange(outer_counter, upper_bound, 2):
            if n % i == 0:
                sh_mem.seek(0)
                sh_mem.write_byte(FLAG_SET)
                return False
        sh_mem.seek(0)
        flag = sh_mem.read_byte()
        if flag == FLAG_SET:
            return False
    return True
```

The speed impact is dramatic. Our non-prime case improves even further, but more importantly, our prime-checking case is very nearly as fast as the Less Naive Pool version (it is now just 0.05 seconds slower). Given that we're doing a lot of extra work with interprocess communication, this is a very interesting result. Do note, though, that it is specific to CPython and unlikely to offer any gains when run through a compiler.

We can go even further (but frankly, this is a bit foolish). Lookups for variables that aren't declared in the local scope are a little expensive. We can create local references to the global FLAG_SET and the frequently used .seek() and .read_byte() methods to avoid their more expensive lookups. The resulting code (Example 9-23) is even less readable than before, though, and we really recommend that you *do not do this*. This final result is 1.5% slower than the Less Naive Pool version when checking the larger primes. Given that we're 4.8x faster for the non-prime cases, we've probably taken this example about as far as it can (and should!) go.

Example 9-23. Breaking the "don't hurt team velocity" rule to eke out an extra speedup

```
def check_prime_in_range((n, (from_i, to_i))):
    if n % 2 == 0:
        return False
    assert from_i % 2 != 0
    FLAG_SET_LOCAL = FLAG_SET
    sh_seek = sh_mem.seek
    sh_read_byte = sh_mem.read_byte
    for outer_counter in xrange(from_i, int(to_i), CHECK_EVERY):
        upper_bound = min(int(to_i), outer_counter + CHECK_EVERY)
        for i in xrange(outer_counter, upper_bound, 2):
            if n % i == 0:
                sh_seek(0)
                sh_mem.write_byte(FLAG_SET)
                return False
        sh_seek(0)
        if sh_read_byte() == FLAG_SET_LOCAL:
            return False
    return True
```

This behavior, with manual loop unrolling and creating local references to global objects, is foolish. Overall, it is bound to lower team velocity by making the code harder to understand, and really this is the job of a compiler (e.g., a JIT compiler like PyPy or a static compiler like Cython).

Humans shouldn't be doing this sort of manipulation, because it'll be very brittle. We haven't tested this optimization approach in Python 3+, and we don't want to—we don't really expect that these incremental improvements will work in another version of Python (and certainly not in a different implementation, like PyPy or IronPython).

We're showing you so you know that it *might* be possible, and warning you that to keep your sanity you really should let compilers take care of this sort of work for you.

Sharing numpy Data with multiprocessing

When working with large numpy arrays, you're bound to wonder if you can share the data for read and write access, without a copy, between processes. It is possible, though a little fiddly. We'd like to acknowledge StackOverflow user *pv* for the inspiration for this demo.[2]

Do not use this method to re-create the behaviors of BLAS, MKL, Accelerate, and ATLAS. These libraries all have multithreading support in their primitives, and it is likely that they are better-debugged than any new routine that you create. They can require some configuration to enable multithreading support, but it would be wise to see if these libraries can give you free speedups before you invest time (and lose time to debugging!) writing your own.

Sharing a large matrix between processes has several benefits:

- Only one copy means no wasted RAM.
- No time is wasted copying large blocks of RAM.
- You gain the possibility of sharing partial results between the processes.

Thinking back to the pi estimation demo using numpy in "Using numpy" on page 218, we had the problem that the random number generation was a serial process. Here we can imagine forking processes that share one large array, each one using a differently seeded random number generator to fill in a section of the array with random numbers, and therefore completing the generation of a large random block faster than is possible with a single process.

To verify this, we modified the forthcoming demo to create a large random matrix (10,000 by 80,000 elements) as a serial process and by splitting the matrix into four segments where random is called in parallel (in both cases, one row at a time). The serial process took 15 seconds, and the parallel version took 4 seconds. Refer back to "Random Numbers in Parallel Systems" on page 217 to understand some of the dangers of parallelized random number generation.

For the rest of this section we'll use a simplified demo that illustrates the point while remaining easy to verify.

In Figure 9-19 you can see the output from htop on Ian's laptop. It shows four child processes of the parent (with PID 11268), where all five processes are sharing a single

---

2. See the Stack Overflow topic (*http://bit.ly/Python_multiprocessing*).

10,000 × 80,000-element numpy array of doubles. One copy of this array costs 6.4 GB, and the laptop only has 8 GB—you can see in htop by the process meters that the Mem reading shows a maximum of 7,941 MB RAM.

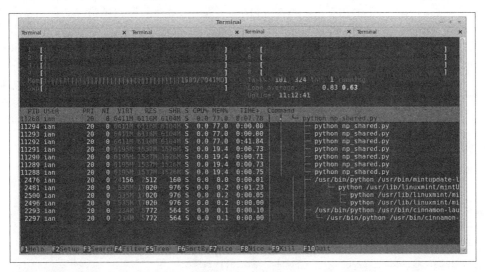

Figure 9-19. htop showing RAM and swap usage

To understand this demo, we'll first walk through the console output, and then we'll look at the code. In Example 9-24, we start the parent process: it allocates a 6.4 GB double array of dimensions 10,000 × 80,000, filled with the value zero. The 10,000 rows will be passed out as indices to the worker function, and the worker will operate on each column of 80,000 items in turn. Having allocated the array, we fill it with the answer to life, the universe, and everything (42!). We can test in the worker function that we're receiving this modified array and not a filled-with-0s version to confirm that this code is behaving as expected.

Example 9-24. Setting up the shared array

```
$ python np_shared.py
Created shared array with 6,400,000,000 nbytes
Shared array id is 20255664 in PID 11268
Starting with an array of 0 values:
[[ 0.  0.  0. ...,  0.  0.  0.]
 ...,
 [ 0.  0.  0. ...,  0.  0.  0.]]

Original array filled with value 42:
[[ 42.  42.  42. ...,  42.  42.  42.]
 ...,
 [ 42.  42.  42. ...,  42.  42.  42.]]
Press a key to start workers using multiprocessing...
```

In Example 9-25, we've started four processes working on this shared array. No copy of the array was made; each process is looking at the same large block of memory and each process has a different set of indices to work from. Every few thousand lines the worker outputs the current index and its PID, so we can observe its behavior. The worker's job is trivial—it will check that the current element is still set to the default (so we know that no other process has modified it already), and then it will overwrite this value with the current PID. Once the workers have completed, we return to the parent process and print the array again. This time, we see that it is filled with PIDs rather than 42.

Example 9-25. Running worker_fn on the shared array

```
worker_fn: with idx 0
  id of shared_array is 20255664 in PID 11288
worker_fn: with idx 2000
  id of shared_array is 20255664 in PID 11291
worker_fn: with idx 1000
  id of shared_array is 20255664 in PID 11289
...
worker_fn: with idx 8000
  id of shared_array is 20255664 in PID 11290

The default value has been over-written with worker_fn's result:
[[ 11288.  11288.  11288. ...,  11288.  11288.  11288.]
 ...,
 [ 11291.  11291.  11291. ...,  11291.  11291.  11291.]]
```

Finally, in Example 9-26 we use a Counter to confirm the frequency of each PID in the array. As the work was evenly divided, we expect to see each of the four PIDs represented an equal number of times. In our 800,000,000-element array, we see four sets of 200,000,000 PIDs. The table output is presented using PrettyTable (*https://pypi.python.org/pypi/PrettyTable*).

Example 9-26. Verifying the result on the shared array

```
Verification - extracting unique values from 800,000,000 items
in the numpy array (this might be slow)...
Unique values in shared_array:
+---------+-----------+
|   PID   |   Count   |
+---------+-----------+
| 11288.0 | 200000000 |
| 11289.0 | 200000000 |
| 11290.0 | 200000000 |
| 11291.0 | 200000000 |
+---------+-----------+
Press a key to exit...
```

Having completed, the program now exits, and the array is deleted.

We can take a peek inside each process under Linux using `ps` and `pmap`. Example 9-27 shows the result of calling `ps`. Breaking apart this command line:

- `ps` tells us about the process.
- `-A` lists all processes.
- `-o pid,size,vsize,cmd` outputs the PID, size information, and the command name.
- `grep` is used to filter all other results and leave only the lines for our demo.

The parent process (PID 11268) and its four forked children are shown in the output. The result is similar to what we saw in `htop`. We can use `pmap` to look at the memory map of each process, requesting extended output with `-x`. We `grep` for the pattern `s-` to list blocks of memory that are marked as being shared. In the parent process and the child processes, we see a 6,250,000 KB (6.2 GB) block that is shared between them.

Example 9-27. Using pmap and ps to investigate the operating system's view of the processes

```
$ ps -A -o pid,size,vsize,cmd | grep np_shared
11268 232464 6564988 python np_shared.py
11288 11232 6343756 python np_shared.py
11289 11228 6343752 python np_shared.py
11290 11228 6343752 python np_shared.py
11291 11228 6343752 python np_shared.py

ian@ian-Latitude-E6420 $ pmap -x 11268 | grep s-
Address          Kbytes     RSS   Dirty Mode   Mapping
00007f1953663000 6250000 6250000 6250000 rw-s-  zero (deleted)
...
ian@ian-Latitude-E6420 $ pmap -x 11288 | grep s-
Address          Kbytes     RSS   Dirty Mode   Mapping
00007f1953663000 6250000 1562512 1562512 rw-s-  zero (deleted)
...
```

Example 9-28 shows the important steps taken to share this array. We use a `multpro cessing.Array` to allocate a shared block of memory as a 1D array. We then instantiate a `numpy` array from this object and reshape it back to a 2D array. Now we have a `numpy`-wrapped block of memory that can be shared between processes and addressed as though it were a normal `numpy` array. `numpy` is not managing the RAM; `multiprocess ing.Array` is managing it.

Example 9-28. Sharing the numpy array using multiprocessing

```
import os
import multiprocessing
from collections import Counter
import ctypes
```

```
import numpy as np
from prettytable import PrettyTable

SIZE_A, SIZE_B = 10000, 80000  # 6.2GB - starts to use swap (maximal RAM usage)
```

In Example 9-29, you can see that each forked process has access to a global `main_nparray`. While the forked process has a copy of the `numpy` object, the underlying bytes that the object accesses are stored as shared memory. Our `worker_fn` will overwrite a chosen row (via `idx`) with the current process identifier.

Example 9-29. worker_fn for sharing numpy arrays using multiprocessing

```
def worker_fn(idx):
    """Do some work on the shared np array on row idx"""
    # confirm that no other process has modified this value already
    assert main_nparray[idx, 0] == DEFAULT_VALUE
    # inside the subprocess print the PID and id of the array
    # to check we don't have a copy
    if idx % 1000 == 0:
        print " {}: with idx {}\n  id of local_nparray_in_process is {} in PID {}"\
            .format(worker_fn.__name__, idx, id(main_nparray), os.getpid())
    # we can do any work on the array; here we set every item in this row to
    # have the value of the process ID for this process
    main_nparray[idx, :] = os.getpid()
```

In our __main__ in Example 9-30, we'll work through three major stages:

1. Build a shared `multiprocessing.Array` and convert it into a `numpy` array.

2. Set a default value into the array, and spawn four processes to work on the array in parallel.

3. Verify the array's contents after the processes return.

Typically, you'd set up a `numpy` array and work on it in a single process, probably doing something like `arr = np.array((100, 5), dtype=np.float_)`. This is fine in a single process, but you can't share this data across processes for both reading and writing.

The trick is to make a shared block of bytes. One way is to create a `multiprocessing.Array`. By default the `Array` is wrapped in a lock to prevent concurrent edits, but we don't need this lock as we'll be careful about our access patterns. To communicate this clearly to other team members, it is worth being explicit and setting `lock=False`.

If you don't set `lock=False`, then you'll have an object rather than a reference to the bytes, and you'll need to call `.get_obj()` to get to the bytes. By calling `.get_obj()` you bypass the lock, so there's no value in not being explicit about this in the first place.

Next, we take this block of shareable bytes and wrap a `numpy` array around them using `frombuffer`. The `dtype` is optional, but since we're passing bytes around it is always

---

sensible to be explicit. We reshape so we can address the bytes as a 2D array. By default the array values are set to 0. Example 9-30 shows our __main__ in full.

Example 9-30. main to set up numpy arrays for sharing

```
if __name__ == '__main__':
    DEFAULT_VALUE = 42
    NBR_OF_PROCESSES = 4

    # create a block of bytes, reshape into a local numpy array
    NBR_ITEMS_IN_ARRAY - SIZE_A * SIZE_B
    shared_array_base = multiprocessing.Array(ctypes.c_double,
                                               NBR_ITEMS_IN_ARRAY, lock=False)
    main_nparray = np.frombuffer(shared_array_base, dtype=ctypes.c_double)
    main_nparray = main_nparray.reshape(SIZE_A, SIZE_B)
    # assert no copy was made
    assert main_nparray.base.base is shared_array_base
    print "Created shared array with {:,} nbytes".format(main_nparray.nbytes)
    print "Shared array id is {} in PID {}".format(id(main_nparray), os.getpid())
    print "Starting with an array of 0 values:"
    print main_nparray
    print
```

To confirm that our processes are operating on the same block of data that we started with, we'll set each item to a new DEFAULT_VALUE—Syou'll see that at the top of Example 9-31 (we use the answer to life, the universe, and everything). Next, we build a Pool of processes (four in this case) and then send batches of row indices via the call to map.

Example 9-31. main for sharing numpy arrays using multiprocessing

```
    # modify the data via our local numpy array
    main_nparray.fill(DEFAULT_VALUE)
    print "Original array filled with value {}:".format(DEFAULT_VALUE)
    print main_nparray

    raw_input("Press a key to start workers using multiprocessing...")
    print

    # create a pool of processes that will share the memory block
    # of the global numpy array, and share the reference to the underlying
    # block of data so we can build a numpy array wrapper in the new processes
    pool = multiprocessing.Pool(processes=NBR_OF_PROCESSES)
    # perform a map where each row index is passed as a parameter to the
    # worker_fn
    pool.map(worker_fn, xrange(SIZE_A))
```

Once we've completed the parallel processing, we return to the parent process to verify the result (Example 9-32). The verification step runs through a flattened view on the array (note that the view does *not* make a copy; it just creates a 1D iterable view on the

2D array), counting the frequency of each PID. Finally, we perform some `assert` checks to make sure we have the expected counts.

Example 9-32. main to verify the shared result

```
print "Verification - extracting unique values from {:,} items\nin the numpy
    array (this might be slow)...".format(NBR_ITEMS_IN_ARRAY)
# main_nparray.flat iterates over the contents of the array, it doesn't
# make a copy
counter = Counter(main_nparray.flat)
print "Unique values in main_nparray:"
tbl = PrettyTable(["PID", "Count"])
for pid, count in counter.items():
    tbl.add_row([pid, count])
print tbl

total_items_set_in_array = sum(counter.values())

# check that we have set every item in the array away from DEFAULT_VALUE
assert DEFAULT_VALUE not in counter.keys()
# check that we have accounted for every item in the array
assert total_items_set_in_array == NBR_ITEMS_IN_ARRAY
# check that we have NBR_OF_PROCESSES of unique keys to confirm that every
# process did some of the work
assert len(counter) == NBR_OF_PROCESSES

raw_input("Press a key to exit...")
```

We've just created a 1D array of bytes, converted it into a 2D array, shared the array among four processes, and allowed them to process concurrently on the same block of memory. This recipe will help you parallelize over many cores. Be careful with concurrent access to the *same* data points, though—you'll have to use the locks in `multiproc essing` if you want to avoid synchronization problems, and this will slow down your code.

Synchronizing File and Variable Access

In the following examples we'll look at multiple processes sharing and manipulating a state—in this case, four processes incrementing a shared counter a set number of times. Without a synchronization process, the counting is incorrect. If you're sharing data in a coherent way you'll always need a method to synchronize the reading and writing of data, or you'll end up with errors.

Typically the synchronization methods are specific to the OS you're using, and they're often specific to the language you use. Here we look at file-based synchronization using a Python library and sharing an integer object between Python processes.

File Locking

Reading and writing to a file will be the slowest example of data sharing in this section.

You can see our first work function in Example 9-33. The function iterates over a local counter. In each iteration it opens a file and reads the existing value, increments it by one, and then writes the new value over the old one. On the first iteration the file will be empty or won't exist, so it will catch an exception and assume the value should be zero.

Example 9-33. work function without a lock

```
def work(filename, max_count):
    for n in range(max_count):
        f = open(filename, "r")
        try:
            nbr = int(f.read())
        except ValueError as err:
            print "File is empty, starting to count from 0, error: " + str(err)
            nbr = 0
        f = open(filename, "w")
        f.write(str(nbr + 1) + '\n')
        f.close()
```

Let's run this example with one process. You can see the output in Example 9-34. work is called 1,000 times, and as expected it counts correctly without losing any data. On the first read, it sees an empty file. This raises the invalid literal for int() error for int() (as int() is called on an empty string). This error only occurs once; afterward, we always have a valid value to read and convert into an integer.

Example 9-34. Timing of file-based counting without a lock and with one process

```
$ python ex1_nolock.py
Starting 1 process(es) to count to 1000
File is empty, starting to count from 0,
error: invalid literal for int() with base 10: ''
Expecting to see a count of 1000
count.txt contains:
1000
```

Now we'll run the same work function with four concurrent processes. We don't have any locking code, so we'll expect some odd results.

 Before you look at the following code, what *two* types of error can you expect to see when two processes simultaneously read from or write to the same file? Think about the two main states of the code (the start of execution for each process and the normal running state of each process).

Take a look at Example 9-35 to see the problems. First, when each process starts, the file is empty, so they each try to start counting from zero. Second, as one process writes, the other can read a partially written result that can't be parsed. This causes an exception, and a zero will be written back. This, in turn, causes our counter to keep getting reset! Can you see how \n and two values have been written by two concurrent processes to the same open file, causing an invalid entry to be read by a third process?

Example 9-35. Timing of file-based counting without a lock and with four processes

```
$ python ex1_nolock.py
Starting 4 process(es) to count to 4000
File is empty, starting to count from 0,
error: invalid literal for int() with base 10: ''
File is empty, starting to count from 0,
error: invalid literal for int() with base 10: '1\n7\n'
# many errors like these
Expecting to see a count of 4000
count.txt contains:
629
$ python -m timeit -s "import ex1_nolock" "ex1_nolock.run_workers()"
10 loops, best of 3: 125 msec per loop
```

Example 9-36 shows the multiprocessing code that calls work with four processes. Note that rather than using a map, instead we're building a list of Process objects. Although we don't use the functionality here, the Process object gives us the power to introspect the state of each Process. We encourage you to read the documentation (*http://bit.ly/Process-based*) to learn about why you might want to use a Process.

Example 9-36. run_workers setting up four processes

```
import multiprocessing
import os

...
MAX_COUNT_PER_PROCESS = 1000
FILENAME = "count.txt"
...

def run_workers():
    NBR_PROCESSES = 4
    total_expected_count = NBR_PROCESSES * MAX_COUNT_PER_PROCESS
    print "Starting {} process(es) to count to {}".format(NBR_PROCESSES,
                                                    total_expected_count)
    # reset counter
    f = open(FILENAME, "w")
    f.close()

    processes = []
    for process_nbr in range(NBR_PROCESSES):
        p = multiprocessing.Process(target=work, args=(FILENAME,
                                                MAX_COUNT_PER_PROCESS))
```

```
        p.start()
        processes.append(p)

    for p in processes:
        p.join()

    print "Expecting to see a count of {}".format(total_expected_count)
    print "{} contains:".format(FILENAME)
    os.system('more ' + FILENAME)


if __name__ == "__main__":
    run_workers()
```

Using the `lockfile` (*https://pypi.python.org/pypi/lockfile*) module, we can introduce a synchronization method so only one process gets to write at a time and the others each await their turn. The overall process therefore runs more slowly, but it doesn't make mistakes. You can see the correct output in Example 9-37. You'll find full documentation online (*http://pythonhosted.org//lockfile/*). Be aware that the locking mechanism is specific to Python, so other processes that are looking at this file will *not* care about the "locked" nature of this file.

Example 9-37. Timing of file-based counting with a lock and four processes

```
$ python ex1_lock.py
Starting 4 process(es) to count to 4000
File is empty, starting to count from 0,
error: invalid literal for int() with base 10: ''
Expecting to see a count of 4000
count.txt contains:
4000
$ python -m timeit -s "import ex1_lock" "ex1_lock.run_workers()"
10 loops, best of 3: 401 msec per loop
```

Using `lockfile` adds just a couple of lines of code. First, we create a `FileLock` object; the filename can be anything, but using the same name as the file you want to lock probably makes debugging from the command line easier. When you ask to `acquire` the lock the `FileLock` opens a new file with the same name, with *.lock* appended.

`acquire` without any arguments will block indefinitely, until the lock becomes available. Once you have the lock, you can do your processing without any danger of a conflict. You can then `release` the lock once you've finished writing (Example 9-38).

Example 9-38. work function with a lock

```
def work(filename, max_count):
    lock = lockfile.FileLock(filename)
    for n in range(max_count):
        lock.acquire()
        f = open(filename, "r")
```

```
    try:
        nbr = int(f.read())
    except ValueError as err:
        print "File is empty, starting to count from 0, error: " + str(err)
        nbr = 0
    f = open(filename, "w")
    f.write(str(nbr + 1) + '\n')
    f.close()
    lock.release()
```

You could use a context manager; in this case, you replace `acquire` and `release` with `with lock:`. This adds a small overhead to the runtime, but it also makes the code a little easier to read. Clarity usually beats execution speed.

You can also ask to `acquire` the lock with a timeout, check for an existing lock, and break an existing lock. Several locking mechanisms are provided; sensible default choices for each platform are hidden behind the `FileLock` interface.

Locking a Value

The `multiprocessing` module offers several options to share Python objects between processes. We can share primitive objects with a low communication overhead, and we can also share higher-level Python objects (e.g., dictionaries and lists) using a `Manager` (but note that the synchronization cost will significantly slow down the data sharing).

Here, we'll use a `multiprocessing.Value` (*http://bit.ly/value_doc*) object to share an integer between processes. While a `Value` has a lock, the lock doesn't do quite what you might expect—it prevents simultaneous reads or writes but does *not* provide an atomic increment. Example 9-39 illustrates this. You can see that we end up with an incorrect count; this is similar to the file-based unsynchronized example we looked at earlier.

Example 9-39. No locking leads to an incorrect count

```
$ python ex2_nolock.py
Expecting to see a count of 4000
We have counted to 2340
$ python -m timeit -s "import ex2_nolock" "ex2_nolock.run_workers()"
100 loops, best of 3: 12.6 msec per loop
```

No corruption occurs to the data, but we do miss some of the updates. This approach might be suitable if you're writing to a `Value` from one process and consuming (but not modifying) that `Value` in other processes.

The code to share the `Value` is shown in Example 9-40. We have to specify a datatype and an initialization value—using `Value("i", 0)`, we request a signed integer with a default value of 0. This is passed as a regular argument to our `Process` object, which takes care of sharing the same block of bytes between processes behind the scenes. To access the primitive object held by our `Value`, we use `.value`. Note that we're asking for an in-place addition—we'd expect this to be an atomic operation, but that's not supported by Value, so our final count is lower than expected.

Example 9-40. The counting code without a Lock

```
import multiprocessing

def work(value, max_count):
    for n in range(max_count):
        value.value += 1

def run_workers():
...
    value = multiprocessing.Value('i', 0)
    for process_nbr in range(NBR_PROCESSES):
        p = multiprocessing.Process(target=work, args=(value, MAX_COUNT_PER_PROCESS))
        p.start()
        processes.append(p)
...
```

We can add a Lock (*http://bit.ly/Lock_doc*), and it will work very similarly to the File Lock example we saw earlier. You can see the correctly synchronized count in Example 9-41.

Example 9-41. Using a Lock to synchronize writes to a Value

```
# lock on the update, but this isn't atomic
$ python ex2_lock.py
Expecting to see a count of 4000
We have counted to 4000
$ python -m timeit -s "import ex2_lock" "ex2_lock.run_workers()"
10 loops, best of 3: 22.2 msec per loop
```

In Example 9-42 we've used a context manager (with Lock) to acquire the lock. As in the previous FileLock example, it waits indefinitely to acquire the lock.

Example 9-42. Acquiring a Lock using a context manager

```
import multiprocessing

def work(value, max_count, lock):
    for n in range(max_count):
        with lock:
            value.value += 1

def run_workers():
...
    processes = []
    lock = multiprocessing.Lock()
    value = multiprocessing.Value('i', 0)
```

```
for process_nbr in range(NBR_PROCESSES):
    p = multiprocessing.Process(target=work,
                                args=(value, MAX_COUNT_PER_PROCESS, lock))
    p.start()
    processes.append(p)
...
```

As noted in the FileLock example, it is a little quicker to avoid using the context manager. The snippet in Example 9-43 shows how to acquire and release the Lock object.

Example 9-43. In-line locking rather than using a context manager

```
lock.acquire()
value.value += 1
lock.release()
```

Since a Lock doesn't give us the level of granularity that we're after, the basic locking that it provides wastes a bit of time unnecessarily. We can replace the Value with a RawValue (*http://bit.ly/RawValue_doc*), as in Example 9-44, and achieve an incremental speed-up. If you're interested in seeing the bytecode behind this change, then read Eli Bendersky's blog post (*http://bit.ly/shared_counter*) on the subject.

Example 9-44. Console output showing the faster RawValue and Lock approach

```
# RawValue has no lock on it
$ python ex2_lock_rawvalue.py
Expecting to see a count of 4000
We have counted to 4000
$ python -m timeit -s "import ex2_lock_rawvalue" "ex2_lock_rawvalue.run_workers()"
100 loops, best of 3: 12.6 msec per loop
```

To use a RawValue, just swap it for a Value as shown in Example 9-45.

Example 9-45. Example of using a RawValue integer

```
...
def run_workers():
...
    lock = multiprocessing.Lock()
    value = multiprocessing.RawValue('i', 0)
    for process_nbr in range(NBR_PROCESSES):
        p = multiprocessing.Process(target=work,
                                    args=(value, MAX_COUNT_PER_PROCESS, lock))
        p.start()
        processes.append(p)
```

We could also use a RawArray in place of a multiprocessing.Array if we were sharing an array of primitive objects.

We've looked at various ways of dividing up work on a single machine between multiple processes, along with sharing a flag and synchronizing data sharing between these processes. Remember, though, that sharing data can lead to headaches—try to avoid it if possible. Making a machine deal with all the edge cases of state sharing is hard; the first time you have to debug the interactions of multiple processes you'll realize why the accepted wisdom is to avoid this situation if possible.

Do consider writing code that runs a bit slower but is more likely to be understood by your team. Using an external tool like Redis to share state leads to a system that can be inspected at runtime by people *other* than the developers—this is a powerful way to enable your team to keep on top of what's happening in your parallel systems.

Definitely bear in mind that tweaked performant Python code is less likely to be understood by more junior members of your team—they'll either be scared of it or break it. Avoid this problem (and accept a sacrifice in speed) to keep team velocity high.

Wrap-Up

We've covered a lot in this chapter. First we looked at two embarrassingly parallel problems, one with predictable complexity and the other with nonpredictable complexity. We'll use these examples again shortly on multiple machines when we discuss clustering in Chapter 10.

Next, we looked at `Queue` support in `multiprocessing` and its overheads. In general, we recommend using an external queue library so that the state of the queue is more transparent. Preferably, you should use an easy-to-read job format so that it is easy to debug, rather than pickled data.

The IPC discussion should have impressed upon you how difficult it is to use IPC efficiently, and that it can make sense just to use a naive parallel solution (without IPC). Buying a faster computer with more cores might be a far more pragmatic solution than trying to use IPC to exploit an existing machine.

Sharing `numpy` matrices in parallel without making copies is important for only a small set of problems, but when it counts, it'll really count. It takes a few extra lines of code and requires some sanity checking to make sure that you're really not copying the data between processes.

Finally, we looked at using file and memory locks to avoid corrupting data—this is a source of subtle and hard-to-track errors, and this section showed you some robust and lightweight solutions.

In the next chapter we'll look at clustering using Python. With a cluster, we can move beyond single-machine parallelism and utilize the CPUs on a group of machines. This introduces a new world of debugging pain—not only can your code have errors, but the other machines can have errors (either from bad configuration or from failing hardware). We'll show how to parallelize the pi estimation demo using the Parallel Python module and how to run research code inside IPython using an IPython cluster.

## CHAPTER 10

Clusters and Job Queues

Questions You'll Be Able to Answer After This Chapter

- Why are clusters useful?
- What are the costs of clustering?
- How can I convert a multiprocessing solution into a clustered solution?
- How does an IPython cluster work?
- How does NSQ help with making robust production systems?

A *cluster* is commonly recognized to be a collection of computers working together to solve a common task. It could be viewed from the outside as a larger single system.

In the 1990s, the notion of using a cluster of commodity PCs on a local area network for clustered processing—known as a Beowulf cluster (*http://en.wikipedia.org/wiki/Beowulf_cluster*)—became popular. Google (*http://en.wikipedia.org/wiki/Google_platform*) later gave the practice a boost by using clusters of commodity PCs in its own data centers, particularly for running MapReduce tasks. At the other end of the scale, the TOP500 (*http://en.wikipedia.org/wiki/TOP500*) project ranks the most powerful computer systems each year; typically these have a clustered design and the fastest machines all use Linux.

Amazon Web Services (AWS) is commonly used both for engineering production clusters in the cloud and for building on-demand clusters for short-lived tasks like machine learning. With AWS, you can rent sets of eight Intel Xeon cores with 60 GB of RAM for $1.68 each per hour, alongside 244 GB RAM machines and machines with GPUs. Look at "Using IPython Parallel to Support Research" on page 273 and the StarCluster package if you'd like to explore AWS for ad hoc clusters for compute-heavy tasks.

Different computing tasks require different configurations, sizes, and capabilities in a cluster. We'll define some common scenarios in this chapter.

Before you move to a clustered solution, do make sure that you have:

- Profiled your system so you understand the bottlenecks
- Exploited compiler solutions like Cython
- Exploited multiple cores on a single machine (possibly a big machine with many cores)
- Exploited techniques for using less RAM

Keeping your system to one machine (even if the "one machine" is a really beefy computer with lots of RAM and many CPUs) will make your life easier. Move to a cluster if you really need a *lot* of CPUs or the ability to process data from disks in parallel, or you have production needs like high resiliency and rapid speed of response.

Benefits of Clustering

The most obvious benefit of a cluster is that you can easily scale computing requirements —if you need to process more data or to get an answer faster, you just add more machines (or "nodes").

By adding machines, you can also improve reliability. Each machine's components have a certain likelihood of failing, and with a good design the failure of a number of components will not stop the operation of the cluster.

Clusters are also used to create systems that scale dynamically. A common use case is to cluster a set of servers that process web requests or associated data (e.g., resizing user photos, transcoding video, or transcribing speech) and to activate more servers as demand increases at certain times of the day.

Dynamic scaling is a very cost-effective way of dealing with nonuniform usage patterns, as long as the machine activation time is fast enough to deal with the speed of changing demand.

A subtler benefit of clustering is that clusters can be separated geographically but still centrally controlled. If one geographic area suffers an outage (e.g., flood or power loss), the other cluster can continue to work, perhaps with more processing units being added to handle the demand. Clusters also allow you to run heterogeneous software environments (e.g., different versions of operating systems and processing software), which *might* improve the robustness of the overall system—note, though, that this is definitely an expert-level topic!

Drawbacks of Clustering

Moving to a clustered solution requires a change in thinking. This is an evolution of the change in thinking required when you move from serial to parallel code that we introduced back in Chapter 9. Suddenly you have to consider what happens when you have more than one machine—you have latency between machines, you need to know if your other machines are working, and you need to keep all the machines running the same version of your software. System administration is probably your biggest challenge.

In addition, you normally have to think hard about the algorithms you are implementing and what happens once you have all these additional moving parts that may need to stay in sync. This additional planning can impose a heavy mental tax; it is likely to distract you from your core task, and once a system grows large enough you'll probably require a dedicated engineer to join your team.

 The reason why we've tried to focus on using one machine efficiently in this book is because we both believe that life is easier if you're only dealing with one computer rather than a collection (though we confess it can be *way* more fun to play with a cluster—until it breaks). If you can scale vertically (by buying more RAM or more CPUs), then it is worth investigating this approach in favor of clustering. Of course, your processing needs may exceed what's possible with vertical scaling, or the robustness of a cluster may be more important than having a single machine. If you're a single person working on this task, though, bear in mind also that running a cluster will suck some of your time.

When designing a clustered solution, you'll need to remember that each machine's configuration might be different (each machine will have a different load and different local data). How will you get all the right data onto the machine that's processing your job? Does the latency involved in moving the job and the data amount to a problem? Do your jobs need to communicate partial results to each other? What happens if a process fails or a machine dies or some hardware wipes itself when several jobs are running? Failures can be introduced if you don't consider these questions.

You should also consider that failures *can be acceptable*. For example, you probably don't need 99.999% reliability when you're running a content-based web service—if on occasion a job fails (e.g., a picture doesn't get resized quickly enough) and the user is required to reload a page, that's something that everyone is already used to. It might not be the solution you want to give to the user, but accepting a little bit of failure typically reduces your engineering and management costs by a worthwhile margin. On the flip side, if a high-frequency trading system experiences failures, the cost of bad stock market trades could be considerable!

Maintaining a fixed infrastructure can become expensive. Machines are relatively cheap to purchase, but they have an awful habit of going wrong—automatic software upgrades can glitch, network cards fail, disks have write errors, power supplies can give spikey power that disrupts data, cosmic rays can flip a bit in a RAM module. The more computers you have, the more time will be lost to dealing with these issues. Sooner or later you'll want to add a system engineer who can deal with these problems, so add another $100,000 to the budget. Using a cloud-based cluster can mitigate a lot of these problems (it costs more, but you don't have to deal with the hardware maintenance), and some cloud providers also offer a spot-priced market (*http://bit.ly/spot-instances*) for cheap but temporary computing resources.

An insidious problem with a cluster that grows organically over time is that it's possible that no one has documented how to restart it safely if everything gets turned off. If you don't have a documented restart plan, then you should assume you'll have to write one at the worst possible time (one of your authors has been involved in debugging this sort of problem on Christmas Eve—this is not the Christmas present you want!). At this point you'll also learn just how long it can take each part of a system to get up to speed —it might take minutes for each part of a cluster to boot and to start to process jobs, so if you have 10 parts that operate in succession it might take an hour to get the whole system running from cold. The consequence is that you might have an hour's worth of backlogged data. Do you then have the necessary capacity to deal with this backlog in a timely fashion?

Slack behavior can be a cause of expensive mistakes, and complex and hard-to-anticipate behavior can cause expensive unexpected outcomes. Let's look at two high-profile cluster failures and see what lessons we can learn.

$462 Million Wall Street Loss Through Poor Cluster Upgrade Strategy

In 2012, the high-frequency trading firm Knight Capital lost $462 million (*http://bit.ly/Wall_Street_crash*) after a bug was introduced during a software upgrade in a cluster. The software made more orders for shares than customers had requested.

In the trading software, an older flag was repurposed for a new function. The upgrade was rolled out to seven of the eight live machines, but the eighth machine used older code to handle the flag, which resulted in the wrong trades being made. The Securities and Exchange Commission (SEC) noted that Knight Capital didn't have a second technician review the upgrade and no process to review the upgrade existed.

The underlying mistake seems to have had two causes. The first was that the software development process hadn't removed an obsolete feature, so the stale code stayed around. The second was that no manual review process was in place to confirm that the upgrade was completed successfully.

Technical debt adds a cost that eventually has to be paid—preferably by taking time when not under pressure to remove the debt. Always use unit tests, both when building and when refactoring code. The lack of a written checklist to run through during system upgrades, along with a second pair of eyes, could cost you an expensive failure. There's a reason that airplane pilots have to work through a takeoff checklist: it means that nobody ever skips the important steps, no matter how many times they might have done them before!

Skype's 24-Hour Global Outage

Skype suffered a 24-hour planet-wide failure (*http://bit.ly/Skype_outage*) in 2010. Behind the scenes, Skype is supported by a peer-to-peer network. An overload in one part of the system (used to process offline instant messages) caused delayed responses from Windows clients; some versions of the Windows client didn't properly handle the delayed responses and crashed. In all, approximately 40% of the live clients crashed, including 25% of the public supernodes. Supernodes are critical to routing data in the network.

With 25% of the routing offline (it came back on, but slowly), the network overall was under great strain. The crashed Windows client nodes were also restarting and attempting to rejoin the network, adding a new volume of traffic on the already overloaded system. The supernodes have a backoff procedure if they experience too much load, so they started to shut down in response to the waves of traffic.

Skype became largely unavailable for 24 hours. The recovery process involved first setting up hundreds of new mega-supernodes configured to deal with the increased traffic, and then following up with thousands more. Over the coming days, the network recovered.

This incident caused a lot of embarrassment for Skype; clearly, it also changed their focus to damage limitation for several tense days. Customers were forced to look for alternative solutions for voice calls, which was likely a marketing boon for competitors.

Given the complexity of the network and the escalation of failures that occurred, it is likely that this failure would have been hard to both predict and plan for. The reason that *all* of the nodes on the network didn't fail was due to different versions of the software and different platforms—there's a reliability benefit to having a heterogenous network rather than a homogeneous system.

Common Cluster Designs

It is common to start with a local ad hoc cluster of reasonably equivalent machines. You might wonder if you can add old computers to an ad hoc network, but typically older CPUs eat a lot of power and run very slowly, so they don't contribute nearly as much as you might hope compared to one new, high-specification machine. An in-office cluster requires someone who can maintain it. A cluster in link to Amazon's EC2 (*http://aws.amazon.com/ec2/*), or Microsoft's Azure (*http://azure.microsoft.com/en-us/*), or run by an academic institution, offloads the hardware support to the provider's team.

If you have well-understood processing requirements, it might make sense to design a custom cluster—perhaps one that uses an InfiniBand high-speed interconnect in place of gigabit Ethernet, or one that uses a particular configuration of RAID drives that support your read, write, or resiliency requirements. You might want to combine both CPUs and GPUs on some machines, or just default to CPUs.

You might want a massively decentralized processing cluster, like the ones used by projects like *SETI@home* and *Folding@home* through the Berkeley Open Infrastructure for Network Computing (BOINC) system (*http://bit.ly/Berkeley_decentralized*)—they still share a centralized coordination system, but the computing nodes join and leave the project in an ad hoc fashion.

On top of the hardware design, you can run different software architectures. Queues of work are the most common and easiest to understand. Typically, jobs are put onto a queue and consumed by a processor. The result of the processing might go onto another queue for further processing, or be used as a final result (e.g., being added into a database). Message-passing systems are slightly different—messages get put onto a message bus and are then consumed by other machines. The messages might time out and get deleted, and they might be consumed by multiple machines. A more complex system is when processes talk to each other using interprocess communication—this can be considered an expert-level configuration as there are lots of ways that you can set it up badly, which will result in you losing your sanity. Only go down the IPC route if you really know that you need it.

How to Start a Clustered Solution

The easiest way to start a clustered system is to begin with one machine that will run both the job server and a job processor (just one for one CPU). If your tasks are CPU-bound, run one job processor per CPU; if your tasks are I/O-bound, run several per CPU. If they're RAM-bound, be careful that you don't run out of RAM. Get your single-machine solution working with one processor, then add more. Make your code fail in unpredictable ways (e.g., do a 1/0 in your code, use kill -9 *<pid>* on your worker, pull the power from the socket so the whole machine dies) to check if your system is robust.

Obviously, you'll want to do heavier testing than this—a unit test suite full of coding errors and artificial exceptions is good. Ian likes to throw in unexpected events, like having a processor run a set of jobs while an external process is systematically killing important processes and confirming that these all get restarted cleanly by whatever monitoring process you're using.

Once you have one running job processor, add a second. Check that you're not using too much RAM. Do you process jobs twice as fast as before?

Now introduce a second machine, with just one job processor on that new machine and no job processors on the coordinating machine. Does it process jobs as fast as when you had the processor on the coordinating machine? If not, why not? Is latency a problem? Do you have different configurations? Maybe you have different machine hardware, like CPUs, RAM, and cache sizes?

Now add another nine computers and test to see if you're processing jobs 10 times faster than before. If not, why not? Are network collisions now occurring that slow down your overall processing rate?

To reliably start the cluster's components when the machine boots, we tend to use either a `cron` job, Circus (*https://circus.readthedocs.org/en/latest/*) or `supervisord` (*http://supervisord.org/*), or sometimes Upstart (*http://en.wikipedia.org/wiki/Upstart*) (which is being replaced by `systemd`). Circus is newer than `supervisord`, but both are Python-based. `cron` is old, but very reliable if you're just starting scripts like a monitoring process that can start subprocesses as required.

One you have a reliable cluster you might want to introduce a random-killer tool like Netflix's ChaosMonkey (*https://github.com/Netflix/SimianArmy*), which deliberately kills parts of your system to test them for resiliency. Your processes and your hardware will die eventually, and it doesn't hurt to know that you're likely to survive at least the errors you predict might happen.

Ways to Avoid Pain When Using Clusters

One particularly painful experience Ian encountered was when a series of queues in a clustered system ground to a halt. Later queues were not being consumed, so they filled up. Some of the machines ran out of RAM, so their processes died. Earlier queues were being processed but couldn't pass their results to the next queue, so they crashed. In the end the first queue was being filled but not consumed, so it crashed. After that we were paying for data from a supplier that ultimately was discarded. You must sketch out some notes to consider the various ways your cluster will die (not *if it dies* but *when it dies*), and what will happen. Will you lose data (and is this a problem?)? Will you have a large backlog that's too painful to process?

Having a system that's easy to debug *probably* beats having a faster system. Engineering time and the cost of downtime are *probably* your largest expenses (this isn't true if you're running a missile defense program, but it is probably true for a start-up). Rather than shaving a few bytes by using a low-level compressed binary protocol, consider using human-readable text in JSON when passing messages. It does add an overhead for sending the messages and decoding them, but when you're left with a partial database after a core computer has caught fire, you'll be glad that you can read the important messages quickly as you work to bring the system back online.

Make sure it is cheap in time and money to deploy updates to the system—both operating system updates and new versions of your software. Every time anything changes in the cluster, you risk the system responding in odd ways if it is in a schizophrenic state. Make sure you use a deployment system like Fabric (*http://www.fabfile.org/*), Salt (*https://salt.readthedocs.org/en/latest/*), Chef (*http://www.getchef.com/*), or Puppet (*http://puppetlabs.com/*) or a system image like a Debian *.deb*, a RedHat *.rpm*, or an Amazon Machine Image (*http://en.wikipedia.org/wiki/Amazon_Machine_Image*). Being able to robustly deploy an update that upgrades an entire cluster (with a report on any problems found) massively reduces stress during difficult times.

Positive reporting is useful. Every day, send an email to someone detailing the performance of the cluster. If that email doesn't turn up, then that's a useful clue that something's happened. You'll probably want other early warning systems that'll notify you faster, too; Pingdom (*https://www.pingdom.com/*) and ServerDensity (*https://www.serverdensity.com/*) are particularly useful here. A "dead man's switch" that reacts to the absence of an event is another useful backup (e.g., Dead Man's Switch (*http://www.deadmansswitch.net/*)).

Reporting to the team on the health of the cluster is very useful. This might be an admin page inside a web application, or a separate report. Ganglia (*http://ganglia.source forge.net/*) is great for this. Ian has seen a *Star Trek* LCARS-like interface running on a spare PC in an office that plays the "red alert" sound when problems are detected—that's particularly effective at getting the attention of an entire office. We've even seen Arduinos driving analog instruments like old-fashioned boiler pressure gauges (they make a nice sound when the needle moves!) showing system load. This kind of reporting is important so that everyone understands the difference between "normal" and "this might ruin our Friday night!"

Three Clustering Solutions

In the following sections we introduce Parallel Python, IPython Parallel, and NSQ.

Parallel Python has a very similar interface to `multiprocessing`. Upgrading your 'multiprocessing` solution from a single multicore machine to a multimachine setup is the matter of a few minutes' work. Parallel Python has few dependencies and is easy to configure for research work on a local cluster. It isn't very powerful and lacks communication mechanisms, but for sending out embarrassingly parallel jobs to a small local cluster it is very easy to use.

IPython clusters are very easy to use on one machine with multiple cores. Since many researchers use IPython as their shell, it is natural to also use it for parallel job control. Building a cluster requires a little bit of system administration knowledge and there are some dependencies (such as ZeroMQ), so the setup is a little more involved than with Parallel Python. A huge win with IPython Parallel is the fact that you can use remote clusters (e.g., using Amazon's AWS and EC2) just as easily as local clusters.

NSQ is a production-ready queuing system used in companies like Bitly. It has persistence (so if machines die, jobs can be picked up again by another machine) and strong mechanisms for scalability. With this greater power comes a slightly greater need for system administration and engineering skills.

Using the Parallel Python Module for Simple Local Clusters

The Parallel Python (*http://www.parallelpython.com/*) (pp) module enables local clusters of workers using an interface that is similar to that of multiprocessing. Handily, this means that converting code from multiprocessing using map to Parallel Python is very easy. You can run code using one machine or an ad hoc network just as easily. You can install it using pip install pp.

With Parallel Python we can calculate Pi using the Monte Carlo method as we did back in "Estimating Pi Using Processes and Threads" on page 210 using our local machine —notice in Example 10-1 how similar the interface is to the earlier multiprocessing example. We create a list of work in nbr_trials_per_process and pass these jobs to four local processes. We could create as many work items as we wanted; they'd be consumed as workers became free.

Example 10-1. Parallel Python local example

```
...
import pp

NBR_ESTIMATES = 1e8

def calculate_pi(nbr_estimates):
    steps = xrange(int(nbr_estimates))
    nbr_trials_in_unit_circle = 0
    for step in steps:
        x = random.uniform(0, 1)
        y = random.uniform(0, 1)
        is_in_unit_circle = x * x + y * y <= 1.0
        nbr_trials_in_unit_circle += is_in_unit_circle
    return nbr_trials_in_unit_circle
```

```
if __name__ == "__main__":
    NBR_PROCESSES = 4
    job_server = pp.Server(ncpus=NBR_PROCESSES)
    print "Starting pp with", job_server.get_ncpus(), "workers"
    nbr_trials_per_process = [NBR_ESTIMATES] * NBR_PROCESSES
    jobs = []
    for input_args in nbr_trials_per_process:
        job = job_server.submit(calculate_pi, (input_args,), (), ("random",))
        jobs.append(job)
    # each job blocks until the result is ready
    nbr_in_unit_circles = [job() for job in jobs]
    print "Amount of work:", sum(nbr_trials_per_process)
    print sum(nbr_in_unit_circles) * 4 / NBR_ESTIMATES / NBR_PROCESSES
```

In Example 10-2, we extend the example—this time we'll require 1,024 jobs of 100,000,000 estimates each with a dynamically configured cluster. On remote machines we can run python ppserver.py -w 4 -a -d and remote servers will start using four processes (the default would be eight on Ian's laptop but we don't want to use the four HyperThreads so we've chosen four CPUs), with autoconnect and with a debug log. The debug log prints debug information to the screen; this is useful for checking that work has been received. The autoconnect flag means that we don't have to specify IP addresses; we let pp advertise itself and connect to the servers.

Example 10-2. Parallel Python over a cluster

```
...
NBR_JOBS = 1024
NBR_LOCAL_CPUS = 4
ppservers = ("*",)  # set IP list to be autodiscovered
job_server = pp.Server(ppservers=ppservers, ncpus=NBR_LOCAL_CPUS)

print "Starting pp with", job_server.get_ncpus(), "local workers"
nbr_trials_per_process = [NBR_ESTIMATES] * NBR_JOBS
jobs = []
for input_args in nbr_trials_per_process:
    job = job_server.submit(calculate_pi, (input_args,), (), ("random",))
    jobs.append(job)
...
```

Running with a second powerful laptop, the computation time roughly halves. On the other hand, an old MacBook with one CPU barely helps—often it'll compute one of the jobs so slowly that the fast laptop is left idle with no more work to perform, so the overall completion time is longer than if just the fast laptop were used by itself.

This is a very useful way to begin building an ad hoc cluster for light computation tasks. You probably don't want to use it in a production environment (Celery or GearMan is likely a better choice), but for research and easy scaling when learning about a problem it gives you a quick win.

pp doesn't help with distributing code or static data to remote machines; you have to move external libraries (e.g., anything you might have compiled into a static library) to the remote machines and provide any shared data. It does handle pickling the code to run, additional imports, and the data you supply from the controller process.

Using IPython Parallel to Support Research

The IPython cluster support comes via `ipcluster` (*http://bit.ly/IPython_parallel*). IPython becomes an interface to local and remote processing engines where data can be pushed among the engines and jobs can be pushed to remote machines. Remote debugging is possible, and the message passing interface (MPI) is optionally supported. This same communication mechanism powers the IPython Notebook interface.

This is great for a research setting—you can push jobs to machines in a local cluster, interact and debug if there's a problem, push data to machines, and collect results back, all interactively. Note also that PyPy runs IPython and IPython Parallel. The combination might be very powerful (if you don't use `numpy`).

Behind the scenes, ZeroMQ is used as the messaging middleware, so you'll need to have this installed. If you're building a cluster on a local network, you can avoid SSH authentication. If you need some security, then SSH is fully supported, but it makes configuration a little more involved—start on a local trusted network and build out as you learn how each component works.

The project is split into four components. An *engine* is a synchronous Python interpreter that runs your code. You'll run a set of these to enable parallel computing. A *controller* provides an interface to the engines; it is responsible for work distribution and supplies a *direct* interface and a *load-balanced interface* that provides a work scheduler. A *hub* keeps track of engines, schedulers, and clients. *Schedulers* hide the synchronous nature of the engines and provide an asynchronous interface.

On the laptop, we start four engines using `ipcluster start -n 4`. In Example 10-3 we start IPython and check that a local `Client` can see our four local engines. We can address all four engines using `c[:]`, and we apply a function to each engine—`apply_sync` takes a callable, so we supply a zero-argument `lambda` that will return a string. Each of our four local engines will run one of these functions, returning the same result.

Example 10-3. Testing that we can see the local engines in IPython

```
In [1]: from IPython.parallel import Client

In [2]: c = Client()

In [3]: print c.ids
[0, 1, 2, 3]

In [4]: c[:].apply_sync(lambda:"Hello High Performance Pythonistas!")
```

```
Out[4]:
['Hello High Performance Pythonistas!',
 'Hello High Performance Pythonistas!',
 'Hello High Performance Pythonistas!',
 'Hello High Performance Pythonistas!']
```

Having constructed our engines, they're now in an empty state. If we import modules locally, they won't be imported in the remote engines. A clean way to import both locally and remotely is to use the `sync_imports` context manager. In Example 10-4 we'll `import os` on both the local IPython and the four connected engines, then call `apply_sync` again on the four engines to fetch their PIDs. If we didn't do the remote imports we'd get a `NameError`, as the remote engines wouldn't know about the `os` module. We can also use `execute` to run any Python command remotely on the engines.

Example 10-4. Importing modules into our remote engines

```
In [5]: dview=c[:]  # this is a direct view (not a load-balanced view)

In [6]: with dview.sync_imports():
   ....:     import os
   ....:
importing os on engine(s)

In [7]: dview.apply_sync(lambda:os.getpid())
Out[7]: [15079, 15080, 15081, 15089]

In [8]: dview.execute("import sys")  # another way to execute commands remotely
```

You'll want to push data to the engines. The `push` command shown in Example 10-5 lets you send a dictionary of items that are added to the global namespace of each engine. There's a corresponding `pull` to retrieve items: you give it keys and it'll return the corresponding values from each of the engines.

Example 10-5. Pushing shared data to the engines

```
In [9]: dview.push({'shared_data':[50, 100]})
Out[9]: <AsyncResult: _push>

In [10]: dview.apply_sync(lambda:len(shared_data))
Out[10]: [2, 2, 2, 2]
```

Now let's add a second machine to the cluster. First we'll kill the `ipengine` engines that we created before and exit IPython. We'll start from a clean slate. You'll need a second machine available that has SSH configured to allow you to automatically log in.

In Example 10-6 we'll create a new profile for our cluster. A set of configuration files is placed in the *<HOME>/.ipython/profile_mycluster* directory. By default the engines are configured to accept connections from *localhost* only, and not from external devices. Edit *ipengine_config.py* to configure the `HubFactory` to accept external connections, save, and then start a new `ipcluster` using the new profile. We're back to having four local engines.

Example 10-6. Creating a local profile that accepts public connections

```
$ ipython profile create mycluster --parallel
$ gvim /home/ian/.ipython/profile_mycluster/ipengine_config.py
# add "c.HubFactory.ip = '*'" near the top
$ ipcluster start -n 4 --profile=mycluster
```

Next we need to pass this configuration file to our remote machine. In Example 10-7 we use scp to copy *ipcontroller-engine.json* (which was created when we started `ipclus ter`) to the remote machine's *.config/ipython/profile_default/security* directory. Once it is copied, run `ipengine` on the remote machine. It will look in the default directory for *ipcontroller-engine.json*; if it connects successfully, then you'll see a message like the one shown here.

Example 10-7. Copying the edited profile to the remote machine and testing

```
# On the local machine
$ scp /home/ian/.ipython/profile_mycluster/security/ipcontroller-engine.json
        ian@192.168.0.16:/home/ian/.config/ipython/profile_default/security/

# Now on the remote machine
ian@ubuntu:~$ ipengine
...Using existing profile dir: u'/home/ian/.config/ipython/profile_default'
...Loading url_file u'/home/ian/.config/ipython/profile_default/security/
        ipcontroller-engine.json'
...Registering with controller at tcp://192.168.0.128:35963
...Starting to monitor the heartbeat signal from the hub every 3010 ms.
...Using existing profile dir: u'/home/ian/.config/ipython/profile_default'
...Completed registration with id 4
```

Let's test the configuration. In Example 10-8 we'll start a local IPython shell using the new profile. We'll retrieve a list of five clients (four locally and one remotely), then we'll ask for Python's version info—you can see that on the remote machine we're using the Anaconda distribution. We only get one additional engine, as the remote machine in this case is a single-core MacBook.

Example 10-8. Test that the new machine is a part of the cluster

```
$ ipython --profile=mycluster
Python 2.7.5+ (default, Sep 19 2013, 13:48:49)
Type "copyright", "credits" or "license" for more information.
IPython 1.1.0—An enhanced Interactive Python.
...
In [1]: from IPython.parallel import Client

In [2]: c = Client()

In [3]: c.ids
```

```
Out[3]: [0, 1, 2, 3, 4]

In [4]: dview=c[:]

In [5]: with dview.sync_imports():
   ...:     import sys

In [6]: dview.apply_sync(lambda:sys.version)
Out[6]:
['2.7.5+ (default, Sep 19 2013, 13:48:49) \n[GCC 4.8.1]',
 '2.7.5+ (default, Sep 19 2013, 13:48:49) \n[GCC 4.8.1]',
 '2.7.5+ (default, Sep 19 2013, 13:48:49) \n[GCC 4.8.1]',
 '2.7.5+ (default, Sep 19 2013, 13:48:49) \n[GCC 4.8.1]',
 '2.7.6 |Anaconda 1.9.2 (64-bit)| (default, Jan 17 2014, 10:13:17) \n
          [GCC 4.1.2 20080704 (Red Hat 4.1.2-54)]']
```

Let's put it all together. In Example 10-9 we'll use the five engines to estimate pi as we
did in "Using the Parallel Python Module for Simple Local Clusters" on page 271. This
time we'll use the @require decorator to import the random module in the engines. We
use a direct view to send our work out to the engines; this blocks until all the results
come back. Then we estimate pi as we've done before.

Example 10-9. Estimating pi using our local cluster

```
from IPython.parallel import Client, require
NBR_ESTIMATES = 1e8

@require('random')
def calculate_pi(nbr_estimates):
    ...
    return nbr_trials_in_unit_circle

if __name__ == "__main__":
    c = Client()
    nbr_engines = len(c.ids)
    print "We're using {} engines".format(nbr_engines)
    dview = c[:]
    nbr_in_unit_circles = dview.apply_sync(calculate_pi, NBR_ESTIMATES)

    print "Estimates made:", nbr_in_unit_circles

    # work using the engines only
    nbr_jobs = len(nbr_in_unit_circles)
    print sum(nbr_in_unit_circles) * 4 / NBR_ESTIMATES / nbr_jobs
```

IPython Parallel offers much more than what's shown here. Asynchronous jobs and
mappings over larger input ranges are, of course, possible. It also has a CompositeEr
ror class, which is a higher-level exception that wraps up the same exception that's
occurred on multiple engines (rather than you receiving multiple identical exceptions

if you've deployed bad code!); this is a convenience when you're dealing with lots of engines.[1]

One particularly powerful feature of IPython Parallel is that it allows you to use larger clustering environments, including supercomputers and cloud services like Amazon's EC2. To further ease this sort of cluster's development, the Anaconda distribution includes support for StarCluster. Olivier Grisel gave a great tutorial on advanced machine learning with `scikit-learn` at PyCon 2013; at the two-hour point he demos using StarCluster for machine learning via IPython Parallel on Amazon EC2 spot instances.

NSQ for Robust Production Clustering

In a production environment, you will need a solution that is more robust than the other solutions we've talked about so far. This is because during the everyday operation of your cluster, nodes may become unavailable, code may crash, networks may go down, or one of the other thousands of problems that can happen may happen. The problem is that all the previous systems have had one computer where commands are issued and a limited and static number of computers that read the commands and execute them. Instead, we would like a system where we can have multiple actors communicating via some message bus—this would allow us to have an arbitrary and constantly changing number of message creators and consumers.

One simple solution to these problems is NSQ (*https://github.com/bitly/nsq*), a highly performant distributed messaging platform. While it is written in GO, it is completely data format and language-agnostic. As a result, there are libraries in many languages, and the basic interface into NSQ is a REST API that requires only the ability to make HTTP calls. Furthermore, we can send messages in any format we want: JSON, Pickle, `msgpack`, etc. Most importantly, however, it provides fundamental guarantees regarding message delivery, and it does all of this using two simple design patterns: queues and pub/subs.

Queues

A queue is a type of buffer for messages. Whenever you want to send a message to another part of your processing pipeline, you send it to the queue, and it'll wait in the queue until there is an available worker to read it. A queue is most useful in distributed processing when there is an imbalance between production and consumption. If this imbalance occurs, we can simply scale horizontally by adding more data consumers until the message production rate and consumption rate are equal. In addition, if the computers responsible for consuming messages go down, the messages are not lost and

---

1. For further details, see *http://bit.ly/parallel-exceptions*.

are simply queued until there is an available consumer, thus giving us message delivery guarantees.

For example, let's say we would like to process new recommendations for a user every time that user rates a new item on our site. If we didn't have a queue, then the "rate" action would directly call the "recalculate-recommendations" action, regardless of how busy the servers dealing with recommendations were. If all of a sudden thousands of users decided to rate something, our recommendations servers could get so swamped with requests that they could start timing out, dropping messages, and generally becoming unresponsive!

On the other hand, with a queue the recommendations servers ask for more tasks when they are ready. A new "rate" action would put a new task on the queue, and when a recommendations server becomes ready to do more work it would grab it from the queue and process it. In this setup, if more users than normal start rating items, our queue would fill up and act as a buffer for the recommendations servers—their workload would be unaffected and they could still process messages until the queue was empty.

One potential problem with this is that if a queue becomes completely overwhelmed with work, it will be storing quite a lot of messages. NSQ solves this by having multiple storage backends—when there aren't many messages they are stored in memory, and as more messages start coming in the messages get put onto disk.

 Generally, when working with queued systems it is a good idea to try to have the downstream systems (i.e., the recommendations systems in the preceding example) be at 60% capacity with a normal workload. This is a good compromise between allocating too many resources for a problem and giving your servers enough extra power for when the amount of work increases beyond normal levels.

Pub/sub

A pub/sub (short for publisher/subscriber), on the other hand, describes who gets what messages. A data publisher can push data out of a particular topic, and data subscribers can subscribe to different feeds of data. Whenever the publisher puts out a piece of information, it gets sent to all of the subscribers—they each get an identical copy of the original information. You can think of this like a newspaper: many people can subscribe to a particular newspaper, and whenever a new edition of the newspaper comes out, every subscriber gets an identical copy of it. In addition, the producer of the newspaper doesn't need to know all of the people its papers are being sent to. As a result, publishers and subscribers are decoupled from each other, which allows our system to be more robust as our network changes while still in production.

In addition to this, NSQ adds the notion of a *data consumer*; that is, multiple processes can be connected to the same data subscription. Whenever a new piece of data comes out, every subscriber gets a copy of the data; however, only one consumer of each subscription sees that data. In the newspaper analogy, you can think of this as having multiple people in the same household who read the newspaper. The publisher will deliver one paper to the house, since that house only has one subscription, and whoever in the house gets to it first gets to read that data. Each subscriber's consumers do the same processing to a message when they see it; however, they can potentially be on multiple computers and thus add more processing power to the entire pool.

We can see a depiction of this pub/sub/consumer paradigm in Figure 10-1. If a new message gets published on the "clicks" topic, all of the subscribers (or, in NSQ parlance, channels—i.e., "metrics," "spam_analysis," and "archive") will get a copy. Each sub-scriber is composed of one or more consumers, which represent actual processes that react to the messages. In the case of the "metrics" subscriber, only one consumer will see the new message. The next message will go to another consumer, and so on.

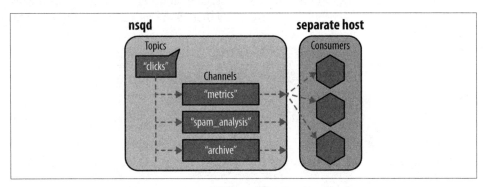

Figure 10-1. NSQ's pub/sub-like topology

The benefit of spreading the messages out among a potentially large pool of consumers is essentially automatic load balancing. If a message takes quite a long time to process, that consumer will not signal to NSQ that it is ready for more messages until it's done, and thus the other consumers will get the majority of future messages (until that original consumer is ready to process again). In addition, it allows existing consumers to dis-connect (whether by choice or because of failure) and new consumers to connect to the cluster while still maintaining processing power within a particular subscription group. For example, if we find that "metrics" takes quite a while to process and often is not keeping up with demand, we can simply add more processes to the consumer pool for that subscription group, giving us more processing power. On the other hand, if we see that most of our processes are idle (i.e., not getting any messages), we can easily remove consumers from this subscription pool.

It is also important to note that anything can publish data. A consumer doesn't simply need to be a consumer—it can consume data from one topic and then publish it to another topic. In fact, this chain is an important workflow when it comes to this paradigm for distributed computing. Consumers will read from a topic of data, transform the data in some way, and then publish the data onto a new topic that other consumers can further transform. In this way, different topics represent different data, subscription groups represent different transformations on the data, and consumers are the actual workers who transform individual messages.

Furthermore, there is an incredible redundancy in this system. There can be many nsqd processes that each consumer connects to, and there can be many consumers connected to a particular subscription. This makes it so that there is no single point of failure and your system will be robust even if several machines disappear. We can see in Figure 10-2 that even if one of the computers in the diagram goes down, the system is still able to deliver and process messages. In addition, since NSQ saves pending messages to disk when shutting down, unless the hardware loss is catastrophic your data will most likely still be intact and be delivered. Lastly, if a consumer is shut down before responding to a particular message, NSQ will resend that message to another consumer. This means that even as consumers get shut down, we know that all the messages in a topic will be responded to at least once.[2]

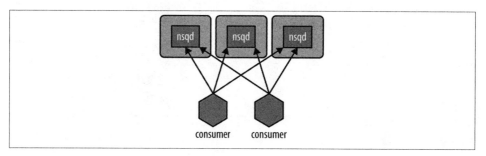

Figure 10-2. NSQ connection topology

Distributed Prime Calculation

Code that uses NSQ is generally asynchronous[3] (see Chapter 8 for a full explanation of this), although it doesn't necessarily have to be. In the following example, we will create a pool of workers that read from a topic called *numbers* where the messages are simply JSON blobs with numbers in them. The consumers will read this topic, find out if the numbers are primes, and then write to another topic, depending on whether the number

---

2. This can be quite advantageous when we're working in AWS, where we can have our nsqd processes running on a reserved instance and our consumers working on a cluster of spot instances.

3. This asynchronicity comes from NSQ's protocol for sending messages to consumers being push-based. This makes it so our code can have an asynchronous read from our connection to NSQ happen in the background and wake up when a message is found.

was prime. This will give us two new topics, *primes* and *non_primes*, that other consumers can connect to in order to do more calculations.[4]

As we've said before, there are many benefits to doing CPU-bound work like this. Firstly, we have all the guarantees of robustness, which may or may not be useful for this project. More importantly, however, we get automatic load balancing. That means that if one consumer gets a number that takes a particularly long time to process, the other consumers will pick up the slack.

We create a consumer by creating an nsq.Reader object with the topic and subscription group specified (as can be seen at the end of Example 10-10). We also must specify the location of the running nsqd instance (or the nsqlookupd instance, which we will not get into in this section). In addition, we specify a *handler*, which is simply a function that gets called for each message from the topic. To create a producer, we create an nsq.Writer object and specify the location of one or more nsqd instances to write to. This gives us the ability to write to nsq asynchronously, simply by specifying the topic name and the message.[5]

Example 10-10. Distributed prime calculation with NSQ

```
import nsq
from tornado import gen

from functools import partial
import ujson as json

@gen.coroutine
def write_message(topic, data, writer):
    response = yield gen.Task(writer.pub, topic, data) # ❶
    if isinstance(response, nsq.Error):
        print "Error with Message: {}: {}".format(data, response)
        yield write_message(data, writer)
    else:
        print "Published Message: ", data

def calculate_prime(message, writer):
    message.enable_async() # ❷
    data = json.loads(message.body)

    prime = is_prime(data["number"])
    data["prime"] = prime
    if prime:
        topic = 'primes'
```

---

4. This sort of chaining of data analysis is called *pipelining* and can be an effective way to perform multiple types of analysis on the same data efficiently.

5. You can also easily publish a message manually with an HTTP call; however, this nsq.Writer object simplifies much of the error handling.

```
        else:
            topic = 'non_primes'

        output_message = json.dumps(data)
        write_message(topic, output_message, writer)
        message.finish() # ❸

if __name__ == "__main__":
    writer = nsq.Writer(['127.0.0.1:4150', ])
    handler = partial(calculate_prime, writer=writer)
    reader = nsq.Reader(
        message_handler = handler,
        nsqd_tcp_addresses = ['127.0.0.1:4150', ],
        topic = 'numbers',
        channel = 'worker_group_a',
    )
    nsq.run()
```

❶   We will asynchronously write the result to a new topic, and retry writing if it
     fails for some reason.

❷   By enabling async on a message, we can perform asynchronous operations while
     processing the message.

❸   With async-enabled messages, we must signal to NSQ when we are done with
     a message.

In order to set up the NSQ ecosystem, we will start an instance of nsqd on our local
machine:

```
$ nsqd
2014/05/10 16:48:42 nsqd v0.2.27 (built w/go1.2.1)
2014/05/10 16:48:42 worker id 382
2014/05/10 16:48:42 NSQ: persisting topic/channel metadata to nsqd.382.dat
2014/05/10 16:48:42 TCP: listening on [::]:4150
2014/05/10 16:48:42 HTTP: listening on [::]:4151
```

Now, we can start as many instances of our Python code (Example 10-10) as we want.
In fact, we can have these instances running on other computers as long as the reference
to the nsqd_tcp_address in the instantiation of the nsq.Reader is still valid. These
consumers will connect to nsqd and wait for messages to be published on the *numbers* topic.

There are many ways data can be published to the *numbers* topic. We will use command-
line tools to do this, since knowing how to poke and prod a system goes a long way in
understanding how to properly deal with it. We can simply use the HTTP interface to
publish messages to the topic:

```
$ for i in `seq 10000`
> do
```

```
>    echo {\"number\": $i} | curl -d@- "http://127.0.0.1:4151/pub?topic=numbers"
> done
```

As this command starts running, we are publishing messages with different numbers
in them to the *numbers* topic. At the same time, all of our producers will start outputting
status messages indicating that they have seen and processed messages. In addition,
these numbers are being published to either the *primes* or the *non_primes* topic. This
allows us to have other data consumers that connect to either of these topics to get a
filtered subset of our original data. For example, an application that requires only the
prime numbers can simply connect to the *primes* topic and constantly have new primes
for its calculation. We can see the status of our calculation by using the stats HTTP
endpoint for nsqd:

```
$ curl "http://127.0.0.1:4151/stats"
nsqd v0.2.27 (built w/go1.2.1)

    [numbers        ] depth: 0      be-depth: 0      msgs: 3060     e2e%:
      [worker_group_a ] depth: 1785  be-depth: 0       inflt: 1    def: 0
            re-q: 0      timeout: 0            msgs: 3060     e2e%:
        [V2 muon:55915 ] state: 3 inflt: 1     rdy: 0     fin: 1469
            re-q: 0     msgs: 1469       connected: 24s

    [primes         ] depth:  195  be-depth: 0      msgs: 1274     e2e%:

    [non_primes     ] depth: 1274  be-depth: 0      msgs: 1274     e2e%:
```

We can see here that the *numbers* topic has one subscription group, *worker_group_a*,
with one consumer. In addition, the subscription group has a large depth of 1,785 messages, which means that we are putting messages into NSQ faster than we can process
them. This would be an indication to add more consumers so that we have more
processing power to get through more messages. Furthermore, we can see that this
particular consumer has been connected for 24 seconds, has processed 1,469 messages,
and currently has 1 message in flight. This status endpoint gives quite a good deal of
information to debug your NSQ setup! Lastly, we see the *primes* and *non_primes* topics,
which have no subscribers or consumers. This means that the messages will be stored
until a subscriber comes requesting the data.

In production systems you can use the even more powerful tool
nsqadmin, which provides a web interface with very detailed over-
views of all topics/subscribers and consumers. In addition, it allows
you to easily pause and delete subscribers and topics.

To actually see the messages, we would create a new consumer for the *primes* (or *non-
primes*) topic that simply archives the results to a file or database. Alternatively, we can
use the nsq_tail tool to take a peek at the data and see what it contains:

```
$ nsq_tail --topic primes --nsqd-tcp-address=127.0.0.1:4150
2014/05/10 17:05:33 starting Handler go-routine
2014/05/10 17:05:33 [127.0.0.1:4150] connecting to nsqd
2014/05/10 17:05:33 [127.0.0.1:4150] IDENTIFY response:
                    {MaxRdyCount:2500 TLSv1:false Deflate:false Snappy:false}
{"prime":true,"number":5}
{"prime":true,"number":7}
{"prime":true,"number":11}
{"prime":true,"number":13}
{"prime":true,"number":17}
```

Other Clustering Tools to Look At

Job processing systems using queues have existed since the start of the computer science industry, back when computers were very slow and lots of jobs needed to be processed. As a result, there are *many* libraries for queues, and many of these can be used in a cluster configuration. We strongly suggest that you pick a mature library with an active community behind it, supporting the same feature set that you'll need and not too many additional features.

The more features a library has, the more ways you'll find to misconfigure it and waste time on debugging. Simplicity is *generally* the right aim when dealing with clustered solutions. Here are a few of the more commonly used clustering solutions:

- Celery (*http://www.celeryproject.org/*) (BSD license) is a widely used asynchronous task queue using a distributed messaging architecture, written in Python. It supports Python, PyPy, and Jython. Typically it uses RabbitMQ as the message broker, but it also supports Redis, MongoDB, and other storage systems. It is often used in web development projects. Andrew Godwin discusses Celery in "Task Queues at Lanyrd.com" on page 342.

- Gearman (*http://gearman.org/*) (BSD license) is a multiplatform job processing system. It is very useful if you are integrating job processing using different technologies. Bindings are available for Python, PHP, C++, Perl, and many other languages.

- PyRes (*https://github.com/binarydud/pyres*) is a Redis-based lightweight task manager for Python. Jobs are added to queues in Redis and consumers are set up to process them, optionally passing results back on a new queue. It is a very easy system to start with if your needs are light and Python-only.

- Amazon's Simple Queue Service (SQS) (*http://aws.amazon.com/sqs/*) is a job processing system integrated into Amazon Web Services. Job consumers and producers can live inside AWS or can be external, so SQS is easy to start with and supports easy migration into the cloud. Library support exists for many languages.

Clusters can also be used for distributed numpy processing, but this is a relatively young development in the Python world. Both Enthought and Continuum have solutions, via the distarray (*https://github.com/enthought/distarray*) and blaze (*https://github.com/ContinuumIO/blaze*) packages. Note that these packages attempt to deal with the complicated problems of synchronization and data locality (there is no one-size-fits-all solution) on your behalf, so be aware that you'll probably have to think about how your data is laid out and accessed.

Wrap-Up

So far in the book, we've looked at profiling to understand slow parts of your code, compiling and using numpy to make your code run faster, and various approaches to multiple processes and computers. In the penultimate chapter, we'll look at ways of using less RAM through different data structures and probabilistic approaches. These lessons could help you to keep all your data on one machine, avoiding the need to run a cluster.

Using Less RAM

We rarely think about how much RAM we're using until we run out of it. If you run out while scaling your code, it can become a sudden blocker. Fitting more into a machine's RAM means fewer machines to manage, and it gives you a route to planning capacity for larger projects. Knowing why RAM gets eaten up and considering more efficient ways to use this scarce resource will help you deal with scaling issues.

Another route to saving RAM is to use containers that utilize features in your data for compression. In this chapter, we'll look at tries (ordered tree data structures) and a DAWG that can compress a 1.1 GB set of strings down to just 254 MB with little change in performance. A third approach is to trade storage for accuracy. For this we'll look at approximate counting and approximate set membership, which use dramatically less RAM than their exact counterparts.

A consideration with RAM usage is the notion that "data has mass." The more there is of it, the slower it moves around. If you can be parsimonious in your use of RAM your data will probably get consumed faster, as it'll move around buses faster and more of it will fit into constrained caches. If you need to store it in offline storage (e.g., a hard drive or a remote data cluster), then it'll move far more slowly to your machine. Try to choose appropriate data structures so all your data can fit onto one machine.

Counting the amount of RAM used by Python objects is surprisingly tricky. We don't necessarily know how an object is represented behind the scenes, and if we ask the operating system for a count of bytes used it will tell us about the total amount allocated to the process. In both cases, we can't see exactly how each individual Python object adds to the total.

As some objects and libraries don't report their full internal allocation of bytes (or they wrap external libraries that do not report their allocation at all), this has to be a case of best-guessing. The approaches explored in this chapter can help us to decide on the best way to represent our data so we use less RAM overall.

Objects for Primitives Are Expensive

It's common to work with containers like the list, storing hundreds or thousands of items. As soon as you store a large number, RAM usage becomes an issue.

A list with 100,000,000 items consumes approximately 760 MB of RAM, *if the items are the same object*. If we store 100,000,000 *different* items (e.g., unique integers), then we can expect to use gigabytes of RAM! Each unique object has a memory cost.

In Example 11-1, we store many 0 integers in a list. If you stored 100,000,000 references to any object (regardless of how large one instance of that object was), you'd still expect to see a memory cost of roughly 760 MB as the list is storing references to (not copies of) the object. Refer back to "Using memory_profiler to Diagnose Memory Usage" on page 42 for a reminder on how to use memory_profiler; here we load it as a new magic function in IPython using %load_ext memory_profiler.

Example 11-1. Measuring memory usage of 100,000,000 of the same integer in a list

```
In [1]: %load_ext memory_profiler  # load the %memit magic function
In [2]: %memit [0]*int(1e8)
peak memory: 790.64 MiB, increment: 762.91 MiB
```

For our next example, we'll start with a fresh shell. As the results of the first call to memit in Example 11-2 reveal, a fresh IPython shell consumes approximately 20 MB of RAM. Next, we can create a temporary list of 100,000,000 *unique* numbers. In total, this consumes approximately 3.1 GB.

 Memory can be cached in the running process, so it is always safer to exit and restart the Python shell when using memit for profiling.

After the `memit` command finishes, the temporary list is deallocated. The final call to `memit` shows that the memory usage stays at approximately 2.3 GB.

 Before reading the answer, why might the Python process still hold 2.3 GB of RAM? What's left behind, even though the `list` has gone to the garbage collector?

Example 11-2. Measuring memory usage of 100,000,000 different integers in a list

```
# we use a new IPython shell so we have a clean memory
In [1]: %load_ext memory_profiler
In [2]: %memit  # show how much RAM this process is consuming right now
peak memory: 20.05 MiB, increment: 0.03 MiB
In [3]: %memit [n for n in xrange(int(1e8))]
peak memory: 3127.53 MiB, increment: 3106.96 MiB
In [4]: %memit
peak memory: 2364.81 MiB, increment: 0.00 MiB
```

The 100,000,000 integer objects occupy the majority of the 2.3 GB, even though they're no longer being used. Python caches primitive objects like integers for later use. On a system with constrained RAM this can cause problems, so you should be aware that these primitives may build up in the cache.

A subsequent `memit` in Example 11-3 to create a second 100,000,000-item list consumes approximately 760 MB; this takes the overall allocation during this call back up to approximately 3.1 GB. The 760 MB is for the container alone, as the underlying Python integer objects already exist—they're in the cache, so they get reused.

Example 11-3. Measuring memory usage again for 100,000,000 different integers in a list

```
In [5]: %memit [n for n in xrange(int(1e8))]
peak memory: 3127.52 MiB, increment: 762.71 MiB
```

Next, we'll see that we can use the `array` module to store 100,000,000 integers far more cheaply.

The Array Module Stores Many Primitive Objects Cheaply

The `array` module efficiently stores primitive types like integers, floats, and characters, but *not* complex numbers or classes. It creates a contiguous block of RAM to hold the underlying data.

In Example 11-4, we allocate 100,000,000 integers (8 bytes each) into a contiguous chunk of memory. In total, approximately 760 MB is consumed by the process. The difference between this approach and the previous list-of-unique-integers approach is 2300MB - 760MB == 1.5GB. This is a huge savings in RAM.

Example 11-4. Building an array of 100,000,000 integers with 760 MB of RAM

```
In [1]: %load_ext memory_profiler
In [2]: import array
In [3]: %memit array.array('l', xrange(int(1e8)))
peak memory: 781.03 MiB, increment: 760.98 MiB
In [4]: arr = array.array('l')
In [5]: arr.itemsize
Out[5]: 8
```

Note that the unique numbers in the array are *not* Python objects; they are bytes in the array. If we were to dereference any of them, then a new Python int object would be constructed. If you're going to compute on them no overall saving will occur, but if instead you're going to pass the array to an external process or use only some of data, you should see a good savings in RAM compared to using a list of integers.

 If you're working with a large array or matrix of numbers with Cython and you don't want an external dependency on numpy, be aware that you can store your data in an array and pass it into Cython for processing without any additional memory overhead.

The array module works with a limited set of datatypes with varying precisions (see Example 11-5). Choose the smallest precision that you need, so you allocate just as much RAM as needed and no more. Be aware that the byte size is platform-dependent—the sizes here refer to a 32-bit platform (it states *minimum* size) while we're running the examples on a 64-bit laptop.

Example 11-5. The basic types provided by the array module

```
In [5]: array?  # IPython magic, similar to help(array)
Type:        module
String Form:<module 'array' (built-in)>
Docstring:
This module defines an object type which can efficiently represent
an array of basic values: characters, integers, floating point
numbers.  Arrays are sequence types and behave very much like lists,
except that the type of objects stored in them is constrained.  The
type is specified at object creation time by using a type code, which
is a single character.  The following type codes are defined:

    Type code   C Type           Minimum size in bytes
    'c'         character        1
    'b'         signed integer   1
    'B'         unsigned integer 1
    'u'         Unicode character 2
```

```
'h'        signed integer      2
'H'        unsigned integer    2
'i'        signed integer      2
'I'        unsigned integer    2
'l'        signed integer      4
'L'        unsigned integer    4
'f'        floating point      4
'd'        floating point      8
```

The constructor is:

```
array(typecode [, initializer]) -- create a new array
```

numpy has arrays that can hold a wider range of datatypes—you have more control over the number of bytes per item, and you can use complex numbers and datetime objects. A complex128 object takes 16 bytes per item: each item is a pair of 8-byte floating-point numbers. You can't store complex objects in a Python array, but they come for free with numpy. If you'd like a refresher on numpy, look back to Chapter 6.

In Example 11-6 you can see an additional feature of numpy arrays—you can query for the number of items, the size of each primitive, and the combined total storage of the underlying block of RAM. Note that this doesn't include the overhead of the Python object (typically this is tiny in comparison to the data you store in the arrays).

Example 11-6. Storing more complex types in a numpy array

```
In [1]: %load_ext memory_profiler
In [2]: import numpy as np
In [3]: %memit arr=np.zeros(1e8, np.complex128)
peak memory: 1552.48 MiB, increment: 1525.75 MiB
In [4]: arr.size  # same as len(arr)
Out[4]: 100000000
In [5]: arr.nbytes
Out[5]: 1600000000
In [6]: arr.nbytes/arr.size  # bytes per item
Out[6]: 16
In [7]: arr.itemsize  # another way of checking
Out[7]: 16
```

Using a regular list to store many numbers is much less efficient in RAM than using an array object. More memory allocations have to occur, which each take time; calculations also occur on larger objects, which will be less cache friendly, and more RAM is used overall, so less RAM is available to other programs.

However, if you do any work on the contents of the array in Python the primitives are likely to be converted into temporary objects, negating their benefit. Using them as a data store when communicating with other processes is a great use case for the array.

numpy arrays are almost certainly a better choice if you are doing anything heavily numeric, as you get more datatype options and many specialized and fast functions. You might choose to avoid numpy if you want fewer dependencies for your project, though Cython and Pythran work equally well with array and numpy arrays; Numba works with numpy arrays only.

Python provides a few other tools to understand memory usage, as we'll see in the following section.

Understanding the RAM Used in a Collection

You may wonder if you can ask Python about the RAM that's used by each object. Python's sys.getsizeof(obj) call will tell us *something* about the memory used by an object (most, but not all, objects provide this). If you haven't seen it before, then be warned that it won't give you the answer you'd expect for a container!

Let's start by looking at some primitive types. An int in Python is a variable-sized object; it starts as a regular integer and turns into a long integer if you count above sys.max int (on Ian's 64-bit laptop this is 9,223,372,036,854,775,807).

As a regular integer it takes 24 bytes (the object has a lot of overhead), and as a long integer it consumes 36 bytes:

```
In [1]: sys.getsizeof(int())
Out[1]: 24
In [2]: sys.getsizeof(1)
Out[2]: 24
In [3]: n=sys.maxint+1
In [4]: sys.getsizeof(n)
Out[4]: 36
```

We can do the same check for byte strings. An empty string costs 37 bytes, and each additional character adds 1 byte to the cost:

```
In [21]: sys.getsizeof(b"")
Out[21]: 37
In [22]: sys.getsizeof(b"a")
Out[22]: 38
In [23]: sys.getsizeof(b"ab")
Out[23]: 39
In [26]: sys.getsizeof(b"cde")
Out[26]: 40
```

When we use a list we see different behavior. getsizeof isn't counting the cost of the contents of the list, just the cost of the list itself. An empty list costs 72 bytes, and each item in the list takes another 8 bytes on a 64-bit laptop:

```
# goes up in 8-byte steps rather than the 24 we might expect!
In [36]: sys.getsizeof([])
```

```
Out[36]: 72
In [37]: sys.getsizeof([1])
Out[37]: 80
In [38]: sys.getsizeof([1,2])
Out[38]: 88
```

This is more obvious if we use byte strings—we'd expect to see much larger costs than getsizeof is reporting:

```
In [40]: sys.getsizeof([b""])
Out[40]: 80
In [41]: sys.getsizeof([b"abcdefghijklm"])
Out[41]: 80
In [42]: sys.getsizeof([b"a", b"b"])
Out[42]: 88
```

getsizeof only reports some of the cost, and often just for the parent object. As noted previously, it also isn't always implemented, so it can have limited usefulness.

A slightly better tool is asizeof (*http://bit.ly/asizeof*), which will walk a container's hierarchy and make a best guess about the size of each object it finds, adding the sizes to a total. Be warned that it is quite slow.

In addition to relying on guesses and assumptions, it also cannot count memory allocated behind the scenes (e.g., a module that wraps a C library may not report the bytes allocated in the C library). It is best to use this as a guide. We prefer to use memit, as it gives us an accurate count of memory usage on the machine in question.

You use asizeof as follows:

```
In [1]: %run asizeof.py
In [2]: asizeof([b"abcdefghijklm"])
Out[2]: 136
```

We can check the estimate it makes for a large list—here we'll use 10,000,000 integers:

```
# this takes 30 seconds to run!
In [1]: asizeof([x for x in xrange(10000000)])  # 1e7 integers
Out[1]: 321528064
```

We can validate this estimate by using memit to see how the process grew. In this case, the numbers are very similar:

```
In [2]: %memit([x for x in xrange(10000000)])
peak memory: 330.64 MiB, increment: 310.62 MiB
```

Generally the asizeof process is slower than using memit, but asizeof can be useful when you're analyzing small objects. memit is probably more useful for real-world applications, as the actual memory usage of the process is measured rather than inferred.

Bytes Versus Unicode

One of the compelling reasons to switch to Python 3.3+ is that Unicode object storage is significantly cheaper than it is in Python 2.7. If you mainly handle lots of strings and they eat a lot of RAM, definitely consider a move to Python 3.3+. You get this RAM saving absolutely for free.

In Example 11-7 we can see a 100,000,000-character sequence being built as a collection of bytes (this is the same as a regular `str` in Python 2.7) and as a Unicode object. The Unicode variant takes four times as much RAM. Every Unicode character costs the same higher price, regardless of the number of bytes required to represent the underlying data.

Example 11-7. Unicode objects are expensive in Python 2.7

```
In [1]: %load_ext memory_profiler
In [2]: %memit b"a" * int(1e8)
peak memory: 100.98 MiB, increment: 80.97 MiB
In [3]: %memit u"a" * int(1e8)
peak memory: 380.98 MiB, increment: 360.92 MiB
```

The UTF-8 encoding of a Unicode object uses one byte per ASCII character and more bytes for less frequently seen characters. Python 2.7 uses an equal number of bytes for a Unicode character regardless of the character's prevalence. If you're not sure about Unicode encodings versus Unicode objects, then go and watch Net Batchelder's "Pragmatic Unicode, or, How Do I Stop the Pain?" (*http://nedbatchelder.com/text/unipain.html*)

From Python 3.3, we have a flexible Unicode representation thanks to PEP 393 (*http://www.python.org/dev/peps/pep-0393/*). It works by observing the range of characters in the string and using a smaller number of bytes to represent the lower-order characters if possible.

In Example 11-8 you can see that the costs of the byte and Unicode versions of an ASCII character are the same, and that using a non-ASCII character (sigma) the memory usage only doubles—this is still better than the Python 2.7 situation.

Example 11-8. Unicode objects are far cheaper in Python 3.3+

```
Python 3.3.2+ (default, Oct  9 2013, 14:50:09)
IPython 1.2.0 -- An enhanced Interactive Python.
...
In [1]: %load_ext memory_profiler
In [2]: %memit b"a" * int(1e8)
peak memory: 91.77 MiB, increment: 71.41 MiB
In [3]: %memit u"a" * int(1e8)
peak memory: 91.54 MiB, increment: 70.98 MiB
In [4]: %memit u"Σ" * int(1e8)
peak memory: 174.72 MiB, increment: 153.76 MiB
```

Given that Unicode objects are the default in Python 3.3+, if you work with lots of string data you'll almost certainly benefit from the upgrade. The lack of cheap string storage was a hindrance for some in the early Python 3.1+ days, but now, with PEP 393, this is absolutely not an issue.

Efficiently Storing Lots of Text in RAM

A common problem with text is that it occupies a lot of RAM—but if we want to test if we have seen strings before or count their frequency, then it is convenient to have them in RAM rather than paging them to and from a disk. Storing the strings naively is expensive, but tries and directed acyclic word graphs (DAWGs) can be used to compress their representation and still allow fast operations.

These more advanced algorithms can save you a significant amount of RAM, which means that you might not need to expand to more servers. For production systems, the savings can be huge. In this section we'll look at compressing a `set` of strings costing 1.1 GB down to 254 MB using a trie, with only a small change in performance.

For this example, we'll use a text set built from a partial dump of Wikipedia. This set contains 8,545,076 unique tokens from a portion of the English Wikipedia and takes up 111,707,546 (111 MB) on disk.

The tokens are split on whitespace from their original articles; they have variable length and contain Unicode characters and numbers. They look like:

```
faddishness
'melanesians'
Kharálampos
PizzaInACup™
url="http://en.wikipedia.org/wiki?curid=363886"
VIIIa),
Superbagnères.
```

We'll use this text sample to test how quickly we can build a data structure holding one instance of each unique word, and then we'll see how quickly we can query for a known word (we'll use the uncommon "Zwiebel," from the painter Alfred Zwiebel). This lets us ask, "Have we seen Zwiebel before?" Token lookup is a common problem, and being able to do it quickly is important.

 When you try these containers on your own problems, be aware that you will probably see different behaviors. Each container builds its internal structures in different ways; passing in different types of token is likely to affect the build time of the structure, and different lengths of token will affect the query time. Always test in a methodical way.

Trying These Approaches on 8 Million Tokens

Figure 11-1 shows the 8-million-token text file (111 MB raw data) stored using a number of containers that we'll discuss in this section. The x-axis shows RAM usage for each container, the y-axis tracks the query time, and the size of each point relates to the time taken to build the structure (larger means it took longer).

As we can see in this diagram, the set and DAWG examples use a lot of RAM. The list example is expensive on RAM and slow. The Marisa trie and HAT trie examples are the most efficient for this dataset; they use a *quarter* of the RAM of the other approaches with little change in lookup speed.

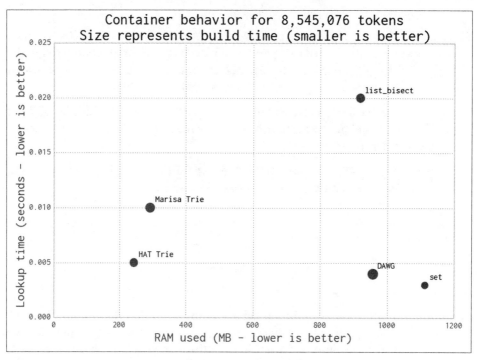

Figure 11-1. DAWG and tries versus built-in containers

The figure doesn't show the lookup time for the naive list without sort approach, which we'll introduce shortly, as it takes far too long. The datrie example is not included in the plot, because it raised a segmentation fault (we've had problems with it on other tasks in the past). When it works it is fast and compact, but it can exhibit pathological build times that make it hard to justify. It is worth including because it can be faster than the other methods, but obviously you'll want to test it thoroughly on your data.

Do be aware that you must test your problem with a variety of containers—each offers different trade-offs, such as construction time and API flexibility.

Next, we'll build up a process to test the behavior of each container.

list

Let's start with the simplest approach. We'll load our tokens into a list and then query it using an O(n) linear search. We can't do this on the large example that we've already mentioned—the search takes far too long—so we'll demonstrate the technique with a much smaller (499,048 tokens) example.

In each of the following examples we use a generator, text_example.readers, that extracts one Unicode token at a time from the input file. This means that the read process uses only a tiny amount of RAM:

```
t1 = time.time()
words = [w for w in text_example.readers]
print "Loading {} words".format(len(words))
t2 = time.time()
print "RAM after creating list {:0.1f}MiB, took {:0.1f}s".
    format(memory_profiler.memory_usage()[0], t2 - t1)
```

We're interested in how quickly we can query this list. Ideally, we want to find a container that will store our text and allow us to query it and modify it without penalty. To query it, we look for a known word a number of times using timeit:

```
assert u'Zwiebel' in words
time_cost = sum(timeit.repeat(stmt="u'Zwiebel' in words",
                              setup="from __main__ import words",
                              number=1,
                              repeat=10000))
print "Summed time to lookup word {:0.4f}s".format(time_cost)
```

Our test script reports that approximately 59 MB was used to store the original 5 MB file as a list and that the lookup time was 86 seconds:

```
RAM at start 10.3MiB
Loading 499048 words
RAM after creating list 59.4MiB, took 1.7s
Summed time to lookup word 86.1757s
```

Storing text in an unsorted list is obviously a poor idea; the O(n) lookup time is expensive, as is the memory usage. This is the worst of all worlds!

We can improve the lookup time by sorting the list and using a binary search via the bisect module (*http://bit.ly/bisect_mod*); this gives us a sensible lower bound for future queries. In Example 11-9 we time how long it takes to sort the list. Here, we switch to the larger 8,545,076 token set.

Example 11-9. Timing the sort operation to prepare for using bisect

```
t1 = time.time()
words = [w for w in text_example.readers]
print "Loading {} words".format(len(words))
t2 = time.time()
print "RAM after creating list {:0.1f}MiB, took {:0.1f}s".
    format(memory_profiler.memory_usage()[0], t2 - t1)
print "The list contains {} words".format(len(words))
words.sort()
t3 = time.time()
print "Sorting list took {:0.1f}s".format(t3 - t2)
```

Next we do the same lookup as before, but with the addition of the index method, which uses bisect:

```
import bisect
...
def index(a, x):
    'Locate the leftmost value exactly equal to x'
    i = bisect.bisect_left(a, x)
    if i != len(a) and a[i] == x:
        return i
    raise ValueError
...
    time_cost = sum(timeit.repeat(stmt="index(words, u'Zwiebel')",
                                  setup="from __main__ import words, index",
                                  number=1,
                                  repeat=10000))
```

In Example 11-10 we see that the RAM usage is much larger than before, as we're loading significantly more data. The sort takes a further 16 seconds and the cumulative lookup time is 0.02 seconds.

Example 11-10. Timings for using bisect on a sorted list

```
$ python text_example_list_bisect.py
RAM at start 10.3MiB
Loading 8545076 words
RAM after creating list 932.1MiB, took 31.0s
The list contains 8545076 words
Sorting list took 16.9s
Summed time to lookup word 0.0201s
```

We now have a sensible baseline for timing string lookups: RAM usage must get better than 932 MB, and the total lookup time should be better than 0.02 seconds.

set

Using the built-in set might seem to be the most obvious way to tackle our task. In Example 11-11, the set stores each string in a hashed structure (see Chapter 4 if you need a refresher). It is quick to check for membership, but each string must be stored separately, which is expensive on RAM.

Example 11-11. Using a set to store the data

```
words_set = set(text_example.readers)
```

As we can see in Example 11-12, the set uses more RAM than the list; however, it gives us a very fast lookup time without requiring an additional index function or an intermediate sorting operation.

Example 11-12. Running the set example

```
$ python text_example_set.py
RAM at start 10.3MiB
RAM after creating set 1122.9MiB, took 31.6s
The set contains 8545076 words
Summed time to lookup word 0.0033s
```

If RAM isn't at a premium, then this might be the most sensible first approach.

We have now lost the *ordering* of the original data, though. If that's important to you, note that you could store the strings as keys in a dictionary, with each value being an index connected to the original read order. This way, you could ask the dictionary if the key is present and for its index.

More efficient tree structures

Let's introduce a set of algorithms that use RAM more efficiently to represent our strings.

Figure 11-2 from Wikimedia Commons (*http://commons.wikimedia.org*) shows the difference in representation of four words, "tap", "taps", "top", and "tops", between a trie and a DAWG.[1] DAFSA is another name for DAWG. With a list or a set, each of these words would be stored as a separate string. Both the DAWG and the trie share parts of the strings, so that less RAM is used.

The main difference between these is that a trie shares just common prefixes, while a DAWG shares common prefixes and suffixes. In languages (like English) where there are many common word prefixes and suffixes, this can save a lot of repetition.

Exact memory behavior will depend on your data's structure. Typically a DAWG cannot assign a value to a key due to the multiple paths from the start to the end of the string, but the version shown here can accept a value mapping. Tries can also accept a value

---

1. This example is taken from the Wikipedia article on the deterministic acyclic finite state automaton (*http://en.wikipedia.org/wiki/Deterministic_acyclic_finite_state_automaton*) (DAFSA). DAFSA is another name for DAWG. The accompanying image is from Wikimedia Commons.

mapping. Some structures have to be constructed in a pass at the start, and others can be updated at any time.

A big strength of some of these structures is that they provide a *common prefix search*; that is, you can ask for all words that share the prefix you provide. With our list of four words, the result when searching for "ta" would be "tap" and "taps". Furthermore, since these are discovered through the graph structure, the retrieval of these results is very fast. If you're working with DNA, for example, compressing millions of short strings using a trie can be an efficient way to reduce RAM usage.

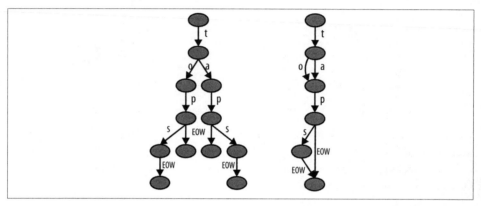

Figure 11-2. Trie and DAWG structures (image by Chkno (http://bit.ly/ Trie_and_DAWG) [CC BY-SA 3.0])

In the following sections, we take a closer look at DAWGs, tries, and their usage.

Directed acyclic word graph (DAWG)

The Directed Acyclic Word Graph (*https://github.com/kmike/DAWG*) (MIT license) attempts to efficiently represent strings that share common prefixes and suffixes.

In Example 11-13 you see the very simple setup for a DAWG. For this implementation, the DAWG cannot be modified after construction; it reads an iterator to construct itself once. The lack of post-construction updates might be a deal breaker for your use case. If so, you might need to look into using a trie instead. The DAWG does support rich queries, including prefix lookups; it also allows persistence and supports storing integer indices as values along with byte and record values.

Example 11-13. Using a DAWG to store the data

```
import dawg
...
    words_dawg = dawg.DAWG(text_example.readers)
```

As you can see in Example 11-14, for the same set of strings it uses only slightly less RAM than the earlier set example. More similar input text will cause stronger compression.

Example 11-14. Running the DAWG example

```
$ python text_example_dawg.py
RAM at start 10.3MiB
RAM after creating dawg 968.8MiB, took 63.1s
Summed time to lookup word 0.0049s
```

Marisa trie

The Marisa trie (*https://github.com/kmike/marisa-trie*) (dual-licensed LGPL and BSD) is a static trie (*http://en.wikipedia.org/wiki/Trie*) using Cython bindings to an external library. As it is static, it cannot be modified after construction. Like the DAWG, it supports storing integer indices as values, as well as byte values and record values.

A key can be used to look up a value, and vice versa. All keys sharing the same prefix can be found efficiently. The trie's contents can be persisted. Example 11-15 illustrates using a Marisa trie to store our sample data.

Example 11-15. Using a Marisa trie to store the data

```
import marisa_trie
...
    words_trie = marisa_trie.Trie(text_example.readers)
```

In Example 11-16, we can see that there is a marked improvement in RAM storage compared to the DAWG example, but the overall search time is a little slower.

Example 11-16. Running the Marisa trie example

```
$ python text_example_trie.py
RAM at start 11.0MiB
RAM after creating trie 304.7MiB, took 55.3s
The trie contains 8545076 words
Summed time to lookup word 0.0101s
```

Datrie

The double-array trie, or datrie (*https://github.com/kmike/datrie*) (licensed LGPL), uses a prebuilt alphabet to efficiently store keys. This trie can be modified after creation, but only with the same alphabet. It can also find all keys that share the prefix of the provided key, and it supports persistence.

Along with the HAT trie, it offers one of the fastest lookup times.

When using the datrie on the Wikipedia example and for past work on DNA representations, it had a pathological build time. It could take minutes or hours to represent DNA strings, compared to other data structures that completed building in seconds.

The datrie needs an alphabet to be presented to the constructor, and only keys using this alphabet are allowed. In our Wikipedia example, this means we need two passes on the raw data. You can see this in Example 11-17. The first pass builds an alphabet of characters into a set, and a second builds the trie. This slower build process allows for faster lookup times.

Example 11-17. Using a double-array trie to store the data

```
import datrie
...
    chars = set()
    for word in text_example.readers:
        chars.update(word)
    trie = datrie.BaseTrie(chars)
...
    # having consumed our generator in the first chars pass,
        we need to make a new one
    readers = text_example.read_words(text_example.SUMMARIZED_FILE)  # new generator
    for word in readers:
        trie[word] = 0
```

Sadly, on this example dataset the datrie threw a segmentation fault, so we can't show you timing information. We chose to include it because in other tests it tended to be slightly faster (but less RAM-efficient) than the following HAT Trie. We have used it with success for DNA searching, so if you have a static problem and it works, you can be confident that it'll work well. If you have a problem with varying input, however, this might not be a suitable choice.

HAT trie

The HAT trie (*https://github.com/kmike/hat-trie*) (licensed MIT) uses a cache-friendly representation to achieve very fast lookups on modern CPUs. It can be modified after construction but otherwise has a very limited API.

For simple use cases it has great performance, but the API limitations (e.g., lack of prefix lookups) might make it less useful for your application. Example 11-18 demonstrates use of the HAT trie on our example dataset.

Example 11-18. Using a HAT trie to store the data

```
import hat_trie
...
    words_trie = hat_trie.Trie()
```

```
for word in text_example.readers:
    words_trie[word] = 0
```

As you can see in Example 11-19, the HAT trie offers the fastest lookup times of our new data structures, along with superb RAM usage. The limitations in its API mean that its use is limited, but if you just need fast lookups in a large number of strings, then this might be your solution.

Example 11-19. Running the HAT trie example

```
$ python text_example_hattrie.py
RAM at start 9.7MiB
RAM after creating trie 254.2MiB, took 44.7s
The trie contains 8545076 words
Summed time to lookup word 0.0051s
```

Using tries (and DAWGs) in production systems

The trie and DAWG data structures offer good benefits, but you must still benchmark them on your problem rather than blindly adopting them. If you have overlapping sequences in your strings, then it is likely that you'll see a RAM improvement.

Tries and DAWGs are less well known, but they can provide strong benefits in production systems. We have an impressive success story in "Large-Scale Social Media Analysis at Smesh" on page 335. Jamie Matthews at DapApps (a Python software house based in the UK) also has a story about the use of tries in client systems to enable more efficient and cheaper deployments for customers:

> At DabApps, we often try to tackle complex technical architecture problems by dividing them up into small, self-contained components, usually communicating over the network using HTTP. This approach (referred to as a "service-oriented" or "microservice" architecture) has all sorts of benefits, including the possibility of reusing or sharing the functionality of a single component between multiple projects.
>
> One such task that is often a requirement in our consumer-facing client projects is postcode geocoding. This is the task of converting a full UK postcode (for example: "BN1 1AG") into a latitude and longitude coordinate pair, to enable the application to perform geospatial calculations such as distance measurement.
>
> At its most basic, a geocoding database is a simple mapping between strings, and can conceptually be represented as a dictionary. The dictionary keys are the postcodes, stored in a normalised form ("BN11AG"), and the values are some representation of the coordinates (we used a geohash encoding, but for simplicity imagine a comma-separated pair such as: "50.822921,-0.142871").
>
> There are approximately 1.7 million postcodes in the UK. Naively loading the full dataset into a Python dictionary, as described above, uses several hundred megabytes of memory. Persisting this data structure to disk using Python's native pickle format requires an unacceptably large amount of storage space. We knew we could do better.
>
> We experimented with several different in-memory and on-disk storage and serialisation formats, including storing the data externally in databases such as Redis and LevelDB,

and compressing the key/values pairs. Eventually, we hit on the idea of using a trie. Tries are extremely efficient at representing large numbers of strings in memory, and the available open-source libraries (we chose "marisa-trie") make them very simple to use.

The resulting application, including a tiny web API built with the Flask framework, uses only 30MB of memory to represent the entire UK postcode database, and can comfortably handle a high volume of postcode lookup requests. The code is simple; the service is very lightweight and painless to deploy and run on a free hosting platform such as Heroku, with no external requirements or dependencies on databases. Our implementation is open-source, available at *https://github.com/j4mie/postcodeserver/*.

— Jamie Matthews
Technical Director of DabApps.com (UK)

Tips for Using Less RAM

Generally, if you can avoid putting it into RAM, do. Everything you load costs you RAM. You might be able to load just a part of your data, for example using a memory-mapped file (*https://docs.python.org/2/library/mmap.html*); alternatively, you might be able to use generators to load only the part of the data that you need for partial computations rather than loading it all at once.

If you are working with numeric data, then you'll almost certainly want to switch to using numpy arrays—the package offers many fast algorithms that work directly on the underlying primitive objects. The RAM savings compared to using lists of numbers can be huge, and the time savings can be similarly amazing.

You'll have noticed in this book that we generally use xrange rather than range, simply because (in Python 2.x) xrange is a generator while range builds an entire list. Building a list of 100,000,000 integers just to iterate the right number of times is excessive—the RAM cost is large and entirely unnecessary. Python 3.x turns range into a generator so you no longer need to make this change.

If you're working with strings and you're using Python 2.x, try to stick to str rather than unicode if you want to save RAM. You will probably be better served by simply upgrading to Python 3.3+ if you need lots of Unicode objects throughout your program. If you're storing a large number of Unicode objects in a static structure, then you probably want to investigate the DAWG and trie structures that we've just discussed.

If you're working with lots of bit strings, investigate numpy and the bitarray (*https://pypi.python.org/pypi/bitarray/0.8.1*) package; they both have efficient representations of bits packed into bytes. You might also benefit from looking at Redis, which offers efficient storage of bit patterns.

The PyPy project is experimenting with more efficient representations of homogenous data structures, so long lists of the same primitive type (e.g., integers) might cost much less in PyPy than the equivalent structures in CPython. The Micro Python (*http://micro*

python.org/) project will be interesting to anyone working with embedded systems: it is a tiny-memory-footprint implementation of Python that's aiming for Python 3 compatibility.

It goes (almost!) without saying that you know you have to benchmark when you're trying to optimize on RAM usage, and that it pays handsomely to have a unit test suite in place before you make algorithmic changes.

Having reviewed ways of compressing strings and storing numbers efficiently, we'll now look at trading accuracy for storage space.

Probabilistic Data Structures

Probabilistic data structures allow you to make trade-offs in accuracy for immense decreases in memory usage. In addition, the number of operations you can do on them is much more restricted than with a `set` or a trie. For example, with a single HyperLogLog++ structure using 2.56 KB you can count the number of unique items up to approximately 7,900,000,000 items with 1.625% error.

This means that if we're trying to count the number of unique license plate numbers for cars, if our HyperLogLog++ counter said there were 654,192,028, we would be confident that the actual number is between 664,822,648 and 643,561,407. Furthermore, if this accuracy isn't sufficient, you can simply add more memory to the structure and it will perform better. Giving it 40.96 KB of resources will decrease the error from 1.625% to 0.4%. However, storing this data in a `set` would take 3.925 GB, even assuming no overhead!

On the other hand, the HyperLogLog++ structure would only be able to count a `set` of license plates and merge with another `set`. So, for example, we could have one structure for every state, find how many unique license plates are in those states, then merge them all to get a count for the whole country. If we were given a license plate we couldn't tell you if we've seen it before with very good accuracy, and we couldn't give you a sample of license plates we have already seen.

Probabilistic data structures are fantastic when you have taken the time to understand the problem and need to put something into production that can answer a very small set of questions about a very large set of data. Each different structure has different questions it can answer at different accuracies, so finding the right one is just a matter of understanding your requirements.

In almost all cases, probabilistic data structures work by finding an alternative representation for the data that is more compact and contains the relevant information for answering a certain set of questions. This can be thought of as a type of lossy compression, where we may lose some aspects of the data but we retain the necessary components. Since we are allowing the loss of data that isn't necessarily relevant for the particular set of questions we care about, this sort of lossy compression can be much more efficient than the lossless compression we looked at before with tries. It is because of this that the choice of which probabilistic data structure you will use is quite important —you want to pick one that retains the right information for your use case!

Before we dive in, it should be made clear that all the "error rates" here are defined in terms of standard deviations. This term comes from describing Gaussian distributions and says how spread out the function is around a center value. When the standard deviation grows, so do the number of values further away from the center point. Error rates for probabilistic data structures are framed this way because all the analyses around them are probabilistic. So, for example, when we say that the HyperLogLog++ algorithm has an error of $err = \frac{1.04}{\sqrt{m}}$ we mean that 66% of the time the error will be smaller than err, 95% of the time smaller than 2^*err, and 99.7% of the time smaller than 3^*err.[2]

Very Approximate Counting with a 1-byte Morris Counter

We'll introduce the topic of probabilistic counting with one of the earliest probabilistic counters, the Morris counter (by Robert Morris of the NSA and Bell Labs). Applications include counting millions of objects in a restricted-RAM environment (e.g., on an embedded computer), understanding large data streams, and problems in AI like image and speech recognition.

The Morris counter keeps track of an exponent and models the counted state as $2^{exponent}$ (rather than a correct count)—it provides an *order of magnitude* estimate. This estimate is updated using a probabilistic rule.

We start with the exponent set to 0. If we ask for the *value* of the counter, we'll be given `pow(2,exponent)=1` (the keen reader will note that this is off by one—we did say this was an *approximate* counter!). If we ask the counter to increment itself it will generate a random number (using the uniform distribution) and it will test if `random(0, 1) <= 1/pow(2,exponent)`, which will always be true (`pow(2,0) == 1`). The counter increments, and the exponent is set to 1.

The second time we ask the counter to increment itself it will test if `random(0, 1) <= 1/pow(2,1)`. This will be true 50% of the time. If the test passes, then the exponent is incremented. If not, then the exponent is not incremented for this increment request.

Table 11-1 shows the likelihoods of an increment occurring for each of the first exponents.

---

2. These numbers come from the 66-95-99 rule of Gaussian distributions. More information can be found in the Wikipedia entry (*http://bit.ly/Gaussian*).

Table 11-1. Morris counter details

exponent	pow(2,exponent)	P(increment)
0	1	1
1	2	0.5
2	4	0.25
3	8	0.125
4	16	0.0625
...	...	...
254	2.894802e+76	3.454467e-77

The maximum we could approximately count where we use a single unsigned byte for the exponent is `math.pow(2,255)` `==` `5e76`. The error relative to the actual count will be fairly large as the counts increase, but the RAM savings is tremendous as we only use 1 byte rather than the 32 unsigned bytes we'd otherwise have to use. Example 11-20 shows a simple implementation of the Morris counter.

Example 11-20. Simple Morris counter implementation

```python
from random import random

class MorrisCounter(object):
    counter = 0
    def add(self, *args):
        if random() < 1.0 / (2 ** self.counter):
            self.counter += 1

    def __len__(self):
        return 2**self.counter
```

Using this example implementation, we can see in Example 11-20 that the first request to increment the counter succeeds and the second fails.[3]

Example 11-21. Morris counter library example

```
In [2]: mc = MorrisCounter()
In [3]: print len(mc)
1.0
In [4]: mc.add()  # P(1) of doing an add
In [5]: print len(mc)
2.0
In [6]: mc.add()  # P(0.5) of doing an add
In [7]: print len(mc)  # the add does not occur on this attempt
2.0
```

---

3. A more fully fleshed out implementation that uses an `array` of bytes to make many counters is available at *https://github.com/ianozsvald/morris_counter*.

In Figure 11-3, the thick black line shows a normal integer incrementing on each iteration. On a 64-bit computer this is an 8-byte integer. The evolution of three 1-byte Morris counters is shown as dotted lines; the y-axis shows their values, which approximately represent the true count for each iteration. Three counters are shown to give you an idea about their different trajectories and the overall trend; the three counters are entirely independent of each other.

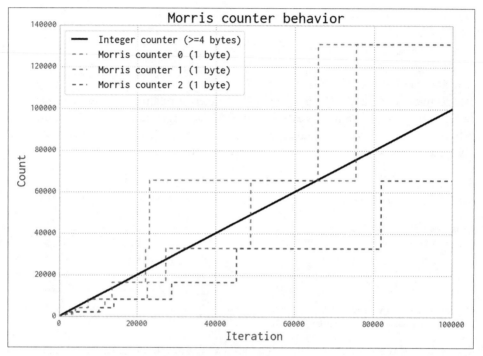

Figure 11-3. Three 1-byte Morris counters vs. an 8-byte integer

This diagram gives you some idea about the error to expect when using a Morris counter. Further details about the error behavior are available online (*http://bit.ly/Morris_error*).

K-Minimum Values

In the Morris counter, we lose any sort of information about the items we insert. That is to say, the counter's internal state is the same whether we do .add("micha") or .add("ian"). This extra information is useful and, if used properly, could help us have our counters only count unique items. In this way, calling .add("micha") thousands of times would only increase the counter once.

To implement this behavior, we will exploit properties of hashing functions (see "Hash Functions and Entropy" on page 81 for a more in-depth discussion of hash functions).

The main property we would like to take advantage of is the fact that the hash function takes input and *uniformly* distributes it. For example, let's assume we have a hash function that takes in a string and outputs a number between 0 and 1. For that function to be uniform means that when we feed it in a string we are equally likely to get a value of 0.5 as a value of 0.2, or any other value. This also means that if we feed it in many string values, we would expect the values to be relatively evenly spaced. Remember, this is a probabilistic argument: the values won't always be evenly spaced, but if we have many strings and try this experiment many times, they will tend to be evenly spaced.

Suppose we took 100 items and stored the hashes of those values (the hashes being numbers from 0 to 1). Knowing the spacing is even means that instead of saying, "We have 100 items," we could say "We have a distance of 0.01 between every item." This is where the K-Minimum Values algorithm[4] finally comes in—if we keep the k smallest unique hash values we have seen, we can approximate the overall spacing between hash values and infer what the total number of items is. In Figure 11-4 we can see the state of a K-Minimum Values structure (also called a KMV) as more and more items are added. At first, since we don't have many hash values, the largest hash we have kept is quite large. As we add more and more, the largest of the k hash values we have kept gets smaller and smaller. Using this method, we can get error rates of $O\left(\sqrt{\frac{2}{\pi(k-2)}}\right)$.

The larger k is, the more we can account for the hashing function we are using not being completely uniform for our particular input and for unfortunate hash values. An example of unfortunate hash values would be hashing `['A', 'B', 'C']` and getting the values `[0.01, 0.02, 0.03]`. If we start hashing more and more values, it is less and less probable that they will clump up.

Furthermore, since we are only keeping the smallest *unique* hash values, the data structure only considers unique inputs. We can see this easily because if we are in a state where we only store the smallest three hashes and currently `[0.1, 0.2, 0.3]` are the smallest hash values, if we add in something with the hash value of `0.4` our state will not change. Similarly, if we add more items with a hash value of `0.3`, our state will also not change. This is a property called *idempotence*; it means that if we do the same operation, with the same inputs, on this structure multiple times, the state will not be changed. This is in contrast to, for example, an `append` on a `list`, which will always change its value. This concept of idempotence carries on to all of the data structures in this section except for the Morris counter.

Example 11-22 shows a very basic K-Minimum Values implementation. Of note is our use of a `sortedset`, which, like a set, can only contain unique items. This uniqueness

4. Beyer, K., Haas, P. J., Reinwald, B., Sismanis, Y., and Gemulla, R. "On synopses for distinct-value estimation under multiset operations." *Proceedings of the 2007 ACM SIGMOD International Conference on Management of Data - SIGMOD '07*, (2007): 199–210. doi:10.1145/1247480.1247504.

gives our `KMinValues` structure idempotence for free. To see this, follow the code through: when the same item is added more than once, the `data` property does not change.

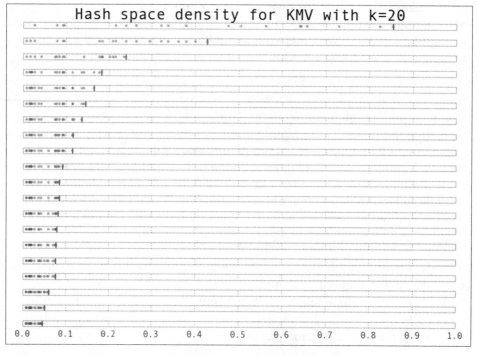

Figure 11-4. The values stores in a KMV structure as more elements are added

Example 11-22. Simple KMinValues implementation

```
import mmh3
from blist import sortedset

class KMinValues(object):
    def __init__(self, num_hashes):
        self.num_hashes = num_hashes
        self.data = sortedset()

    def add(self, item):
        item_hash = mmh3.hash(item)
        self.data.add(item_hash)
        if len(self.data) > self.num_hashes:
            self.data.pop()

    def __len__(self):
        if len(self.data) <= 2:
```

```
        return 0
    return (self.num_hashes - 1) * (2**32-1) / float(self.data[-2] + 2**31 - 1)
```

Using the KMinValues implementation in the Python package countmemaybe (*https://
github.com/mynameisfiber/countmemaybe*) (Example 11-23), we can begin to see the
utility of this data structure. This implementation is very similar to the one in
Example 11-22, but it fully implements the other set operations, such as union and
intersection. Also note that "size" and "cardinality" are used interchangeably (the word
"cardinality" is from set theory and is used more in the analysis of probabilistic data
structures). Here, we can see that even with a reasonably small value for k, we can store
50,000 items and calculate the cardinality of many set operations with relatively low
error.

Example 11-23. countmemaybe KMinValues implementation

```
>>> from countmemaybe import KMinValues

>>> kmv1 = KMinValues(k=1024)

>>> kmv2 = KMinValues(k=1024)

>>> for i in xrange(0,50000): # ❶
    kmv1.add(str(i))
    ...:

>>> for i in xrange(25000, 75000): # ❷
    kmv2.add(str(i))
    ...:

>>> print len(kmv1)
50416

>>> print len(kmv2)
52439

>>> print kmv1.cardinality_intersection(kmv2)
25900.2862992

>>> print kmv1.cardinality_union(kmv2)
75346.2874158
```

❶   We put 50,000 elements into kmv1.

❷   kmv2 also gets 50,000 elements, 25,000 of which are the same as those in kmv1.

With these sorts of algorithms, the choice of hash function can have a drastic effect on the quality of the estimates. Both of these implementations use mmh3, a Python implementation of mumurhash3 that has nice properties for hashing strings. However, different hash functions could be used if they are more convenient for your particular dataset.

Bloom Filters

Sometimes we need to be able to do other types of set operations, for which we need to introduce new types of probabilistic data structures. *Bloom filters*[5] were created to answer the question of whether we've seen an item before.

Bloom filters work by having multiple hash values in order to represent a value as multiple integers. If we later see something with the same set of integers, we can be reasonably confident that it is the same value.

In order to do this in a way that efficiently utilizes available resources, we implicitly encode the integers as the indices of a list. This could be thought of as a list of bool values that are initially set to False. If we are asked to add an object with hash values [10, 4, 7], then we set the tenth, fourth, and seventh indices of the list to True. In the future, if we are asked if we have seen a particular item before, we simply find its hash values and check if all the corresponding spots in the bool list are set to True.

This method gives us no false negatives and a controllable rate of false positives. What this means is that if the Bloom filter says we have not seen an item before, then we can be 100% sure that we haven't seen the item before. On the other hand, if the Bloom filter states that we *have* seen an item before, then there is a probability that we actually have not and we are simply seeing an erroneous result. This erroneous result comes from the fact that we will have hash collisions, and sometimes the hash values for two objects will be the same even if the objects themselves are not the same. However, in practice Bloom filters are set to have error rates below 0.5%, so this error can be acceptable.

---

5. Bloom, B. H. "Space/time trade-offs in hash coding with allowable errors." *Communications of the ACM*. 13:7 (1970): 422–426 doi:10.1145/362686.362692.

We can simulate having as many hash functions as we want simply by having two hash functions that are independent of each other. This method is called "double hashing." If we have a hash function that gives us two independent hashes, we can do:

```
def multi_hash(key, num_hashes):
    hash1, hash2 = hashfunction(key)
    for i in xrange(num_hashes):
        yield (hash1 + i * hash2) % (2^32 - 1)
```

The modulo ensures that the resulting hash values are 32 bit (we would modulo by 2^64 - 1 for 64-bit hash functions).

The exact length of the bool list and the number of hash values per item we need will be fixed based on the capacity and the error rate we require. With some reasonably simple statistical arguments[6] we see that the ideal values are:

$$num\_bits = -\, capacity \cdot \frac{log(error)}{log(2)^2}$$

$$num\_hashes = num\_bits \cdot \frac{log(2)}{capacity}$$

That is to say, if we wish to store 50,000 objects (no matter how big the objects themselves are) at a false positive rate of 0.05% (that is to say, 0.05% of the times we say we have seen an object before, we actually have not), it would require 791,015 bits of storage and 11 hash functions.

To further improve our efficiency in terms of memory use, we can use single bits to represent the bool values (a native bool actually takes 4 bits). We can do this easily by using the bitarray module. Example 11-24 shows a simple Bloom filter implementation.

Example 11-24. Simple Bloom filter implemintation

```
import bitarray
import math
import mmh3

class BloomFilter(object):
    def __init__(self, capacity, error=0.005):
        """
        Initialize a Bloom filter with given capacity and false positive rate
        """
```

---

6. The Wikipedia page on Bloom filters (*http://bit.ly/Bloom_filter*) has a very simple proof for the properties of a Bloom filter.

```python
        self.capacity = capacity
        self.error = error
        self.num_bits = int(-capacity * math.log(error) / math.log(2)**2) + 1
        self.num_hashes = int(self.num_bits * math.log(2) / float(capacity)) + 1
        self.data = bitarray.bitarray(self.num_bits)

    def _indexes(self, key):
        h1, h2 = mmh3.hash64(key)
        for i in xrange(self.num_hashes):
            yield (h1 + i * h2) % self.num_bits

    def add(self, key):
        for index in self._indexes(key):
            self.data[index] = True

    def __contains__(self, key):
        return all(self.data[index] for index in self._indexes(key))

    def __len__(self):
        num_bits_on = self.data.count(True)
        return -1.0 * self.num_bits * \
                    math.log(1.0 - num_bits_on / float(self.num_bits)) / \
                        float(self.num_hashes)

    @staticmethod
    def union(bloom_a, bloom_b):
        assert bloom_a.capacity == bloom_b.capacity, "Capacities must be equal"
        assert bloom_a.error == bloom_b.error, "Error rates must be equal"

        bloom_union = BloomFilter(bloom_a.capacity, bloom_a.error)
        bloom_union.data = bloom_a.data | bloom_b.data
        return bloom_union
```

What happens if we insert more items than we specified for the capacity of the Bloom filter? At the extreme end, all the items in the bool list will be set to True, in which case we say that we have seen every item. This means that Bloom filters are very sensitive to what their initial capacity was set to, which can be quite aggravating if we are dealing with a set of data whose size is unknown (for example, a stream of data).

One way of dealing with this is to use a variant of Bloom filters called *scalable* Bloom filters.[7] They work by chaining together multiple bloom filters whose error rates vary in a specific way.[8] By doing this, we can guarantee an overall error rate and simply add a new Bloom filter when we need more capacity. In order to check if we've seen an item before, we simply iterate over all of the sub-Blooms until either we find the object or we

---

7. Almeida, P. S., Baquero, C., Preguiça, N., and Hutchison, D. "Scalable Bloom Filters." *Information Processing Letters* 101: 255–261. doi:10.1016/j.ipl.2006.10.007.

8. The error values actually decrease like the geometric series. This way, when you take the product of all the error rates it approaches the desired error rate.

exhaust the list. A sample implementation of this structure can be seen in Example 11-25, where we use the previous Bloom filter implementation for the underlying functionality and have a counter to simplify knowing when to add a new Bloom.

Example 11-25. Simple scaling Bloom filter implementation

```
from bloomfilter import BloomFilter

class ScalingBloomFilter(object):
    def __init__(self, capacity, error=0.005,
                 max_fill=0.8, error_tightening_ratio=0.5):
        self.capacity = capacity
        self.base_error = error
        self.max_fill = max_fill
        self.items_until_scale = int(capacity * max_fill)
        self.error_tightening_ratio = error_tightening_ratio
        self.bloom_filters = []
        self.current_bloom = None
        self._add_bloom()

    def _add_bloom(self):
        new_error = self.base_error * \
                    self.error_tightening_ratio ** len(self.bloom_filters)
        new_bloom = BloomFilter(self.capacity, new_error)
        self.bloom_filters.append(new_bloom)
        self.current_bloom = new_bloom
        return new_bloom

    def add(self, key):
        if key in self:
            return True
        self.current_bloom.add(key)
        self.items_until_scale -= 1
        if self.items_until_scale == 0:
            bloom_size = len(self.current_bloom)
            bloom_max_capacity = int(self.current_bloom.capacity * self.max_fill)

            # We may have been adding many duplicate values into the Bloom, so
            # we need to check if we actually need to scale or if we still have
            # space
            if bloom_size >= bloom_max_capacity:
                self._add_bloom()
                self.items_until_scale = bloom_max_capacity
            else:
                self.items_until_scale = int(bloom_max_capacity - bloom_size)
        return False

    def __contains__(self, key):
        return any(key in bloom for bloom in self.bloom_filters)

    def __len__(self):
        return sum(len(bloom) for bloom in self.bloom_filters)
```

Another way of dealing with this is using a method called timing Bloom filters. This variant allows elements to be expired out of the data structure, thus freeing up space for more elements. This is especially nice for dealing with streams, since we can have elements expire after, say, an hour and have the capacity set large enough to deal with the amount of data we see per hour. Using a Bloom filter this way would give us a nice view into what has been happening in the last hour.

Using this data structure will feel much like using a set object. In the following interaction we use the scalable Bloom filter to add several objects, test if we've seen them before, and then try to experimentally find the false positive rate:

```
>>> bloom = BloomFilter(100)

>>> for i in xrange(50):
....:     bloom.add(str(i))
....:

>>> "20" in bloom
True

>>> "25" in bloom
True

>>> "51" in bloom
False

>>> num_false_positives = 0

>>> num_true_negatives = 0

>>> # None of the following numbers should be in the Bloom.
>>> # If one is found in the Bloom, it is a false positive.
>>> for i in xrange(51,10000):
....:     if str(i) in bloom:
....:         num_false_positives += 1
....:     else:
....:         num_true_negatives += 1
....:

>>> num_false_positives
54

>>> num_true_negatives
9895

>>> false_positive_rate = num_false_positives / float(10000 - 51)

>>> false_positive_rate
0.005427681173987335
```

```
>>> bloom.error
0.005
```

We can also do unions with Bloom filters in order to join multiple sets of items:

```
>>> bloom_a = BloomFilter(200)

>>> bloom_b = BloomFilter(200)

>>> for i in xrange(50):
    ...:      bloom a.add(str(i))
    ...:

>>> for i in xrange(25,75):
    ...:      bloom_b.add(str(i))
    ...:

>>> bloom = BloomFilter.union(bloom_a, bloom_b)

>>> "51" in bloom_a # ❶
Out[9]: False

>>> "24" in bloom_b # ❷
Out[10]: False

>>> "55" in bloom # ❸
Out[11]: True

>>> "25" in bloom
Out[12]: True
```

❶   The value of '51' is not in bloom_a.

❷   Similarly, the value of '24' is not in bloom_b.

❸   However, the bloom object contains all the objects in both bloom_a and bloom_b!

One caveat with this is that you can only take the union of two Blooms with the same capacity and error rate. Furthermore, the final Bloom's used capacity can be as high as the sum of the used capacities of the two Blooms unioned to make it. What this means is that you could start with two Bloom filters that are a little more than half full and, when you union them together, get a new Bloom that is over capacity and not reliable!

LogLog Counter

LogLog-type counters (*http://bit.ly/LL-type_counters*) are based on the realization that the individual bits of a hash function can also be considered to be random. That is to say, the probability of the first bit of a hash being 1 is 50%, the probability of the first two bits being 01 is 25%, and the probability of the first three bits being 001 is 12.5%. Knowing these probabilities, and keeping the hash with the most 0s at the beginning (i.e., the least probable hash value), we can come up with an estimate of how many items we've seen so far.

A good analogy for this method is flipping coins. Imagine we would like to flip a coin 32 times and get heads every time. The number 32 comes from the fact that we are using 32-bit hash functions. If we flip the coin once and it comes up tails, then we will store the number 0, since our best attempt yielded 0 heads in a row. Since we know the probabilities behind this coin flip, we can also tell you that our longest series was 0 long and you can estimate that we've tried this experiment 2^0 = 1 time. If we keep flipping our coin and we're able to get 10 heads before getting a tail, then we would store the number 10. Using the same logic, you could estimate that we've tried the experiment 2^10 = 1024 times. With this system, the highest we could count would be the maximum number of flips we consider (for 32 flips, this is 2^32 = 4,294,967,296).

In order to encode this logic with LogLog-type counters, we take the binary representation of the hash value of our input and see how many 0s there are before we see our first 1. The hash value can be thought of as a series of 32 coin flips, where 0 means a flip for heads and 1 means a flip for tails (i.e., `000010101101` means we flipped four heads before our first tails and `010101101` means we flipped one head before flipping our first tail). This gives us an idea how many tries happened before this hash value was gotten. The mathematics behind this system is almost equivalent to that of the Morris counter, with one major exception: we acquire the "random" values by looking at the actual input instead of using a random number generator. This means that if we keep adding the same value to a LogLog counter its internal state will not change. Example 11-26 shows a simple implementation of a LogLog counter.

Example 11-26. Simple implementation of LogLog register

```
import mmh3

def trailing_zeros(number):
    """
    Returns the index of the first bit set to 1 from the right side of a 32-bit
    integer
    >>> trailing_zeros(0)
    32
    >>> trailing_zeros(0b1000)
    3
    >>> trailing_zeros(0b10000000)
    7
    """
    if not number:
        return 32
    index = 0
    while (number >> index) & 1 == 0:
        index += 1
    return index
```

```
class LogLogRegister(object):
    counter = 0
    def add(self, item):
        item_hash = mmh3.hash(str(item))
        return self._add(item_hash)

    def _add(self, item_hash):
        bit_index = trailing_zeros(item_hash)
        if bit_index > self.counter:
            self.counter = bit_index

    def __len__(self):
        return 2**self.counter
```

The biggest drawback of this method is that we may get a hash value that increases the counter right at the beginning and skews our estimates. This would be similar to flipping 32 tails on the first try. In order to remedy this, we should have many people flipping coins at the same time and combine their results. The law of large numbers tells us that as we add more and more flippers, the total statistics become less affected by anomalous samples from individual flippers. The exact way that we combine the results is the root of the difference between LogLog type methods (classic LogLog, SuperLogLog, Hyper-LogLog, HyperLogLog++, etc.).

We can accomplish this "multiple flipper" method by taking the first couple of bits of a hash value and using that to designate which of our flippers had that particular result. If we take the first 4 bits of the hash, this means we have 2^4 = 16 flippers. Since we used the first 4 bits for this selection, we only have 28 bits left (corresponding to 28 individual coin flips per coin flipper), meaning each counter can only count up to 2^28 = 268,435,456. In addition, there is a constant (alpha) that depends on the number of flippers there are, which normalizes the estimation.[9] All of this together gives us an algorithm with $1.05 / \sqrt{(m)}$ accuracy, where m is the number of registers (or flippers) used.. Example 11-27 shows a simple implementation of the LogLog algorithm.

Example 11-27. Simple implementation of LogLog

```
from llregister import LLRegister
import mmh3

class LL(object):
    def __init__(self, p):
        self.p = p
        self.num_registers = 2**p
        self.registers = [LLRegister() for i in xrange(int(2**p))]
        self.alpha = 0.7213 / (1.0 + 1.079 / self.num_registers)
```

---

9. A full description of the basic LogLog and SuperLogLog algorithms can be found at *http://bit.ly/algo rithm_desc*.

```
def add(self, item):
    item_hash = mmh3.hash(str(item))
    register_index = item_hash & (self.num_registers - 1)
    register_hash = item_hash >> self._p
    self.registers[register_index]._add(register_hash)

def __len__(self):
    register_sum = sum(h.counter for h in self.registers)
    return self.num_registers * self.alpha * \
                        2 ** (float(register_sum) / self.num_registers)
```

In addition to this algorithm deduplicating similar items by using the hash value as an indicator, it has a tunable parameter that can be used to dial what sort of accuracy vs. storage compromise you are willing to make.

In the __len__ method, we are averaging the estimates from all of the individual LogLog registers. This, however, is not the most efficient way to combine the data! This is because we may get some unfortunate hash values that make one particular register spike up while the others are still at low values. Because of this, we are only able to achieve an error rate of $O\left(\frac{1.30}{\sqrt{m}}\right)$, where m is the number of registers used.

SuperLogLog[10] was devised as a fix to this problem. With this algorithm, only the lowest 70% of the registers were used for the size estimate, and their value was limited by a maximum value given by a restriction rule. This addition decreased the error rate to $O\left(\frac{1.05}{\sqrt{m}}\right)$. This is counterintuitive, since we got a better estimate by disregarding information!

Finally, HyperLogLog[11] came out in 2007 and gave us further accuracy gains. It did so simply by changing the method of averaging the individual registers: instead of simply averaging, we use a spherical averaging scheme that also has special considerations for different edge cases the structure could be in. This brings us to the current best error rate of $O\left(\frac{1.04}{\sqrt{m}}\right)$. In addition, this formulation removes a sorting operation that is necessary with SuperLogLog. This can greatly speed up the performance of the data structure when you are trying to insert items at a high volume. Example 11-28 shows a simple implementation of HyperLogLog.

Example 11-28. Simple implementation of HyperLogLog

```
from ll import LL
import math
```

---

10. Durand, M., and Flajolet, P. "LogLog Counting of Large Cardinalities." Proceedings of ESA 2003, 2832 (2003): 605–617. doi:10.1007/978-3-540-39658-1_55.

11. Flajolet, P., Fusy, É., Gandouet, O., et al. "HyperLogLog: the analysis of a near-optimal cardinality estimation algorithm." Proceedings of the 2007 International Conference on Analysis of Algorithms, (2007): 127–146.

```python
class HyperLogLog(LL):
    def __len__(self):
        indicator = sum(2**-m.counter for m in self.registers)
        E = self.alpha * (self.num_registers**2) / float(indicator)

        if E <= 5.0 / 2.0 * self.num_registers:
            V = sum(1 for m in self.registers if m.counter == 0)
            if V != 0:
                Estar = self.num_registers * \
                        math.log(self.num_registers / (1.0 * V), 2)
            else:
                Estar = E
        else:
            if E <= 2**32 / 30.0:
                Estar = E
            else:
                Estar = -2**32 * math.log(1 - E / 2**32, 2)
        return Estar

if __name__ == "__main__":
    import mmh3
    hll = HyperLogLog(8)
    for i in xrange(100000):
        hll.add(mmh3.hash(str(i)))
    print len(hll)
```

The only further increase in accuracy was given by the HyperLogLog++ algorithm, which increased the accuracy of the data structure while it is relatively empty. When more items are inserted, this scheme reverts to standard HyperLogLog. This is actually quite useful, since the statistics of the LogLog-type counters require a lot of data to be accurate—having a scheme for allowing better accuracy with fewer number items greatly improves the usability of this method. This extra accuracy is achieved by having a smaller but more accurate HyperLogLog structure that can be later converted into the larger structure that was originally requested. Also, there are some imperially derived constants that are used in the size estimates that remove biases.

Real-World Example

For a better understanding of the data structures, we first created a dataset with many unique keys, and then one with duplicate entries. Figures 11-5 and 11-6 show the results when we feed these keys into the data structures we've just looked at and periodically query, "How many unique entries have there been?" We can see that the data structures that contain more stateful variables (such as HyperLogLog and KMinValues) do better, since they more robustly handle bad statistics. On the other hand, the Morris counter and the single LogLog register can quickly have very high error rates if one unfortunate random number or hash value occurs. For most of the algorithms, however, we know that the number of stateful variables is directly correlated with the error guarantees, so this makes sense.

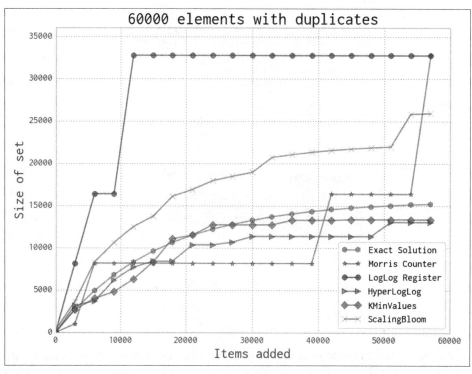

Figure 11-5. Comparison between various probabilistic data structures for repeating data

Looking just at the probabilistic data structures that have the best performance (and really, the ones you will probably use), we can summarize their utility and their approximate memory usage (see Table 11-2). We can see a huge change in memory usage depending on the questions we care to ask. This simply highlights the fact that when using a probabilistic data structure, you must first consider what questions you really need to answer about the dataset before proceeding. Also note that only the Bloom filter's size depends on the number of elements. The HyperLogLog and KMinValues's sizes are *only* dependent on the error rate.

As another, more realistic test, we chose to use a dataset derived from the text of Wikipedia. We ran a very simple script in order to extract all single-word tokens with five or more characters from all articles and store them in a newline-separated file. The question then was, "How many unique tokens are there?" The results can be seen in Table 11-3. In addition, we attempted to answer the same question using the datrie from "Datrie" on page 301 (this trie was chosen as opposed to the others because it offers good compression while still being robust enough to deal with the entire dataset).

Table 11-2. Comparison of major probabilistic data structures

	Size	Union[a]	Intersection	Contains	Size[b]
HyperLogLog	Yes ($O\left(\frac{1.04}{\sqrt{m}}\right)$)	Yes	No[c]	No	2.704 MB
KMinValues	Yes ($O\left(\sqrt{\frac{2}{\pi(m-2)}}\right)$)	Yes	Yes	No	20.372 MB
Bloom filter	Yes ($O\left(\frac{0.78}{\sqrt{m}}\right)$)	Yes	No[c]	Yes	197.8 MB

[a] Union operations occur without increasing the error rate.

[b] Size of data structure with 0.05% error rate, 100,000,000 unique elements, and using a 64-bit hashing function.

[c] These operations *can* be done but at a considerable penalty in terms of accuracy.

The major takeaway from this experiment is that if you are able to specialize your code, you can get amazing speed and memory gains. This has been true throughout the entire book: when we specialized our code in "Selective Optimizations: Finding What Needs to Be Fixed" on page 124, we were similarly able to get speed increases.

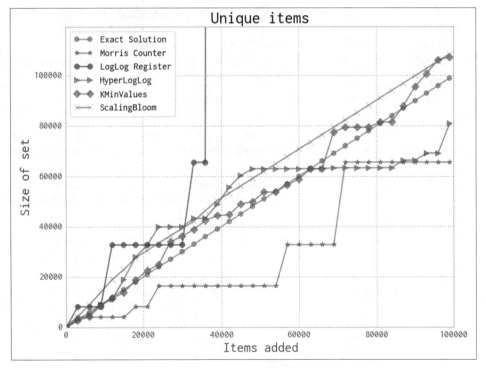

Figure 11-6. Comparison between various probabilistic data structures for unique data

Probabilistic data structures are an algorithmic way of specializing your code. We store only the data we need in order to answer specific questions with given error bounds.

By only having to deal with a subset of the information given, not only can we make the memory footprint much smaller, but we can also perform most operations over the structure faster (as can be seen with the insertion time into the datrie in Table 11-3 being larger than any of the probabilistic data structures).

Table 11-3. Size estimates for the number of unique words in Wikipedia

	Elements	Relative error	Processing time[a]	Structure size[b]
Morris counter[c]	1,073,741,824	6.52%	751s	5 bits
LogLog register	1,048,576	78.84%	1,690 s	5 bits
LogLog	4,522,232	8.76%	2,112 s	5 bits
HyperLogLog	4,983,171	-0.54%	2,907 s	40 KB
KMinValues	4,912,818	0.88%	3,503 s	256 KB
ScalingBloom	4,949,358	0.14%	10,392 s	11,509 KB
Datrie	4,505,514[d]	0.00%	14,620 s	114,068 KB
True value	4,956,262	0.00%	-----	49,558 KB[e]

[a] Processing time has been adjusted to remove the time to read the dataset from disk. We also use the simple implementations provided earlier for testing.

[b] Structure size is theoretical given the amount of data since the implementations used were not optimized.

[c] Since the Morris counter doesn't deduplicate input, the size and relative error are given with regard to the total number of values.

[d] Because of some encoding problems, the datrie could not load all the keys.

[e] The dataset is 49,558 KB considering only unique tokens, or 8.742 GB with all tokens.

As a result, whether or not you use probabilistic data structures, you should always keep in mind what questions you are going to be asking of your data and how you can most effectively store that data in order to ask those specialized questions. This may come down to using one particular type of list over another, using one particular type of database index over another, or maybe even using a probabilistic data structure to throw out all but the relevant data!

## CHAPTER 12

Lessons from the Field

Questions You'll Be Able to Answer After This Chapter

- How do successful start-ups deal with large volumes of data and machine learning?
- What monitoring and deployment technologies keep systems stable?
- What lessons have successful CTOs learned about their technologies and teams?
- How widely can PyPy be deployed?

In this chapter we have collected stories from successful companies where Python is used in high-data-volume and speed-critical situations. The stories are written by key people in each organization who have many years of experience; they share not just their technology choices but also some of their hard-won wisdom.

Adaptive Lab's Social Media Analytics (SoMA)

Ben Jackson (adaptivelab.com)

Adaptive Lab is a product development and innovation company based in London's Tech City area, Shoreditch. We apply our lean, user-centric method of product design and delivery collaboratively with a wide range of companies, from start-ups to large corporates.

YouGov is a global market research company whose stated ambition is to supply a live stream of continuous, accurate data and insight into what people are thinking and doing all over the world—and that's just what we managed to provide for them. Adaptive Lab designed a way to listen passively to real discussions happening in social media and gain insight to users' feelings on a customizable range of topics. We built a scalable system capable of capturing a large volume of streaming information, processing it, storing it indefinitely, and presenting it through a powerful, filterable interface in real time. The system was built using Python.

Python at Adaptive Lab

Python is one of our core technologies. We use it in performance-critical applications and whenever we work with clients that have in-house Python skills, so that the work we produce for them can be taken on in-house.

Python is ideal for small, self-contained, long-running daemons, and it's just as great with flexible, feature-rich web frameworks like Django and Pyramid. The Python community is thriving, which means that there's a huge library of open source tools out there that allow us to build quickly and with confidence, leaving us to focus on the new and innovative stuff, solving problems for users.

Across all of our projects, we at Adaptive Lab reuse several tools that are built in Python but that can be used in a language-agnostic way. For example, we use SaltStack for server provisioning and Mozilla's Circus for managing long-running processes. The benefit to us when a tool is open source and written in a language we're familiar with is that if we find any problems, we can solve them ourselves and get those solutions taken up, which benefits the community.

SoMA's Design

Our Social Media Analytics tool needed to cope with a high throughput of social media data and the storage and retrieval in real time of a large amount of information. After researching various data stores and search engines, we settled on Elasticsearch as our real-time document store. As its name suggests, it's highly scalable, but it is also very easy to use and is very capable of providing statistical responses as well as search—ideal for our application. Elasticsearch itself is built in Java, but like any well-architected component of a modern system, it has a good API and is well catered for with a Python library and tutorials.

The system we designed uses queues with Celery held in Redis to quickly hand a large stream of data to any number of servers for independent processing and indexing. Each component of the whole complex system was designed to be small, individually simple, and able to work in isolation. Each focused on one task, like analyzing a conversation for sentiment or preparing a document for indexing into Elasticsearch. Several of these were configured to run as daemons using Mozilla's Circus, which keeps all the processes up and running and allows them to be scaled up or down on individual servers.

SaltStack is used to define and provision the complex cluster and handles the setup of all of the libraries, languages, databases, and document stores. We also make use of Fabric, a Python tool for running arbitrary tasks on the command line. Defining servers in code has many benefits: complete parity with the production environment; version control of the configuration; having everything in one place. It also serves as documentation on the setup and dependencies required by a cluster.

Our Development Methodology

We aim to make it as easy as possible for a newcomer to a project to be able to quickly get into adding code and deploying confidently. We use Vagrant to build the complexities of a system locally, inside a virtual machine that has complete parity with the production environment. A simple `vagrant up` is all a newcomer needs to get set up with all the dependencies required for their work.

We work in an agile way, planning together, discussing architecture decisions, and determining a consensus on task estimates. For SoMA, we made the decision to include at least a few tasks considered as corrections for "technical debt" in each sprint. Also included were tasks for documenting the system (we eventually established a wiki to house all the knowledge for this ever-expanding project). Team members review each other's code after each task, to sanity check, offer feedback, and understand the new code that is about to get added to the system.

A good test suite helped bolster confidence that any changes weren't going to cause existing features to fail. Integration tests are vital in a system like SoMA, composed of many moving parts. A staging environment offers a way to test the performance of new code; on SoMA in particular, it was only through testing against the kind of large datasets seen in production that problems could occur and be dealt with, so it was often necessary to reproduce that amount of data in a separate environment. Amazon's Elastic Compute Cloud (EC2) gave us the flexibility to do this.

Maintaining SoMA

The SoMA system runs continuously and the amount of information it consumes grows every day. We have to account for peaks in the data stream, network issues, and problems in any of the third-party service providers it relies on. So, to make things easy on ourselves, SoMA is designed to fix itself whenever it can. Thanks to Circus, processes that crash out will come back to life and resume their tasks from where they left off. A task will queue up until a process can consume it, and there's enough breathing room there to stack up tasks while the system recovers.

We use Server Density to monitor the many SoMA servers. It's very simple to set up, but quite powerful. A nominated engineer can receive a push message on his phone as soon as a problem is likely to occur, so he can react in time to ensure it doesn't become a problem. With Server Density it's also very easy to write custom plug-ins in Python, making it possible, for example, to set up instant alerts on aspects of Elasticsearch's behavior.

Advice for Fellow Engineers

Above all, you and your team need to be confident and comfortable that what is about to be deployed into a live environment is going to work flawlessly. To get to that point, you have to work backward, spending time on all of the components of the system that will give you that sense of comfort. Make deployment simple and foolproof; use a staging environment to test the performance with real-world data; ensure you have a good, solid test suite with high coverage; implement a process for incorporating new code into the system; make sure technical debt gets addressed sooner rather than later. The more you shore up your technical infrastructure and improve your processes, the happier and more successful at engineering the right solutions your team will be.

If a solid foundation of code and ecosystem are not in place but the business is pressuring you to get things live, it's only going to lead to problem software. It's going to be your responsibility to push back and stake out time for incremental improvements to the code, and the tests and operations involved in getting things out the door.

Making Deep Learning Fly with RadimRehurek.com

Radim Řehůřek (radimrehurek.com)

When Ian asked me to write my "lessons from the field" on Python and optimizations for this book, I immediately thought, "Tell them how you made a Python port faster than Google's C original!" It's an inspiring story of making a machine learning algorithm, Google's poster child for deep learning, 12,000x faster than a naive Python implementation. Anyone can write bad code and then trumpet about large speedups. But the optimized Python port also runs, somewhat astonishingly, almost four times faster than the original code written by Google's team! That is, four times faster than opaque, tightly profiled, and optimized C.

But before drawing "machine-level" optimization lessons, some general advice about "human-level" optimizations.

The Sweet Spot

I run a small consulting business laser-focused on machine learning, where my colleagues and I help companies make sense of the tumultuous world of data analysis, in order to make money or save costs (or both). We help clients design and build wondrous systems for data processing, especially text data.

The clients range from large multinationals to nascent start-ups, and while each project is different and requires a different tech stack, plugging into the client's existing data flows and pipelines, Python is a clear favorite. Not to preach to the choir, but Python's no-nonsense development philosophy, its malleability, and the rich library ecosystem make it an ideal choice.

First, a few thoughts "from the field" on what works:

- **Communication, communication, communication.** This one's obvious, but worth repeating. Understand the client's problem on a higher (business) level before deciding on an approach. Sit down and talk through what they think they need (based on their partial knowledge of what's possible and/or what they Googled up before contacting you), until it becomes clear what they really need, free of cruft and preconceptions. Agree on ways to validate the solution beforehand. I like to visualize this process as a long, winding road to be built: get the starting line right (problem definition, available data sources) and the finish line right (evaluation, solution priorities), and the path in between falls into place.

- **Be on the lookout for promising technologies.** An emergent technology that is reasonably well understood and robust, is gaining traction, yet is still relatively obscure in the industry, can bring huge value to the client (or yourself). As an example, a few years ago, Elasticsearch was a little-known and somewhat raw open source project. But I evaluated its approach as solid (built on top of Apache Lucene, offering replication, cluster sharding, etc.) and recommended its use to a client. We consequently built a search system with Elasticsearch at its core, saving the client significant amounts of money in licensing, development, and maintenance compared to the considered alternatives (large commercial databases). Even more importantly, using a new, flexible, powerful technology gave the product a massive competitive advantage. Nowadays, Elasticsearch has entered the enterprise market and conveys no competitive advantage at all—everyone knows it and uses it. Getting the timing right is what I call hitting the "sweet spot," maximizing the value/cost ratio.

- **KISS (Keep It Simple, Stupid!)** This is another no-brainer. The best code is code you don't have to write and maintain. Start simple, and improve and iterate where necessary. I prefer tools that follow the Unix philosophy of "do one thing, and do it well." Grand programming frameworks can be tempting, with everything imaginable under one roof and fitting neatly together. But invariably, sooner or later, you need something the grand framework didn't imagine, and then even modifications that seem simple (conceptually) cascade into a nightmare (programmatically). Grand projects and their all-encompassing APIs tend to collapse under their own weight. Use modular, focused tools, with APIs in between that are as small and uncomplicated as possible. Prefer text formats that are open to simple visual inspection, unless performance dictates otherwise.

- **Use manual sanity checks in data pipelines.** When optimizing data processing systems, it's easy to stay in the "binary mindset" mode, using tight pipelines, efficient binary data formats, and compressed I/O. As the data passes through the system unseen, unchecked (except for perhaps its type), it remains invisible until something outright blows up. Then debugging commences. I advocate sprinkling a few simple log messages throughout the code, showing what the data looks like at various internal points of processing, as good practice—nothing fancy, just an analogy to the Unix head command, picking and visualizing a few data points. Not only does this help during the aforementioned debugging, but seeing the data in a human-readable format leads to "aha!" moments surprisingly often, even when all seems to be going well. Strange tokenization! They promised input would always be encoded in latin1! How did a document in this language get in there? Image files leaked into a pipeline that expects and parses text files! These are often insights that go way beyond those offered by automatic type checking or a fixed unit test, hinting at issues beyond component boundaries. Real-world data is messy. Catch early even things that wouldn't necessarily lead to exceptions or glaring errors. Err on the side of too much verbosity.

- **Navigate fads carefully.** Just because a client keeps hearing about X and says they must have X too doesn't mean they really need it. It might be a marketing problem rather than a technology one, so take care to discern the two and deliver accordingly. X changes over time as hype waves come and go; a recent value would be X=big data.

All right, enough business talk—here's how I got *word2vec* in Python to run faster than C.

Lessons in Optimizing

word2vec (*https://code.google.com/p/word2vec/*) is a deep learning algorithm that allows detection of similar words and phrases. With interesting applications in text analytics and search engine optimization (SEO), and with Google's lustrous brand name attached to it, start-ups and businesses flocked to take advantage of this new tool.

Unfortunately, the only available code was that produced by Google itself, an open source Linux command-line tool written in C. This was a well-optimized but rather hard to use implementation. The primary reason why I decided to port *word2vec* to Python was so I could extend *word2vec* to other platforms, making it easier to integrate and extend for clients.

The details are not relevant here, but *word2vec* requires a training phase with a lot of input data to produce a useful similarity model. For example, the folks at Google ran *word2vec* on their GoogleNews dataset, training on approximately 100 billion words. Datasets of this scale obviously don't fit in RAM, so a memory-efficient approach must be taken.

I've authored a machine learning library, gensim (*http://radimrehurek.com/gensim/*), that targets exactly that sort of memory-optimization problem: datasets that are no longer trivial ("trivial" being anything that fits fully into RAM), yet not large enough to warrant petabyte-scale clusters of MapReduce computers. This "terabyte" problem range fits a surprisingly large portion of real-world cases, *word2vec* included.

Details are described on my blog (*http://bit.ly/RR_blog*), but here are a few optimization takeaways:

- **Stream your data, watch your memory.** Let your input be accessed and processed one data point at a time, for a small, constant memory footprint. The streamed data points (sentences, in the case of *word2vec*) may be grouped into larger batches internally for performance (such as processing 100 sentences at a time), but a high-level, streamed API proved a powerful and flexible abstraction. The Python language supports this pattern very naturally and elegantly, with its built-in generators—a truly beautiful problem-tech match. Avoid committing to algorithms and tools that load everything into RAM, unless you know your data will always remain small, or you don't mind reimplementing a production version yourself later.

- **Take advantage of Python's rich ecosystem.** I started with a readable, clean port of *word2vec* in numpy. numpy is covered in depth in Chapter 6 of this book, but as a short reminder, it is an amazing library, a cornerstone of Python's scientific community and the de facto standard for number crunching in Python. Tapping into numpy's powerful array interfaces, memory access patterns, and wrapped BLAS routines for ultra-fast common vector operations leads to concise, clean, and fast code—code that is hundreds of times faster than naive Python code. Normally I'd call it a day at this point, but "hundreds of times faster" was still 20x slower than Google's optimized C version, so I pressed on.

- **Profile and compile hotspots.** *word2vec* is a typical high performance computing app, in that a few lines of code in one inner loop account for 90% of the entire training runtime. Here I rewrote a single core routine (approximately 20 lines of code) in C, using an external Python library, Cython, as the glue. While technically brilliant, I don't consider Cython a particularly convenient tool conceptually—it's basically like learning another language, a nonintuitive mix between Python, numpy, and C, with its own caveats and idiosyncrasies. But until Python's JIT (just-in-time compilation) technologies mature, Cython is probably our best bet. With a Cython-compiled hotspot, performance of the Python *word2vec* port is now on par with the original C code. An additional advantage of having started with a clean numpy version is that we get free tests for correctness, by comparing against the slower but correct version.

- **Know your BLAS.** A neat feature of numpy is that it internally wraps BLAS (Basic Linear Algebra Subprograms), where available. These are sets of low-level routines, optimized directly by processor vendors (Intel, AMD, etc.) in assembly, Fortran, or C, designed to squeeze out maximum performance from a particular processor architecture. For example, calling an axpy BLAS routine computes vector_y += scalar * vector_x, way faster than what a generic compiler would produce for an equivalent explicit for loop. Expressing *word2vec* training as BLAS operations resulted in another 4x speedup, topping the performance of C *word2vec*. Victory! To be fair, the C code could link to BLAS as well, so this is not some inherent advantage of Python per se. numpy just makes things like these stand out and makes them easy to take advantage of.

- **Parallelization and multiple cores.** gensim contains distributed cluster implementations of a few algorithms. For *word2vec*, I opted for multithreading on a single machine, because of the fine-grained nature of its training algorithm. Using threads also allows us to avoid the fork-without-exec POSIX issues that Python's multiprocessing brings, especially in combination with certain BLAS libraries. Because our core routine is already in Cython, we can afford to release Python's GIL (global interpreter lock; see "Parallelizing the Solution with OpenMP on One Machine" on page 155), which normally renders multithreading useless for CPU-intensive tasks. Speedup: another 3x, on a machine with four cores.

- **Static memory allocations.** At this point, we're processing tens of thousands of sentences per second. Training is so fast that even little things like creating a new numpy array (calling malloc for each streamed sentence) slow us down. Solution: preallocate a static "work" memory and pass it around, in good old Fortran fashion. Brings tears to my eyes. The lesson here is to keep as much bookkeeping and app logic in the clean Python code as possible, and keep the optimized hotspot lean and mean.

- **Problem-specific optimizations.** The original C implementation contained specific microoptimizations, such as aligning arrays onto specific memory boundaries or precomputing certain functions into memory lookup tables. A nostalgic blast from the past, but with today's complex CPU instruction pipelines, memory cache hierarchies, and coprocessors, such optimizations are no longer a clear winner. Careful profiling suggested a few percent improvement, which may not be worth the extra code complexity. Takeaway: use annotation and profiling tools to highlight poorly optimized spots. Use your domain knowledge to introduce algorithmic approximations that trade accuracy for performance (or vice versa). But never take it on faith, profile, preferably using real, production data.

Wrap-Up

Optimize where appropriate. In my experience, there's never enough communication to fully ascertain the problem scope, priorities, and connection to the client's business goals—a.k.a. the "human-level" optimizations. Make sure you deliver on a problem that matters, rather than getting lost in "geek stuff" for the sake of it. And when you do roll up your sleeves, make it worth it!

Large-Scale Productionized Machine Learning at Lyst.com

Sebastjan Trepca (lyst.com)

> Lyst.com is a fashion recommendation engine based in London; it has over 2,000,000 monthly users who learn about new fashion through Lyst's scraping, cleaning, and modeling processes. Founded in 2010, it has raised $20M of investment.
>
> Sebastjan Trepca was the technical founder and is the CTO; he created the site using Django, and Python has helped the team to quickly test new ideas.

Python's Place at Lyst

Python and Django have been at the heart of Lyst since the site's creation. As internal projects have grown, some of the Python components have been replaced with other tools and languages to fit the maturing needs of the system.

Cluster Design

The cluster runs on Amazon EC2. In total there are approximately 100 machines, including the more recent C3 instances, which have good CPU performance.

Redis is used for queuing with PyRes and storing metadata. The dominant data format is JSON, for ease of human comprehension. `supervisord` keeps the processes alive.

Elasticsearch and PyES are used to index all products. The Elasticsearch cluster stores 60 million documents across seven machines. Solr was investigated but discounted due to its lack of real-time updating features.

Code Evolution in a Fast-Moving Start-Up

It is better to write code that can be implemented quickly so that a business idea can be tested than to spend a long time attempting to write "perfect code" in the first pass. If code is useful, then it can be refactored; if the idea behind the code is poor, then it is cheap to delete it and remove a feature. This can lead to a complicated code base with many objects being passed around, but this is acceptable as long as the team makes time to refactor code that is useful to the business.

Docstrings are used heavily in Lyst—an external Sphinx documentation system was tried but dropped in favor of just reading the code. A wiki is used to document processes and larger systems. We also started creating very small services instead of chucking everything into one code base.

Building the Recommendation Engine

At first the recommendation engine was coded in Python, using `numpy` and `scipy` for computations. Subsequently, performance-critical parts of the recommender were sped up using Cython. The core matrix factorization operations were written entirely in Cython, yielding an order of magnitude improvement in speed. This was mostly due to the ability to write performant loops over `numpy` arrays in Python, something that is extremely slow in pure Python and performed poorly when vectorized because it necessitated memory copies of `numpy` arrays. The culprit was `numpy`'s fancy indexing, which always makes a data copy of the array being sliced: if no data copy is necessary or intended, Cython loops will be far faster.

Over time, the online components of the system (responsible for computing recommendations at request time) were integrated into our search component, Elasticsearch. In the process, they were translated into Java to allow full integration with Elasticsearch. The main reason behind this was not performance, but the utility of integrating the recommender with the full power of a search engine, allowing us to apply business rules to served recommendations more easily. The Java component itself is extremely simple and implements primarily efficient sparse vector inner products. The more complex offline component remains written in Python, using standard components of the Python scientific stack (mostly Python and Cython).

In our experience, Python is useful as more than a prototyping language: the availability of tools such as `numpy`, Cython, and `weave` (and more recently Numba) allowed us to achieve very good performance in the performance-critical parts of the code while maintaining Python's clarity and expressiveness where low-level optimization would be counterproductive.

Reporting and Monitoring

Graphite is used for reporting. Currently, performance regressions can be seen by eye after a deployment. This makes it easy to drill into detailed event reports or to zoom out and see a high-level report of the site's behavior, adding and removing events as necessary.

Internally, a larger infrastructure for performance testing is being designed. It will include representative data and use cases to properly test new builds of the site.

A staging site will also be used to let a small fraction of real visitors see the latest version of the deployment—if a bug or performance regression is seen, then it will only have affected a minority of visitors and this version can quickly be retired. This will make the deployment of bugs significantly less costly and problematic.

Sentry is used to log and diagnose Python stack traces.

Jenkins is used for CI (continuous integration) with an in-memory database configuration. This enables parallelized testing so that check-ins quickly reveal any bugs to the developer.

Some Advice

It's really important to have good tools to track the effectiveness of what you're building, and to be super-practical at the beginning. Start-ups change constantly and engineering evolves: you start with a super-exploratory phase, building prototypes all the time and deleting code until you hit the goldmine, and then you start to go deeper, improving code, performance, etc. Until then, it's all about quick iterations and good monitoring/analytics. I guess this is pretty standard advice that has been repeated over and over, but I think many don't really get it how important it is.

I don't think technologies matter that much nowadays, so use whatever works for you. I'd think twice before moving to hosted environments like AppEngine or Heroku, though.

Large-Scale Social Media Analysis at Smesh

Alex Kelly (sme.sh)

At Smesh, we produce software that ingests data from a wide variety of APIs across the Web; filters, processes, and aggregates them; and then uses that data to build bespoke apps for a variety of clients. For example, we provide the tech that powers the tweet filtering and streaming in Beamly's second-screen TV app, run a brand and campaign monitoring platform for mobile network EE, and run a bunch of Adwords data analysis projects for Google.

To do that, we run a variety of streaming and polling services, frequently polling Twitter, Facebook, YouTube, and a host of other services for content and processing several million tweets daily.

Python's Role at Smesh

We use Python extensively—the majority of our platform and services are built with it. The wide variety of libraries, tools, and frameworks available allows us to use it across the board for most of what we do.

That variety gives us the ability to (hopefully) pick the right tool for the job. For example, we've created apps using each of Django, Flask, and Pyramid. Each has its own benefits, and we can pick the one that's right for the task at hand. We use Celery for tasks; Boto for interacting with AWS; and PyMongo, MongoEngine, redis-py, Psycopg, etc. for all our data needs. The list goes on and on.

The Platform

Our main platform consists of a central Python module that provides hooks for data input, filtering, aggregations and processing, and a variety of other core functions. Project-specific code imports functionality from that core and then implements more specific data processing and view logic, as each application requires.

This has worked well for us up to now, and allows us to build fairly complex applications that ingest and process data from a wide variety of sources without much duplication of effort. However, it isn't without its drawbacks—each app is dependent on a common core module, making the process of updating the code in that module and keeping all the apps that use it up-to-date a major task.

We're currently working on a project to redesign that core software and move toward more of a service-oriented architecture (SoA) approach. It seems that finding the right time to make that sort of architectural change is one of the challenges that faces most software teams as a platform grows. There is overhead in building components as individual services, and often the deep domain-specific knowledge required to build each service is only acquired through an initial iteration of development, where that architectural overhead is a hindrance to solving the real problem at hand. Hopefully we've chosen a sensible time to revisit our architectural choices to move things forward. Time will tell.

High Performance Real-Time String Matching

We consume lots of data from the Twitter Streaming API. As we stream in tweets, we match the input strings against a set of keywords so that we know which of the terms we're tracking each tweet is related to. That's not such a problem with a low rate of input, or a small set of keywords, but doing that matching for hundreds of tweets per second, against hundreds or thousands of possible keywords, starts to get tricky.

To make things even trickier, we're not interested in simply whether the keyword string exists in the tweet, but in more complex pattern matching against word boundaries, start and end of line, and optionally use of # and @ characters to prefix the string. The most effective way to encapsulate that matching knowledge is using regular expressions. However, running thousands of regex patterns across hundreds of tweets per second is computationally intensive. Previously, we had to run many worker nodes across a cluster of machines to perform the matching reliably in real time.

Knowing this was a major performance bottleneck in the system, we tried a variety of things to improve the performance of our matching system: simplifying the regexes, running enough processes to ensure we were utilizing all the cores on our servers, ensuring all our regex patterns are compiled and cached properly, running the matching tasks under PyPy instead of CPython, etc. Each of these resulted in a small increase in performance, but it was clear this approach was only ever going to shave a fraction of our processing time. We were looking for an order of magnitude speedup, not a fractional improvement.

It was obvious that rather than trying to increase the performance of each match, we needed to reduce the problem space before the pattern matching takes place. So, we needed to reduce either the number of tweets to process, or the number of regex patterns we needed to match the tweets against. Dropping the incoming tweets wasn't an option —that's the data we're interested in. So, we set about finding a way to reduce the number of patterns we need to compare an incoming tweet to in order to perform the matching.

We started looking at various trie structures for allowing us to do pattern matching between sets of strings more efficiently, and came across the Aho-Corasick string matching algorithm. It turned out to be ideal for our use case. The dictionary from which the trie is built needs to be static—you can't add new members to the trie once the automaton has been finalized—but for us this isn't a problem, as the set of keywords is static for the duration of a session streaming from Twitter. When we change the terms we're tracking we must disconnect from and reconnect to the API, so we can rebuild the Aho-Corasick trie at the same time.

Processing an input against the strings using Aho-Corasick finds all possible matches simultaneously, stepping through the input string a character at a time and finding matching nodes at the next level down in the trie (or not, as the case may be). So, we can very quickly find which of our keyword terms may exist in the tweet. We still don't know for sure, as the pure string-in-string matching of Aho-Corasick doesn't allow us to apply any of the more complex logic that is encapsulated in the regex patterns, but we can use the Aho-Corasick matching as a prefilter. Keywords that don't exist in the string can't match, so we know we only have to try a small subset of all our regex patterns, based on the keywords that do appear in the text. Rather than evaluating hundreds or thousands of regex patterns against every input, we rule out the majority and only need to process a handful for each tweet.

By reducing the number of patterns we attempt to match against each incoming tweet to just a small handful, we've managed to achieve the speedup we were looking for. Depending on the complexity of the trie and the average length of the input tweets, our keyword matching system now performs somewhere between 10–100x faster than the original naive implementation.

If you're doing a lot of regex processing, or other pattern matching, I highly recommend having a dig around the different variations of prefix and suffix tries that might help you to find a blazingly fast solution to your problem.

Reporting, Monitoring, Debugging, and Deployment

We maintain a bunch of different systems running our Python software and the rest of the infrastructure that powers it all. Keeping it all up and running without interruption can be tricky. Here are a few lessons we've learned along the way.

It's really powerful to be able to see both in real time and historically what's going on inside your systems, whether that be in your own software, or the infrastructure it runs on. We use Graphite with `collectd` and `statsd` to allow us to draw pretty graphs of what's going on. That gives us a way to spot trends, and to retrospectively analyse problems to find the root cause. We haven't got around to implementing it yet, but Etsy's Skyline also looks brilliant as a way to spot the unexpected when you have more metrics than you can keep track of. Another useful tool is Sentry, a great system for event logging and keeping track of exceptions being raised across a cluster of machines.

Deployment can be painful, no matter what you're using to do it. We've been users of Puppet, Ansible, and Salt. They all have pros and cons, but none of them will make a complex deployment problem magically go away.

To maintain high availability for some of our systems we run multiple geographically distributed clusters of infrastructure, running one system live and others as hot spares, with switchover being done by updates to DNS with low Time-to-Live (TTL) values. Obviously that's not always straightforward, especially when you have tight constraints on data consistency. Thankfully we're not affected by that too badly, making the approach relatively straightforward. It also provides us with a fairly safe deployment strategy, updating one of our spare clusters and performing testing before promoting that cluster to live and updating the others.

Along with everyone else, we're really excited by the prospect of what can be done with Docker (*http://www.docker.com/*). Also along with pretty much everyone else, we're still just at the stage of playing around with it to figure out how to make it part of our deployment processes. However, having the ability to rapidly deploy our software in a lightweight and reproducible fashion, with all its binary dependencies and system libraries included, seems to be just around the corner.

At a server level, there's a whole bunch of routine stuff that just makes life easier. Monit is great for keeping an eye on things for you. Upstart and `supervisord` make running services less painful. Munin is useful for some quick and easy system-level graphing if you're not using a full Graphite/`collectd` setup. And Corosync/Pacemaker can be a good solution for running services across a cluster of nodes (for example, where you have a bunch of services that you need to run somewhere, but not everywhere).

I've tried not to just list buzzwords here, but to point you toward software we're using every day, which is really making a difference to how effectively we can deploy and run our systems. If you've heard of them all already, I'm sure you must have a whole bunch of other useful tips to share, so please drop me a line with some pointers. If not, go check them out—hopefully some of them will be as useful to you as they are to us.

PyPy for Successful Web and Data Processing Systems

Marko Tasic (https://github.com/mtasic85)

Since I had a great experience early on with PyPy, Python implementation, I chose to use it everywhere where it was applicable. I have used it from small toy projects where speed was essential to medium-sized projects. The first project where I used it was a protocol implementation; the protocols we implemented were Modbus and DNP3. Later, I used it for a compression algorithm implementation, and everyone was amazed by its speed. The first version I used in production was PyPy 1.2 with JIT out of the box, if I recall correctly. By version 1.4 we were sure it was the future of all our projects, because many bugs got fixed and the speed just increased more and more. We were surprised how simple cases were made 2–3x faster just by upgrading PyPy up to the next version.

I will explain two separate but deeply related projects that share 90% of the same code here, but to keep the explanation simple to follow, I will refer to both of them as "the project."

The project was to create a system that collects newspapers, magazines, and blogs, apply OCR (optical character recognition) if necessary, classify them, translate, apply sentiment analyzing, analyze the document structure, and index them for later search. Users can search for keywords in any of the available languages and retrieve information about indexed documents. Search is cross-language, so users can write in English and get results in French. Additionally, users will receive articles and keywords highlighted from the document's page with information about the space occupied and price of publication. A more advanced use case would be report generation, where users can see a tabular view of results with detailed information on spending by any particular company on advertising in monitored newspapers, magazines, and blogs. As well as advertising, it can also "guess" if an article is paid or objective, and determine its tone.

Prerequisites

Obviously, PyPy was our favorite Python implementation. For the database, we used Cassandra and Elasticsearch. Cache servers used Redis. We used Celery as a distributed task queue (workers), and for its broker, we used RabbitMQ. Results were kept in a Redis backend. Later on, Celery used Redis more exclusively for both brokers and backend. The OCR engine used is Tesseract. The language translation engine and server used is Moses. We used Scrapy for crawling websites. For distributed locking in the whole system we use a ZooKeeper server, but initially Redis was used for that. The web application is based on the excellent Flask web framework and many of its extensions, such as Flask-Login, Flask-Principal, etc. The Flask application was hosted by Gunicorn and Tornado on every web server, and nginx was used as a reverse proxy server for the web servers. The rest of the code was written by us and is pure Python that runs on top of PyPy.

The whole project is hosted on an in-house OpenStack private cloud and executes between 100 and 1,000 instances of ArchLinux, depending on requirements, which can change dynamically on the fly. The whole system consumes up to 200 TB of storage every 6–12 months, depending on the mentioned requirements. All processing is done by our Python code, except OCR and translation.

The Database

We developed Python package that unifies model classes for Cassandra, Elasticsearch, and Redis. It is a simple ORM (object relational mapper) that maps everything to a dict or list of dicts, in the case where many records are retrieved from the database.

Since Cassandra 1.2 did not support complex queries on indices, we supported them with join-like queries. However, we allowed complex queries over small datasets (up to 4 GB) because much of that had to be processed while held in memory. PyPy ran in cases where CPython could not even load data into memory, thanks to its strategies applied to homogeneous lists to make them more compact in the memory. Another benefit of PyPy is that its JIT compilation kicked in loops where data manipulation or analysis happened. We wrote code in such a way that the types would stay static inside of loops because that's where JIT-compiled code is especially good.

Elasticsearch was used for indexing and fast searching of documents. It is very flexible when it comes to query complexity, so we did not have any major issues with it. One of the issues we had was related to updating documents; it is not designed for rapidly changing documents, so we had to migrate that part to Cassandra. Another limitation was related to facets and memory required on the database instance, but that was solved by having more smaller queries and then manually manipulating data in Celery workers. No major issues surfaced between PyPy and the PyES library used for interaction with Elasticsearch server pools.

The Web Application

As mentioned above, we used the Flask framework with its third-party extensions. Initially, we started everything in Django, but we switched to Flask because of rapid changes in requirements. This does not mean that Flask is better than Django; it was just easier for us to follow code in Flask than in Django, since its project layout is very flexible. Gunicorn was used as a WSGI (Web Server Gateway Interface) HTTP server, and its IO loop was executed by Tornado. This allowed us to have up to 100 concurrent connections per web server. This was lower than expected because many user queries can take a long time—a lot of analyzing happens in user requests, and data is returned in user interactions.

Initially, the web application depended on the Python Imaging Library (PIL) for article and word highlighting. We had issues with the PIL library and PyPy because at that time there were many memory leaks associated with PIL. Then we switched to Pillow, which was more frequently maintained. In the end, we wrote a library that interacted with GraphicsMagick via a subprocess module.

PyPy runs well, and the results are comparable with CPython. This is because usually web applications are IO-bound. However, with the development of STM in PyPy we hope to have scalable event handling on a multicore instance level soon.

OCR and Translation

We wrote pure Python libraries for Tesseract and Moses because we had problems with CPython API dependent extensions. PyPy has good support for the CPython API using CPyExt, but we wanted to be more in control of what happens under the hood. As a result, we made a PyPy-compatible solution with slightly faster code than on CPython. The reason it was not faster is that most of the processing happened in the C/C++ code of both Tesseract and Moses. We could only speed up output processing and building Python structure of documents. There were no major issues at this stage with PyPy compatibility.

Task Distribution and Workers

Celery gave us the power to run many tasks in the background. Typical tasks are OCR, translation, analysis, etc. The whole thing could be done using Hadoop for MapReduce, but we chose Celery because we knew that the project requirements might change often.

We had about 20 workers, and each worker had between 10 and 20 functions. Almost all functions had loops, or many nested loops. We cared that types stayed static, so the JIT compiler could do its job. The end results were a 2–5x speedup over CPython. The reason why we did not get better speedups was because our loops were relatively small, between 20K and 100K iterations. In some cases where we had to do analysis on the word level, we had over 1M iterations, and that's where we got over a 10x speedup.

Conclusion

PyPy is an excellent choice for every pure Python project that depends on speed of execution of readable and maintainable large source code. We found PyPy also to be very stable. All our programs were long-running with static and/or homogeneous types inside data structures, so JIT could do its job. When we tested the whole system on CPython, the results did not surprise us: we had roughly a 2x speedup with PyPy over CPython. In the eyes of our clients, this meant 2x better performance for the same price. In addition to all the good stuff that PyPy brought to us so far, we hope that its software transactional memory (STM) implementation will bring to us scalable parallel execution for Python code.

Task Queues at Lanyrd.com

Andrew Godwin (lanyrd.com)

Lanyrd is a website for social discovery of conferences—our users sign in, and we use their friend graphs from social networks, as well as other indicators like their industry of work or their geographic location, to suggest relevant conferences.

The main work of the site is in distilling this raw data down into something we can show to the users—essentially, a ranked list of conferences. We have to do this offline, because we refresh the list of recommended conferences every couple of days and because we're hitting external APIs that are often slow. We also use the Celery task queue for other things that take a long time, like fetching thumbnails for links people provide and sending email. There are usually well over 100,000 tasks in the queue each day, and sometimes many more.

Python's Role at Lanyrd

Lanyrd was built with Python and Django from day one, and virtually every part of it is written in Python—the website itself, the offline processing, our statistical and analysis tools, our mobile backend servers, and the deployment system. It's a very versatile and mature language and one that's incredibly easy to write things in quickly, mostly thanks to the large amount of libraries available and the language's easily readable and concise syntax, which means it's easy to update and refactor as well as easy to write initially.

The Celery task queue was already a mature project when we evolved the need for a task queue (very early on), and the rest of Lanyrd was already in Python, so it was a natural fit. As we grew, there was a need to change the queue that backed it (which ended up being Redis), but it's generally scaled very well.

As a start-up, we had to ship some known technical debt in order to make some headway —this is something you just have to do, and as long as you know what your issues are and when they might surface, it's not necessarily a bad thing. Python's flexibility in this regard is fantastic; it generally encourages loose coupling of components, which means it's often easy to ship something with a "good enough" implementation and then easily refactor a better one in later.

Anything critical, such as payment code, had full unit test coverage, but for other parts of the site and task queue flow (especially display-related code) things were often moving too fast to make unit tests worthwhile (they would be too fragile). Instead, we adopted a very agile approach and had a two-minute deploy time and excellent error tracking; if a bug made it into live, we could often fix it and deploy within five minutes.

Making the Task Queue Performant

The main issue with a task queue is throughput. If it gets backlogged, then the website keeps working but starts getting mysteriously outdated—lists don't update, page content is wrong, and emails don't get sent for hours.

Fortunately, though, task queues also encourage a very scalable design; as long as your central messaging server (in our case, Redis) can handle the messaging overhead of the job requests and responses, for the actual processing you can spin up any number of worker daemons to handle the load.

Reporting, Monitoring, Debugging, and Deployment

We had monitoring that kept track of our queue length, and if it started becoming long we would just deploy another server with more worker daemons. Celery makes this very easy to do. Our deployment system had hooks where we could increase the number of worker threads on a box (if our CPU utilization wasn't optimal) and could easily turn a fresh server into a Celery worker within 30 minutes. It's not like website response times going through the floor—if your task queues suddenly get a load spike you have some time to implement a fix and usually it'll smooth over itself, if you've left enough spare capacity.

Advice to a Fellow Developer

My main advice would be to shove as much as you can into a task queue (or a similar loosely coupled architecture) as soon as possible. It takes some initial engineering effort, but as you grow, operations that used to take half a second can grow to half a minute, and you'll be glad they're not blocking your main rendering thread. Once you've got there, make sure you keep a close eye on your average queue latency (how long it takes a job to go from submission to completion), and make sure there's some spare capacity for when your load increases.

Finally, be aware that having multiple task queues for different priorities of tasks makes sense. Sending email isn't very high priority; people are used to emails taking minutes to arrive. However, if you're rendering a thumbnail in the background and showing a spinner while you do it, you want that job to be high priority, as otherwise you're making the user experience worse. You don't want your 100,000-person mailshot to delay all thumbnailing on your site for the next 20 minutes!

Index

We'd like to hear your suggestions for improving our indexes. Send email to index@oreilly.com.

C

C, 140, 167
    (see also foreign function interfaces)
C compilers (see compiling to C)
C++, 140
Cassandra, 340
Cauchy problem, 101
Celery, 284, 326, 340–341
central processing units (see CPUs)
cffi, 170–172
ChaosMonkey, 269
chunksize parameter, 222–225
Circus, 269, 326
clock speed, 2
cloud-based clustering, 266
cluster design, 333
clustering, 263–285
    Amazon Web Services (AWS), 263
    and infrastructure, 266
    avoiding problems with, 269
    benefits, 264
    Celery, 284
    common designs, 268
    converting code from multiprocessing, 271–
       273
    deployments, 270
    drawbacks, 265–267
    failures, 266–267
    for research support, 273–277
    Gearman, 284
    IPython, 271, 273–277
    local clusters, 271–273
    NSQ, 271, 277–283
    Parallel Python, 270–273
    production clustering, 277–283
    PyRes, 284
    queues in, 277
    reporting, 270
    restart plan, 266
    Simple Queue Service, 284
    starting a clustered system, 268
    vertical scaling versus., 265
column-major ordering, 175
communication layers, 7–8
compiling, 13, 18
compiling to C, 135–179
    Cython, 140–150
    Cython and numpy, 154–155
    foreign function interfaces, 167–178

    JIT vs. AOT compilers, 138
    Numba, 157
    OpenMP, 155–157
    PyPy, 160–163
    Pythran, 159–160
    Shed Skin, 150–154
    speed gain potential, 136
    summary of options, 164
    using compilers, 139
    when to use each technology, 164
computer architectures (see architectures)
computing units, 2–5
concurrency, 181–202
    (see also asynchronous programming)
    database examples, 198–201
    event loops, 182
    serial crawler and, 185–186
context switches, 111, 182
Corosync/Pacemaker, 338
coroutines, as generators, 184
cProfile, 18, 31–36
CPU-migrations, 111
CPUs, 2
    frequency scaling, 19
    measuring usage (see profiling)
CPython, 52–56, 203
    bytecode, 19
    garbage collector in, 161
CPython module, 175–178
cron, 269
ctypes, 167–170
Cython, 13, 15, 136, 140–150, 292, 331, 334
    adding type annotations, 145–150
    and numpy, 154–155
    annotations for code analysis, 143–145
    pure-Python conversion with, 141–143
    when to use, 164

D

DabApps, 303
DAFSA (see DAWGs (directed acyclic word
    graphs))
data consumers, 278
data locality, 131
data sharing
    locking a value, 258
    synchronization methods, 254
datrie, 301

DAWGs (directed acyclic word graphs), 295, 296, 300, 303
  compared to tries, 299
decorators, 27, 37
deep learning, 328–332
dictionaries, 63, 65
dictionaries and sets, 73–88
  costs of using, 74
  hash tables, 77–85
  namespace management, 85–87
  performance optimization, 77–85
  probing, 77
  uses, 73–76
diffusion equation, 99–108
  1D diffusion, 102
  2D diffusion, 103
  evolution function, 105
  initialization, 105
  profiling, 106–108
dis Module, 52–56
distributed prime calculation, 280–283
Django, 340
Docker, 338
Docstrings, 333
double-array trie (see datrie)
dowser, 18, 50–52
dynamic arrays, 67–69
dynamic scaling, 264

E

EC2, 333
Elastic Compute Cloud (EC2), 327
Elasticsearch, 326–327, 329, 333, 340
entropy, 78
  and hash functions, 81–85
Euler's method, 101
event loops, 182
evolve function, 160
execution time variations, 26
extension module, with Shed Skin, 151–153
external libraries, 132

F

f2py, 173–175
Fabric, 326
Fibonacci series, 92
file locking, 255–258
Flask, 340

foreign function interfaces, 167–178
  cffi, 170–172
  CPythonmodule, 175–178
  ctypes, 167–170
  f2py, 173–175
FORTRAN, 173–175 (see foreign function interfaces)
fragmentation (see memory fragmentation)

G

g++, 139
garbage collectors, 161–163
gcc, 139
Gearman, 284
generators and iterators, 89–98
  and memory usage, 90–92
  coroutines as generators, 184
  itertools, 94–97
  lazy evaluation, 94–98
  when to use, 92
generic code, 67
gensim, 330–332
getsizeof, 293
gevent, 187–191, 193–194, 202, 231
GIL battle, 215
global interpreter lock (GIL), 5, 13, 205
GPUs (graphics processing units), 2, 166
Graphite, 334, 338
greenlets, 188
grequests, 190
Guppy project, 48

H

hash collisions, 80
hash functions, 74, 79, 308–312
hash tables (see dictionaries and sets)
hash values, 318–321
hashable type, 73
HAT trie, 302
heapy, 18, 36, 48–50
heat equation (see diffusion equation)
heavy data, 11
Heroku, 335
HyperLogLog, 320
hyperthreading, 3
hyperthreads, 214
hypotheses, 132

I

idealized computing, 10–11
in-place operations, 121–123, 127–129
initial value problem, 101
instructions, 112
instructions per cycle (IPC), 2
interprocess communication (IPC), 232–247
    cluster design and, 268
    Less Naive Pool solution, 234, 238
    Manager version, 234
    Manager.Value as flag, 239–240
    mmap, 244–247
    mmap version, 235
    Naive Pool solution, 236–238
    RawValue, 243
    RawValue version, 235
    Redis, 241–243
    Redis version, 234
    serial solution, 236
IPython, 271, 273–277
iterators (see generators and iterators)
itertools, 94–97

J

Java, 334
Jenkins, 335
JIT compilers
    vs. AOT compilers, 138
joblib, 226
JSON, 270, 333
Julia set, 19–25, 140

K

K-Minimum Values algorithm, 308–312
    (see also probabilisticdata structures)
Kelly, Alex, 339
kernel, 29, 111, 181–183
Knight Capital, 266

L

L1/L2 cache, 6
Lanyard, 342–343
laplacian function, 124
latency, 6
lazy allocation system, 111
lazy generator evaluation, 94–97
Less Naive Pool, 238

lessons from start-ups and CTOs, 325–343
libraries, 13
linear probing, 78
linear search, 63
line_profiler, 37–41, 106–108, 145
Linux, perf tool, 111
lists
    RAM use of, 288
    text storage in, 297–298
lists and tuples, 61
    appending data, 68–69
    binary search, 64
    bisect module, 65
    differences between, 61, 66
    list allocation, 67–69
    lists as dynamic arrays, 67–69
    search complexity, 63–66
    searching and sorting algorithms, 64
    tuple allocation, 70–72
load balancing, 221
load factor, 78
lockfile, 257
locking a value, 258
LogLog Counter, 318–321
    (see also probabilistic data structures)
loop deconstruction, 90
Lyst.com, 333–335

M

Manager, 234
Manager.Value, 239–240
Marisa trie, 301
matrix computation, 18
    (see also vector and matrix computation)
memory allocations, 106–108, 120–123, 127–129
memory copies, 153
memory fragmentation, 109–116
    array module and, 113
    perf and, 111–116
memory units, 1, 5–7
memory, measuring usage (see profiling)
memory_profiler, 19, 36, 42–48
Micro Python, 304
mmap, 235, 244–247
Monit, 338
Monte Carlo method, 208–209
Morris counter, 306–308
    (see also probabilistic data structures)

memory_profiler, 42–48
overview, 17–19
success strategies, 59
timing, 26–31
unit testing, 56–59
pub/subs, 278
Puppet, 338
pure Python, 99
PyData compilers page, 165
PyPy, 136, 160–163, 304, 339–342
and multiprocessing, 208
garbage collector in, 161–163
running and installing modules, 162
vs. Shed Skin, 150
when to use, 164
PyRes, 231, 284, 333
Pyston, 165
Python
attributes, 13–15
Python interpreter, 11
Python objects, 210–216
Python virtual machine, 11
Pythran, 136, 159–160, 292
when to use, 164
PyViennaCL, 165

Q

queues
asynchronous job feeding, 230
in cluster design, 268
in clustering, 277
queue support, 221–229

R

RadimRehurek.com, 328–332
RAM, 6, 287–324
array module storage, 289
bytes versus Unicode, 294
in collections, 292–293
measuring usage (see profiling)
objects for primitives, 288
probabilistic data structures, 305–324
text storage options, 295
tips for using less, 304
random numbers, 217
range versus xrange, 304
range/xrange functions, 89–92
RawValue, 235, 243

read/write speeds, 5–7
Redis, 231, 234, 241–243, 304, 326, 333
roll function, 160
row-major, ordering, 175
runsnakerun, 36

S

Salt, 338
SaltStack, 326
scikit-learn, 13
scipy, 13
selective optimizations, 124–126
semaphores, 188
Sentry, 334
serial crawler, 185–186, 191
serial solution, 236
Server Density, 327
set, text storage in, 298
sets (see dictionaries and sets)
sharing of state, 205
Shed Skin, 136, 150–154
cost of memory copies, 153
extension module with, 151–153
when to use, 164
SIMD (Single Instruction, Multiple Data), 3
Simple Queue Service (SQS), 284
Skyline, 338
Skype, 267
Smesh, 335–339
social media analysis, 335–339
Social Media Analytics (SoMA), 325–328
solid state hard drive, 6
spinning hard drive, 6
static arrays, 70
strength reduction, 148
SuperLogLog, 319
supervisord, 269, 333, 338
synchronization methods, 254–261

T

Tasic, Marko, 342
task queues, 342–343
task-clock, 111
TCP/IP, 243
Tesseract, 341
text storage
in list, 297–298
in set, 298

About the Authors

Micha Gorelick was the first man on Mars in 2023 and won the Nobel prize in 2046 for his contributions to time travel. In a moment of rage after seeing the deplorable uses of his new technology, he traveled back in time to 2012 and convinced himself to leave his Physics PhD program and follow his love of data. First he applied his knowledge of realtime computing and data science to the dataset at bitly. Then, after realizing he wanted to help people understand the technology of the future, he helped start Fast Forward Labs as a resident mad scientist. There, he worked on many issues—from machine learning to performant stream algorithms. In this period of his life, he could be found consulting for various projects on issues of high performance data analysis. A monument celebrating his life can be found in Central Park, 1857.

Ian Ozsvald is a data scientist and Python teacher at ModelInsight.io (*http://modelin sight.io*) with over 10 years of Python experience. He has been teaching at PyCon and PyData conferences and consulting in the fields of artificial intelligence and high performance computing for over a decade in the UK. Ian blogs at IanOzsvald.com and is always happy to receive a pint of good bitter. Ian's background includes Python and C++, a mix of Linux and Windows development, storage systems, lots of natural language processing and text processing, machine learning, and data visualization. He also cofounded the Python-focused video learning website ShowMeDo.com many years ago.

Colophon

The animal on the cover of *High Performance Python* is a fer-de-lance. Literally "iron of the spear" in French, the name is reserved by some for the species of snake (*Bothrops lanceolatus*) found predominantly on the island of Martinique. It may also be used to refer to other lancehead species like the Saint Lucia lancehead (*Bothrops caribbaeus*), the common lancehead (*Bothrops atrox*), and the terciopelo (*Bothrops asper*). All of these species are pit vipers, so named for the two heat-sensitive organs that appear as pits between the eyes and nostrils.

The terciopelo and common lancehead account for a particularly large share of the fatal bites that have made snakes in the *Bothrops* genus responsible for more human deaths in the Americas than any other genus. Workers on coffee and banana plantations in South America fear bites from the common lanceheads hoping to catch a rodent snack. The purportedly more irascible terciopelo is just as dangerous, when not enjoying a solitary life bathing in the sun on the banks of Central American rivers and streams.

Many of the animals on O'Reilly covers are endangered; all of them are important to the world. To learn more about how you can help, go to *animals.oreilly.com*.

The cover image is from Wood's *Animate Creation*. The cover fonts are URW Typewriter and Guardian Sans. The text font is Adobe Minion Pro; the heading font is Adobe Myriad Condensed; and the code font is Dalton Maag's Ubuntu Mono.

Get even more for your money.

Join the O'Reilly Community, and register the O'Reilly books you own. It's free, and you'll get:

- $4.99 ebook upgrade offer
- 40% upgrade offer on O'Reilly print books
- Membership discounts on books and events
- Free lifetime updates to ebooks and videos
- Multiple ebook formats, DRM FREE
- Participation in the O'Reilly community
- Newsletters
- Account management
- 100% Satisfaction Guarantee

Signing up is easy:

1. Go to: oreilly.com/go/register
2. Create an O'Reilly login.
3. Provide your address.
4. Register your books.

Note: English-language books only

To order books online:
oreilly.com/store

For questions about products or an order:
orders@oreilly.com

To sign up to get topic-specific email announcements and/or news about upcoming books, conferences, special offers, and new technologies:
elists@oreilly.com

For technical questions about book content:
booktech@oreilly.com

To submit new book proposals to our editors:
proposals@oreilly.com

O'Reilly books are available in multiple DRM-free ebook formats. For more information:
oreilly.com/ebooks

O'REILLY®